"Alan Gelb's book is wri_____ detail and nuance. It _____ wonderful read."

D0445832

"SPELLBINDING fro_____ to finish, it is a chilling true-life tale of murder that raises disturbing questions about the American judicial system. A first-rate, must-read work."

—Christopher Anderson,
author of *The Serpent's Tooth*

"AN ABSOLUTELY RIVETING BOOK. I literally couldn't put it down and stayed up till 4 AM reading it! Alan Gelb brilliantly searches out the forces which led to a young man's brutal murder of his father...READ IT!"

—Dinitia Smith, author of
Remember This

"Alan Gelb has written a complex and compelling book. It is all at once a detective story, a family drama, a tale about small town life, and, not least, an autobiography of sorts—and it succeeds impressively on all these varied levels. One reads each page with interest, and with eager anticipation for what comes next."

—Howard Blum, author of
Wanted: The Search for Nazis in America and *I Pledge Allegiance: The Walker Family Spy Case*

"A compelling, well-written true story of casual violence, explosive hatred, a disintegrating family and an unobservant culture, reminding us that things are seldom what they seem."

—Jack Early, author of
Donato and Daughter

MOST LIKELY TO SUCCEED

Multiple Murder
and the Elusive Search
for Justice in an American Town

ALAN GELB

ST. MARTIN'S PAPERBACKS

Published by arrangement with Penguin Books USA

MOST LIKELY TO SUCCEED

Copyright © 1990 by Alan Gelb.
Teaser for *Bad Company* copyright © 1990 by Steve Wick.

Cover photo courtesy of Harvey McCagg, *The Independent*

Library of Congress Catalog Card Number: 89-71412

ISBN: 0-312-92566-2

Printed in the United States of America

Dutton hardcover edition/August 1990
St. Martin's Paperbacks edition/July 1991

10 9 8 7 6 5 4 3 2 1

For my parents

ACKNOWLEDGMENTS

In the course of writing this book, I relied on the cooperation and openness of many people. As a result of these murders, there were many who felt the impulse to retreat in the face of further exposure; I wish to thank all those members of the Canaan and Chatham communities, anonymous and noted, who trusted me enough to overcome this impulse and to share with me their insights and memories. Everything in this book is based on facts collected through interviews, transcripts, newspaper accounts, or my firsthand observation of events. There are no reconstructed scenes and no efforts to "dramatize" what is a sufficiently dramatic event.

Special thanks to the attorneys Eugene Keeler, Charles Wilcox, and Nancy Snyder; Joan Yowe; Judge John G. Leaman; and the staff of the Columbia County court. I would like to acknowledge the cooperation and contributions of the Gates family; the Brahm family; and Sally and Stanley Joseph. Assisting me as well in this effort were Barry Leiwant, who offered his legal knowledge; Joanne Gerstel and Joel Merker, who provided me with a workplace at a critical time; Jan Weber, for her insights and camaraderie; and the members of the press who shared with me their information and interpretations. I would also like to mention the help and support of our friends C. L. and Dan Fornari and Janie Trumpy, who eased our transition into this community that became our home. My great appreciation to my agent, Ellen Levine, and her superb staff, and to my distinguished editor, Joyce Engelson. The contribution of copy editor Bill Reynolds was invaluable, and thanks too to Angela Palmisono. I would also like to note the help and support of Michaela Hamilton. And, of course, special mention must be made of my family, who stood up good-humoredly, supportively, and lovingly during an experience that was underscored with stress and, at times, even fear.

I have wandered in many lands, seeking the lost regions from which my birth into this world exiled me, and the company of creatures such as I myself . . .
—GEORGE BERNARD SHAW, *Caesar and Cleopatra*

As I walk'd through the wilderness of this world, I lighted on a certain place. . . .
—JOHN BUNYAN, *Pilgrim's Progress*

Before Man is life and death, good and evil: that which he shall choose shall be given him.　　—Ecclesiasticus 15:18

INTRODUCTION

The easternmost town in the New York foothills of the Berkshire Mountains is Canaan, and one of the oldest sections of Canaan is Frisbie Street, settled in 1770 by Gideon Frisbie, who emigrated from Canaan, Connecticut. Here, in the northern section of Columbia County, Gideon Frisbie found narrow fertile valleys, deposits of deep-blue slate, and clear, deep Whiting's Pond, later renamed Queechy Lake, a six-hundred-acre body of water that even now, over two hundred years later, is as much a lure for summer renters from Manhattan as it was for Frisbie himself. Fronting on what was once the Albany-Boston stagecoach route, Frisbie Street, many of whose residents live in eighteenth- and nineteenth-century homes, overlooks a steady traffic of tractor-trailers on the New York State Thruway. But for all the interstate trucking that goes on below, Frisbie Street remains essentially a quiet place, running from the hamlet of East Chatham eastward to County Route 5 in Canaan. From there, one picks up the misnamed Peaceful Valley Road, site of a fiery single-car accident that claimed two lives central to this story, and then it is just a few miles farther to the Massachusetts state line.

Running off of Frisbie Street is Maple Drive, a 2.2-mile dirt horseshoe of some sixteen homes, ranging from hunting cabins and raised ranches to estates. Roughly one-quarter of the homeowners are weekenders, a percentage that reflects the demographic changes in the Columbia County population at large. In the past, the identities of Canaan and East Chatham were formed by agriculture and railroads; now these towns are flourishing as second-home resorts for people drawn to the area by real-estate ads that promote the region as "Hamptons North" or "The Hunt Country." And yet, while it is now possible to buy croissants and balsamic vinegar alongside the Freihofer's Parker House rolls and the Heinz Distilled White, Canaan and East Chatham maintain an unspoiled country feeling. This is still a place of church suppers and turkey shoots and big breakfasts and waitresses who call you "hon" and towheaded kids exploring the midway at the Chatham Fair and autumn leaf bonfires and 4-H and Little League and prom queens and Dairy Queens and deer carcasses atop pickup trucks and everything else that stands for continuity and order and values in this part of the world.

The East Chatham post office has been hung with stars-and-stripes curtains, and lollipops are freely distributed to anyone who looks even vaguely underage. Slattery's, the general store, lacks a cracker barrel but does have its resident assembly of codgers who can play checkers or discuss the state of the world at will. Outside The Bakery, a restaurant where everyone seems to wind up for breakfast, people leave hundreds of dollars' worth of tools and equipment in their pickup trucks, and those seen locking their doors will soon find themselves fodder for the gossip mill. On Maple Drive, whose residents have an East Chatham mailing address but who pay taxes to the Town of Canaan, it is not only unusual but perhaps unthinkable to lock your doors. Even with an occasional theft on the road, the act still seems unwarranted. Even after a multiple murder, the doors go unlocked on Maple Drive.

These towns—Canaan and Chatham, of which East Chatham, along with Old Chatham, North Chatham, and Chatham Center are satellites—are close-knit communities. As in all small towns, the connections are everywhere, forming a web. You nod to people in the streets here; some men even tip their hats. You stop for pedestrians—there is no question as to who has the right-of-way. If someone cuts you off while driving—which rarely happens—you don't lean out your window and shout your choicest profanity, because the person you would be profaning might be your neighbor's cousin or your plumber's aunt and it will come back to haunt you. After all, everyone knows you have, let's say, a beige Taurus, 1986. But more inhibiting than the danger of being found out is the fact that the person in the other car is a person. Not an anonymous creature, but a person whom you've probably seen at the bank or the supermarket or on line at the movies. So you let that person drive on and you keep your harsh words for encounters in other parts of the world, for this is a part of the world where there is still some real measure of goodness and kindness and decency.

But all this goodness and kindness and decency does not mitigate against the fact that there is darkness present, nor does it deny the fact that, when the short days and long nights arrive, there comes along the road a feeling of primordial loneliness and unease. It is at these moments—mostly at twilight, when the eyes are playing tricks, when the remains of a dead hickory loom like a frenzied witch, or before the shadowy, blunt-snouted thing shuffling in the bushes reveals itself to be an opossum—that those of us caught on winding country roads hurry home. There we sit, on those long winter nights, listening now and again to the piercing screams that sound like a woman in pain until we learn, from someone with more experience but not necessarily less capacity for being spooked, that what we are listening to is the cry of a pheasant. At those times we who live here accept that unease as a condition in the natural order of things. And so we light our candles, play music, watch television, mull cider, or do whatever we have to do in our ongoing and mostly futile effort to ward off the encroachment of the profound unknown.

On Saturday, December 13, 1986, the weather was clear and frigid on Maple Drive. We were nearly at the end of our season up here, getting ready, by the next weekend, to close up the house for the winter, drain the pipes, and repair to Manhattan, where my wife and I lived with our two young sons. It would be difficult to spend the next three months in our small, cramped apartment without the weekly relief of getting away to the country, but we didn't feel capable of coping with the exigencies of snow plowing, maintaining minimum temperatures to protect the pipes from bursting, and all the other things you have to worry about when the building superintendent isn't taking care of you.

December 13 started out an ordinary day, filled with the usual simple pleasures and burdens. We watched the chickadees, who wouldn't deign to fly south, root in for the winter; we took a bracing walk through white birches and stout hemlocks. Everywhere in the air was the fruity smell of burning applewood from the stove, and the cold, clear weather lent a crystalline clarity that was almost startlingly beautiful. But we had all of our last-minute chores and errands to attend to. We were awaiting a parade of service people; we had to pack our belongings to be brought back to the city; and we had to shop for dinner, as our last houseguests of the year were coming later that day.

It was midmorning by the time we left to do our shopping. We had decided to leave our two boys at home with their baby-sitter, but then, as we turned onto Maple Drive, we saw, not fifty feet away, a pickup truck parked along the side of the road. Such a sight is admittedly not a rare sight on a country road, but this was not hunting season, nor were the two occupants of the truck people I had ever seen before, nor were they people whose looks I liked. In fact, as my wife and I turned around and drove past them once more, we decided we liked their looks so little that it was not a good idea for us to be leaving the kids with their baby-sitter just now. We pulled up the driveway and found other chores to undertake. By the time we set out again, the truck was gone and we would probably never have thought of it again if the events of that evening had turned out differently.

Our houseguests drove in that afternoon with their two children, and so began The Basic Visit. This means an excursion of some sort by day—a modest hike or a drive over to Lenox, Massachusetts, the resort town twelve miles away that is the summer home of the Boston Symphony Orchestra. By night, we had Act Two of The Basic Visit, which is inevitably a big "country" dinner.

The memory of the evening has become what is at once a remote and vivid mix of images for me: the icy thrust of the wind as I went out to get firewood; the searing taste of Stolichnaya Peppar vodka; the warming smell of cider mulled for the children; the sounds of those same tired children as their fortunes waned in a late-night Monopoly game. And then, after the children were put to sleep, the spectacle of the parents in various postures of fatigue on the living room furniture. We said good-night to our guests around midnight, then went upstairs and fell asleep as soon as our heads hit the pillows.

It was just after two o'clock in the morning when my wife nudged me awake. "I hear something," she whispered.

"Go to sleep," I said. "It's the wind."

"No," she said. "There's a car."

I got out of bed and looked out the window. For sure, a car was parked there. A police car, its dome light flashing.

Suddenly there was a pounding on the door. I threw on a robe and headed downstairs. As I opened the door, admitting a blast of subzero air, I saw the taut pale faces of the two deputy sheriffs, their flashlights and badges held aloft. "There's been a crime on the road," one of them announced.

"Did you hear anything unusual tonight?" asked the other.

"What crime?" my wife asked, from halfway down the stairs.

"We can't give you any specific information," one of them replied, so incredibly wired that he was almost bug-eyed.

"Wait a minute. You're scaring us!" said my wife, speaking now for our guests as well, who had come out onto the landing. "You can't just come in here and tell us there's been a crime and not tell us what's happened!"

The deputies looked at each other. "There's been a homicide," one of them said. "But don't worry. There are fifty police cars on the road."

"Where was it?" I asked.

"I'm sorry, sir, but we can't tell you that. We have a suspect, but the investigation is still pending," the deputy said. "Now, did you hear anything unusual tonight?"

We all looked at each other. "No," I said for the group. "Not that we were aware of."

They jotted something down and then told us to stay indoors and not to go out in the morning until we checked in with the sheriff's department. And again, as they left, they told us "not to worry."

We didn't listen to them. We worried. "Maybe we should leave tonight," said our friend Barbara, but that would have meant waking the kids, so we decided against it. After some rationalization, we figured that whoever had done whatever had happened was already far away. And so, after sitting up for a while, we all went back to bed.

"I'm not going to be able to sleep," said my wife.

"We can take turns staying up," I suggested.

"What do you think really happened?" she asked me.

The first thought that flashed through my mind had to do with one or more homicidal maniacs—an upstate version of the Manson gang—but I wasn't about to tell her that. Anyway, everyone knows that statistics indicate most homicides are family affairs.

"It must have been a domestic squabble that got out of hand," I said. "A jealous wife, or a jealous husband."

"Maybe it was drug-related," said my wife. "But did you see those cops? They looked so freaked out."

"You go to sleep," I told her. "I'll sit up."

In a few minutes, to my surprise, she was asleep. As I sat in the club chair by the window, I listened to her breathing heavily. I really wasn't afraid at that point, and, of course, I was very tired, but I felt I had made her a promise and so I tried to stay up. But I couldn't. It had been too long a day, too many errands, too many kids, too much food and wine. Sometime after 3:00 A.M., I felt my eyes begin to close and, shirking the sentry duty I had promised to perform, I allowed the sleep to come.

I woke early and started putting together the country breakfast that was part of The Basic Visit. When I'd gotten the pancake batter mixed and had set the griddle to heating up, I decided to call the sheriff's office.

"I live on Maple Drive," I told the officer who picked up, "and the deputies who were here last night said I should check in with you in the morning about the homicide."

"You mean the homicides," the officer bluntly replied. "There were four people who died on Maple Drive last night."

"Four people?" I repeated. "Can you tell me where?"

No, he could not. With the investigation still pending, the exact location could not be divulged, but I was reminded that if I knew anything or could remember anything unusual, I should call back.

I hung up and tried to absorb what I had just heard. A murder that I had assumed to be an isolated incident, freakish, a crime of passion, was suddenly four murders, a massacre, an abomination.

"Did you call?" asked my wife as she entered the kitchen.

I turned to look at her. "They killed four people on the road last night," I told her, and she sat down in a chair.

Once we told our friends what had happened, it was quickly decided that we should forgo the pancake breakfast, and we got ourselves together with extreme dispatch. The children wanted to know why we had to leave so soon. We had no reason we felt we could share with them, and so we just barked at them and told them to hurry along. But, before we left, we made two more phone calls.

I called back the sheriff's department and reported to the officer on duty that I had seen two men parked in a pickup truck. I hadn't liked the looks of them, I said. The officer asked me for details about the truck, and I could only be vague.

My wife placed the other call to a neighbor with whom we had only a glancing acquaintanceship. Mary-Lynn Bedford lived in a beautiful old house restored by her husband. She told my wife that the murders had occurred at the log home of Robert Gates, directly across the road from them and three driveways down from us. The victims, she said, were Bob Gates, his girlfriend, his teenage son, and his three-year-old nephew. "Poor little Jason," said Mary-Lynn, referring to the slain child. "I used to baby-sit for him all the time. Please come by sometime soon," she added. "It's important for people on this road to know each other."

"That's where Wyley Gates lived," my wife whispered to me as she hung up.

"Who?" I asked.

"Wyley Gates. You remember—he mowed our lawn."

I had never met him—my wife had handled that one-time employment—but I could visualize him, as I had often seen him atop the rider-mower at the home of his grandmother, who lived next door to Mary-Lynn.

"I can't believe it," my wife said. "I just talked to him about baby-sitting for the kids."

Now I remembered more. She had told me what a quiet, studious young man he seemed to be, and how convenient it would be to have a baby-sitter right on the road (although he had also said that he had "a very busy schedule" and would have to think about it).

"And now he's dead," my wife murmured. "God, how horrible."

We finally got everything into the car and set out for

home. As we headed back to Manhattan the children fell asleep, and my wife and I took this opportunity to talk.

"It feels so close," she said.

"It is so close."

"I mean, I can't believe that the boy I talked to just last week is now . . ."

She closed her eyes and I drove on.

Twenty minutes later I heard a news report out of Poughkeepsie. "Authorities have arrested Wyley Gates in the murders of four people in Canaan, New York last night . . ."

"Wake up!" I cried to my wife. "Wake up!"

For my wife, coming out of a deep sleep, the news must have been even more dreamlike than it was for me.

"Gates, seventeen, the salutatorian of the Chatham High School, was arraigned this morning in Stockport and re-manded to the custody of the Columbia County Jail in Hudson, New York . . ."

"I don't believe it," my wife said as they gave us details. The teenage-boy victim, whom we had assumed to be Wyley, was in fact his older brother, Robert, Jr., with whom we were unacquainted.

"Sheriff Paul Proper said that another person was being questioned in the case but did not comment on a possible motive for the murders or reveal the source of the murder weapon . . ."

"I can't believe this is happening," my wife said.

"Wait," I said, silencing her, and together we hung on to every word and then played with the dial to find more information wherever we could.

In the next few days, we learned that Wyley Gates, whom the media dubbed the "Computer Whiz Kid," was not the only suspect. Another boy, Damian Rossney, a junior at Chatham High School, had been arrested. Authorities had been led to Rossney by a third boy, Miles McDonald, who had been involved in a robbery of the Robert Gates residence on December 4, wherein ammunition and guns were stolen, including the alleged murder weapon, a Walther PPK .380. McDonald, granted immunity, gave an account of a target-practice session with the murder weapon at the home of yet another boy, John Bailey, also of East Chatham, also of Chatham High School. In the months ahead, it would become apparent that at least two other boys at Chatham High knew something of the plans to commit murder, and many members of the community were convinced that knowledge of the impending event had been even more widespread.

As I followed the news accounts in the wake of these murders, I realized that this crime was very different from what I had first imagined it to be. I had assumed that this was a case of a boy who had, in the turmoil of adolescence, reached his breaking point and, in a crime of passion, destroyed those around him. Shocking, horrible, awful . . . but not necessarily unique. But, in fact, the evidence that emerged suggested that this was a highly premeditated crime, involving plotting that was sometimes fanciful, sometimes grimly realistic. The evidence indicated that the murders might not be the work of a sole perpetrator, but, rather, were the result of a group effort. In the end, there would be more than one boy standing trial for the murders of Robert Gates, his son Bobby, his nephew Jason, and his companion Cheryl Brahm.

When my wife and I returned to our house after that winter, as the fiddleheads were pushing their way up through the ground and the branches of the fruit trees were swollen with pink and white buds, the town was still deep in shock. One of their own—and, as class salutatorian, one of their best—was sitting in the Hudson jail, awaiting a murder trial that promised to be the most sensational in the county's history. As we drove along Maple Drive, so full of promise on this early spring day, my wife turned to me. "How can anyone who lives on this road and comes home every day to this kind of beauty come to murder?" she wondered.

The question may have been naïve, but I believe it was in the minds of everyone who lived in this community. How had it come to be? How do you live in a place like this, a place of beauty, serenity, stability, and continuity, and come to murder? By the time the trials were over, the questions still lingered on, in some ways more pronounced than ever.

"Maybe what we're dealing with here," I said to my wife, as we braked for a family of wild turkeys crossing the road, "is a question of evil."

The turkeys darted crazily into the woods, and then it was very quiet. The sun was out; there was a light wind; and everywhere was the pervasive odor of grass, water, springtime warmth, and the faint excrescence of rot. As we moved slowly down the road the word *evil*, like a sudden black cloud, hung there, not yet an answer—there would never be any real answers—but at least a place to begin.

PART

ONE

1

Summer in Columbia County is a tonic for most everyone who experiences it. It is the payoff after a winter of rigor and a mud season whose assault of primordial ooze and fetid aromas gives way to a notoriously short spring. But when summer comes, the citizens of Chatham and Canaan become convinced that they are living in the right place at the right time. The fields are planted with corn and melons, and the roadside is lined with a succession of tawny daylilies, sky-blue chicory, and Queen Anne's lace. Days that seem endless are interrupted by brief interludes of firefly-filled darkness, to return once again to mornings scored by the chittering chorus of wrens and finches. There are lakes and streams and, increasingly, swimming pools; there are baseball diamonds and tennis courts and riding trails. For the culturally inclined there are the nearby music and dance festivals at Tanglewood, Jacob's Pillow, and Saratoga, and for those fixed at the other end of the cultural spectrum, there is the summer season of stock-car racing at the Lebanon Speedway. Even the essential sadness of summer's end is softened by the climax provided

by the Chatham Fair, one of the oldest and largest agricul-
tural fairs in the state. Truly, it would be no hyperbole on
the part of the local Chamber of Commerce to extoll the
Chatham area as a summer vacationland.

But the summer of 1986 was no tonic and no pleasure
for a seventeen-year-old resident named Wyley Gates. Wyley, born in the county, had been away from it only for a
few years when he went to live, after his parents' divorce,
with his mother, Kristi, in her native California. As he was
later to relate, the thing he missed most when he was in
California was the beauty of Columbia County, where his
love of animals and nature had more chance of being
satisfied than it did in the shopping mall/parking lot terrain
out west. On Maple Drive, where Wyley resided with his
father, Robert, familiarly called Bob; his father's live-in
companion, Cheryl Brahm; and his older brother, Robert,
Jr., known as Bobby, that natural beauty was as evident as
it was anywhere in the county, but it wasn't enough to make
Wyley happy. For as long as he could remember, Wyley
would later reveal, he had not been happy living on Maple
Drive.

This unhappiness overwhelmed any number of reasons
why Wyley should have felt good about himself. For one
thing, he was an outstanding member of his high school
class. Academically, he was ranked number two, and had
every reason to expect to be the class salutatorian, if not
valedictorian, upon graduation the following year. Furthermore, he would be applying to college on the added strength
of significant extracurricular achievement. For a number of
years, he had been playing in the trumpet section of the
school band, and this summer he was practicing to such an
extent that he felt he had a good shot at making the first
trumpet chair when he got back to school in the fall. He
had, as well, been elected vice-president of the student
senate, and would serve in that capacity in the coming year.
This was a particular stretch for him, as he had never sought
elected office before and, in fact, had never really felt
comfortable with people. But he had enlisted a popular

member of the class to run with him as president on a ticket, and they had been elected; and so, on paper, it now appeared as though he were truly a leader among his peers. On the basis of his determination and his innate talents, he could well expect to be named "Most Likely to Succeed" in the senior yearbook.

None of these achievements, however, made the summer easier for him, and perhaps the bottom line was that it would have been easier if there had been no summer altogether. He had never really enjoyed these summer interludes, for what they represented was time, unlimited by the imposed structure of school obligations, when he was put to work at the discretion of his father. Bob Gates, who himself had grown up on Maple Drive, was thoroughly imbued with a personal work ethic, one that he intended to pass on to his sons. And so, for Wyley, the summers were filled with work, work, and more work, mainly the maintenance of the grounds at the log cabin Bob Gates had built himself and at the homes of his grandmother and his great-aunt, both of whom lived on the road, and the maintenance of cars, trucks, and machinery at Robert Gates Enterprises, his father's business, which was located in a building nearby on Route 295.

It was not just the work that irritated Wyley and made the summer less than summer should have been for a seventeen-year-old boy. There was, as well, the tension that resulted from having Cheryl Brahm living in the same house with him. Cheryl, who had been on the scene ever since Wyley and his brother had returned from California, was utterly devoted to Bob, and although a strong streak of what might be termed misogyny ran through Bob's makeup, it was generally thought that he, in his way, was devoted to her as well. Cheryl, who worked in a clerical position for the State Department of Taxation and Finance in Albany, took her "stepmothering" role seriously, but to Wyley this attractive, vivacious woman in her midthirties was not only a lightweight, an annoyance, a "reader of romance novels," but was, more significantly, the woman who had stepped into the position that rightfully belonged to his mother, whom he regarded as a person of intelligence and refinement.

What made matters worse was that Wyley had had such high hopes for this summer before his senior year. It had been his wish to attend summer school in Boston, perhaps taking a course in oceanography, but his father had vetoed that plan on account of the expense. Instead, Bob had suggested that Wyley take the course in California, spending the summer with his mother and establishing residency there so that he could apply in the state university system when the time came next year. Bob would pay the tuition for the summer course if Kristi would pay the airfare. For one reason or another—Wyley said he never asked his mother; others claimed that the airfare money was not forthcoming—the plan didn't pan out. And so here he was down at the garage alongside his father's cronies, with whom he rarely deigned to converse, being asked to do menial chores that he did in as slow and unmotivated a way as possible, so as to show his father that he had his own way of doing things, a way that had nothing to do with whatever "ethic" his father was trying to impose upon him.

In the summer of 1986—that long, hot summer—the pattern of simmering resentment between Bob and Wyley Gates was being replaced with a new pattern that could best be described as a pitched battle.

If there was nothing else for which Wyley could respect his father, he could at least respect him as a tough adversary. Bob Gates had a reputation for wanting things done the way *he* wanted them done. Moreover, he had built up, from the bottom, a considerable business for himself. If his life thus far had had more than its share of complications—a bad marriage, a messy divorce, family tragedy—at least he could find a stabilizing force in his work.

To Bob, working was as much a life function as breathing or eating or sleeping. Dick Klingler, a farmer in Canaan who doubled as the town supervisor and, at one time, the town justice, remembered his friend Bob as "a very hard worker and the epitome of the capitalist." But "capitalism," in Bob's case, did not translate into a mercenary attitude about money. "Money he had no regard for. If you were down and out and needed a thousand dollars, he'd reach into his pocket and take it right out," Klingler recalled. "He worked so hard for his money but yet he seemed to work for the joy of working. Money was not the object."

For Bob, the joy of working specifically meant working with an entrepreneurial gleam in his eye. For over twenty years, he had worked for Hudson Handling, a road-salt business in Hudson, New York, founded by Bob's mentor and lifelong neighbor on Maple Drive, Robert C. Kellam. Bob started out with Hudson Handling running the loader and doing labor jobs, but through the years worked his way along in the company until he was essentially its manager. As a subsidiary business, Bob, in partnership with Kellam, established Kelgate, a company that furnished stockpile coverings, operating out of the garage that Bob owned on Route 295, in East Chatham. The garage, on ten acres, had been established with Bob's personal funds, but with the understanding that Hudson Handling would be feeding Bob its machinery and equipment for repair, thus covering Bob's initial investment. Bob also intended to rent space to a variety of tenants—already occupying a place in the garage was a motorcycle shop owned by Bob's good friend Richard "Skip" Huvar—and eventually to expand the property into some kind of minimall, which Bob and Dick Klingler referred to, half kiddingly, as "Gatesmall."

The fact that Bob's position with Hudson Handling allowed enough room for him to pursue his entrepreneurial bent had to do not only with the mentor-protégé relationship Bob had forged in his youth with Robert Kellam but also, in great measure, with Bob's own managerial style. "He was just that kind of person who could kind of sit back and run the operation and not have to be physically apparent to everybody every minute of the day," observed his friend and co-worker Dave Frick. To some of the men who worked with him, Bob seemed to have a quick and easy style. Frick, who kiddingly recalled him as a "ballbuster," said, "He just had a knack about him. He could really come down hard on you and make you feel good about it. People would get cranked maybe for the instant, and then be all right."

There were some, however, who didn't feel good about Bob's "ballbusting" and who felt, in fact, that Bob could be a harsh taskmaster. Dennis Gawron, one of Robert Gates, Jr.,'s closest friends, also worked for Kelgate and remembered Bob as a man who was sometimes difficult to deal with. According to Gawron, Bob would set him up with something to do and then take off, expecting it to be done when he returned. Gawron had memories of toiling in ninety-five-degree heat down at the garage, working almost to the point where he was ready to drop, and then having Bob come back to accuse him of being slow. This demanding attitude was both inflicted upon and instilled in young Bobby, who had briefly attended Hudson Valley Community College before working full-time at Kelgate. In Gawron's opinion, Bobby and his father were very much alike. "They had this attitude once in a while," he recalled, "that you couldn't do anything right."

Another great strength of Bob's, in addition to his energy and his entrepreneurial spirit, was an innate understanding of machinery. Dick Klingler's son, Jim, an engineer employed by Kelgate, recalled a time when they were working in Newark, using an unfamiliar piece of equipment. "Within two minutes of getting the machine from the kid who brought it over to us to use, Bob could run it better than the kid, and the kid had been using it for days," Klingler said. "He just understood machinery."

Respect for hard work and a knowledge of the way things work were two paramount tenets in the gospel according to Bob Gates, and he was intent on getting his sons to adopt that gospel. Bobby was not a problem—he had never been a shining light academically and he clearly had made the decision to emulate his father as closely as he could—but Wyley was a different story altogether. This was a boy whose interest in technology extended not to machinery that needed axle grease and motor oil, but to the clean universe of computers. Computers were his joy and his solace, and he spent many hours in front of them, so many that his father had taken to making derisive comments about his son's "computer hands." Bob regarded this summer before Wyley's senior year as a last-ditch opportunity to drum some sense into the obstinate head of that gifted but strange son of his, and it was this game plan that led Bob and Dick Klingler to have what Klingler remembered as the closest thing they ever had to a serious disagreement.

According to Klingler, Wyley came to Bob with a plan to go to either Boston to take college summer courses or to California to be with his mother, and Bob said no to both plans. Klingler told Bob that he was making the wrong decision. "The boy hates it here—you're not going to get any work out of him," Klingler remembered telling his friend. "I said, 'Let him go . . . let him further his education and it's going to be a lot easier the whole way through.' " But Bob, even though he acknowledged the truth in what his friend suggested, wouldn't play along with Wyley. "He said, 'Wyley has to understand that the entire world is not just sitting in front of a computer screen all day or doing what one wants to do'," recalled Klingler. " 'There are certain things that you have to do through life that may turn out to be disagreeable. I understand fully that Wyley hates the business, is never going to follow in the business, and will never have anything to do with it. I have enough money to send Wyley to any college he wants to go to and I will.' But he said, 'However, before he goes to college, he has to clearly understand that there are other facets to living too, that you have to know how to change the oil in your car, you have to know how to take care of a car, there are other things that have to be learned. He should spend this summer learning some of those things—working in the shop and doing a few of the things he may find disagreeable.' "

And so, in the summer of 1986, Wyley stayed on Maple Drive, enrolled in a course of disagreeability, and commenced a silent warfare with his father. Dave Frick remembered going down to the garage in those days and finding Wyley put to work by his father on one task or another that he found objectionable. One time, Frick, an outgoing man who claimed he always tried to find a good word for a boy who he felt was profoundly strange, found Wyley working on a farm tractor. He offered some advice to the boy. "I said, 'Wyley, you want me to show you how you can do that a little bit easier, save yourself some grief?' " Frick recalled. "He gives me one of them nasty snarly looks, like why didn't I just go somewheres and he was going to do whatever he had to do just to waste as much time as he could."

Whenever and wherever Wyley could act out, he would. Frick remembered Bob complaining to him about how Wyley would mow a lawn. "You know that kid will make mowing that lawn last a week," Bob told Dave. "He'll just go back and forth, back and forth, just so that he can say he's mowing the lawn like I told him to do." When it came to working on the ceiling down at the garage, Bob complained to his friends that "that goddamn Wyley, he just stood there all day long, staring at the ceiling, hoping it was going to glue itself to the wall."

"He was so rebellious," said Dick Klingler, "and he hated working in that garage so much that if he went down there and Bob, let's say, gave him a disc off a tractor that had to be cleaned up, Wyley would clean one side, lay it down, fold his hands, and stare at the ceiling. He would not do one single thing down there unless he was told every single move to make. . . . He acted like a prisoner."

But, for all the tension and bad feelings that were being engendered between father and son, no one who worked down at the garage with Bob, Bobby, and Wyley remembered any kind of abuse dealt Wyley by his father. If anything, in light of Wyley's stony intransigence and strategy of calculated indolence, Bob was regarded as indulgent, never really "getting on his case." Dave Frick and his wife, Louise, who had known Wyley all his life, had some tentative talks with Bob and Cheryl about the boy.

"He was strange," Louise said of Wyley. "He really was. Bob would come over sometimes and bring Wyley with him. And I'll never forget this. One day Bob sat there and Wyley stood right over there in the corner and he just stared at the ceiling for two hours. If he said hi to us when he came indoors, that was all he said. And he'd stand there and stare and stare, and I'd look at him and think, There's something wrong with that kid."

But, despite efforts that they made to bring Wyley's strangeness to their friend's attention, Bob wouldn't hear of it. "He'd always say, 'The boys. They'll grow out of it.' But he wouldn't yell at the kids," said Louise. "I yell at my kids all the time and he'd say, 'Calm down, Louise. Calm down.' "

Some thought Bob was giving Wyley the room he needed, but there may have been more to it than that. "Many, many times Robert used to tell us that one of these days Wyley was going to get very upset and he said, 'He's going to kill everybody, he's going to blow everybody away,' " recalled Dorothy Donnelley, the companion of Bob's friend Skip Huvar and a frequent visitor to the log house. "And I said, 'What do you mean "everybody"?' He said 'anybody that's in his way at the time.' " Bob's suspicion, according to Donnelley, was one that was voiced repeatedly. "We questioned him many times, over and over again, because he used to say it all the time. He said, 'He's just that type of person. Keeps everything bottled up, doesn't talk to anybody, and one of these days he's going to get really angry and kill everybody. He'll take a gun and kill everybody or he'll just do something, blow everybody up, or something. It might be the whole world, it might be just us, it might be who knows?' he said. 'But he's gonna do it.' "

For Wyley, the summer of 1986 was redeemed by one person, and his name was Damian Rossney. As a freshman, Damian, who would be a junior in the coming year at Chatham High, had been sent up by his parents from Ossining, in suburban Westchester County, to live with his aunt and uncle, Sally and Stanley Joseph, of Colane Road in Canaan. Soon after he arrived, Damian encountered Wyley in the computer lab at the high school and questioned the studious older boy on the use of the Apple computer. This casual beginning served as the ignition for the first real friendship that Wyley had ever experienced.

Although he was respected by his high school peers, Wyley's relationships never made that leap beyond to friendship or, failing that, social interaction. What Wyley was waiting for—and what, unfortunately and depressingly, he doubted he would ever be able to find in his socially dreary environs—was a like-minded soul. A superior being, in fact, who evinced the same sort of intellectual capacity on which Wyley prided himself. And then, miraculously, that person came along, and it was Damian. At that time physically unprepossessing and a year Wyley's junior, Damian was, by all accounts, extremely bright (his I.Q. would later test at 158) and had a glint in his eye for trouble—of the mischievous variety, it was initially thought. Linda Renken, who taught him in classes, thought of him as being "a bit of a wiseguy, kind of devilish . . . what can I get away with? sort of thing." When he first came into the school, he was a discipline problem. "He just tended to be extremely obnoxious," Renken recalled, "and if you asked him to do something he'd just say, 'Why?' "

The glue that really bound Wyley and Damian together in this new, and for Wyley, ground-breaking friendship was their love of computers, and computer games in particular. It was on a program called The Mind Prober that Wyley forged a profile of his new friend.

**Mr. D.R. is an enthusiastic, innovative person who can always find a new way to skin a cat. He is likely to keep his friends talking about his new projects and endeavors. If you want to work or play with him, you'll have to hustle—he's not the sort of person who will waste time waiting around for others.

**Mr. D.R. may be a handful. He is likely to pick and choose his friends with little regard for the impact they make on others. He's a risk-taker who may do things of which his peers only dream.

**Mr. D.R. can get new projects on the road. A high energy performer, Mr. D.R. has the self confidence necessary to be a school leader. His social skills are strong enough to get even the most reluctant group started on a new task.

**What makes Mr. D.R. tick? He secretly craves admiration and success, which he defines as power over people and resources.

Damian, in turn, contributed to a profile of Wyley:

**"Goal-centered" is a good way to describe Mr. W.G. His preoccupation with a project at hand will override social pleasantries or the feelings of others. He can be easily annoyed at those who get in the way of attaining his goals.

**Mr. W.G. may get involved with a group of young people whose interests mesh with his own. Without taking much time to "learn the ropes" within the group, he is likely to persuade the others to center their activities around his particular interests.

**If the fire gets too hot, Mr. W.G. is prone to react in impulsive, even reckless ways. On occasion, he may not consider the difference between right and wrong and find himself in a bigger mess than when he started.

**Mr. W.G. is willing to take chances. He's intrigued by potentially risky pursuits that offer excitement and stimulation . . . He is likely to participate in activities that offer him a chance to compete with others in a win or lose contest. How he plays the game is unimportant to him, because winning is all that matters.

**What makes Mr. W.G. tick? Mr. W.G. considers
life a series of challenges. If there are none facing
him at the moment, he'll seek them out. He plays
to win, whether the game is serious or for pleasure.

In the summer of 1986—that long and difficult summer—
Wyley Gates cultivated his friendship with Damian Rossney
and saw it thrive. In the fall, when school started up again
and when Wyley Gates—number two in his class, vice-
president of the student senate—stood poised on the brink
of a year of great promise for him, that friendship would
intensify and other boys would cluster around them, forming
a constellation—indeed, a kind of fraternity—that was a far
cry from the isolation to which Wyley had so long been
confined.

2

In offering directions to anyone traveling to my house for the first time, I always tell them to keep an eye out for the home of Vivian Gates, because it is there that they will have to bear left, and it is a landmark that cannot be missed. A large white Greek Revival home, set high on a hill, overlooking a pond, it is the single most imposing residence on a road of many excellent homes. Its broad sweep of lawn, stately columns, and clipped yew hedges all conspire to convey the picture of a high standard of country living. Parked among the assorted passenger cars and vans is a rider-mower used to mow the eighty-five acres that Mrs. Gates still owns on the road and, amid that acreage, at a high point overlooking the house, is a small graveyard of lichenous shifting tombstones. This is the family plot, of the sort that adjoins many old New England homes, and one that has seen, in recent years, too many tragic and untimely additions.

For over forty years, the Gates family has been a presence on Maple Drive, a short time by the standards of many locals who mark their stay in generations and centuries, but long enough to put down roots that would have gone deep save for the bizarre and seemingly random series of violent events that have afflicted the family. The arrival in East Chatham of Louis Gates III and his wife, Vivian, was marked by the sort of searching optimism that characterized so many young couples in the years following the Second World War. Vivian, a native of New Orleans, had followed her husband around the country while he served with the army; by the time they returned to live with Louis's family in Pelham, New York, just north of the Bronx, they were the parents of a son, also named Louis, and a daughter Viki. Lou—creative, high-strung, intense—wanted a different kind of life from that which Pelham could provide, and, as he had always loved the countryside, he proceeded to look for a home farther north of the New York City metropolitan area. He was familiar with the Chatham area through an uncle who owned a home and acreage on Maple Drive, and so, when the house and property adjacent to his uncle's became available—that large white house on the hill, spacious enough for a big family—Lou and Vivian made their move.

Lou, a draftsman, or, as he preferred to describe himself, an architect, albeit without a degree, went to work for the state, and the next few years saw the births of their sons Robert, Steven, and Bill. When Lou Gates left his job with the state and went to work for independent architects in nearby Pittsfield, Massachusetts, financial pressures caused Vivian to take a job as well. Fortunately, while matriculated at Newcomb College of Tulane University, where she had studied art, Vivian had enrolled in teaching courses, and this qualification enabled her to secure a teaching position at the elementary level in the nearby Claverack and Greenport school systems. Before long, however, Vivian's teaching career was interrupted. "The first year I taught I got pregnant," she recalled. "And that was Dane." Dane was the last of her six children, and, in time, she resumed her teaching career and went on to enjoy a lengthy tenure, well remembered for her skills and her general qualities of warmth and patience.

Gordon Ringer, who would later become the Chatham High School music instructor for both Bobby Gates and his brother Wyley, was a student of Vivian's. "It was almost like having a second grandmother or mother when you were in class with her," recalled Ringer. "She'd do everything to help you, like button up your coat if you had to go outside. She was always very supportive."

Lou Gates's reputation in the community, however, was painted in considerably darker tones. Neighbors wishing to remain anonymous described him as "nasty" and "miserable." Even those who barely knew him seemed to have the sense of his being a difficult man, and those who one would have assumed were close to him, such as the men who were his honorary pallbearers, were not necessarily so. One of Lou Gates's honorary pallbearers, the former proprietor of the East Chatham general store, described him as "a fine gentleman," but another, an attorney who had had some dealings with Gates, never knew he had been so honored until I told him and couldn't quite understand why he had been so designated. Bob Gates's close friend Dick Klingler, perhaps Canaan's least anonymous citizen, recalled a particularly unpleasant business experience with Lou Gates.

Klingler sold him a tractor and thereafter Gates kept finding things wrong with it, which he felt that Klingler should repair for nothing. "Finally, one day, right outside my barn here, he came down and he said he broke a guard hitting a rock and I should replace it," Klingler recalled. "After all these complaints it was the straw that broke the camel's back. And I said, 'Look, this isn't perpetual care. If you want to drive it into a dozen rocks, fine and dandy with me.' We got into quite a donnybrook out in the middle of the road. Finally, I just pulled out of it and said, 'That's the way it's going to be, take it or leave it.'" Gates took it, without another word. "He went off down the road and our relationship from then on was always very cordial and I never had any more trouble from him," said Klingler. "I think the point came down to that he was a testing kind of person."

Within his own family, Lou Gates was remembered as

a caring and providing father, but even here his difficult personality traits were gingerly acknowledged. "I think we can all be difficult at times," said Evelyn Prescott, the older of Lou's two sisters. "He was maybe a little more difficult, yes he was." Lou's younger sister, Dorothy Dooley, added, "He certainly had his own opinions about things and ideas about things." Gates's "difficult" personality led him into an unfortunate fracas with the East Chatham Fire Department, one of the institutional mainstays of this hamlet. Lou Gates had been asked to design a room in the firehouse and what resulted was, in the words of one neighbor, a "ruckus."

"They had drawn up plans to put a commercial kitchen in the firehouse—it cost quite a bit—and Lou decided he had a friend who could do it cheaper," said Betty Brorup, a member of the Ladies' Auxiliary of the East Chatham firehouse and for years the village postmistress. "And it's really a terrible mess . . . he put three stoves in and they weren't any good, and he'd never make it right for us. . . . The sliding doors never worked and it ended up costing us more money than it would have if we put that commercial kitchen in from the start." It was an incident that people remembered for years. "The firemen were very, very upset with him," said Mrs. Brorup. "In a small town, you do something like that, for a community that really can't afford it, that leaves very bad feelings."

These incidents could, conceivably, be written off as the normal wear and tear of small-town relationships, but, in fact, material that later emerged during the trial of Wyley Gates conveyed a portrait of Lou Gates as a man who, more than being difficult or even nasty, suffered from severe psychological problems. Indeed, the Gates home, despite the close-knit relationships of the siblings and the interference run by Vivian Gates, was marked by the tension created by its extremely exacting head of household. Bob Gates's close friend Dave Frick remembered that Bob and his sister Viki and all the other Gates family members he knew said that "Lou was tough." A neighbor recalled Lou Gates "screaming and yelling" all the time. Evelyn Prescott said that her brother was "a little on the strict side and I don't think his kids went for that too much." To close friends, even more of the truth was divulged. "Bob told me his father was mean," said Don DeLapp, a friend of Bob's for over twenty years. "He said, 'My father said something to you once, if you weren't moving he'd jack your ass.' " Indeed, DeLapp felt that Bob bent over backward not to follow his father's example. "Part of the reason Bob was so good to his kids was because he didn't want to be like his father was," said DeLapp.

With a haunting inevitability, Lou Gates's sons left home at an early age. His eldest son, Louis, joined the navy. Another son, Steven, served in Vietnam. As for Bob, the regular conflict in which he found himself with his father led to his being sent to California to live with Vivian's sister. Of the relationship between Lou Gates and his sons, Dick Klingler conjectured that "when they came of age, they just got as far away from him as they could." But perhaps not far enough, for, with all the distance that Bob put between himself and his father, he still carried the scars of this conflicted relationship and, to a degree that remains questionable, he replicated this dynamic in his relationships with his own sons.

Bob attended junior college while in California but dropped out, at age nineteen, to marry Kristi Holcomb, then a lissome sixteen-year-old from Concord, north of Oakland. Kristi's mother came from a Norwegian community in Minnesota; she and Kristi's father were divorced and, to Wyley, his maternal grandfather would remain a shadowy figure. Shortly after Kristi and Bob were married, their first son, Bobby, Jr., was born. They stayed for a while in California, but Bob was aching to get back east, and so, with his young family in tow, he returned to Columbia County, staying first with his parents and then renting a place in the hamlet of Craryville, some twenty miles south of Chatham.

While residing in Craryville, a second son was born and they named him Wyley. Bob, Kristi, and the boys moved back up to East Chatham, first to a house on Frisbie Street, then into an apartment in Chatham while they built their log cabin. Vivian Gates often wondered why her husband never specifically commented on their son's homespun cabin, which seemed at such incongruous odds with the stately dwelling in which they had reared their own children. "One of the things he used to say, when there was a mess in the house, is 'You people should live in a log cabin.' I wondered if Bobby built it because of that," she said.

In fact, the log cabin, in direct view of the dignified Greek Revival home, may have represented more than a flaunting gesture in the face of the autocratic patriarch. It could be seen as a definite statement that Bob Gates's life would contain none of the grandiosity or pretension of his father's life (psychiatric testimony at the Gates trial would reveal Lou Gates's intense interest in tracing his lineage to the royal bloodlines of Europe). Indeed, in a distinctly downward cycle of educational and social aspiration and attainment, most of the Gates children established life-styles very different from that of their parents. Within Wyley's social circle at school, Bob Gates was regarded as a "biker," as was Wyley's young uncle Dane Gates. Bob Gates's brother-in-law Howard Hatch, the husband of his sister Viki, was described by a neighbor as a decent man, but uncouth and backwoods. "He used to have these coonhounds all the time," said the neighbor. "Bob used to say to us, 'My God, I wish he'd get rid of those damned dogs, they bark all night.' " The dichotomy between the kind of life that Vivian Gates had set out to make for herself and the life that her daughter Viki was leading was striking to this observer. "Considering this is Mrs. Gates's daughter," the neighbor said, "it doesn't fit . . . It isn't 'like mother, like daughter.' "

Nor, in significant ways, was it "like mother, like son." Whereas Vivian Gates had gotten her college degree from a fine university, of her sons, neither Steven, Dane, nor Bob completed college. To me, the schizoid nature of the family became readily apparent when I went to interview Mrs. Gates at her home. There, in the magazine rack, were a number of issues of the *Kenyon Review*, a scholarly literary journal. In what percentage of American homes would one find a collection of *Kenyon Review*s? A minute percentage, and fewer still were such homes where the next generation went on to lead lives of heavy labor, trucking, stock-car racing, and the other elements of a rural blue-collar way of life. Clearly, there was a polarization within the family, a polarization that, perhaps, had given rise to the alienated identity of a grandson named Wyley.

Wyley, again and again, would make a point of identifying with his grandmother. Vivian, he claimed, was an intellectual, as was his mother, whereas the men in his family were not. And, like himself, his grandmother was a survivor. According to the court testimony that would raid the privacy of the Gates family in the months ahead, she had had to be. Testimony revealed that her husband was an emotionally disturbed individual who had physically abused her and their children. In the course of this testimony, severe behavioral disorders were ascribed as well to at least three of her sons. And through it all—through all the horror and all the tragedy—Mrs. Gates would present a face to the world that was alternately described as becalmed or benumbed or bewildered, but rarely as bereft or bereaved. To one psychiatrist, Vivian Gates would confess the incredibly difficult time she had showing her children affection. This stood, of course, in marked contrast to the memories of someone like former student Gordon Ringer, who remarked on her warmth and supportiveness. Perhaps her flat affect and her inability to express affection were outgrowths of the trauma of living with a man who was abusive to her and her children. One of those children, Viki Hatch, when asked if she could trace to her father the seeds of violence in her family history, responded, "If I was to be honest about it, yes."

If the juxtaposition of the homely log cabin and the elegant Greek Revival house set high on a hill symbolized the deeply schizoid nature of the family, the log cabin represented, as well, for Wyley's father and, briefly, for

Wyley's mother, that recognizable piece of the American dream called the private family dwelling. Although it remained unfinished—some of the rooms were never given doors and the electrical wiring in places was left naked—Bob had worked hard on it, doing it just as he wanted it done, and at his side was Kristi, young and beautiful and increasingly lonely, helping to build it every inch of the way, log by log. But for all of the labor that had gone into it, for all the blood, toil, and sweat, it lacked some essential mortar, some homebound, hearthside warmth that would hold it all together. In the weeks following the murders, on her first trip back to Maple Drive in many years, Kristi Gates told her former mother-in-law something she had never permitted herself to express before. "It should have burned down long ago," she said of the log cabin.

What Wyley's mother didn't know at the time was that the torching of the dwelling had been a contingency considered by Wyley and his friends. But they decided against it, not wanting to lower "property values." Oddly enough, despite its having served as the crucible for his murderous intentions, the log cabin was much cherished by Wyley. A psychiatrist who interviewed him after the murders said that Wyley really thought he would just go back to the house and continue living there, and that he was very protective of it.

The plaintiveness of Kristi Gates's remark was emblematic of her experience living on Maple Drive. Making her way in the large, close-knit Gates family proved an overwhelming assignment for her. Bob's sister Viki, who lived for many years with her husband Howard and their four daughters next to the log cabin, had as much contact with Kristi as anyone in the family had in those years. "Kristi was difficult to talk to," Viki recalled. "At first I thought it was because she'd come from California and she was in a strange area where she didn't know anybody. For the longest time you'd try to talk to her and get one-word answers or ignored altogether. Most of us gave up after a while. Bob got mad because nobody would talk to her." Evelyn Prescott, Bob's aunt, corroborated Viki Hatch's characterization of Wyley's mother. "She was the type of person that if you walked into a room, she wouldn't acknowledge you," said Mrs. Prescott. "If you spoke to her, she'd talk to you." Louise Frick recalled a visit to the log cabin when she and Kristi were both young mothers with, ostensibly, much in common. "When we first met them, I had just had our youngest son and Bob invited us over there one Sunday," she said. "My oldest one was playing with the kids and Kristi was sitting there and she wouldn't say a word to me. All that time, she would not say one word to me! Just like Wyley. And I wound up sitting there talking to the baby." Other friends had similar experiences with Bob's wife, describing her either as cold and aloof or as a "space cadet." Bob used to complain that when his friends would come over to the house for dinner, Kristi would serve a meal, clean up, and then, while everyone was still at the table talking, she would take a book and go sit in the living room.

A deep sense of dissatisfaction and unhappiness began to grip the snug log cabin. Kristi's questing for something beyond her life in East Chatham was confusing to Bob, who would open up to friends about it. One friend from that period recalls Bob talking about her black moods, wherein she would complain endlessly that she didn't know what she wanted to do with her life. "Bob would suggest to her that if you don't know what you want to do, why don't you do this or try this?" Dave Frick said. "Why don't you go back to college or why don't you try this and see if that's what you want to do? Try different things. Because," Frick added, "Bob wasn't afraid to try anything."

But Kristi found herself in a crisis situation, on a downward spiral that was life-threatening. Vivian Gates recalled an evening when she was baby-sitting for her grandsons at her house and Bob ran in, terribly upset, to ask her if the boys could spend the night. Not until material emerged at the trial did Mrs. Gates discover that that night, which she only vaguely remembered, was, in fact, the night that Kristi had ingested approximately one hundred aspirin tablets in an attempt to commit suicide.

Beyond the black moods, however, there were other complications. Although she could be extremely withdrawn and depressed, there was, as well, a manic side to Kristi that was marked by her being very outgoing and attractive to men and that pointed to multiple relationships. A family member recalled a long-ago party. "Kristi was throwing herself all over this guy, with his wife there," said the relative. "I know if it were my wife I would have been embarrassed to tears."

With the situation having deteriorated beyond repair, Bob moved out of the cabin he had built and for a time Kristi stayed on in the house. She looked for work in Albany, but it was her desire to return to California with her two little boys. "I don't think she was a very devoted mother," suggested a family member, "but she did have an affectionate side." And so to Antioch, California, north of Oakland, traveled Bobby, Jr., ten, and Wyley, eight, bewildered and with only each other for companionship and support. They stayed for two years and when they returned, it was generally felt, they were very different . . . particularly Wyley.

Bob's experience with marriage had left him scarred. "Bob never trusted another woman after that. Ever," recalled Dick Klingler. "It was one of his quirks." Bob told a neighbor that women were only good for two things, one of which was obvious, the other of which was raising children until they reached a "tolerable" age. But Bob, for all his nascent misogyny, was an attractive man, active, physical, and available. It wasn't long after Kristi left for California that Bob found himself in another relationship, one that would last, through periods of upheaval, until the end of his life . . . and hers.

Cheryl Brahm was born in 1950, in Niverville, a working-class community of faded pastel bungalows clustered alongside a lake ten miles west of East Chatham. One of six children, Cheryl, bright and attractive, was employed as a nurse's aide at the Barnwell Nursing Home in neighboring

Valatie. At nineteen, she married Anson Dubois, a carpenter eight years her senior. Before she was thirty, the marriage had ended. Like Bob Gates, she had married young and had divorced young and, like Bob Gates, she had no great respect for the institution of marriage and no pressing desire to repeat her mistake.

In fact, Cheryl viewed the period following her divorce as a rich time of change in her life. With her marriage over, unfettered by children she had been unable to conceive, and with her long tenure at Barnwell at an end due to her involvement in a unionization effort, she was free to start all over again. Her sister-in-law Mame Brahm, to whom she was close, recalled the Cheryl of that period. "She got her initiative; she was growing as a woman; she got involved in everything; and she was changing," said Mame. "She wanted to grow—now she was going to live on her own! She was going to be her own fulfilled person. She was going to support herself—the New Woman of the 'seventies era." She turned to nearby Albany, as so many in Columbia County do, first taking a mail-room job and then, after passing her high school equivalency test, successfully taking the civil service examination. When this led to a secretarial position with the New York State Department of Taxation and Finance, Cheryl became one of that legion whose very appellation—"state workers"—was often used as a put-down by Bob Gates, man of action, man of the outdoors.

Neither Bob's sarcasm nor his misogyny, however, kept Cheryl from pursuing a relationship with him. A chance meeting at a tavern in Chatham had reintroduced Bob to Cheryl, and Cheryl, who had known and admired Bob from high school, was soon in love. "Cheryl thought the world of him," recalled their friend Dorothy Donnelley. "She would do anything for him. I mean, she just adored him." But neither of them, as their history suggested, was particularly easy to live with, so their relationship had its problems. Bob, in the words of a close friend of Cheryl's, "liked to bust on people . . . he was pretty chauvinistic . . . he liked a good argument and he knew how to get you, to go after you, and get a rise out of you." As for Cheryl, a family member described her as having been "very nervous . . . she'd bite her nails down to no end," and a friend suggested that even though Cheryl, at five feet, six inches and 120 pounds, was very slender, almost delicate physically, "there was something about her that if you knew she was mad, you wouldn't want to mess with her . . . she'd be a formidable candidate just because she could get mad enough." But the attraction between them was undeniable. In fact, Cheryl was reputed to have told a friend that once you had been with a Gates man, it was never the same with anyone else. This strong attraction led Cheryl, in the opinion of one of her friends, to suffer anxiety about Bob's traveling on the road so much and the seductions to which he might be exposed there. That anxiety caused Cheryl to become, in the words of a neighbor, "obsessive" about her appearance. "Her whole thing was staying thin for Bob," said the neighbor. "Bob used to lift weights, a very macho guy, muscley, had to do exercise because he drove his trucks so much, and so that was what was important to her, to look good for Bobby."

In the beginning, she kept her own apartment in the village of Kinderhook, coming to stay with him days here, days there, weeks here, weeks there. They had fun together, especially riding on Bob's motorbike, a pursuit that they found carefree and without any of the prototypically sinister overtones. "Robert enjoyed it," recalled Dorothy Donnelley, who often rode with them. "He used to ride fast now and then, no big deal. Not being bad, running people off the road or anything like that. He never wore a black jacket. He didn't wear anything black."

But there were rocky interludes too, when Cheryl would move back to her apartment and Bob would complain to his friends that he was used to living alone and couldn't alter his ways to suit a woman. A neighbor remembered him returning from one of his frequent trips and stating that it was a good thing he wasn't married, because he didn't like being tied down and if he were married he wouldn't be able to go away. "I pointed out that here he was with Cheryl and he had been away and he said, 'Oh, but everything changes when you're married,'" the neighbor recalled.

"Bobby had this feeling that marriage meant confinement. He couldn't do what he wanted to do."

In response to Bob's kneejerk reluctance to commitment, his friends championed Cheryl. "From time to time, there would be problems, like in any kind of relationship," Dave Frick said, "and Bob would say, 'Well, what do you think?' And I'd say, 'Bob, I don't live with her but I just can't see a woman better suited to the way you do things.' "

Bob's family also regarded Cheryl warmly. Cheryl and Vivian Gates had an excellent relationship. "Bob had his mother on a pedestal and Cheryl adored her just like Bob did," recalled Mame Brahm. "Cheryl had this great admiration for Vivian. She was educated, supposed to be in the fine arts . . . she really admired her. When she shopped, she had to be more particular for what she got for her than being particular for what she gave to anyone else."

With her characteristic energy and buoyancy, Cheryl fully entered into the heart of the Gates clan as Kristi had never been able to do. "Cheryl was a terrific person," said Viki Hatch. "A real bubbly, terrific kind of person. Big smile . . . always helping out if she could. I was working and had the girls and she'd come up just about every night and ask if everything was all right and if she could help out with something. She was just a giving person, that's all."

Cheryl's close relationship with the four Hatch daughters was very much in character for a woman whom everyone described as having been particularly gifted with children. Although she would never have her own—in addition to her unsuccessful attempts to conceive during her marriage, Bob had had a vasectomy after the birth of Wyley—children were a special source of pleasure for her. Viki Hatch remarked that Cheryl was "very gifted with babies and kids." Louise Frick thought that Cheryl was "real good with kids . . . so patient at it." Another friend, Barbara DeLapp, noted that "Cheryl loved everybody. If someone needed her, she was there. She kind of just had a motherly instinct."

In fact, all of her patience and all of her talent would be required of her in the years ahead on Maple Drive, for she had become an unspecified but very real and present figure of authority to two Gates grandsons and, in time, would seek to become the adoptive mother of a third. It was a daunting task she had set for herself, made even more so by the enmity of the Gates boys, an enmity that she could neither understand nor, despite all her best efforts, do anything to control.

3

There are few, if any, young children whose lives and personalities are not radically altered by the divorce of their parents. Judith S. Wallerstein and Sandra Blakeslee, in their widely read *Second Chances: Men, Women, and Children a Decade After Divorce*, studied sixty families, following them from the time of divorce to five and then ten years later. They found that the majority of the children they studied could not concentrate in school, had trouble making friends, and suffered a wide range of behavioral problems. Even after ten years, many of these children of divorced parents continued to do poorly, entering adulthood as worried, underachieving, self-deprecating, and sometimes angry young men and women. Children tend to do well if their mothers and fathers resume their parenting roles, manage to put aside differences, and afford them a continuing relationship with both parents, but, overall, most children from divorced families are on a downward course. Indeed, Wallerstein stated that "it would be hard to find another group—except, perhaps, the victims of a natural disaster—who suffered such a rate of sudden serious psychological problems."

Those who knew Wyley before he went off with his brother to California at the age of eight, to live with a mother who had herself manifested clinical symptoms of extreme emotional disturbance, believed him to be a very different child when he returned to Maple Drive at the age of ten. Viki Hatch saw the change immediately. "Before he went to California, we could kind of relate," she recalled. "But when he came back he was different." Don DeLapp remembered that "when they came back here, they wouldn't say boo. They both looked like they were deathly afraid of everything."

The time in California had been a kind of anxious twilight. Wyley and Bobby, Jr., were left alone for hours on end, during which time they were fixed to the television. They also found themselves the target of neighborhood kids who saw them as strange and alien. In later years, Bobby related to a close friend just how awful the experience had been: every day on their way home from school, they were beaten up by neighborhood kids. Dr. Anthony Marchionne, a clinical psychologist who spent forty-five hours with Wyley after the murders, reflected on this period in Wyley's life. "I think that his mother's reality circumstance, her actual living circumstance, was a shock to Wyley," said Marchionne. "She was living in a trailer, dating different men. Additionally, I don't think she was giving him an unusual level of support at the time."

At the age of ten, on a trip back east, Wyley came to a fork in the road: Did he want to live with his mother or his father? According to a family member, Bob made it Wyley's decision. "I remember trying to get him to stay here, feeling like his family was around him, not liking what I'd heard about things in California, the way the kids watched TV while Kristi was out, alone most of the time," a relative recalled. "Wyley finally told Kristi that he was going to stay with Bob, but I remember feeling that it was too big a job for a kid his age."

For both Wyley and Bobby, the return to Maple Drive

proved an enormous adjustment. Whereas they essentially had been on their own in California—or, at least, left to their own devices, with the narcotizing TV furnishing a background—they now suddenly found themselves at the behest of this demanding and commanding person who was their father. "They were taken out of one house—a quiet, quiet environment," recalled a family friend, "and they get off an airplane and here they are in the middle of a salt yard with tractor trailers and payloaders digging away, and this is your father, you know? And you could see it on their faces—like 'Ma, what are we gonna do now?' "

Bob was aware that his sons were quiet to the point of being withdrawn and tried to spend as much time with them as he could. Often he would take them on the interstate runs his business required him to make. But sometimes that would prove impossible, and Bob, like any single parent, which is essentially what he was, with Kristi living on the West Coast, had to create a support system for himself. Fortunately, his sister Viki and her family lived next door, and he had his mother and father just across the road. Unfortunately, however, the Gates family was experiencing their own severe pressures. Bob's brother Steven, a Vietnam veteran who had been known locally as "Boogaloo," cracked up his van upon his return from active duty. "His car went off a cliff, according to the cops," said a family member. "And they really don't know what happened, if he was forced off the road or what." Steven's injuries resulted in severe neurological damage that, to this day, have required his institutionalization. This tragedy was followed by the long illness of Lou Gates, who had developed leukemia and who died in 1981, at the age of sixty-six.

Bob recognized that he needed one sure place to turn, and that the only way he could get what he needed was by having a woman full-time in his life, even if that meant a curtailment of his freedom. And so, with the return of the boys to Maple Drive, the relationship between Cheryl and Bob accelerated rapidly, so much that when Bob was away from home, it was Cheryl who suddenly, inexplicably, and perhaps threateningly became the substitute figure of authority to the boys, and, consequently, the focal point of their animosity.

"Cheryl never wanted the kids to think she was taking their mother's place," Louise Frick recalled. "She always said that. Especially with Wyley. . . . She said she wasn't his mother and she had no intention of trying to be his mother. She was going to try and guide him and everything but she wasn't going to push herself on him."

At the time that Cheryl became a "stepmother" to Bob Gates's sons, Bobby was twelve and Wyley was ten. In the ensuing years, after their return back east, they would see little of their mother, although both of them continued to profess fond feelings toward her. "I think Cheryl realized that the kids were hurt," said a friend of Cheryl's. "Their mother would do things like go on a vacation and send them cards saying, 'Having a wonderful time' . . . she'd forget birthdays, Christmas." And then, not long after their return east, Kristi gave birth to an out-of-wedlock daughter, providing Wyley with a half sister for whom he would profess a continuing fondness as well.

As for Cheryl, she threw herself into the role of the woman of the house. She was compulsive about housekeeping, and the log cabin was always spotless, which was no mean task with the kids coming in and out. She made curtains for the windows, and she and Bob enjoyed collecting antiques. In other respects, however, Bob and Cheryl could be lackadaisical about their environment. The love life of Bob and Cheryl, which Cheryl portrayed to her friends as being a lusty one, was, one imagines, occasionally in evidence, or at least audible, to young boys living in a house that lacked doors that would have insured privacy.

But, to give her her due, Cheryl took her domestic responsibilities seriously. Even though Bob and the boys teased her relentlessly about her cooking, she saw herself as the nurturer. "She always had things like a square meal for the boys," noted Barbara DeLapp. "If they were hungry or not, they left the house with lunch."

Moreover, recognizing Wyley's signature mode of withdrawal early on, she made, at least in the eyes of her friends, particular efforts to connect to him. "She spent a lot of time with him and tried to understand him," Barbara DeLapp pointed out. "She used to say, 'What do you want to do about Christmas? Do you want to get your mother something? Do you want to get your brother something?' She would take him shopping. When he wanted to learn how to drive, she taught him how to drive." Mame Brahm agreed that Cheryl was protective of Wyley and really loved him. "She would never accept him hating her," said Mame. "She wouldn't think anybody could hate that bad to harm her. She knew that he resisted her because he wanted his natural mother . . . she wanted his love so bad."

But she wasn't to get it. Even though some observers characterized Cheryl as a "confidante" for Wyley, those closer to the scene reported a basic and continual antipathy that never lightened and that was, to some extent, shared by Bobby, Jr., as well.

A power struggle was going on in the house and, clearly and frustratingly for Cheryl, it was not a struggle that she was going to be able to win. And yet she fought for her proper place in the home. To her, the issue of being "respected" was cardinal, and she regularly made into a charged issue the fact that she wasn't being respected by the boys, reporting to their father, when he returned from his travels, any slights she felt she had suffered. The tension between Cheryl and the boys was compounded by the boys' suspicion that Cheryl "snooped" in their rooms when they were out, looking for something she could use against them. Bobby's friend Dennis Gawron remembered times when Bob was away and "we'd be working down at the garage and Cheryl would call up Bobby wondering what we were doing and why did he have his father's truck down there and things like that." This surveillance was somewhat ironic, as other employees of Bob's remembered that the garage, in Bob's absence, could only be locked up by Bobby or Wyley, as they—and, significantly, not Cheryl—were the holders of the keys. Indeed, Viki Hatch felt that there was a built-in problem with Cheryl's situation in the house. "If she said something to them," Mrs. Hatch recalled, "Bob would tell her to leave them alone. Remember, she was the intruder."

As far as Bobby was concerned, a good deal of his resentment toward Cheryl may have been misplaced anger he was feeling toward his father. Although Bobby had made, in his adolescence, a decision, conscious or unconscious, to identify with Robert, their relationship still had its problems. In the aftermath of the murders, some media accounts sought to demonstrate that they had arisen out of a clear-cut situation in which Wyley was set against his father and his brother. Jim Klingler, who worked at Kelgate with Robert and Bobby, Jr., discounts this. "The newspapers said Bob and Bob, Jr., were really tight and Wyley was the outsider," said Klingler. "And that wasn't really the case at all. Bob, Jr., caught hell plenty of times for various things. It wasn't like he had ice cream and Wyley got gravel to eat."

Klingler also noted that Bobby was having second thoughts about continuing to work at Kelgate. "Bobby decided more or less that he wanted to go back to school when he had a chance," said Klingler. "I don't think he felt that he wanted to work forever in his father's garage." Several friends of the family, however, cited the fact that Bobby owed his father a large sum of money. Bobby's friends warned him that if he continued to borrow money, he would never be able to go off on his own. But Bobby got in deeper and deeper. Wyley, on the other hand, was described as "tight as hell," lending his brother money and then charging him interest. Clearly, Wyley was not going to provide an avenue out of Bobby's spiraling debt to his father.

Even the areas of interest that Bob and Bobby shared were often fraught with undue intensity. One such interest, which Bob saw as an activity that he and the boys could enjoy together, was stock-car racing. In looking for a way to relate to his sons when they returned from California, Bob had bought the boys dirtbikes, which Bobby enjoyed but Wyley rejected. Then Bob introduced his sons to snow-mobiles, and again Bobby took up the hobby and Wyley

declined. Next came the stock cars. Bob's younger brother
Dane had taken up stock-car racing and had introduced
Bob to it, and Bob enjoyed working on the cars. Fiddling
with old cars and motorbikes had always been his greatest
love. He wanted to pass that kind of pleasure on to his
sons—he built each of them his own stock car—and for a
while it appeared he had an avid adherent in Bobby at least.
"I watched Bobby," remembered Don DeLapp, "and I said,
'Boy, you know, Bob, that kid's got it, he's gonna be good.
That kid can go to the top.' " But again, as far as Wyley was
concerned, the boy was having none of what interested his
father. "After Bob built the race cars, I said, 'How's Wyley
doing?' " DeLapp recalled. "And Bob said, 'Well, I got him
to drive twice and I think it scared him.' And I said, 'Well,
the best thing to do is just leave him be. Different people
take things different ways.' "

Bobby, Jr.,'s racing career went well for a while. He
had a couple of good wins, but mostly he placed second or
third. At the end of the season in 1986, however, Bobby
wasn't sure whether he would continue. To DeLapp, he
expressed interest in getting a Chevy—the car to beat—but
to his closest friend, Dennis Gawron, a much more discouraged picture presented itself. "He was real good for a while
and then just the last season he raced he wasn't doing very
well at all," said Gawron. "And he took a lot of riding from
his father about that." It was a prohibitively expensive hobby
for Bobby—his father agreed to pay for all the car repairs,
but Bobby had to pay the entrance fee, which was approximately eleven dollars, and for the high-octane gas, which
ran two dollars a gallon—and this was every Saturday night
in the summer, quite a financial commitment for a young
man earning what Bobby was earning.

And so the stock-car racing, which had been seized
upon as a means to bring father and sons closer together,
in fact represented yet another example of the way that
Bob Gates sought to imprint his will on his sons. They were
the only children he would ever have and he wanted them
to do things the way he thought they should be done. The
stress of living with a father who always wanted things done

"the right way" had to come out somewhere. Inevitably, it
was easier for the boys to express their anger and resentment
not to their father, but to Cheryl—the eternal outsider, the
eternal "intruder." Sometimes the resentment would reach
a head and find an overt form of expression. One relative
of Cheryl's remembered a time when Cheryl came to her
swimming pool with Bobby and Wyley, when they were still
quite young. Horseplay between Cheryl and the boys quickly
escalated into an opportunity to get in some real, powerful
licks at this woman who exerted an unwelcome influence
over their lives, and Cheryl, in pain and tears, had to take
refuge in the relative's house.

But mostly the resentment found expression in continual contempt and derision. Dennis Gawron, who liked
Cheryl, used to have conversations with her when he visited
Bobby at the log cabin. "Bobby could never understand it—
like, 'What are you talking to *her* for?' " Gawron recalled.
Cheryl, whom friends describe as having been attentive and
supportive of Bobby's and Wyley's extracurricular pursuits,
would sometimes appear at the stock-car races at the Lebanon Speedway, but her attendance was unappreciated.
"Bobby would just look like, 'What's *she* doing here?' " Gawron related.

Eventually, the enmity between Bobby and Cheryl
lessened. To some extent, this was a result of Bobby's
growing older and more mature emotionally, and striving
for a closer identification with his father and his father's
way of life. Partly, however, the détente was struck when
that enmity erupted into actual physical violence. A friend
remembered a time when Bob was away, leaving Cheryl, as
always, with the family responsibilities. Bobby "gave Cheryl
lip" and Cheryl slapped him right across the face. Cheryl
was very upset, as was Bobby, and Bobby went down to the
garage, where he had a heart-to-heart with his father's
buddy. "I had a little talk with him," the friend recalled,
"and told him that here's a woman who's bending over
backwards, keeping your house clean; she's good to you;
she's nice to you; you don't have to pull that bullshit. Then

Bobby went back and apologized to her and after that incident they got real close."

But whereas Bobby found himself eventually coming around to an understanding with Cheryl, Wyley remained staunchly resistant. In fact, based on statements that Wyley made to Viki Hatch's daughters, they knew that "he would never accept her." Every manner of chore became a battle-field where Wyley was concerned. Mowing the lawn, taking out the garbage, bringing the clothes downstairs . . . all of it. "They had to beg him to do it," recalled Barbara DeLapp. "He had no interest in it. Because it took him away from what he wanted to do." Even a little thing like Cheryl's insistence that he get out of the car to pump the gas when they pulled into a service station became just another bone that stuck in Wyley's craw.

Throughout his adolescence, Wyley's contempt and hatred festered and grew. "He began to perceive that these people—his father and his brother and Cheryl—were very inferior human beings," Dr. Marchionne noted. "Particularly Cheryl. She was weak. She tried to quit smoking twenty times and couldn't do it. She worked for the state of New York and she was just lazy." In fact, Dr. Marchionne realized, she wasn't that way at all. "This was a really involved woman," he pointed out. "She really took pride in that house."

To a cousin—one of the very few people whom Wyley used as a confidante—he was open about his full-blown hatred of Cheryl. Indeed, he told her that he wanted to torture Cheryl, that this was his life mission. But, as far as Cheryl was concerned, the intensity of Wyley's feelings toward her went unnoted or, at least, uncommented on by her. Evelyn Prescott could only recall one time when Cheryl ever verbalized any concern about Wyley. It came during a visit when Cheryl was selling sweaters on consignment. "We were talking about the sweaters," Mrs. Prescott recalled, "and then about Wyley. They were having some trouble with Wyley." But what was presented by Cheryl—difficulties surrounding Wyley's unauthorized use of the family's ve-hicles—was perceived as nothing more than ordinary adolescent cutting-up . . . "sowing his oats," as Mrs. Prescott put it. There seemed no aspect of fear expressed on that afternoon of the sweater sale, nor on any other afternoon, for no one seemed to feel that Wyley was a person capable of anything sinister. "He was the last person in the world anyone would suspect," Mrs. Prescott remarked, "because he was so quiet . . . he certainly wasn't a person of violence, in my opinion."

While he may not have been seen as violent, only the most complacent of observers could have failed to see that Wyley was an unusual child, an unhappy child, perhaps even a seriously disturbed child. Indeed, there were times when Wyley made his "difference" known in a fully overt and even aggressive manner. For instance, Vivian Gates had brought Wyley and Bobby to St. Luke's Episcopal Church in Chatham upon the boys' return from California. There they took instruction and were baptized and confirmed. They then went on to become, briefly, acolytes. When Wyley was approximately thirteen, he announced to his religious instructors that he considered all of this stuff basically a lot of garbage, and suggested that a person couldn't be very bright if he or she believed in all this. This was a forthright statement indeed from a boy just barely entering adolescence, but Douglas Alamillo, a deacon of St. Luke's Church, always felt there was something "different" about Wyley. "He always had a sly grin if he had any expression on his face at all," Alamillo recalled. Shortly thereafter, Wyley and Bobby, Jr., left the church altogether. According to Alamillo, Bobby, whom he remembered as quiet, did so at Wyley's behest. "My impression was Wyley really ran the show," said Alamillo. "Bobby waited to see what Wyley would do and then followed his lead." Rumor had it that Wyley burned his religious articles as a further statement of his lack of religious conviction, but this may well have been apocryphal. In any event, Wyley's leaving the church could not have caused his father any anguish, as Bob Gates never put in an appearance at St. Luke's; but Vivian has remained an active member of the parish, as has Evelyn Prescott.

Mrs. Prescott's husband, in fact, died in church, and this precipitated one of the few genuine displays of emotion from Wyley that anyone could recall. "The day my husband died—he dropped dead in church—Wyley was there," Mrs. Prescott remembered. "And when I came home, after the hospital, we went straight to Vivian's house and he was walking back and forth and back and forth and I knew he wanted to tell me he was sorry or express his sympathy but he just couldn't bring himself to do it. And I was so in shock, I didn't say anything to him. And once after that, when we were coming home and I mentioned that day to him, he got so upset that I quickly got off of it." Thereafter, Wyley lapsed back into the pattern of noncommunication that was typical of his interaction with his family. Often, Mrs. Prescott would drive Wyley home from school when he had missed the bus, and the drives were invariably silent. "He'd ride all the way home and not say boo to me if I didn't ask him something. And then he would respond and then he'd grow quiet again. Then he'd get out of the car and say thank you and go," she recalled. "I used to think to myself, Gee, Wyley, I'm your aunt! Can't you talk to me?"

"We all realized that Wyley didn't have an easy time holding conversations with people," Vivian Gates told me. "And when he got older, in high school, my daughter was quite worried about him, his being in his room so much. I remember Dane once bought him one of those remote-control airplanes—trying to get him outdoors. Everyone was always trying to find ways to get Wyley outdoors."

Despite these indicators, however, it does not appear that a real focus was ever trained on Wyley. This may have had to do with the inevitable human and familial urge to deny what is disturbing about our loved ones; but, perhaps even more significantly in this case, it must be remembered that the growing pathology of Wyley, which some family members had convinced themselves was mere idiosyncrasy, was vying for attention in the family with a series of tragic upheavals that were occurring with an appalling regularity. The terrible accident and subsequent incapacitation of Steven Gates; the painful, prolonged death of Lou Gates . . .

these gave way on September 15, 1985, to a tragedy that would occupy the family's attention from then on.

Vivian and Lou's youngest son, Dane, was a handsome young man who, in the eyes of family friends, was cut from the same cloth as his older brother Bob, to whom he was very close. "Daredevils," Louise Frick said of the two Gates brothers. "They weren't afraid to try anything. Stock-car racing, motorcycles, all that stuff." According to Don De-Lapp, "Dane liked to have fun, like any kid; he liked to be with his friends. He enjoyed tinkering with motorcycles. He'd buy an old truck, fix it up. Bob and Dane enjoyed things like that and they did a lot of stuff like that together. Bob and Dane were close."

Under Bob's wing, Dane went to work for Hudson Handling, running the salt facility down in Beacon, New York, and married Georgia Groudas of East Chatham. Their first and only child, Jason, was born on March 6, 1983.

The lives of the Gates and Groudas families were tied up together in a number of strange, even macabre knots. Georgia Groudas's brother Paul worked at one time for Bob Gates and was maimed in an accident. "He was unloading rail cars," recalled Dave Frick, "and he slipped and his foot went under the wheel of the rail car and the rail car rolled over his foot." Paul lost the foot, and was urged, it is said, by Bob Gates to sue the railroad for negligence. People in the community remembered too that Paul's wife, Laurie, had been romantically involved with Dane Gates before her marriage, and this relationship represented still another point of intersection between the two families. According to a family friend, Dane was a "crazy driver" and Laurie was always arguing with him to slow down. "He had told her that he was going to die before he was twenty-five," said the friend. "And she said, 'Well, why don't you slow down and maybe you won't?' But he had this thing that he was going to die young."

Dane's restlessness continued as a factor in his marriage, and he and Georgia suffered problems typical of many young marrieds. Mary-Lynn Bedford, who lived across the street from the log house, remembered a telling exchange between Dane and Georgia. "I was sitting with my eldest little girl on the front lawn, nursing her, and Georgia came up," Bedford recalled. "She was going down the road and stopped to talk to me, and we discussed breast feeding and all the rest of it, and I remember that Dane came along at that time and I said, 'Oh, by the way, we're having another, I'm pregnant again.' And Dane turned to Georgia and said, 'Don't you ever have another one.' He said, 'One is enough, this has been an awful experience, and really we don't need any more. It costs too much.' "

Dane, at twenty-five, was a contemporary of his niece Viki-Lynn Hatch, the eldest daughter of Viki and Howard Hatch. Indeed, Dane and Georgia were half of a regular foursome with Viki-Lynn and her boyfriend Ray Palmer. Ray, twenty, a local boy who worked as a welder and raced stock cars, was a good friend, as well, of Bobby, Jr.,'s. Bobby and Ray, in fact, used to fantasize about leaving it all behind to go work out west somewhere.

On the night that Ray and Viki-Lynn announced their engagement, the foursome celebrated at Jackson's Town House, a restaurant and bar in Old Chatham. There was dancing and drinking that evening, and, around 2:00 A.M., Dane suggested that they all drive over to Depot 22, an all-night truck stop on nearby Route 22.

In an account that Viki-Lynn gave to a family friend, she reportedly suggested to her. Uncle Dane that he had been drinking excessively and shouldn't drive, but he protested that he could handle it. The four of them got into the car and they took off. The route to Depot 22 was one they had all traveled innumerable times. Up Frisbie, across County Route 5, to Peaceful Valley Road, where Viki-Lynn's paternal grandmother lived. Peaceful Valley Road, a dirt concourse that runs 2.5 miles, parallel to the New York State Thruway, is dark and winding and full of potholes. The car hit one of the potholes, left the south side of the road, and traveled several hundred feet, hitting trees before bursting into flames. According to the family friend, Viki-Lynn was flung from the car and lay on the road, badly injured, listening to the cries of those entrapped and feeling that if she could only get up she could save them. But she couldn't get up and they weren't saved. In fact, reports indicated that Dane, Georgia, and Ray Palmer had died instantly, charred to the point where the only unburned flesh on Georgia Gates was beneath her wedding ring. As for the ring that Ray had given Viki-Lynn, the diamond was dislodged when she was thrown and was never found.

The tragedy was enormous. Three young lives snuffed out, and a two-year-old left orphaned. For Bob Gates, the tragedy was complicated by guilt because, before the accident, dissension had crept into his relationship with his brother. "Dane was back here working for Bob and they had a terrible argument that summer," recalled Mary-Lynn Bedford. "They didn't get along all summer. And after the death, Bob took over and tried to handle everything because he felt guilty about not having straightened things out with Dane before he died. He said he took it worse than his mother."

Viki-Lynn was hospitalized with chest injuries and a head laceration and Wyley sent her a stuffed German shepherd. "She was amazed," said Vivian Gates, "that Wyley should have these feelings for her." (After the murders of his family, while Wyley was in the Hudson jail, he got an angry letter from Viki-Lynn, then living in Texas, and, to mollify her, he had his grandmother search out another stuffed dog to send her.) As for the death of his Uncle Dane, it was one more link in the chain of violence that was running through his family, but not necessarily a violence that he saw as unique to the Gates men. "He happened to like Dane," noted Dr. Anthony Marchionne, "but I don't think he would have seen what happened as uniquely violent to them. I think he'd see it as part of the masculine process and he didn't want any part of it. 'If this is what you have to do to be a man—drive motorcycles, wear black leather jackets, carry a gun—I don't want to do it.' " This feeling of not wanting to be a part of this particular lineage may have furnished one reason for Wyley's conspicuous absence at Dane's funeral. "He didn't come to the funeral like everyone else," Vivian Gates recalled. "He stayed home. Wyley wanted to stay home—that's the way he handled it." In fact, Sally Joseph, Damian's aunt, remembered Damian remarking to her that he thought it was strange that Wyley was in school right after the incident. "Apparently, he didn't take a day off or anything from school," said Mrs. Joseph.

As a reaction to the accident, Viki Hatch, who at the time was the Canaan town clerk, and her husband, Howard, sold their house directly adjacent to the log cabin and moved to Canajoharie, outside of Schenectady, over an hour away. The move proved to be significant in Wyley's life, as there had been much involvement between Wyley and the Hatches over the years. That involvement may have been confusing or even troubling for Wyley at times, since Howard Hatch was an avid hunter, and Wyley detested hunting. But, despite this, the proximity of the Hatches was clearly valued by Wyley. "It was traumatic when they moved away," Vivian Gates said. "He didn't have this place to go to talk to people." The person he talked to most had been his cousin Tina, several years his junior. "She spent more time with Wyley because he was able to relate to her feminine interests," Dr. Marchionne explained. "He liked her because they had an elitist attitude. They would talk about buying Gucci shoes and clothes and dressing very well, driving expensive cars, things of this nature." In time he would commit to somebody else with an elitist attitude—Damian Rossney—but for now Tina was gone, along with her sisters, and Wyley was left with no one on the road he cared very much about, except for his grandmother.

A little more than a year later, after the murders in the log cabin, Dr. Marchionne had occasion to interview both Wyley and his grandmother. "I was struck by the remarkable similarity between Wyley's affect and Vivian's affect," he recalled. "I think Wyley's was essentially flat but so was hers. Particularly as we talked about what had happened to her other sons—just this incredible bombardment of tragedy. I, of course, was focusing on the murder of her son and just the year before she had lost a son in an automobile accident and she had another son terribly injured in another accident, and I got nothing that suggested a sadness. It was just kind of matter-of-fact—these are things that happen to people and you don't react to them other than to take care of them, to bury them."

Others who were closer to her speak not of a "lack of affect" but, rather, of a quiet, private nature that is not given to showing emotion. Her sister-in-law Dorothy Dooley characterized her as "an unreal lady. She's a very strong person. She has to be a very strong person with everything she's gone through. She's always had the attitude that she will get through this thing . . . no matter how bad anything was she felt it would be over and something would take care of it or something would happen and that she would get through it." Her sister-in-law Evelyn Prescott added, "She was keeping her chin up. She always does. An amazing person. We can't figure out how she does it. She just thinks she has to see it through and she will see it through. She's very strong that way." In fact, when Wyley found himself in jail, in an atmosphere so base for one who considered himself so superior, he attributed to his grandmother his ability to get through the experience. Like his grandmother, he explained to me, he had the ability to survive.

With Dane and Georgia dead, there was the question—the very big question—of what to do with Jason. In the beginning the care of little Jason Gates was equably divided between the Gates and Groudas families. Vivian was with him in the morning while his other grandmother worked as a domestic, and during the rest of the day, when Vivian worked at the liquor store that she had bought after the death of her husband, the child stayed with Deloras Groudas, returning to the Gates home in the evening.

Although the care of Jason was officially divided between Vivian Gates and Deloras Groudas, the little boy spent a great deal of time with Bob and Cheryl. Don DeLapp recalled that Jason "was all Gates. The spitting image of his father. And Bob took him everywhere." Jim Klingler, who in his work for Kelgate was often down at the garage on 295, remembered Jason as "an awfully good little kid. A lot of little kids are kind of whiny and difficult in a situation where you really expect them to stay and play by themselves. But Jason was just as happy as a clam to be at the garage. He had two toy trucks down there and he would sit and watch us work, never a peep out of him."

But, despite the fact of their time together and despite the family likeness, there was not, to some observers at least, any particularly special bond between Bob and his nephew. "I never saw Bob walking down the street with Jason on his shoulders," said Mary-Lynn Bedford, who used to baby-sit for Jason almost daily. "I never saw that fatherly thing like, 'Here, I have another son.'"

As in the case of Wyley and Bobby, it fell to Cheryl to see to the care and feeding of yet another Gates boy. And, as with the other Gates boys, she worried about his eating. "She used to get upset because Jason was not a good eater," remembered Barbara DeLapp. "That used to bother her." As Cheryl was childless, it might be speculated that she looked on Jason as the child she never had, but this hypothesis is discounted by those closest to her, who did not feel that Cheryl regarded Jason as a surrogate. "Cheryl was the type of person that just kind of took things as they came," explained a friend.

As time went on, the custody arrangement between the Gates and the Groudas families began to fray. Deloras Groudas wished to adopt Jason, but, as she was in the middle of a divorce, it was decided that her son Paul and his wife Laurie should put in for adoption. But Paul and Laurie already had three small children, and members of the Gates family worried about how well Jason would fare in an environment in which he would have to compete for attention. "I really didn't like the idea of Jason going to Paul and Laurie because they had three little kids and were having a hard time from what I understood surviving on his business," Mrs. Hatch recalled.

The issue of Jason drove a wedge between the families and threatened friendships of long standing. Dennis Gawron, Bobby, Jr., and Peter Groudas, Georgia's younger brother, were all close friends. Gawron remembered that the death of Dane and Georgia drew Bobby, Jr., and Peter very close. But once the custody issue began, the two boys found their relationship severely strained. "I heard both sides of it," Gawron recalled. "I heard from Bobby that the Groudases shouldn't have him because of the situation over there, the money wasn't that good, and then I heard on the Groudas side that Bob and Cheryl wouldn't be good for him because of their marital situation, and Bob was on the road a lot and they didn't feel that Cheryl really wanted him. Between the two families there was very much conflict. A clash, definitely."

So much pain and so much love was centered around this child that there was little chance of finding a solution that would please everyone. "There were so many people that were trying to pull that poor child in each direction. The Groudases and Mrs. Gates and Bobby and Cheryl," recalled family friend Dave Frick. "Everybody had the same feeling, that this was the only remnant left of that whole particular aspect of the family."

The issue of Jason's custody even created some inter-necine stress within the Gates family. Despite the fact that she knew her brother Bob was planning to seek shared custody with Vivian, Viki Hatch and her husband put in for custody as well. "I felt that even though the laws and outlooks were changing, there might have been a possibility that because Bob and Cheryl were not married they might not have succeeded," Mrs. Hatch explained. The Hatches withdrew from the conflict, however, when it became apparent that in order to successfully win Jason they would have to besmirch the reputations of Bob and Cheryl. "We had been talking to our lawyer who was going to represent us in this," said Mrs. Hatch, "and he said, 'The only way I'm going to take on this case is if you actually say things about Bob' and I said, 'If we're going to be slinging mud at each other, no way.' Bob couldn't believe that it would come to that but I said, 'Bob, I'm going to drop out.' "

It was just as well, for, according to those who knew Bob Gates, he would not have been deterred from the idea of having Jason to himself. "Bobby wanted to possess Jason," a family friend said. "He wanted to get him away from the Groudases because, in his mind, the Groudases were no good." To that end, new arrangements were called for. Cheryl told Barbara DeLapp that she would quit work and stay home with Jason if they won custody. And, to get around the big issue, Bob and Cheryl even talked about marriage.

Marriage was not something either of them sought particularly. Don DeLapp, who remembered Bob as a practical joker, recalled a time when his friend called him from Buffalo to announce that he and Cheryl were on their way back from their honeymoon. "So that weekend we went down, brought a bottle of champagne, and said congratulations to Cheryl," said DeLapp. " 'For what?' she said. I said, 'I thought you and Bob got married.' 'Who told you that?' she said. 'He did,' I said. 'Well, who'd want to marry him anyway?' she said."

But as the custody hearing drew closer, their habitual resistance to the idea of marriage was softening. "It was probably around November, because it was still a really nice night and we were over at Castleton on the bikes," remembered their friend Dorothy Donnelley, "and Cheryl said, 'Bobby and I are going to get married.' And I said, 'Whoa. You *are*?' And she said, 'Yes.' She said, 'We're tired of little Jason being pushed around and he's here and he's there. . . . We're going to get married and we're going to adopt him. And that will put an end to everything. Then he's ours and we'll bring him up and he'll have a life . . . like a little boy life. Which he never had.' "

Two of the Gates sons were lost—Steven, irreparably damaged; Dane, gone forever. What was going wrong? Was it accident? Was it destiny? These are questions that had to be going through the mind of Bob Gates in those awful months following the tragedy on Peaceful Valley Road. Friends of the family remembered hearing Bob talk about "spirits" in the big white house on the hill. They remembered hearing how Georgia claimed to have had a vacuum wrested from her hands while cleaning there. All of this was talk, of course, but after the death of Dane and Georgia, there was more talk. "Robert said in Dane's room, he heard voices, he heard Dane," recalled Dorothy Donnelley. "And little Jason went into that bedroom one time and he was talking and talking and talking just like he was talking to his father. And he said, 'Grandma, come in here, Dad wants you.' It was really very strange." Whatever it was that he heard— whatever message he had received—Bob Gates was determined to have Jason join his family in the log cabin. It was this determination and this effort that preoccupied him in the fall of 1986.

4

The seasons in Columbia County are acutely defined, and by the end of the first week of September, a distinct touch of autumn was in the air. The leaves of the birch trees hung precariously from the branches, and the sky, having lost all trace of its summer haziness, was imbued with a special clear light that at times washed golden over the hills in late afternoon. The Chatham Fair had come and gone. Some of the local kids now had blue ribbons on their bedroom bureaus, commemorating their prize Belgian rabbits or Rhode Island Reds, while others, in a daze of illicit beer and seduced by carnies, had wasted their lawn-mowing or baby-sitting money on games of chance. The wonderful delusion of endless summertime pleasure could no longer be entertained, for already in the air were the sobering auguries of the endless hard winter that was waiting ahead. The school year too was ready to begin, with all its possibilities of new success, new achievement. It was a time to sharpen pencils; to confront pure white sheets of paper; to look into the eye of the future and to feel sanguine about one's chances to grow and prosper.

And, for some, it was the beginning of the senior year, that rare time that marks the end of something familiar and comfortable and the ushering in of a new era of exciting, unknown opportunity.

For Wyley, trapped in a pressure system all his own, the senior year was a last chance to outdo himself, to outstrip the one student whose ranking was higher than his own, to prove himself in music, student government, and academics. The summer—that loathed summer, when he toiled long hours for his father without pay—was over. But, for all its dreariness, he should have been able to look back on the summer and derive some satisfaction from his achievements.

For one thing, Gordon Ringer immediately noticed the improvement in Wyley's trumpet playing, at which he had practiced so hard over the summer. Ringer, who had had Wyley in the band from ninth grade on, every day, five days a week for a full class period, with extra sessions for the marching band and jazz band of which Wyley was a part, charted Wyley's high school music career and had noted his determination to succeed, a determination that even saw him through braces, a particularly troublesome handicap for a trumpet player. But, despite this determination, Wyley, in Ringer's opinion, was limited as to how far he could really go with his music. "One of his goals was to play first chair, and, to be honest, I don't think he would have been able to make it," Ringer said. "Technically he was a wizard. If you asked him to play scales or fingering passages or something technical, he could whip it off better than anybody because I think he could relate to it. But when you tried to talk to him about expression and phrasing—you know, the music coming from inside—that he didn't have."

In this, Ringer distinguished Wyley from Bobby, Jr., who also played under Ringer during his high school years. "Bob had a lot more natural ability musically than Wyley did," Ringer remembered. "His grade in band wasn't really important to him, just the fact that he got to play." Bobby, who had formed a rock band during his brief time as a student at Hudson Valley Community College, was, in Ringer's mind, "a real rock and roller." As such, he went looking for high times or, at least, as high a time as he could find in a small rural town. "I couldn't prove it, but there were times when he came in drunk for rehearsals," said Ringer. "But when it came time for concert time, I knew that if we had to be in every day after school or whatever the week before to get the stuff down, he would be in and he'd learn it." What's more, he had the knack of getting along with people. "If we had a parade at eight o'clock in the morning, he would be the kind of guy where I'd find a cup of black coffee on my desk and he'd smile at me or wink or something to say, 'Hey, I know I could use this, I'm sure you could use it too,' " Ringer recalled.

Although Wyley lacked his brother's natural musicality, his organizational ability and discipline took him a certain distance. All of his dutiful practicing had paid off at the end of his junior year when he got one of the top three ratings for his trumpet selection at the New York State School Music Association competition, an adjudicated event. This success spurred him on and, before the summer, he had asked Ringer to supply him with music and books with which to practice. Upon his return to school in the fall of 1986, Wyley's playing was, in Ringer's opinion, far superior.

A fellow member of the first-trumpet section was Jim Andrews, who was also Wyley's lab partner in physics. Andrews, who had known Wyley since the seventh grade, thought of him as "a likable guy. There wasn't anybody in the school who disliked him. Easy to get along with, hard worker . . . very quiet, though." Andrews regarded Wyley as one of the most intelligent students in the class, distinguished by the way he carried himself and the way he did his work—"always wanting to do one step more than anyone else—that's the way he was." In Andrews's opinion, this did not stigmatize Wyley or set him apart from his peers in any negative way. Any comments about Wyley's being "a brain" were made not, in Andrews's opinion, to mock him, but, rather, were offered as recognition that Wyley really was better than anybody else. "I think kids were not really picking on him but making [his specialness] noticeable to everybody else," Andrews commented. "I mean, they were all doing it in good fun, and Wyley knew it, calling him like 'brain' and stuff like that. I think he liked it, actually."

Generally, those who found themselves in regular contact with Wyley came away with very positive impressions of him. "He was intelligent," recalled Zachary Gobel, who ran as president of the student senate on the ticket that featured Wyley as vice-president. "He had a weird kind of sense of humor. He did a lot of funny things. You know, kind of mumbled under his breath. He wasn't a person to be in the front of the scene; it didn't seem like he wanted a lot of attention. It seemed like he was always behind the scenes and consequently only a few people would hear, but he was funny." This quality of Wyley's—his wry, dry humor—was picked up on by others. "He would look away very often," recalled one of his teachers, "but then when he did look you in the eye, there was that unmistakable twinkle. Once I had this problem with my computer and I asked Wyley if he could help me fix it, but he said he knew there was an extra one in the computer department. He actually went and got it for me even when the computer department had said they didn't have one. He had the twinkle in his eye like 'You and I have just beaten the system together.' "

There were few, however, who could get close to him. Teachers described him as "very, very quiet" or remarked on the fact that he had "no body language" or commented that "to get him to crack a smile, or even to frown, was very difficult." One teacher who was able to detect a body language described it as a "posture that said, 'I am of you but I am not with you.' " Jim Andrews remembered him always studying. "When he was in school, he would work—homework and stuff—and when he was out of school he would do homework and stuff," said Andrews. "There wasn't really time for him to communicate with other people." English teacher Louise Lincoln, who taught Wyley both in her advanced-placement English course that senior year and for three years in her homeroom, had ample opportunity to observe him. "He was shy; he was a loner," Lincoln recalled. "But he coped with himself, with who he was. He was never a victim. There are shy people who are victims and he did not ever give me the sense that he was a victim. No one ever picked on Wyley in that sense. They ignored him to a large extent, as he did them. He went his own way."

In this senior class of 125 students, however, a boy of Wyley's capabilities, no matter what personality wrinkles he had, would inevitably engender some measure of respect. "Respect is the right word. Because he could stand for himself," Lincoln commented. "He was never the weird kid. He may have been different. He always wore a tie and a cotton shirt versus a T-shirt, but not that strange or different. Maybe it was a differentness that we knew because it had always been; it was just a part of us and of our identity. Like one polka dot on a dress or a shirt. Maybe not quite the perfect circle, but that's OK, it's one among many, it's part of the pattern."

Wyley took his student government activities seriously, and, even in the next few months, when his absences from school were increasing and he was falling behind with his assignments, he held up his end of the responsibilities of his office. The four students in the administration and the two faculty advisers met at least once a week, and according to Gobel, "Wyley was there and was doing what he should be doing." His diligence in music was also sustained during this fall semester. "He was very, very up as far as his musical studies were concerned," remembered Gordon Ringer. "Very up, very positive. Even when he had a cold. That year we had a veterans' parade in November and we had to parade in the snow. I mean, the plows were going down the street in front of us. We were playing for the local American Legion. Other kids were really grumbling but he was hanging in there, just the fact that he was playing was enough. He was the first one there when I opened up the band room. Wyley never missed a lesson."

But, despite his efforts to hold it all together, things began to unravel for Wyley on his return to school. And the place where the unraveling manifested itself was the place where he had always been sure to excel, the area that had, in fact, given birth to his identity. In the fall of 1986,

Wyley, ranked number two in his high school class, began to falter academically.

Reports of Wyley's innate intelligence varied from teacher to teacher. "He was wonderful," noted a teacher who taught him in his senior year. "Very intelligent, a little laid back. He knew and everybody else always knew that he had the answers." Doris Gearing, who taught him social studies, singled out his writing skills. "He'd write beautifully," she noted. "Very articulate. Very very bright." Gearing qualified this specialness, however. "If he was superb, it only came out in his writing," she said, "because it was never in the classroom. He rarely would come out with a statement that would show such insight that the other students didn't see it." Linda Renken, who ran the computer lab of which Wyley was so much a part, also regarded him with a certain reserve. "I think his intellectual ability came from the fact that he was willing to put forth the effort," Renken said. "There are some kids who are brilliant and from them it requires no effort. Wyley was the type of student who was interested in learning and put forth the effort to acquire any knowledge that you wanted him to acquire. I would say he was bright enough but I'm sure his I.Q. wasn't really very high."

Louise Lincoln put his academic achievements squarely in the context of his class. "The class of 'eighty-seven was probably the most dismal class intellectually that we'd had in a number of years," said Lincoln, who had taught at Chatham High School for seventeen years. "And I smile when they talk about Wyley as an honor student and so intellectual. It has to be a matter of comparison. I thought he was adequate. He could have developed much more."

Part of his academic success may have had to do with his classroom deportment. "He never caused any problem," noted one teacher. "He was on time, he was responsible, he was reliable, he would not be one to mix in if a particular student wanted to cause trouble. Wyley didn't mix in that. He didn't encourage it. He was aloof from it." But at least one teacher, Louise Lincoln, dated Wyley's academic decline to a signal event in his life. "As a student, he was not doing as well after the death of his uncle," Lincoln said. "People thought he had greater potential, that he wasn't expanding on what was there intellectually. We felt that he gave us cursory work, the top of the head, and for Wyley, because he was linguistically adept, it was enough, compared to the children he was in class with."

If it can be maintained that Wyley's intelligence was not extraordinary—and this contention was supported by intelligence tests administered to him after the murders—then Wyley's academic success can be attributed to his work habits and the lack of competition from his peers. But in the fall semester, his work habits slackened precipitously and he owed assignments right and left.

"Wyley was behind in his work," Lincoln remembered. "His work was handed in later and later and then not at all." This errant behavior was manifested in Mrs. Gearing's criminal-justice class as well. "By the last week of November, he was missing two or three days of school a week," Gearing said. This was a high rate of absenteeism, but, because of school policy at the time, was not noted as such. "We didn't have an attendance policy," said Gearing, "and I had a lot of kids who would go Christmas shopping and their parents would excuse them, so it was not out of the ordinary. As I looked back, I wished I had noticed this, but it was not uncommon for seniors to be missing."

But even among his peers Wyley's slipping academic performance was noted. "His grades weren't what they were," said classmate Desiree Kelleher. "His grades were always among the best. In our calculus class, there weren't really very many of us and we knew that his grades weren't as good, but you could also see that he was doing a lot more extracurricular stuff." By the end of the first quarter, he had received a 65 in calculus and a 78 in physics.

In fact, Wyley was not only sabotaging himself in terms of school performance, but he was also neglecting his college applications. In a discussion I had with Wyley while he was incarcerated at the Columbia County jail, he dismissed his failure to apply to college as just one more manifestation of his habitual procrastination. He also maintained that he never had any guidance on the issue from the high school, even though he was the salutatorian. The fact is that 80 percent of Chatham High School students go on to college, and, among the top ten students in Wyley's graduating class, only one other student besides Wyley did not go on to college, and this was because that student opted for the "life experience" of going to work on Wall Street for a year.

Wyley, in our jailhouse talk, claimed that he never spoke to his father about college plans, or even about whether his father would finance his college career, although he believed that Bob would have been willing to do so. Those close to Bob Gates—his mother, his sister, friends—were absolutely convinced that he would have done so. Wyley talked about going to Ithaca College, he talked about going to Boston University, but Barbara DeLapp remembered a conversation with Wyley that gives some insight into where, in fact, the college issue was headed. Two weeks before this conversation, she had had another conversation with Wyley, in which she cautioned him not to lose track of his college applications. "I said to him, 'Wyley, you really should get going about school because you've got to start applying,' " she recalled. " 'You're a smart kid, but you really have to start thinking about scholarships.' " And then, on the next visit, Barbara was seated in her truck outside the Gates garage and Wyley came over to talk to her. "Wyley acted completely out of character," she said. "We actually had a full-length conversation! He said, 'I'm not going to be able to go to school where I want to.' And I said, 'Well, where do you want to go?' And that's when he said, 'I want to go to Boston but my father won't send me. He wants me to go to Hudson Valley for two years and then if I'm really doing well, I can transfer.' And Wyley was really upset by that. For him to say something to me, he was very upset."

Hudson Valley Community College may have been a fine school in the eyes of the Chatham High guidance counselors, but Wyley perceived it otherwise. To him, it was a school for average kids, and he was not, and never would be, average. In terms of his class standing alone, he was anything but average. He was the salutatorian, a class "brain," the one who always had the answers. And in terms of his internal life and musings, he envisioned himself as extraordinary. A month before the shootings, in an entry in his journal—what he termed his "quasi-memoirs"—he wrote, "I have no doubts as to the importance these papers will have to future generations. More important than Hitler's diaries, if they were ever found." Now he was facing the prospect of going to Hudson Valley, from which his brother—his "average" brother—had dropped out and it was insufferable to think of himself as being part of this wholly undistinguished lineage.

Although on the surface Bob Gates was "all for education," as some of his friends maintained, the message, in fact, seemed to be a mixed one. Mary-Lynn Bedford recalled a time when she tried to congratulate Bob on Wyley's academic achievements. "I said, 'Boy, isn't Wyley doing well?'" Bedford said. "And he got really hepped up, really kind of worked up over it. He said, 'I don't think it's natural for a kid of his age to be a bookworm like that. He stays in his room and all he does is stick his head in those dumb books and worry about this computer stuff when he should be outside, doing some of the things that boys do who are his age.' And here I thought I was being complimentary."

What Bedford observed was an inconsistency that was becoming a hallmark of Bob's interaction with his sons. On the one hand he could be contemptuous, frequently assailing their incompetence. "Bob's favorite saying was that the boys were 'goobers,'" said Viki Hatch. "Bob didn't think that was humiliating, but it was." And Wyley specifically recalled for me such put-downs from his father as "all thumbs" and "computer hands." But then, at other times—or even at the same time—Bob could be flushed with pride for his sons' achievements. "I think Bob could have been more demonstrative," said a family friend, "but you know the report card would go right on the refrigerator and Bob and Cheryl were real proud. They went to open houses at the school, to band concerts, when Wyley was inducted into the honor society." And to his closest friends—those whom perhaps he didn't need to impress with a macho-style indictment of "bookishness"—Bob displayed a pride that was tinged with a very real and wistful kind of regret when it came to Wyley's achievements. "I remember one time Wyley got a report card home from school," recalled Don DeLapp, "and Bob said, 'Jeez, Wyley won this honor thing.' And I said, 'Boy, that's good.' And Bob—he was proud of Wyley, he was. He said, 'He's not like we are.' "

"He said, 'Wyley's going to be a doctor or a lawyer or something. But he's not going to be like we are,' " confirmed Barbara DeLapp. "He was so proud."

But whatever Wyley's aspirations were as he entered Chatham High School in the fall of 1986, they would find themselves at odds with reality. Indeed, reality in the fall of 1986 would be replaced by a heightened sense of unreality as the school term progressed. Before the semester was over, Wyley Gates—class salutatorian, class vice-president, favorite to be named "Most Likely to Succeed"—would be incarcerated in the Columbia County Jail on charges of murder. And, in the eyes and memories of at least two of his teachers, there were unreal moments along the way that seemed so telling in retrospect.

There were two incidents involving Wyley that Doris Gearing remembered distinctly. One of them took place on one of Wyley's last days at Chatham High. With five minutes left at the end of one of her criminal-justice classes, the discussion turned to military convoys and Mrs. Gearing told them that she had heard that some of the equipment is sometimes missing or pilfered in the process. "And Wyley . . . the last thing he said to me—thirty seconds before the bell rings," recalled Mrs. Gearing, "he said, 'Yeah, I can produce an atomic bomb and I can get you the plutonium.' " In that instant, a small measure of Wyley's grandiosity, developing at an alarming rate, was leaked to the outside world.

The teacher's other vivid memory had to do with Halloween that fall. "He came in total camouflage with a ski mask, like he was a terrorist," said Mrs. Gearing. "He had camouflage boots, camouflage outfit, camouflage shirt. He had a hunting belt with knives in it and he had two plastic machine guns. You don't think anything, because the kids dress up for Halloween, some in clown costumes, but it struck me as out of character for Wyley."

Gordon Ringer echoed the eerie sensation set off by Wyley's uncharacteristic appearance that day. "Our last football game was on Halloween, and rather than have everybody dress up in band uniforms, I told everyone to dress up as clowns and dance with the kids and all," Ringer explained. "And Wyley was walking around all day with a noose hanging out, skull of death, and that was something. You would not have expected it."

From the fall of 1986, unreality set up camp on Maple Drive, at Chatham High School, and in the life of Wyley Gates, a boy who had been unfailingly described as peaceful, nonviolent, and nonaggressive, but who harbored within himself some dark and ominous impulses. Whether these impulses were given expression in uncharacteristic costumes or grandiose claims to skullduggery or the persistent intransigence that he exhibited down at his father's garage, they were there. What the adults in his life didn't realize, however, was that Wyley finally had other boys who understood and even shared these impulses. For the first time in Wyley's life, he was not alone.

5

Although he fostered a cerebral, above-it-all identity, Wyley longed for material things as much as any typical American high school student. As much as any of his peers, he wanted a car and, by most accounts, there was a car in his future. In a talk we had at the Columbia County Jail, Wyley told me that his father was planning to buy his brother's car back from Bobby with the idea of making it Wyley's graduation gift in June (although Wyley sardonically added that his family didn't seem to think he really needed a car). Don DeLapp, however, was convinced that the present of the car was more immediately forthcoming. "Bob, just before the shootings, was going to give Wyley his car," said DeLapp. "It was only a matter of two more days and Wyley would have had his own car." But, however far away the car was—a few months or a few weeks or a few days—it was clearly too far away.

The car issue was a raw one and continued throughout the fall as a source of tension. Evelyn Prescott heard about Wyley's unauthorized use of the family's motor vehicles. "I know that he was taking the cars," recalled Mrs. Prescott.

"I know that at that time he was acting out a bit. I remember Cheryl saying something about it, that she was going to speak to Bob about it." Dave and Louise Frick were also aware of Wyley's "acting out" that year. "Toward the end, I think Cheryl was having lots of trouble with Wyley," said Louise Frick. "And then she tried to get Bob to look at the situation more, because he'd always say, 'Leave him alone, you're on them too much, back off.' And then we'd all get together, 'cause she'd figure if she had us with her, she could talk more and he'd listen. And I think toward the end he was listening and deciding there was something wrong with Wyley."

As much as he coveted a car, Wyley coveted, as well, a computer. Bob, in fact, had been coming around to the idea of getting Wyley a computer. Despite all Bob's talk of "computer hands," all the concern about its being "unnatural" for the boy to stay in his room so much, all the effort to get him outside and to put him to work on gears and camshafts so that he would have some "real" knowledge of the "real" world, there was, as well, a kind of headshaking approach to this younger son of his, a sense that the boy was gifted, different, "not like we are." And when Wyley brought up the issue of a computer, there may have even been a begrudging, if unspoken, awareness that computers now represented as much of the "real" world as any technology with which Bob was involved. When Wyley asked Bob for two thousand dollars to buy his own computer, Bob turned to his friend Don DeLapp for advice. "I was welding something down at the garage," DeLapp recalled, "and Bob said, 'Jeez, you know, how much do computers cost?' And I said, 'Jeez, I don't know, I can find out for you.' He says, 'Well, Wyley's got one—some kid wants to sell him one—he wants two thousand for it.' I say, 'Hey, that ain't so bad. I hear they're going for twenty-six hundred, twenty-seven hundred.' So Bob says, 'The kid's done real good. Real smart kid.' And I said, 'If he needs a computer, buy it for him.' "

According to DeLapp, Bob gave Wyley the two thousand dollars, but it turned out that Wyley did not get the computer from another boy at all, but, rather, from Chatham High School. "It was the school's," said Linda Renken of the Apple 2-E that became Wyley's. "He and a couple of the other boys apparently 'acquired' it."

The computer began to occupy an increasingly central place in Wyley's life. Not only did computer science represent a realistic vocational direction—"he could have definitely made a good career out of it for himself," said Renken—but, through the games of strategy and role-playing and simulated risk that Wyley played on computers, he could be assured a trusty avenue of escape from reality. Sitting there in his room, the computer also served as a symbol of what he could now attain if he put his mind to it. His brother's friends remembered that Bobby was capable of bending the rules until he broke them, but that Wyley "never did anything bad." But things were changing, and that prized object on his desk was testimony to the changes. The computer had been easily "acquired" and the possibilities of antisocial behavior were being thoroughly, almost joyfully, plumbed, not only by Wyley but by these other boys who were part of that grand new breed he had never before encountered: friends.

Mr. D.R. is an enthusiastic, innovative person who can always find a new way to skin a cat.

In 1983, Damian asked his aunt and uncle if he could come live with them. "He said he didn't like school down there too much and wasn't doing that well," said Sally Joseph, a psychiatric nurse. Damian told the Josephs that he had never felt comfortable with the other kids in the Ossining schools, that they were "either poor or rich" and he felt like he never fit in. "Every day there would be kids in the halls mugging you for your lunch money, and he didn't develop many close friendships," Mrs. Joseph explained. "He said most of the time he felt a bit nauseous going to school in the morning and felt like he wished he could be part of the wallpaper."

The Josephs had some reservations about this proposed arrangement. "He was only twelve or thirteen at the time and we tried to impress on him that there were no other kids around and it could be quite lonely," said Mrs. Joseph. "He said he didn't care—he loved the woods, he loved the fields." The Josephs recalled that Damian's mother thought it was a good idea, but that his father was a little more reluctant for him to come, as he felt he would miss him terribly. But, in the end, the Rossneys gave their permission, and so Damian came up at the beginning of August 1984 to start his freshman year at Chatham High. For the Josephs, their reservations were soon quelled by the strengths they saw in Damian's character. "I suppose the main reason for having him," said Stanley Joseph, a retired psychologist, "is we thought he was bright, he was not a dependent kid, we knew he liked to read a lot, we knew he could occupy himself without our having to be at his beck and call. We weren't concerned along those lines at all. Another child we might have felt differently about. But we saw him as certainly being able to take care of himself."

Assimilating himself into a new school took some time for Damian. The first friendship he forged was with Miles McDonald; the two boys were drawn to each other, ostensibly, by a shared interest in skiing. Miles wound up spending quite a bit of time around the Joseph home, and Mrs. Joseph was initially struck by how polite the young man was. But, in time, her feelings changed. "Miles went down to visit Damian in Ossining," Mrs. Joseph recalled of a particularly catalytic incident, "and smuggled this BB gun along with him. And so they were out shooting cans and neighborhood dogs or something. Damian's mother called Miles's mother about it, and they hadn't known he'd taken this BB gun along with him. So I was a little more cautious about Miles after that."

Academically, Damian was doing much better than he had been doing in Ossining. After ironing out some academic problems in his initial years, he was doing "fabulously," in Mr. Joseph's words, by his junior year. In fact, his grades at that point qualified him for the honor society, which he was kept out of because of a disciplinary incident involving an altercation in the hall with another student.

In his sophomore year, Damian made his second good friend, Wyley. "I asked Damian about Miles and Wyley," said Mrs. Joseph, "did he like one better than the other, and he said, 'I like them for different things. Miles and I have a better time doing outdoor stuff, athletic stuff, and Wyley and I do computer stuff.' " A great favorite of theirs was the war game Titan, which would go on for days. Even though Wyley never won at Titan, the games remained, in the opinion of the Josephs, generally good-natured. Miles participated as well, and the play almost always took place at the Joseph residence. "In fact, I asked, 'Why don't you ever go to Wyley's house?' " recalled Mrs. Joseph. "And Damian told me, 'Wyley doesn't like to be at his house. He'd rather be here.' " The reasons cited were that Cheryl and Jason were around. As far as the Josephs were concerned, Cheryl, whom they described as very attractive and pleasant, seemed extremely accommodating to Wyley. But they also had the impression that Wyley and his brother teased her mercilessly. As far as Jason was concerned, they had the impression, through Damian, that Wyley didn't like the idea of Jason becoming a member of their household because he would have to share his room with the child.

The Josephs got to see a lot of Wyley, and early on formed their impression of him. "He was very uncomfortable socially," Mrs. Joseph remembered. "We took him out a few times for dinner to a restaurant and Damian would talk to Wyley and Wyley really wouldn't say much." Wyley would answer a question if it was directly put to him, but was otherwise not forthcoming. "When he would be at our house for dinner," said Mrs. Joseph, "it would be a relief to have it over with." Indeed, in the eyes of the Josephs, both mental-health professionals, Wyley manifested "a sort of extreme shyness to the point of social anxiety." Going further, Mr. Joseph said, "We saw him as schizoid . . . just not comfortable with expressing his feelings. Not kind of relating to you with any kind of ease or spontaneity."

Damian, too, in the opinion of the Josephs, recognized Wyley's strangeness. "Damian always described Wyley as weird," said Mr. Joseph, who detected, in the term, a sense of coolness about it—"weird but cool," as it were. But Mrs. Joseph recalled a time when Damian's concern about his friend's peculiarity became quite overt. "Damian asked me once what schizophrenia was," she said, "and when I started to explain it and asked him why, he said, 'Because Wyley told me he was schizophrenic.' So I said, 'Why does Wyley think he's schizophrenic?' 'Well, because he thinks he has a split personality.' "

None of this, however, gave the Josephs serious pause about the friendship, and, in fact, they were pleased with Damian's relationship with the older boy who came across as so responsible. In fact, Wyley's sense of responsibility struck them as nothing less than exemplary. Mrs. Joseph, for instance, recalled asking Damian to warn Wyley to drive slowly and to use seat belts, and Damian replied that she needn't worry because Wyley had an inviolable rule regarding the use of seat belts.

This conscientious use of seat belts—this seeming nod to the sanctity of life—was actually a far cry from the glue that held the two boys together. To Dr. Anthony Marchionne, Wyley would characterize Damian as having "even less regard for people than I do." What's more, Damian had an aggressive social style, which contrasted markedly with Wyley's passive social posture. Although there were people around Wyley who interested him—indeed, at least one of the boys in his class would find himself the recipient of an ardent love letter sent from jail—it was important to Wyley that he not be the one to take the initiative, but, rather, that he be the object of pursuit. Damian pursued Wyley, and Wyley's gratitude proved boundless.

Dr. Marchionne spoke of the "pathological bonding" between these two boys, which he felt had a variety of significances. Chief among them was the fact that the friendship, coming as it did at a time when adolescents have to form their close relationships, kept Wyley from becoming "grossly psychotic." Up until that time, Wyley had not participated in these kinds of relationships with people and he had a harsh view of himself, believing that people simply would not like him. His defense was to emphasize all his nonemotional qualities, and so he portrayed himself to his peer group as hyperintelligent, hyperintellectual, even to the point of correcting minor errors of pronunciation or spelling made by his classmates. But this "coping" was proving inadequate as he moved deeper into adolescence, and then, suddenly and miraculously, along came Damian. Damian was perceived by Wyley as being very bright, and they entered into a dynamic of intellectual competitiveness. "So they begin in typical ways playing video games and who's better and who gets better grades in SATs or I.Q. scores," said Dr. Marchionne, "but Damian has a quality that Wyley does not have and that is to be very aggressive, very assertive, and this connects them. And this is where I saw the pathological bond occur."

To Dr. Marchionne, Wyley expressed an almost eternal gratitude to Damian for taking him out of his loneliness and social isolation and went on to describe a kind of socialization process between himself and Damian that included marathon phone conversations, sometimes lasting three or four hours. These obsessive phone conversations between Damian and Wyley were noted by Bob and Cheryl, and they talked to friends about it. "He and that Damian used to get on the phone and talk for hours, just the two of them, talk for hours and hours and hours," recalled Dorothy Donnelley. "They'd get off the school bus and they'd get on the phone and they'd talk." The degree to which Wyley's patterns of communication altered as a result of his association with Damian was even reflected in court-room testimony offered by Vivian Gates at Wyley's trial. She testified that on the night of the murders, Jason was supposed to have come to her house by eight o'clock. She called the house repeatedly only to get a busy signal, and so she thought that "maybe Wyley was on the phone."

Still, these long phone calls were not, as Dr. Marchionne pointed out, atypical for adolescents and, to some degree, Cheryl and Bob may have thought them just another manifestation of Wyley's characteristic desire to retreat into his own private world, a characteristic also manifested in his hours on end at the video games and in his extraordinarily protracted bathroom interludes ("He liked to spend a lot of time in the bathroom with the water going," a family friend remembered. "And Cheryl'd say, 'What's he *doing* in there?' He really spent an inordinate time in the bathroom, like an hour and a half").

For any or all of these reasons, it was Bob and Cheryl's inclination, in the beginning, to look kindly upon this relationship. "In the beginning, I think Cheryl was really glad that Wyley had found somebody that he could get along with so well," recalled a friend of Cheryl's. "She used to go pick him up, bring him over [to the Josephs], very accommodating to the relationship."

But Cheryl's warm feelings about Damian were soon to dissipate. "Cheryl thought the kid was really strange. There was something about him that she just did not like—she never said what it was," noted Barbara DeLapp. "Damian used to come to get Wyley, and one night the four of us were sitting around the table, and Cheryl said she didn't like him, and at first Bob said something like, 'Don't say too much 'cause Wyley's starting to get out of the house.' Then he said he wasn't too crazy about him either but they didn't like to give specifics."

One family member who did give specifics—at least to his own friends—was Bobby, Jr., who had taken an instant dislike to Damian on account of the youth's "smirk." This uneasy feeling was dramatically heightened for Bobby by an incident that occurred in the summer. "Bobby came home from work and found his .22 rifle lying on his bed and asked Wyley about it," recalled Dennis Gawron. "And Wyley said, 'Oh, Damian had it.' And Bobby said, 'First of all, why did you let Damian crawl around the room and get my rifle?' 'Oh, I don't know,' Wyley said. And Bobby later found out that Damian was just aimlessly shooting it. He shot Howard Hatch's mailbox—there's a hole in it yet. And Bobby's saying, 'Well, why didn't you stop him?' And Wyley says, 'Oh, it's nothing. He just doesn't know any better.' "

Maybe it was an excuse or an accommodation Wyley was making to his new friend. After all, it was during this summer too that Wyley and Damian engaged in "horseplay" that saw Damian cutting Wyley with an open knife and causing him to pass out and fall off a railing. In relating this story to Dr. Marchionne, Wyley was saying, in Dr. Marchionne's opinion, that "he had already by that time seen Damian as a violent person, very careless, and that would simultaneously irritate him and frighten him."

Mr. D. R. can be a handful. . . . He's a risk-taker who may do things of which his peers only dream.

To some at Chatham High School, Damian seemed an average, normal kid, or even better than that. "He used to help us occasionally with a candy sale or whatever," remembered one teacher who was active in school affairs. "He'd come by and help out. I thought he was just a fine kid. Also, always with a smile, never seemed to do anything bizarre." Others, however, held him in considerably less esteem. "Damian's I.Q. was really high," recalled Linda Renken, who saw much of him in the computer lab, "but he was more interested in being a wiseguy, somebody who hoped to have a good time and could get away with as much as he could get away with."

When the allegations regarding Damian's involvement in the criminal case became known, discussions among the teachers corroborated an uneasy feeling that many of them had felt about this student but had not previously verbalized. "All you had to do was listen in the faculty room," remembered one teacher. "What was I hearing? That he was strange. I guess the greatest comparison was to some character in a Stephen King book. Many of the teachers felt that he was very different."

Through Damian, Wyley became friendly with Miles McDonald as well. Miles, also a year Wyley's junior, was an average student, a good athlete, a regular in the computer lab, and, like Wyley, a member of the trumpet section of the school band. "He was quiet, very quiet, but could be very enthusiastic," said Gordon Ringer. "He was one of those guys who had a real hard time making up his mind whether he was going to be a jock or whether he was going to play music."

Although he was described as intelligent and quiet, some of Miles's teachers felt that same sense of discomfort around him that Damian was capable of provoking. "Miles always made me a little uneasy because I didn't know how to read him," said one teacher. "Miles is a very scary person," said another. "He frightens me. He has this awful mean look, and a very snide, very arrogant attitude like, 'How dare you tell me what to do?' He once walked in the front door, stepped up on the first desk, walked across the tops of all the desks, and sat down in his seat. I made him leave the room and come in again. He didn't come in for a while and I was scared. I was afraid of him, I really was."

But the attraction of Wyley to Miles had a subtext different from Wyley's attraction to Damian. To the question of whether Wyley "loved" Damian, Dr. Marchionne responded that "there was no love there. The love is for Miles." When information about Wyley and Damian began to emerge in the aftermath of the crimes, parallels were drawn to Leopold and Loeb, those two boys of another era whose shared sense of superiority led them to murder. And as with Leopold and Loeb, Wyley, too, had a confused sense of sexual identity. "There are certain very strong sexual issues in Wyley's development which he has been confused by for a while," said Dr. Marchionne. "It's almost, if you take a dynamic approach, a sublimation of this sexual power of the aggressor . . . as if whatever possible affectionate feelings he is capable of developing for people, when it comes to Damian these get thwarted into an aggressive response." At the beginning of his sessions with Dr. Marchionne, Wyley presented a total absence of sexuality. He told the psychologist that he never masturbated and had never had an orgasm. But evidence from the Rorschach test administered by Dr. Marchionne indicated that there were some strong sexual themes going on. "He has homosexual feelings that go way back to his childhood," said Marchionne. These homosexual feelings were incorporated into Wyley as a sense of "being different," with this "difference" becoming part and parcel of his developing sense of grandiosity. In other words, in Marchionne's opinion, the "difference"

in his sexual feelings was just another element that contributed to his sense of distance between himself and other
youngsters.

After many sessions, Wyley sketched for the psychologist a more expanded picture of his "love" interests. "Wyley
will not mention names," said Marchionne, "but he was
going to go down a list with me. We named them Love One,
Love Two, and he'd give me a description of them." One
group was composed of his peers—ages sixteen, seventeen,
eighteen. Characteristically, they were all shorter than Wyley; they were all dark-haired and usually more meso-
morphic (a description that fits Miles perfectly). In the other
group were people whom he "hated" but whom he "loved
sexually" and these were men in their late twenties and
early thirties. They were hunters; they were the typical
townspeople; they were people whom he despised socially,
people who killed animals and were indifferent to the
environment. "This is a very interesting paradox," noted
Dr. Marchionne. "Something you see in the paranoid personality, where they find themselves attracted to individuals
for whom they have these markedly negative feelings and
it becomes a little bizarre."

There is no evidence that Wyley acted out sexually with
any of his friends, but, whatever the basis for these friendships, at least, for the first time in his life, he had them.
Wyley, who had spent so many years in isolation; who would
later tell a court psychiatrist that his only memory of his
childhood was an episode in which he had been locked out
of his house; who told another court psychiatrist that every
time he heard someone uttering words that began with *w*
or *wh* he was convinced they were whispering about him,
was, for the first time in his life, no longer alone. For once,
when he entered the school cafeteria, he didn't have to feel
that everyone was looking at him and that there was nowhere
for him to sit. He could sit with Damian; he could sit with
Miles. And, often present at the table—"his" table now—
was another student by the name of John Bailey.

John, who would later give testimony regarding a target-
practice session that he hosted for Damian, Miles, and Wyley

at his grandfather's farm in East Chatham, was, like Damian, another boy who had been sent from one school area—in John's case, Long Island—to live with relatives in another school area, in this case Chatham. John, who lived with his elderly grandparents, had been in the armed services and was having a difficult time of it at Chatham High.

Characterizations of John Bailey offered by his fellow students ran the proverbial gamut. "He was a nice guy," said one. "He was different. I don't think he was harmful or anything." Another student said, "He came in and out of the school. He was just a kind of off-the-wall, flaky guy. I just seem to remember him bouncing up and down the halls, a big smile on his face. I think he was basically a good-hearted person as far as I could tell." A third student said, "Kind of a split personality. There were all kinds of rumors and stuff floating around him."

The difficulties in dealing with John Bailey seemed to be a problem that unified many of the faculty members at Chatham High, although some viewed him more benignly than others. "He was a sketch. He *is* a sketch," said one teacher. "He should have been a Houdini because he did the greatest disappearing acts you'd ever want to see. He was an unusual individual, he really was. Very intelligent, very intuitive. I never expected of him anything bad. I just thought he was really strange."

Whereas Wyley was repeatedly described as the last person one would connect to a violent act, and Damian and Miles were described only in terms of being irritating or disturbing, it was around John Bailey that elements of violence and self-destruction clung. "John had lots of problems," recalled Doris Gearing. "He'd be up and down emotionally." On one occasion, some of Mrs. Gearing's students approached her with their fears that John was suicidal. "I said, 'Well, let's get him down to the nurse,'" she said. "He said he wanted to go home and that he knew where the guns were."

Gordon Ringer never taught John Bailey but remembered him from hall duty as being "the one who could really challenge authority." Bailey's military aspect particularly stood out in Ringer's mind. "He was supposedly going into the army, he was going to be jumping, he was going to be an airborne, he had it all planned out what he was going to do with a life in the military," said Ringer. "He was always walking around with fatigues on and the boots and was really playing the role up." Another teacher who remarked on his military aspect noted that "John had been in the National Guard. John had weaponry. He knew how to shoot very well."

Louise Lincoln remembered John as an "itchy" kind of student. "That is, he couldn't sit still, couldn't keep quiet, didn't read, didn't study," he said. Looking for answers about him, she talked to the school nurse, who was familiar with John's family and who told her that John had been suicidal but that he was much better now than he had been. "I looked at the nurse with astonishment," recalled Mrs. Lincoln. "I had never seen anybody this bad—and he was *better*?"

On several occasions, he came into the school obviously having inflicted punishment on himself. "I remember one time he had marks that looked like maybe from a cigarette lighter from a car, all the way up his arms at regular intervals," said Linda Renken, "and then trying to explain that he was working on an engine and he burned himself that way." This episode was repeated in a slightly different form at another point. "There was one time he had cigarette burns and another time he came in with slashes across the inner parts of his arms, the tender part," said Mrs. Lincoln, who recalled that it was a cold day and that John was wearing a short-sleeved shirt, obviously wanting his wounds to be noticed. "I caught up with him about third period that day and I said, 'John, what have you done?' 'Oh, I tried to crawl through a barbed-wire fence.' Well, these were slashes that were even. And I said, 'No, John, that's not true. Let's go see the nurse and get them cared for,' because they were encrusted with dried fluids. And he ran away . . . 'ran away' meaning that he would go into an empty hallway or the boys' room or whatever. It got to be almost a joke with John except it was never a joke because there was always that potential that he would do himself mortal harm."

Efforts were made continually in his behalf, but generally they were short-term efforts. "His grandfather would have to be called and the dear old man would have to come down and get him," Mrs. Lincoln noted. "We'd have to call the mental-health person. The social worker was there. John didn't get too involved with her but the nurse knew him and we'd depend upon the nurse to help him calm down and talk with him." More broad-spectrum approaches never seemed to get off the ground. "We tried to get him placed somewhere because we felt that he wasn't in good shape and he needed something that we couldn't give him," said Linda Renken, "but it didn't go anywhere. I think he fell through the cracks."

The cracks through which a troubled student might fall had, in the opinion of many of the teachers interviewed, grown wider with each passing year. And, in the opinion of these teachers, the cracks were the result of a general breaking down of the societal fabric.

Doris Gearing, who had taught in Chatham for ten years, noted a definite change in morality and values at the school since the time she had first taught there. "Kids think it's funny to kick each other or hit each other or destroy property," she said. "They have no respect for property. . . . They have no respect for themselves." Gordon Ringer echoed this concern. "I find I spend a lot of my time teaching manners and deportment in the classroom more than I do my subject matter," he said. Both teachers cited the changes in family structure today as a major contributing factor to these problems. "There are a lot of parents around the area now, a lot of people moving into Chatham who commute to Albany or go over to Massachusetts, who are going all over the place," said Ringer, "and a lot of homes where the parents are both working and that supervision doesn't seem to be there."

Doris Gearing also cited the increase in broken homes

and single parents as a factor, but felt, as well, that there was a general decline in the teaching of moral, ethical, and religious values. "These kids don't know how to explain things," she said. "They can't cope with a crisis. No religious background, no religious moral structure. I teach comparative religions in ninth grade, and when I mention the Dead Sea Scrolls or Moses or David, some of these kids don't even know any of this stuff." The result of all this is that teachers now find themselves in the position, on the one hand, of being asked to instill moral standards and values and, on the other hand, being resented for it.

While the abnegation of parental responsibility is there in many subtle ways, it sometimes finds manifest expression when parents farm their children out in these years to live with other relatives. Chatham is recognized as a good school district and so finds itself the recipient of the "difficult child" who has been, in a sense, forfeited by the larger urban schools. If parents of a "difficult child" can find a good small public school and have a relative who lives in the district, they can ship the child to those districts, and if a relative has been assigned custody, the public schools cannot refuse to take that child.

Wyley. Damian. Miles. John Bailey. These were "different" children, operating within a context that was markedly and unfortunately changed from the atmosphere of even ten years earlier. And yet they were not unique in the role-playing and fantasy games in which they indulged. "If I had to say anything about the milieu of the class of eighty-seven, it would be that it was a class that was not in the real world," remarked Louise Lincoln. "It was one gigantic fantasy. The drinking group . . . the 'oh, let's go out and have a good time' group. . . . boys who later had accidents, boys who started college this year and now they've dropped out and some are in the service but they could not face up to reality." In looking for rationales for this lack of rationality, Mrs. Lincoln kept returning to the homes from which these children had sprung. "Plenty of these boys were painfully hurt at home," she said. "We have a John Bailey coming up to us with suicidal tendencies . . . We have a

Damian Rossney sent to us—I don't know why; I don't know what is in that family, but I truly believe something serious is back there. We've got Wyley dealing silently with his pain, and a father picking on him because he was not the he-man, macho, and called the family sissy because he was, if you will, a little brainier than the rest of them. We've got hurting people who happen to cluster."

The facts that would emerge during the trials of Wyley Gates and Damian Rossney would indicate that the murders of Bob Gates, Cheryl Brahm, Robert Gates, Jr., and Jason Gates were an outgrowth of planning and discussion that involved not only the two defendants but Miles McDonald, who allegedly backed out of the plot at the midnight hour, and John Bailey, whose knowledge of "weaponry" provided useful training for the group. The trials of Wyley Gates and Damian Rossney further would indicate that, beyond this group of four, there were other students at Chatham High School who had gleanings of what was planned, whether they took them seriously or, as they professed, did not. Dr. Marchionne, who had access only to Wyley among this group, put forth a theory as to how the crime evolved. "What I saw was that there was developing a pseudo-community," he said, "between Wyley and Damian and Miles and John Bailey and one or two other guys." To enter into this pseudo-community—to buy his initiation into this fraternity—Wyley looked around him until he found that something special that would enable him to gain admittance. "I don't know how to say this—it sounds as if it's the grossest thing in the world," said Marchionne, "but you know how adolescents are notorious for buying attention? Some kids will be very generous—they have cars and will give you a ride wherever you want to go; some other kids will pick up the checks because they want your friendship—and I think that Wyley threw his family in for the friendship and membership in this group. So that as they began to talk about killing and the rest of these kids coalesced around the issue and began to talk about it, it's as if this is Wyley's membership into a peer group he never had."

It wasn't until many, many months after the murders—not until after he had been the center of the longest trial in Columbia County history—that Wyley would be able to say that these boys were not his friends after all.

6

On Saturday, November 15, 1986, Chatham High School was the target of what was later described by the principal, Wesley Brown, as a "mysterious and bizarre burglary." The attractive, modern centerpiece in a complex of educational facilities that includes the elementary school and, a block away, the intermediate school, Chatham High School was described by one teacher as "a little school, a country school. . . . They never had problems like this. They never had stealing. A little vandalism, but no stealing." Now, however, as they were just beginning to discover, Chatham High School most definitely had stealing, and the stealing was underscored by a peculiar, almost perverse tone of prankishness.

When the burglary was reconstructed, it became evident that the burglars had entered the school by key through a door near the science wing. The main administrative office was their first destination, to which they also gained admission with a key, and there the desks of the secretaries were rifled. Minor items were taken—a pocket calculator, a roll of stamps—but all cash was left untouched.

The burglars next climbed on top of a floor safe in the main office, removed a suspended ceiling panel and crawled over a cinder-block wall to gain admission to the vice-principal's office. There they helped themselves to two radios and they then climbed back through the ceiling, carefully replacing the ceiling panel. From there, they went into the principal's office, where their booty included computer paper, a microphone, and blank computer address labels.

The library was the next stop. They jimmied the lock and took a dozen books, which, upon their subsequent recovery, were found to cover such subject matter as witch-craft and brainwashing. Again, cash was left untouched, as they ignored the money collected in overdue fines that was kept in an easily accessible drawer. From the audiovisual room, however, they took money from a drawer that was not, according to the principal, particularly accessible. A message was clearly being sent that the burglars were as much in this for the challenge as for the loot.

Finally, they made their way to the faculty room. Taking a break, they sat down to eat a pizza they'd brought along with them. Before they left the faculty room, the burglars placed a hanging plant in the oven and called it a night.

The effect of this escapade was unsettling. "The mischievous things that were done, like the plant put in the oven or somebody's file cabinet turned upside down, were not really damaging things," said Louise Lincoln, "but piquant things, strangeness." Wesley Brown said, "They did nothing malicious or damaging, but left little signs as if to say, 'See, we can come in when we want and do what we want.'"

The stolen materials from the November 15 robbery were recovered along with items stolen in the December 4 robbery of the Gates log cabin, implicating Wyley Gates, Damian Rossney, and Miles McDonald in the burglaries. The burglaries had become habitual with the boys, and, in fact, Wyley, in a diary entry, made mention of the November 15 robbery as "the third group penetration into Chatham High School," adding that it was, for him, his fifth penetration,

Damian's third, and, as far as Miles was concerned, he had, according to Wyley, "ceased counting." Wyley also told Dr. Marchionne that the group had been contemplating a burglary of the high school in Canajoharie, where the Hatch family lived and where, Wyley knew, there was a large cache of computers.

The computers stolen over the course of these "penetrations" enabled the boys to play the games that were their passion. One game that they played frequently was a video adaptation of Dungeons and Dragons. Conceived in the early 1970s, Dungeons and Dragons (D&D) has been widely condemned by groups who have linked it to incidents of teenage violence and who have sought to have the game banned. The game, whose basic components are a set of special dice and hundreds of pages of instructions, has no winners or losers, and individual games can go on indefinitely, as the fantasies of which the game is composed become more and more elaborate. Involving demons, sorcerers, dragons, and witches who must be conquered in the pursuit of treasure, the game includes detailed manuals on which players rely, using their imaginations to create adventures under the aegis of an experienced game player who is known as The Dungeonmaster. It is The Dungeonmaster who designs the problems that other players will confront; it is The Dungeonmaster who accords the individual players their strength, values, and the weapons they are allowed.

TSR Hobbies, the manufacturer of Dungeons and Dragons, estimates that some four million people play the game. But critics of D&D have linked it to as many as fifty incidents of teenage violence, including murder and suicide. Pat Pulling of Virginia, the mother of a boy whose death was linked to the game, started an organization called Bothered About D&D (BADD). She said that her son, a bright high school junior, had become so obsessed with D&D that his grades suffered and when another player in a long-running game at his school sent him a curse, he interpreted this literally and shot himself through the heart. Pulling asserts that D&D game manuals contain "detailed descriptions of killing, satanic human sacrifice, assassination, sadism, premeditated murder, and curses of insanity." She also states that much of the material comes from witchcraft, demonology, and the occult.

The attack on D&D, which TSR Hobbies spokesman Dieter Sturm said "is being made a scapegoat for the rampant teenage suicide problem," is both of a religious and secular nature. Those who attack it on religious grounds feel that the game is a form of satanism, and indeed the playing of the game on school grounds has been forbidden in at least one Roman Catholic school system. The secular objection to the game is based on the assertion that players become so wrapped up in the fantasies of the game that they lose contact with reality. "The game causes young men to kill themselves and others," stated Dr. Thomas Radecki, a psychiatrist and chairman of the National Coalition on Television Violence. "The kids start living in the fantasy . . . and they can't find their way out of the dungeon." Of course, the vast majority of players do not go on to commit crimes or to become pathologically confused about the difference between reality and fantasy, but TSR Hobbies did come to the decision, as far back as 1983, to include a warning against players identifying too much with their game's characters. "The more the two are kept apart," the manual advises, "the better your games will be."

That Dungeons and Dragons was the inspiration for the crime committed on December 13 is doubtful; that the game, as well as other fantasy-oriented games, was an influence on the boys is probable. Indeed, it was another fantasy game, Infierno—an allusion to hell as depicted by Dante—that provided the code name for the plan to kill Robert Gates.

Beyond the theft of computer facilities that would aid Wyley, Damian, and Miles in realizing their goals, whether phantasmagoric or starkly realistic, the burglaries offered the boys something else that was real, tangible, and valuable, and that was the concrete, hard-core experience that was accrued with each of these "penetrations." Each of these successful forays into the high school helped the boys develop their identities as competent criminals and convinced them that they could do pretty much what they wanted to do. Consequently, it wasn't long before the group was pushing beyond the challenge—or lack of challenge—that Chatham High School provided. Indeed, it would only be a matter of a few short weeks before the prankishness of the November 15 "penetration" was supplanted by the grim seriousness and intent of another burglary whose impact was far more profound.

Months later, in April 1987, in an interview conducted by Dr. Neil Borenstein, clinical director of the Central New York Psychiatric Center and an expert witness for the prosecution in the trial of *The People of New York* v. *Wyley Gates*, Wyley re-created the dialogue that had developed between himself and Damian in the fall of the previous year.

The return to school, Wyley told Dr. Borenstein, had been bitterly disappointing and frustrating, and it was late in September when he first began channeling these frustrations into a new way of thinking. The feelings of distance and estrangement from his father, Cheryl, and, lately, his brother had become transmuted into feelings of intense antipathy that were more and more the focus of his energies, if not his very existence. Bob, Cheryl, Bobby . . . they were the ones who stood between him and his personal fulfillment. With increasingly acute pathology, Wyley became convinced that his personal fulfillment would be the product of what he grandiosely envisioned as his potential role of world leader and as a potent force in the cause of ecology and conservation. Consequently, his shabby, small-minded, ignorant, and inferior family, with their constant, nattering distractions, represented ever-greater stumbling blocks to his academic achievement and warranted, in his mind, their elimination. He asked himself repeatedly this question: Why should I suffer by them instead of the other way around? And so, as he told Dr. Borenstein, he began to toy with the idea of getting rid of them, and this new idea was mentioned to his friend Damian sometime at the end of September or in early October.

Damian, according to Wyley, was willing to help him. The compensation that Wyley allegedly offered for this help was 25 percent of the inheritance that Wyley would receive from his father's estate. Dr. Marchionne, with whom Wyley also discussed the murder plot that was hatched that fall, described the thinking as "so grandiose, it's unbelievable." Wyley told Marchionne that he had estimated his father's estate at between $500,000 and $800,000 (the estate was eventually estimated at approximately $170,000), and that the offer to Damian of 25 percent would ensure his friend roughly $100,000. As for Miles, Wyley told Marchionne that he had offered him 10 percent of Damian's share for driving Damian and, if Miles wound up killing anyone, then he would get 25 percent of Damian's share.

In testimony that Miles McDonald later gave in the trial of Wyley Gates, he stated that he first witnessed a conversation regarding a plan to murder Wyley's father in either the last week of September or the first week of October 1986. Miles had been in the computer room watching Wyley and Damian play Titan. At some point during the game, Wyley let it be known that he was planning to kill his father and his brother. Miles reported there was no further conversation at that time, and nothing more was said until the following week. At that point, once again in the computer room, Wyley mentioned that he had a plan to kill his father and knew how to do it, and again, Miles testified, the conversation went no further. A third conversation in the computer room followed at an unspecified date when Wyley explained the plan in which Damian and Miles would kill his father and brother. Damian and Miles would go to the Kelgate garage on Route 295, whereupon Miles would throw rocks to get Robert and Bobby outside and Damian would be waiting for them with a gun. It was during this third conversation, Miles testified, that he was told that the name of the plan was Infierno.

In Wyley's mind, this triumvirate—Damian, Miles, and

himself—represented a potent combination. Wyley was the "engineer"; Damian was the "genius"; and Miles possessed "aggressive skills." With these varied skills and talents, the trio planned and executed, on December 4, a robbery of the log house on Maple Drive. Wyley, who had already accumulated a number of absences from school, including an entire week in October when he feigned sickness, brought to school that day a fake excuse, as did Miles. The two set off for Colane Road, in Miles's car, to pick up Damian. En route, however, they passed Damian's uncle and, afraid of being seen by him, they turned around and went straight to the log house. But, having arrived there, they felt Damian's absence sorely and so they went to get him. With Damian now in tow, they returned to the log house and the three boys donned gloves—"food service"-type gloves, Miles would later testify, which Damian had provided, bringing along at least a dozen pair. They stood on an overturned canoe to enter the house through the window of Bobby, Jr.'s, room, and then the ransacking began. Damian broke into Robert Gates's gun rack and began to clear out an arsenal of weapons.

The loot was stuffed into duffel bags. In addition to guns and ammunition, it included holsters, a camping hatchet, an onyx ring, some bourbon, two Walkmans, a watch, and cash. The boys left the house through the garage and returned to the car, which was parked at a neighbor's. After they loaded the loot, they went back to the Joseph residence and then to a nearby field where they target-practiced with the stolen firearms. Along the way the six pairs of gloves that were used were thrown into a stream and Damian took the remaining pairs back to his aunt and uncle's house.

In the Josephs' garage, they divvied up the goods, with Wyley essentially sitting by passively as Miles and Damian vied for what each of them wanted. Damian was particularly intent on keeping for himself a Walther PPK .380 automatic pistol. The Walther—a descendant of the 1929 Walther PP ("*Polizei Pistole*") designed for use by German police officers—was a seven-shot, automatic handgun that fired nine-

millimeter or .380-caliber slugs. Miles testified that they
referred to the Walther as "Damian's little toy." Further
testimony suggested that Damian had a particular interest
in the Walther because it was the pistol with which James
Bond, Agent 007, was identified. With the loot divided, the
group broke up for the day, with Miles driving Wyley to a
haircutting appointment in nearby Kinderhook.

The December 4 robbery proved a traumatic event for the
Gates family. On the night of the robbery, Bobby, Jr., went
to the Chatham High School to notify his brother as to what
had happened. Wyley would later report to Dr. Marchionne
that he had been irritated by Bobby's interruption of his
band practice to inform him of the burglary. To Wyley, this
was a measure of Bobby's stupidity. In fact, Bobby was
deeply disturbed by the incident. "He said, 'The creeps
walked all over my bed,' " recalled Dennis Gawron, "and he
was real hurt about it." Gawron, too, remembered that Bob
Gates, whom he saw in the days following the robbery, "was
probably the worst I'd ever seen him."
    In the days ahead, Bob found himself feeling dissatisfied
with the police, who told him that there was not much they
could do about this. Moreover, the burglary of the log house
was not an isolated event. The Kelgate garage had already
been robbed twice and the stress of this third robbery, along
with the stress of Jason's custody situation, was taking its
toll. Nor were there any satisfactory leads. A friend of Bob's
had told him that she had sighted a yellow pickup truck
with white license plates on the road on the day of the
burglary, but the information was sketchy. Bob's personal
hunch was that this was the work of neighborhood hood-
lums, but there wasn't really anything to go on.
    Taking his friend Don DeLapp on the route that the
burglars had used, Bob showed him the tire tracks and
where they had parked the car and how they had stood on
the canoe. To DeLapp, Bob vented his outrage and frustra-
tion, and DeLapp was blunt with him. "Someone's got it
out for you," he told Bob. "Someone is trying to put

you on your knees and believe me, it's someone that you know."

Bob's friend Dave Frick had similar thoughts when Bob told him what had been taken. "I said, 'Well, what did they take from Wyley's room?' " Frick recalled. " 'Cause he told me what they had taken from Bobby and what they had taken from himself and what they had taken from Cheryl and how they had taken the liquor and how they had taken all the guns. 'And what did they take from Wyley?' I asked, knowing that Wyley had all this computer equipment, knowing that if they were really thieves, and were just out to make a haul, well, everybody knows that computers are valuable." But Bob explained that nothing was touched in Wyley's room; that Wyley had had on his good watch and good ring at school that day. Frick told Bob that it all sounded "fishy" to him, but Bob didn't seem able to hear it. According to Louise Frick, however, Cheryl agreed that it was strange that nothing of Wyley's had been taken and she set about getting Bob to open his eyes to the possibilities.

On December 7, Don and Barbara DeLapp came over to Canaan to see their embattled friends. It proved a strange day for them. At the Kelgate garage, Wyley had his uncharacteristically open conversation with Barbara about his father wanting him to go to community college rather than a four-year university. Then there was a brief discussion at the garage about the robbery. Don DeLapp recalled telling Bob, in Wyley's presence, that, in his opinion, the perpetrator was someone he knew. "Bob said, 'Don't say it too much around the kids, I don't want them to hear anything,' " DeLapp remembered. When they all went back to the house afterward, there was more discussion about the robbery. Don asked Bob to think if he had any enemies—people who owed him money or who might otherwise have it in for him. At this point, Barbara got up to go to the bathroom and discovered Wyley lurking around the corner, listening to them. A little bit later, she got up again and again there was Wyley. "When he saw me, he like jumped," she said, "and moved back." A little later, when she went to the refrigerator to put away a bottle of soda, she spotted him again. "He like pretended that he was going into the bathroom. But you could see that he was shocked that I saw him there."

Indeed, December 7 had been a very full day for Wyley, as it was on that day too that he joined Miles and Damian for target practice with the stolen weapons at John Bailey's grandfather's farm. The group had with them the Walther PPK .380, a seven-millimeter rifle, and a .22 pistol, among other firearms. According to Bailey's later testimony, Wyley was unsure of how to use the Walther, how to load it, or how to work the safety. Damian and Bailey showed Wyley what to do. They loaded magazines for him and showed him how to cock it. They shot the weapon into trees, into the air, and at Bailey's grandfather's tractor. An injury common to those who use a Walther PPK .380 was sustained both by Bailey and Wyley. The light firearm kicked back on discharge, cutting their thumbs. Finally, when they were done, Wyley and Damian chatted briefly to each other and then Wyley left with the loaded pistols in the shoulder holster.

Those who knew Bob felt that the impact of the robbery continued to weigh heavily on him. Of his close friends, Don DeLapp was the last to see Bob, on Wednesday, December 10. DeLapp was convinced that "when Bob came to see me on Wednesday, he knew something. 'Cause he really looked like he was in trouble. Just his general manner. He didn't say anything to me. But he had 'scared' written all over his face."

Dave Frick, who had been one of Bob's closest friends for twenty years, had the same feeling. "I think that Bob did find out in the week that we didn't see him," said Frick. "And maybe had confronted Wyley. . . . This is only my own personal feelings because that's the type of person Bob was. . . . When he put his mind to something, he got to the truth of the matter."

Whether Bob Gates knew the truth behind the December 4th robbery is not something that will ever be known. But the time for truths to emerge was running out. As the winter solstice approached, the days were growing shorter, the nights were growing longer, and December 13 was almost at hand.

7

The holiday season was upon them, but for the family of Robert Gates it was not a time of cheer. The December 4 burglary of the log cabin had cast its long shadow over them, and the battle between the Gates family and the Groudases over Jason was cresting. The hotly contested custody of Jason, who had become the recipient of a $124,000 trust fund established after $170,000 had been awarded him in a lawsuit for wrongful death that the Groudases had brought against the estate of Dane Gates, was to be decided at a hearing scheduled for December 18. In addition to the stress of these events, the largely unspoken problem of Wyley was now becoming a spoken one as Wyley's hostility and peculiarity became increasingly overt and intense.

For years, the Gates family had become accustomed to Wyley's disappearing acts at family gatherings, but now that reclusiveness was being supplanted by open displays of anger. Evelyn Prescott was a guest at a holiday dinner when that anger flared up. "We all went over [to the log house] for Thanksgiving dinner," Mrs. Prescott recalled, "and

Cheryl had made one of the pies and Bob said something to Wyley about trying the pie or something. And Wyley said, in clenched tones, 'I don't want it!' Like that, you know? And my sister Dorothy said he had such a look on his face when he said that."

Sally Joseph, too, was aware of the stress going on in the log house, particularly in the week before December thirteenth. Although she was used to the frequent and lengthy phone conversations between Damian and Wyley, it seemed to her that Wyley's calls, in this week, were quite a bit more frequent than usual. When she inquired as to the reasons for this, Damian told her that Wyley had been out of school all week. "I said, 'Oh? Why? Is he sick?' And he said, 'No, he's just been staying home; he doesn't feel like going to school,'" recalled Mrs. Joseph. "And I said, 'Is he depressed?' And Damian said, 'I don't know, maybe he is.'" Mrs. Joseph felt that perhaps Wyley was depressed about living at home, as Damian had told her that Wyley didn't like Cheryl and believed that Jason was usurping his place in the family, and so she impulsively extended an invitation. "Here it was December; Wyley only had another five, six months to go," she said, "and I said, 'Well, why don't you ask Wyley if he wants to live over here?' And Damian was on the phone with Wyley and said, 'My aunt wants to know if you want to live here.'" But Mrs. Joseph never found out what Wyley's response to the invitation was, although she did remember that Damian seemed to quail at the idea, pointing out that she had promised to let him use the extra bedroom for his computer setup. But, despite her nephew's resistance, Mrs. Joseph felt compelled to offer Wyley a lifeline. "We can make an arrangement for Wyley," she remembered telling Damian. "I was serious. I thought the kid might be suicidal."

It was nearing Christmastime, and, as is common in a family rent by divorce, the seasonal cheer was mitigated by the problem of who would go where to spend the holiday with whom. The boys had talked about making a trip to California to see their mother. Dennis Gawron, who was a sounding board for much of Bobby's dissatisfaction with his life, remembered hearing some vague talk about this trip. "There were times when Bobby was very unhappy [at the garage] and he said he just wanted to get out," recalled Gawron. "And he talked about going to California that winter." But according to Dorothy Donnelley, Robert told Bobby that he could either go see his mother for Christmas or go to Daytona for Bike Week, and Bobby chose Daytona. Wyley, on the other hand, to the best of Donnelley's recollection, chose California.

The fact was that no structured plan of visitation had ever been set up for the boys and their mother. Viki Hatch described the visitation schedule as "catch as catch can," owing to expenses over the airline flights. According to Vivian Gates, "Robert had said when they were [living in California] that he would pay for their visits and now, if she wanted them, she'd have to pay." In an interview held at the Elmira Correctional Facility, Wyley told me that neither his mother nor his mother's family ever gave him money, although he regarded her family as being "middle class." Wyley pointed with pride to the fact that his mother had not asked for alimony, and, although he believed that his mother and her family had financial resources, he saw nothing odd in the fact that she never gave him any money. In any event, however, the plan to visit Kristi Gates seems to have gotten lost somewhere along the way. "They were planning to go at Christmas," said Vivian Gates. "They were in my kitchen and I heard Bobby say, 'Wyley and I have plans to go.' And then I didn't hear any more about it and Wyley told me that his brother couldn't afford it." Why Wyley stayed home that Christmas is another question altogether, for, in fact, he later admitted to Dr. Marchionne that he had planned to use the trip to California as his alibi for the murders that he would commission Damian to commit in his absence. In any case, neither Wyley nor Bobby ever made it to California that winter, nor did Bobby make it to Daytona, nor, in fact, did either boy make it to any warm place in the sun. They remained at home, where, like everyone else, they would have to endure the near-arctic weather conditions that had the area in its grip in this second week of December.

The morning of December 13 was particularly frigid, and it took time for the garage to warm up. Jim Klingler was the first to arrive at the shop, where he was joined by Bob and the boys, who got there by eight, and then, at around 9:30, by Skip Huvar, who had opened his motorcycle shop in Bob Gates's garage, and Mike Donnelley, Skip's parts manager and the son of Skip's companion Dorothy Donnelley.

The day had been set aside for improvements. Bob and Skip were in the process of constructing two additions to the garage, one a new storage facility for Skip and the other an office facility. That day the group was working on the office facility, as they had been for the past three or four weekends.

Bob, of course, never minded the weekend work. "That's something people don't understand," remarked Jim Klingler. "Bob could relax while he was doing these things." Wyley, however, who customarily acted, in the words of Dick Klingler, "like a prisoner," was, for some reason, different this Saturday. Dorothy Donnelley remembered her son Mike telling her just how different the usually taciturn Wyley had been that day. "That day, Michael noticed that he was very friendly, very happy. He was just bubbling. He was just like a totally different person," said Donnelley.

But whatever uncharacteristic bonhomie Wyley was evincing that day, it was not shed upon Cheryl. Saturdays were, as a rule, Cheryl's day with Jason, and she had picked him up at Vivian's house around eight o'clock. As was her habit, she showed up with lunch for the boys at the garage. "She did that every Saturday," said Dorothy Donnelley. "She brought for everyone. She brought Wyley tuna salad wrapped up special, because he didn't like what she brought everyone else. This particular day he took it and made some comment as to, 'I don't know why she did this,' and threw it in the garbage. Very hostile about it."

Evidently, Wyley's acting-out in Cheryl's direction did
not preclude his asking her for the use of her car that night.
She agreed, and the day progressed with only minor interruptions. At one point, Cheryl's car refused to start when
she had it parked in front of Slattery's, East Chatham's
general store, and it was towed over to the garage, where
Bobby took out the starter and cleaned it up. The malfunc-
tion did not seem serious, at least not serious enough to
deter Wyley from wanting to use the car that night. The
only other interruption in the workday came when Bob
stopped over at his mother's house for ten minutes at three
o'clock to meet with the custody lawyers. He returned to
the garage after that to get a few more hours of work in.
Skip Huvar left at approximately 4:45 P.M. to get ready for
a Christmas party, and Mike Donnelley and Jim Klingler
had left before that. Bob remained at the garage with his
sons until approximately 5:30.

Returning home to the log cabin, Bob, Bobby, Cheryl,
Jason, and Wyley sat down for a spaghetti dinner. Bob and
Cheryl had had plans to go out that night with Don and
Barbara DeLapp, but a work-related Christmas party that
Barbara had to attend forced a change in plans. So it would
be an at-home evening after all, but that was all right with
them. It was a bitterly cold night; it didn't hurt to stay in.
And, anyway, there were always a hundred different things
to do before Christmas. The Gates family, the Brahm
family—these were large clans, and that meant a lot of
presents to sort and wrap. It wouldn't hurt to be in and get
some of it done. Bobby would be at home tonight too, for
he had no date (that was really just starting; he was late out
of the gate) and the likelihood was slim that he would be
called upon to serve in his capacity as volunteer fireman.
He would spend the evening in the weight room/music
room above the garage, where he could practice on the
drums without disturbing anyone. Little Jason was due to
be returned in a short while to Vivian, but he could play a
little longer with the Lego in the rec room. As for Wyley,
he had plans to go out. Their perpetual shut-in was finally
having something like a social life and, even though Damian

wasn't their idea of an ideal best friend and even though Wyley was giving them more attitude than they felt they deserved, at least he wouldn't be moping around the house tonight. And anyway, he was going to see *Heartbreak Ridge*, the new Clint Eastwood movie—enough said. Cheryl turned over the car keys and Wyley left the house around 6:30.

Around 6:25, Dick Klingler looked at the clock in his kitchen. He was quite sure of the time because his wife was preparing dinner and he asked her how long it would be before it was ready. She told him he had fifteen minutes. "Then I went and called Bob and that must have been around six-thirty," recalled Klingler. Cheryl answered the phone and Dick teased her a little—that was the tenor of their relationship— and then she put Bob on the phone and the conversation ran to the robbery. Klingler told Bob that he had been driving up Frisbie Street that afternoon and a car he had never seen before, a Volkswagen, came tearing out and almost wrongsided his pickup truck as it went on down the road. Bob said he knew the car, that it belonged to a kid up the road who was in the habit of buying and refurbishing wrecks. The two friends then talked about the Christmas party that Klingler proposed Bob host down at "Gatesmall." "We were arguing over who was going to buy the beer," said Klingler, "and finally I decided my fifteen minutes was up because the wife always gets mad at me when I'm late for dinner, so I hung up and came in to eat dinner and I looked at the clock and said to my wife, 'You see, I didn't take more than fifteen minutes,' and it was six-forty."

For Vivian Gates, the evening of December 13 had gotten off to a pleasant start. The sister of her daughter-in-law Mary, her son Bill's wife, had come by to introduce Vivian to her fiancé, and it was good to have company. Despite the fact that she was surrounded by family—her son and his boys lived within walking distance, as did her sister-in-law Evelyn Prescott, who was "like a sister" to her, who knew what it was to be a widow, and who had asked Vivian to join her and her sister Dorothy and brother-in-law Paul for dinner that night, an invitation Vivian declined—despite all this, it was still a very big house for just one person and a dog. Moreover, it was a time of year when the crushing losses that she had suffered—a son and a daughter-in-law dead; her husband dead; another son irreparably damaged—were only accentuated. All told, it was better not to be alone.

But by the time her company had left, the comfortable atmosphere of the evening was just beginning, with the slightest frisson of anxiety, to dissipate. Little Jason, who was supposed to have been returned to her by eight o'clock, had not yet shown up. Surely, she told herself, she shouldn't worry. After all, Bob and Cheryl had probably just gone out somewhere and taken Jason with them. But it was hard not to worry. Her life had been marked by phone calls in the night, and there was, on top of everything else, the strain of the custody situation. And so Vivian, shortly after eight o'clock, began calling her son's house and got a busy signal. She told herself it must be Wyley, who had so recently discovered the telephone, talking to a friend.

But throughout the next few hours, whenever she called the house, she got a busy signal. Although he had been due at eight o'clock, by ten-thirty there was still no sign of Jason. Time and again, she called the cabin; time and again she got a busy signal. Two hours and thirty minutes was a long conversation, even by Wyley's standards these days. And yet she chose to keep her anxieties to herself. At no point during that evening did Vivian call Evelyn Prescott or Dorothy and Paul Dooley or Mary-Lynn Bedford, who lived across from the log house. As her anxieties mounted by the moment, she chose to remain alone in her house with her fears.

The experience of going to the movies at the Crandell Theater in "downtown" Chatham has remained pretty much of a constant through the decades. As you sit in the plush seats, and as the theater darkens for the main attraction, you find yourself embarking effortlessly on that journey into fantasy, a journey that requires so much more effort when you are sitting in one of ten or a dozen shoebox-shaped spaces in a shopping mall. On Saturday night, Wyley, against all odds, made that journey into fantasy, as he watched Clint Eastwood playing a grizzled marine sergeant who whips a ragtag group of flakes into damned good soldiers just in time for the Grenada invasion. The movie was a paean to the traditional values of American manhood, and Wyley must have been aware that this was a movie of which his father would have approved.

Almost two years later, at his own trial, Damian Rossney would testify that Wyley, watching the movie, seemed "completely normal . . . when it was funny, he laughed." To one of the many psychotherapists who would interview him, however, Wyley acknowledged a certain ironic feeling he experienced during the film, as the people sitting around him, watching the shooting on the screen, really didn't have any idea what that kind of shooting was all about, as he now did.

After the movie, as Wyley and Damian emerged, Damian stopped to talk to Miles McDonald, who was waiting in line to get in—a meeting that was allegedly chance—and Wyley, as they spoke, turned away from them, looking up the street, toward the train tracks, toward the tall building known as The Clocktower, the dominant architectural element in the Chatham cityscape. What was he thinking? This crystal cold night; the snug little town; Delson's Department Store, where you buy your underwear and your socks, and Brown's Shoes and the Mini-Chopper, where you buy your lottery ticket, and Chatham Auto Parts, where his brother Bobby had once worked. What was he thinking as he looked up the street? That he would never be able to look at it again this way? That no longer was he just one more town son amid the town fathers?

They went back to Damian's house. Sally and Stanley Joseph were upstairs in the loft area outside their bedroom, watching a movie, when the boys came in around 9:25, and they remembered a lot of kidding back and forth, between Wyley and Damian. The boys excused themselves to go play video games, and then a strange thing happened. Damian came back upstairs to show his aunt a catalog that had come in the mail that day, and Wyley accompanied him. "Very strange," Mrs. Joseph remarked. "Wyley didn't usually put himself in a situation where you talked. He'd usually stay in Damian's room and wait for him or whatever. But he came right up . . . he was smiling. They were both smiling. And I said, 'Well, you guys are pretty excited. How was the movie?' 'Oh, it was a good movie.' " Stanley Joseph also felt that something "strange" was happening then. "If there was any time in our experience with Wyley that we thought that Wyley wanted to say something to us spontaneously," he recalled, "it was that moment."

The other strange thing had to do with Wyley's making a phone call. "He made a phone call at the phone right down from the balcony at the desk," Mrs. Joseph said. "And Damian had a phone in his room, which Wyley would usually use, because it was private, but Wyley came out to call home." She asked Damian who Wyley was calling, and Damian told her he was calling Cheryl to tell her he would be right home. At approximately 10:25 P.M., Wyley said good-night to the Josephs and to his good friend Damian, and in Cheryl's car he headed back to Maple Drive.

At approximately 10:45 P.M., Wyley entered the garage of his grandmother's house, where her German shepherd, King, was confined, and stooped down to pet the dog. "Wyley loved animals," remarked Evelyn Prescott. "He always played with my dog if he was over here." Mrs. Prescott remembered that Wyley himself had once had a dog, but she thought that when the boys went back to California, Bob had taken the dog to the pound. That dog of long ago was called Pogo, and the way Pogo had come to them was etched in Wyley's memory. Once, when riding back from a salt-pile job with his father and his brother, his father stopped somewhere and came back to the car with Pogo. Wyley was never sure whether it had been planned that way by his father or whether it had been an act of pure spontaneity. But Wyley's memory of what happened to Pogo was very different from Mrs. Prescott's memory. The dog had taken off when the boys left for California but, Wyley suspected, it was Pogo whom he saw again, relocated a few miles up the road at a neighbor's house, when he returned to East Chatham. His school bus used to drive by the house where Pogo had taken up residence, Wyley recalled, but it had been so long since Wyley had last seen him that he could never be sure if that large black dog with a blaze of white on its chest was in fact his Pogo or not. Now, as he bent down to pet King, and to release him from his chain, it seemed unimaginable that sometime in the very near future he would be writing from prison, "wondering/hoping" whether King missed him, but realizing too that he probably didn't.

It was just after 10:45 when Vivian Gates looked out her window and saw a car. She thought it must be Cheryl. But when she opened the door, it was Wyley she saw standing there, petting her dog. "They're all dead," he told her. The first thing she could think of was a car accident. They're all dead in a car accident, she thought, and she asked him where the accident had been, and it was then that he told her they had been shot. He told her that Jason too had been shot.

At 10:56 P.M.—approximately ten unaccountable minutes after Wyley had told her that he had found four members of their family dead, or at least, without any medical expertise to draw upon, presumed dead—Vivian Gates called the police. Deputy Sheriff James Sweet, of the Columbia County Sheriff's Department, took the call. Mrs. Gates told him that there had been a shooting at her son's house. She gave him the address, and Deputy Sheriff Sweet then requested the dispatching of the Rescue Squad to that address. Sweet immediately called back to the house and Mrs. Gates told him at that time that her grandson had been the one to make the discovery. Upset because she thought that the officer wasn't taking her seriously and wasn't sending anyone out, Mrs. Gates, a quiet woman, started "talking loudly" on the phone, at which point Officer Sweet asked to talk to Wyley. Wyley got on the phone and stated that he had arrived at the log cabin and had found all four occupants dead. There were no weapons and the only vehicle was his father's pickup truck. He added that he had been to the movies in Chatham.

Then Wyley hung up the phone and he and his grandmother sat on the couch and waited. Many weeks after that moment, Mrs. Gates would have occasion to meet with Dr. Anthony Marchionne. "The only comment that she made about herself which I thought of any consequence," Dr. Marchionne noted, "was that she had an incredibly difficult time showing affection to her children, that she never felt comfortable hugging them." But now, on that profoundly cold and dark December night, she put her arm around Wyley and let him rest his head against her shoulder. When asked as a witness at the subsequent murder trial of her grandson if there had been any conversation, she testified, "I'm not sure. I think I said something like, 'Wyley, it's just you and me now.'" After that there was silence as they waited for someone to come.

PART

TWO

8

Thirteen minutes after Vivian Gates placed her call to the Columbia County Sheriff's Department, Doris Gearing, Wyley's teacher of criminal justice, received a call at her home on New Concord Road, directly across the Thruway from Maple Drive. Mrs. Gearing and her husband, members of the Chatham Rescue Squad, were being dispatched to the Robert Gates residence on Maple Drive. They were told that there were "four down" and were instructed to go immediately to the scene. "We both got our jackets on," Mrs. Gearing recalled. "It was bitter cold . . . a bitter night. We were first on the scene." But, at the instructions of the authorities who followed them, the Gearings were told to remain outside. They never went in to the Gates house that night.

The undersheriff who arrived at the cabin just as the Gearings did was James Bertram, a compact but powerful-looking man of middle age who had served eleven years in this position. Bertram had just fallen asleep in his chair at headquarters when he received a call telling him that there had been a shooting at the Gates residence and that there was the possibility that four people were dead. Now Bertram approached the house, crawling under the porch to look through a small storm window. He saw a woman lying on the floor and, watching her for several moments, the cold almost paralyzing on that bitter night, he could detect no signs of movement. Crawling around to another window, Bertram got a glimpse of two others who appeared to be lifeless, an adult male and a young child who was in front of a TV that was still playing. At that point, Undersheriff Bertram returned to his patrol car and waited for two deputies to arrive. He then entered the house. As he descended the rough, steep stairs to the downstairs room, all he could see were two feet sticking up, which belonged to the white female. Going down into the room, he could see the adult male, lying with his head up against a bar, his arm bloodied, a phone to the right of him. Continuing his search, Bertram, looking to his right, saw the body of the young child, in front of the flickering television. As he had expected, there were no signs of life.

Moving through the house, Bertram came to a weight room, located over the garage. There he found the lifeless body of another white male, lying between a set of drums and the wall. Bertram also found empty casings on the floor of the weight room, as well as a live round. Other casings were found back in the main part of the house, by the entrance stairway, on the stairway itself, and in the rec room.

For Doris Gearing, the wait was interminable. "I was saying to myself, 'Oh, my gosh, I hope it's not Wyley,' " she recalled. The other vivid memory she retains from that cold, clear night was the extraordinary number of shooting stars in the sky.

When Bertram emerged, he confirmed that there were four down, with no signs of life. By this time twelve cars belonging to the sheriff's department were on the scene, with a Chatham Rescue Squad ambulance on hand. But, as it turned out, there was no need for the ambulance that night after all.

With the house secured, Bertram and Sheriff Paul

Proper put out a call to the county coroner and put in a request for assistance from the New York State Police I.D. unit in Poughkeepsie. Meanwhile, District Attorney Eugene Keeler, asleep in his Kinderhook home, got a phone call from the sheriff's department dispatcher. Keeler picked up Nancy Snyder, his assistant D.A., who also lived in Kinderhook, and they headed over to Maple Drive. When they got there, the house was sealed off, with the sheriff, the under-sheriff, the state troopers, members of the sheriff's department, and some local policemen awaiting the arrival of the state police I.D. unit. Going into the house, Keeler saw the bodies for himself. "It was not a bloody mess. It was very tragic, very sad, cold and calculating, whatever was done." His most emotional response was evoked by the figure of Jason. "Seeing the three-and-a-half-year-old in front of the TV set with the snow on it, that bothered me." Otherwise, the crime scene was less gruesome than some he had seen. "The rest was not bloody," he recalled. "There were shots and that sort of thing and blood, but not the magnitude you see in a shotgun wound, where brains are all over the place, blood is usually all over the place, heads blown off, legs blown off. That is a gory mess. These people . . . were shot with a weapon that did not come with a lot of gore to it."

Others on the scene, however, were considerably more shaken than Keeler. Sheriff Proper would tearfully tell reporters that night, "We've had a massacre . . . worse than anything I ever saw in Korea." The coroner, Angelo Nero, also badly shocked, would say that he "had never seen anything like this before." Whatever the emotional reactions were to the murders, these reactions had necessarily to take a backseat to the critical business of taking evidence and pursuing an investigation. And so, in those early hours of December 14, 1986, the Columbia County Sheriff's Department went to work.

At the big white house on the hill, Vivian Gates and Wyley were still seated on the couch, waiting for the police to arrive. Officer Richard Lindmark, of the Chatham police,

was the first on the scene, followed momentarily by Walter
Shook, a criminal investigator with the Columbia County
Sheriff's Department. Shook, a tall man with thinning, lank
blond hair and a long Nordic face, who had been with the
department fourteen years, seven of them as an investigator,
had gotten the call at home at 11:00 P.M. Now, as he entered
the spacious sun porch, so cheery during the day with its
pots of cyclamen and flowering kalanchoe, he saw two people
sitting on a couch, an older, gray-haired woman and a thin,
reddish-haired boy, a grandmother and grandson with a
markedly strong family resemblance. Shook asked Wyley to
tell him exactly what he had found at the log house. Wyley
told him that he had been to see *Heartbreak Ridge* in Chatham
with Damian Rossney; that he went back to Damian's house
to play computer games; and that while he was there he
called home but the line was busy. At around 10:30 P.M.,
Wyley told Shook, he left the Rossney home and arrived
back at the log cabin by 10:45. He entered through the
garage, went into the weight room, saw his brother, checked
his pulse, and found no signs of life. He then went downstairs, saw Cheryl at the foot of the stairs, saw his father
lying with the phone next to him, and Jason in front of the
TV. Checking for signs of life, he found none, so he got
back into Cheryl's car, drove over to his grandmother's,
petted the dog in the garage, and, when Vivian emerged to
see who it was, told her that "he had something to tell her."

Shook found Wyley's affect extraordinarily flat and
unemotional, and this immediately raised his suspicions. As
Wyley related the chronology of events, Shook became aware
of a Band-Aid on the boy's right thumb. When Shook
inquired into it, Wyley explained that as he was getting
ready to leave for the movies, Cheryl asked him to get a
bag of sweaters from the car and that, in so doing, he closed
the car door on his thumb.

With Wyley's cooperation, Shook drew a detailed map
of the log house, and the route that Wyley had taken as he
discovered the bodies. Shook then questioned Wyley in
greater depth as to his precise movements that evening.

Wyley told him that he had gotten home from working at the garage sometime between 5:00 and 5:30, and that the family then sat down for a dinner of spaghetti and meatballs and garlic bread. In the course of what he described as "sparse" conversation—Wyley's language, even in these extreme conditions, remained hyperintellectual and highly controlled—he told his father that Cheryl was letting him use her car to go to the movies. He then changed his clothes, and called Damian at approximately 6:30 to let him know that he would be picking him up at his house. Cheryl then asked Wyley to get the bag of sweaters, which he did, in the process causing the injury to his thumb. He then got into Cheryl's car and arrived at the Joseph residence at 6:45, where he washed his hand and dressed his wound. The two boys then set off for the Crandell Theater, arriving fifteen minutes late to the show.

As they left the Crandell, Wyley recounted, they ran into some friends and chatted and got back to Damian's house at approximately 9:30. At around 10:30, Wyley told Shook, he tried to call home but the phone was busy. He got into his car, left Damian's house, and headed home. And once again, in a manner that Investigator Shook would describe as "calm" and "coherent," Wyley repeated how he had discovered the four bodies that had once been his family.

Back in the cold outside the log house, suspicions and theories were emerging. The police who were present at the scene were aware that the log cabin had been burglarized a little over a week before and that firearms had been stolen. Moreover, it soon became apparent that the wounds on these four bodies were consistent with the type of firearms stolen. Therefore, very early on, the theory emerged that whoever committed the burglary committed the murders as well. Investigator Richard Nesbitt of the state police contacted Chatham High School principal Wesley Brown to see if Wyley Gates had been absent from school on December 4, the day of the burglary. Brown went to the high school to check through the files and got back to Nesbitt with the information that Wyley had indeed been absent that day, as had Damian Rossney and Miles McDonald.

At 11:45 P.M., just as he was getting home, Investigator John Cozzolino, of the Columbia County Sheriff's Department, received a call notifying him that four people were down on Maple Drive. Cozzolino, a rugged-looking man who had been with the department for nine years, three of them as an investigator, went directly to the crime scene and spoke with the sheriff and the undersheriff, who instructed him to go to Vivian Gates's home to assist Walter Shook. Cozzolino, who had grown up in the county, had a passing familiarity with the Gates family. He had gone to school with Vivian's son Steven, whom he remembered as "Boogaloo," and had been one of the officers summoned to the site of the fiery crash on Peaceful Valley Road that had claimed the lives of Dane and Georgia Gates. Arriving at the Gates house, he was told by Shook—they are familiarly known in the department as "Shooky" and "Cozzy"—to go to the Joseph residence and question the Rossney boy about his activities that evening and about the Band-Aid.

Cozzolino and Officer Lindmark, who knew the local roads, set off for the Joseph residence, but it's easy enough to get lost at night in the country and they wound up having to call for directions. They arrived at the Joseph residence at approximately 12:30 A.M. "I honestly couldn't believe it," recalled Sally Joseph, who had been in bed. "I made them show their identification." Once the credentials had been established, the Josephs found the officers "very professional . . . very nice." But their "niceness" did not allay Mrs. Joseph's mounting anxiety, and the next moment would be permanently engraved on her memory.

"Cozzolino said, 'Could you ask Damian to go into his room for a minute?' " she remembered. "And I started to feel something ominous was happening here. So Damian went back to his room and [Cozzolino] said, 'Wyley Gates just went home and found four people dead in his house.' And I thought I was going to faint. I couldn't believe it. I had to ask them a couple of times, 'Are they dead?' "

When Damian was called back in, Cozzolino told him what had happened. "I think Damian said, 'What four people?' " Mrs. Joseph recalled, to which Cozzolino replied Cheryl and Wyley's father and his brother and the baby. "And Damian said, 'What baby?' And then Cozzolino said, 'Well, the three-year-old, Jason.' And Damian said, 'Oh, Jason,' like he was very surprised."

At Cozzolino's request, Damian sketched his activities of December thirteenth. On the morning of that day, he had called the log house and had spoken with Cheryl, who told him that Wyley was down at the garage working with his father. Then, at around 4:30 or 5:00, Damian and Wyley had their conversation relating to the evening's plan of going to the movies, with Wyley telling him that he would have to ask Cheryl if he could use her car. Wyley called back at approximately 6:30, said Damian, to tell him that Cheryl had agreed to let him use the car and that he would pick him up "after he did something for his father." They got to the movie at around 7:15 and after the movie went back to Damian's house to play computer games. Both Damian and the Josephs told Cozzolino that Wyley had left their house around 10:30. Damian said he did not notice any blood or any cut on Wyley's hand, nor had Wyley asked for a Band-Aid while he was in Damian's house. Damian also mentioned that Wyley had tried to call home but that the line was busy, and he volunteered the observation that it was unusual for Wyley to call home before he left the Josephs' house.

Cozzolino asked who Wyley's other friends were, and Damian mentioned Miles. Cozzolino then asked Damian if he ever saw Wyley use any guns, and Damian said something about their once taking a gun off the wall and maybe shooting a round. Finally, Cozzolino asked Damian if he knew anything about the murders, and Damian assured him that he did not. The Josephs, recalling the interview, thought it was "like having a chat . . . it certainly wasn't like he should have read Damian his rights. It was like having a talk 'cause your friend just found this horrible thing and 'We want to ask you about what happened at the theater and all.' " Having concluded the interview, Investigator Cozzolino left his business card, returned to his car, and headed back to Vivian Gates's house.

With Cozzolino gone, the Josephs sat up for a while talking with their nephew. In Damian's opinion, it sounded as if the police thought Wyley committed the crimes. "And he said, 'I don't see how he could have done it,' " recalled Mrs. Joseph, who also recalled that the last thing she said, before they went to bed, was that she thought Wyley had probably done it.

During this time, Vivian Gates got up from her station next to Wyley on the couch and began the wrenching task of notifying family members. Her first call was to Jason's other grandmother, Deloras Groudas. In Mrs. Gates's words, Mrs. Groudas "got hysterical," and so Mrs. Gates called Paul Groudas, Jason's uncle, and told him what had happened, advising him that he should be with his mother. The next call Mrs. Gates made was to her sister-in-law Evelyn Prescott, who was being visited by her sister, Dorothy, and Dorothy's husband Paul Dooley.

Mrs. Prescott and the Dooleys had enjoyed a quiet evening at home after some holiday shopping that afternoon. The quiet, however, was underscored by a sense of activity on the road, of which they had been only subliminally aware. "I thought, Somebody's probably having a party around here, or something like that," said Mrs. Dooley, who had noticed an unusual volume of traffic on the road. "But then I realized later of course it was all police cars."

It was around twelve o'clock when the phone rang and Mrs. Prescott answered. "Viv spoke to us and she said, 'There's been another tragedy,' " Mrs. Prescott remembered. "And I said, 'Oh, no, Viv'—I thought another accident, like Dane's accident." But this time it was not an accident. Mrs. Gates told Mrs. Prescott that "they were all dead" and when Mrs. Prescott asked who, Mrs. Gates named them all. "Well, I was stunned," Mrs. Prescott recalled. "I just handed the phone to my sister, who was standing there."

"Evelyn picked up the phone and was getting more and

more excited," said Mrs. Dooley, "and I went in and said, 'What's the matter? What's going on?' And she said, 'I don't know. I can't understand it. She's talking about everyone being dead. I don't understand it.' She said, 'You take it! You take it!' " And so Mrs. Dooley took the phone and asked Vivian what had happened. "She sounded like a little girl, a very confused little girl, on the other end of the phone," said Mrs. Dooley, "and she said, 'Oh, Dorothy, there's been a terrible tragedy. They're all dead.' 'What do you mean they're all dead?' And she started naming them and it was like there was no end to it." Vivian told her that they had been shot and that Wyley had discovered the bodies and that the only reason Wyley was saved was that he went to a movie. She told her sister-in-law that the police were there questioning them, and Mrs. Dooley told her that they would throw some clothes on and be right over.

As the numbed relatives got dressed, the only thing that kept running through their minds was that it had to have been the work of a lunatic. Who else would kill a child that way? And the terrifying thing was that it was a maniac who could still be loose in the neighborhood. "For a couple of hours I was never so scared in my life," remembered Paul Dooley. "Because I've been through World War Two and Korea both and I had no gun and I didn't think those Keystone Kops could protect anybody."

As they got to their sister-in-law's house, the first person they saw was Wyley. "Wyley was sitting on the end of the couch," remembered Mrs. Prescott, "and Mrs. Groudas was there and she was holding his hand, because she figured he had been through something terrible." Vivian was in and out of the room, Mrs. Prescott recalled, and Wyley just kept his head down the whole time, as if he were in shock. Neither Mrs. Prescott nor the Dooleys, however, attempted to engage their nephew in conversation. "I didn't say a word to him. Nobody did," said Mrs. Prescott. "I thought, you know, for what he'd been through . . . and, anyway, you couldn't get close to Wyley." As far as their sister-in-law went, Mrs. Dooley remembered that Mrs. Gates maintained her composure. "She's an unreal lady," said Mrs. Dooley, "but she had me a little worried because I really felt badly for her. She was in an awful state of shock too. I know she was terribly upset and of course I was worried something was going to happen to her." Mrs. Prescott characterized Mrs. Gates in those early hours of December fourteenth as being "very, very shocked, very quiet . . . but she's a quiet person too, not given to showing emotion." Mostly from that awful night Mrs. Prescott remembers a sense of silence as they sat around. "Everybody had the chills," she said, "because it was a cold night out and on top of that we were shocked."

Mrs. Gates felt they should notify the other members of the family. She called her son Louis in California, and she called her brother so that he could notify their aged mother in New Orleans before she heard it on television. Paul Dooley volunteered to call Viki Hatch.

The Hatches, who had stayed up until approximately 1:30 that morning, awaiting the return of their daughter from a date, were just getting into bed when the phone rang. "Tina answered it and she called us and said, 'Uncle Paul wants to talk to you,'" recalled Viki Hatch. "And we said, 'Uncle Paul?' I knew something was wrong. And Howard got on and he just went white." Hatch told his wife to gather the children together. "He said, 'I only want to say this once,'" Mrs. Hatch said. The news threw them into an immediate state of shock, but Mrs. Hatch thought to contact her husband's brother, a state trooper who might have access to information. Howard called his brother, but he knew nothing of the crime and suggested that someone might be "playing a joke" on them. He offered, however, to make some calls and, before long, he called back with a confirmation of the events. "He wanted to know if Bob was involved in any gangland stuff or drugs or stuff like that and we said not that we knew," recalled Mrs. Hatch. "But it looked like somebody—a hit person—had just come in." At that point, Mrs. Hatch felt that she had better call her mother to see if she wanted them to come down. "Yes, you should come. I think Wyley needs to see other people,"

Vivian told her daughter, and so Viki Hatch and her family got dressed and headed right out.

The trip from the Hatch home outside Schenectady to East Chatham takes a good hour, but this was not a good hour. All members of the family were lost in their own private thoughts. "We didn't even talk," Mrs. Hatch said. "And as soon as we turned onto Frisbie Street, we were afraid of what we were coming into." They were afraid that somebody was still out there, lurking in the dark bushes, waiting with a rage that might still have need of being vented.

At the big white house on the hill, Investigator Shook was continuing his inquiries. He questioned Paul Groudas as to his activities of the day, and Groudas replied that he had been doing carpentry work, which was his regular employment. Shortly, Investigator Cozzolino returned to the house and told Shook that Damian had corroborated Wyley's story of having gone to the Crandell Theater to see *Heartbreak Ridge*, but, Cozzolino added, Damian said Wyley did not get a Band-Aid from him and that he had volunteered as well the information that Wyley's call home from the Joseph residence was uncharacteristic.

Shook decided, at that point, to ask Wyley, who was still sitting impassively on the sun porch, surrounded by grieving and numbed relatives, if he'd be willing to reduce his activities of the evening to a written deposition. Wyley, still "calm" and "coherent," as Shook would describe him being throughout the evening, agreed to do so, and Shook asked Mrs. Gates if there was a quieter spot in the house that they might use. She directed them to the living room/library and closed the doors, leaving Wyley, Shook, and Cozzolino alone in the room. Cozzolino showed Wyley the official deposition form used by Columbia County, and Shook instructed the boy to write out his activities of the evening in chronological order. At approximately 1:45 A.M., Wyley—noting his age as seventeen and his occupation as "student"—began the writing of the deposition and stated as follows:

On Saturday, December 13th, at 5:35 P.M., my
brother, Robert Gates, Jr., and myself arrived at
our house on Maple Drive. After about ten or
fifteen minutes, we ate dinner, having spaghetti,
meatballs, and bread. Jason Gates, Robert Gates,
Jr. and senior, Cheryl Brahm, and myself were
present. Sparse conversation was had, but nothing
of note was said. I informed my father, Robert
Gates, Sr., that I was planning on going to the
movies in either Chatham or Hudson, and that I
had asked Cheryl if I could borrow her car for the
night. She had said that I could before this. Damian
Rossney and myself had planned on going to the
early showing of *Heartbreak Ridge*, starring Clint
Eastwood. After dinner was finished, I got ready
for the movies, called Damian at approximately
6:30 [deleted, initialed, and changed to] 6:25 and
left the house at about 6:30 p.m. After going to
Cheryl's car in the parking lot, I removed a bag of
sweaters from the car at her request, closed my
thumb in the door, and brought the bag into the
house. Cheryl, my father, and my cousin Jason
Gates, were on the lowest level of the house,
apparently watching television. I said that I was
leaving, then went outside. My brother was on the
second story of the garage playing his drum set
with the radio on, and I asked him to take out the
garbage. I then left in Cheryl's car and drove down
Maple Drive onto Goetz Road, and then onto
Frisbee Street. After turning on Frisbee St., I passed
a car going in the opposite direction. However it
was dark and the car's lights prevented me from
clearly seeing it. I believe that it was a mid-size
station wagon. I went via Frisbee St. to East
Chatham where I got on Route 295 towards Canaan. Getting of [sic] on Colane Road, I picked
Damian Rossney up at his aunt and uncle's Stanley
and Sally Joseph's house. I cannot remember at
what time I arrived or left the Josephs' residence,

but after getting a Curad plastic strip for my thumb
and talking to Damian for a couple of minutes, we
both left in Cheryl's car for the Crandell cinema in
Chatham. We reached Chatham without incident,
at approximately 7:15 pm. I had thought that the
movie was scheduled to begin at 7:00, so that we
arrived about fifteen minutes late. We paid admission and watched the movie, which ended late at
about 9:10 pm. We met [deleted, initialed, and
changed to] passed some friends outside the theatre
and then preceeded [sic] to the car. We left the
Mini-Chopper parking lot and travelled along route
295 to Damian's residence without incident, arriving about 9:30. Stan and Sally Joseph were home
then, not being so when I first arrived near seven
o'clock. We went in and played a video game until
most likely 10:15 pm, when I left in Cheryl's car.
I arrived at my house, coming for [deleted, initialed,
and changed to] from Frisbee St. to Maple Drive,
at probably 10:30 pm. I parked opposite from the
garage in the parking area. I noticed that the lights
were on in the second level of the garage. Assuming
that my brother was still playing his drums, as is
not unusual, I walked up the hill and around to
the back entrance of the only entrance to the second
level, situated in the back of the garage. The door
was open and I stepped up onto the floor of the
level, noticing my brother layed on [deleted, initialed, and changed to] lying on his side between
his drum set and the wall behind it. I noticed shell
casings on the floor in front of the doorway, in my
opinion pistol casings. I checked for any signs of
breathing or movement, but found none. I exited
the top level of the garage and went around to the
front of the house. I entered the front door,
noticing that both the storm and main doors were
ajar. I walked to the top of the descending stairwell
between the main entrance and the kitchen. I
looked down the strairs [sic] and saw Cheryl lying

with her feet toward the stairwell, but the rest of
her body was not visible through the side of the
stairwell. I noticed small areas of blood on the stairs
and on the carpeting on the lowest floor. I descended the stairs and saw my father lying in a
corner formed by the wall of the recreation room
and the bar area. I noticed a great deal of blood
on both Cheryl and my father, and I also noticed
that the telephone was on the floor next to him. I
turned around from where I was standing near
the [deleted, initialed, and changed to] inside the
recreation room near the doorway and saw Jason
Gates lying face down about halfway between my
father and the far wall. Cheryl was also face down
toward the floor. I checked for signs of breathing
or other movement, but found none. I went back
up the stairs and exited the building, through the
main door. I believe that I closed the main door,
but left the storm door open. I got into Cheryl's
car and drove to my grandmother's: Vivian Gates'
house. I arrived at her house, parking in front of
her garage. I opened her garage door in order to
see if she was home. Upon my unchaining her dog
she opened the door to the front living room and
greeted me [deleted, initialed, and changed to] said
hello. I went inside and told her in more words
that Cheryl, my father, my brother, and Jason were
all dead (as had appeared to be the case at the
time). After several minutes, she called the operator
and asked for the police.

It took approximately forty-five minutes for Wyley to
complete the writing of this deposition. During that time,
Vivian Gates looked in on them, saw Wyley writing, and
returned to the porch. She sat there for a while, comforting
Deloras Groudas, who wept on Mrs. Gates's shoulder.

Upon the completion of the deposition, at approximately 2:30 A.M., Investigator Shook asked Wyley a number
of questions that he had been formulating as Wyley wrote.

He asked Wyley if he had had a fight with his father that evening and Wyley said he had not. He asked Wyley if he had had a fight with his brother that evening, and again Wyley responded that he hadn't. He asked Wyley if he would be willing to undergo a polygraph examination and to submit his clothing for testing, and Wyley said that he would be. "Did you and your father fight over the car?" Shook asked, and Wyley said they had not. Shook asked Wyley why he had called home from Damian's house, when Damian said he had never done that before, to which Wyley replied that he *had* done that before. "Why did you call Damian at six twenty-five to say you weren't leaving right away?" Shook asked, and Wyley responded that he had called at 6:25 to say he *was* leaving right away. "Where did you get the Band-Aid?" asked Shook, and Wyley said he had gotten it at Damian's. "Did you wash your hands?" Shook asked. Wyley replied that he had washed his hands at Damian's, before putting on the Band-Aid.

As the sequestering of Wyley grew prolonged, Mrs. Gates, still on the sun porch, became increasingly concerned about what was going on in there. "She said, 'Why are they keeping that boy in there so long?'" recalled Dorothy Dooley. "'What's going on?' She was starting to get very concerned. She said, 'He's been through enough without putting him through all of this.'" Mrs. Dooley assured her that the authorities were just trying to gather as much information as they could, but this assurance did little to mitigate Mrs. Gates's agitation. Finally, she got up once again and went into the library. "She didn't come out for a while," Mrs. Dooley recalled, "and I started to feel a little on edge." In the library, Mrs. Gates found Wyley, having completed the deposition and his responses to Shook's questions, now passing the time reading John Bunyan's *Pilgrim's Progress*. She and Cozzolino conversed about the size of the Gates house and the fact that it had two furnaces; about Steven Gates; and about the accident that had claimed the lives of Dane and Georgia. It had been Cozzolino who had gone to the Groudas home to notify Deloras Groudas of the death of her daughter, and it had been Cozzolino who had deterred Mrs. Groudas from seeing her daughter's body. Now Mrs. Gates, with remarkable composure, was showing Cozzolino family photographs displayed on the piano. Two of her sons were gone; a third would never be what he had been; two grandsons had been slaughtered; a daughter-in-law and a woman whom she had regarded as a daughter-in-law had had their lives snuffed out. *So I awoke*, wrote Bunyan, *and behold it was a dream.*

By this time, the log cabin was overrun with officials. Investigator Ralph Gagliardi, of the Identification Section of the New York State Police, had just arrived at the log house and was conferring with Undersheriff Bertram and Investigator William Vick. Vick, who had been with the Columbia County Sheriff's Department for fourteen years, the last eight as an investigator, helped to secure the house, and had already begun the primary canvassing of potential witnesses among the immediate neighbors on the road. It would be Vick's province, according to the delegation of responsibilities set up by the sheriff and undersheriff, to secure the necessary evidence from the crime scene.

Bertram took Investigator Gagliardi on a tour of the log house, and Gagliardi made note that neither money, in plain view, nor such valuables as stereo equipment had been taken, thus indicating that burglary was not a motive. Bertram also pointed out the bullet casings, and Gagliardi and his team took photographs and collected evidence.

By this time too Angelo Nero, the county coroner, had contacted Dr. Baruch J. Davis, who would make the preliminary examinations. Dr. Davis was serving in the capacity of coroner's physician, which meant that his duties were twofold: to make the pronouncement of death and to describe both the physical situation of the victims and the traumas inflicted on their bodies. Dr. Davis, a pathologist since 1954 and a coroner's physician since 1970, first examined Jason Gates, whom he found lying on his chest in the rec room, with the right side of his face in contact with the rug. In his initial examination, Dr. Davis noted several bullet wounds directly visible in the left arm. Getting down on his hands and knees, he turned the body over and found a thin film of blood on the child's face, and superficial lacerations. Among the other observations Dr. Davis made that night were gouges on the pad of Cheryl Brahm's right index finger, parallel lacerations on her left wrist, and bullet-type wounds in the right wrist of Robert Gates, Sr.

Walter Shook returned to the crime scene with the news that Wyley had agreed to take a polygraph examination. Lacking any local facility for such an examination, the sheriff's department asked the state police to set up an examination at Troop K Barracks in Poughkeepsie, some fifty miles south. Shook headed back to Mrs. Gates's house to collect Wyley and bring him down to the Chatham Police Station at the Tracy Memorial Building on Chatham's main street.

But when Investigator Shook told Vivian Gates that they were taking Wyley for a polygraph, she put her arm around her grandson and told them that he had already been through too much. It was three o'clock in the morning, she cried, but they assured her that it would only take an hour and, anyway, Wyley made no protest. In fact, in Shook's opinion, the boy appeared to be getting more and more upset as more relatives showed up, and actually seemed eager to go with them. When Wyley asked to go to the bathroom, however, Shook told Cozzolino to accompany him, wanting to make sure that Wyley didn't wash his hands. It was at that point, when she heard Shook's directive to Cozzolino, that it first occurred to Vivian Gates that her grandson was a suspect in the crime.

For another relative on the scene, Paul Dooley, the awful realization that Wyley was a suspect came in two stages. The first glimmer came when the information emerged that the weapon used was a Walther PPK. Dooley, familiar with the characteristic thumb cut made by improper handling of a Walther, began to put two and two together. And then, when they took Wyley for a polygraph, Dooley fully understood what was going on. "Still, the very idea of it was almost impossible to digest," he said. "You think it's there, but you don't want to believe it. Somebody more macho maybe, somebody with a bad temper. . . ."

Evelyn Prescott, too, remembered her moment of recognition. It came while she was in the kitchen with her sister, after the police had taken away Wyley. "I said, 'Dorothy, do you think that they could be suspecting Wyley?' And she said, 'Oh, be quiet! Don't say such a thing! How can you say such a thing!' " Mrs. Prescott remembered her sister snapping at her. "And I said, 'Well, [Bob and Cheryl] were having some trouble with him.' I knew that he was taking the car and wasn't getting along too well. Still, I didn't have a feeling that it could happen. It was the furthest thing from my mind."

Into the dark and frigid night, investigators Shook and Cozzolino ushered their suspect, dressed in his usual uniform of slacks, neat cotton shirt, and, on the occasion of this night, a white tie. They got into the squad car, Shook in the driver's seat, Wyley in the passenger seat, Cozzolino in the seat behind. Shortly after three o'clock on the morning of December 14, the sheriff's men put on their dome light, read seventeen-year-old Wyley Gates his *Miranda* rights, and pulled away from the big white house to make their way down to the station.

9

For Mame Brahm, Cheryl's sister-in-law, the night had promised to be long, for she was working the eleven-to-seven shift as an aide at Barnwell Nursing Home in Valatie. But what Mame, her husband, Pete, and the rest of the Brahms would soon discover was that this was a night that would have no end to it. "I got a phone call about one o'clock in the morning," recalled Mame. "It was my husband, Pete, and he said that someone murdered Cheryl. He said, 'Cheryl has been murdered.' That's what he said. 'Cheryl has been murdered.' I got hysterical. I couldn't believe it."

Mame left Barnwell immediately and headed for home. "Once the doors parted and I was out in the cold, I was frightened," she remembered. "I felt vulnerable . . . I got outside and I realized how alone I was, how dark and how cold it was."

When Pete called her at Barnwell, he had only told her about Cheryl, but now, arriving home, Mame found out that there were four victims. But the fact that it was Wyley alone who had escaped the massacre did not register with the Brahms at the time. "It didn't enter my mind," said Mame. "I was just concentrating on that one fact: murdered."

Pete and Mame brought their children over to Jim and his wife Gretchen's, and they all sat together, in shock. The theory that kept coming back into their minds during that night was that whoever had burglarized the log house on December 4 had come back to burglarize it again and must have been caught in the act. Jim and Gretchen owned a police scanner, and the family sat there listening to it. With rising concern about where Cheryl's body was and who was identifying it, there was discussion as to whether or not they should go to Vivian Gates's house, but that idea was put aside in favor of ever more pressing problems that were presenting themselves. Chief among these was the question of how to break the news to Cheryl's infirm mother. It was decided that the elder Mrs. Brahm should be allowed to sleep until morning, and that the family should call her doctor to secure tranquilizers for when the time came to tell her the horrible truth.

For the rest of the night, all through those long hours, the Brahms sat stunned, numbed, each of them going over in their minds what had happened. Mame, to whom Cheryl had been as close as to anyone in the family, must have been filled with thoughts of the awful, grim, tragic disappointment that now stood in such stark contrast to Cheryl's ebullience and promise. "She gave her life for Bob," Mame remarked. "I'm telling you honestly and truly, she did . . . she wanted his love so bad."

Among those assembled at Vivian Gates's house, the shock of seeing Wyley spirited away in a police car was now layered on top of the shock created by the murders themselves. "I really can't tell you how I felt at that point," said Dorothy Dooley. "You don't want to believe, when it's your own family, and yet you know if there's a chance, if they're taking him, he had to have said something." Still, denial was natural and very much present. For one thing, the two investigators, Shook and Cozzolino, were described as having been "very mild," "nothing heavy," and "very calm," and, furthermore, they had told the family that Wyley was going with them voluntarily and that the procedure, which would not take long, would "help clear things up." And yet, denial aside, it took someone outside the immediate family to remind Mrs. Gates of the measures that needed to be taken. "I remember Mrs. Groudas saying at the time, 'You better get a lawyer,' when they were going to take him for questioning," recalled Evelyn Prescott. And so, at Mrs. Gates's request, Paul Groudas went to the phone in the hopes of securing representation for Wyley.

Groudas placed a call to Richard Hogle, a young local attorney who had prepared a petition for custody of Jason Gates on behalf of the Gates family. Hogle, who described himself as "about as much of a native as you can be," having lived in the community since the age of four, had received his law degree from Pace University in White Plains, practiced in Westchester County for a time, and then moved back to Columbia County because he "didn't want to be hanging around your violence and criminal elements." He became the partner of an aggressive young attorney named Jay Crimmins—himself brutally murdered the following year, allegedly by the husband of a woman whose divorce he was handling—and then became a solo practitioner with one aspect of his practice revolving around his duties as an assistant county attorney.

Hogle was well acquainted with Bob Gates even before their professional dealings—"Bob was more than an acquaintance and just less than a friend"—and he had been tutoring Cheryl for her real-estate license shortly before her death. He knew Wyley only slightly, having interviewed him in connection with the custody suit and, in fact, ended up deciding not to call on Wyley as a witness, preferring instead to rely on young Bobby Gates for that purpose. Hogle recalled that Wyley had "seemed kind of distant . . . short and guarded" when he had interviewed him some months before the evening of December thirteenth. "I found that strange. I'm used to *lawyers* who are short and guarded and watch their language carefully."

It was at approximately 4:30 in the morning when Groudas awoke Hogle with the news that a "tragedy" claiming the lives of four people had occurred at the Gates residence. Groudas went on to say that the police had taken Wyley for a polygraph test, and that Mrs. Gates wanted someone to look after Wyley's rights. Hogle told Groudas that, since he served as an assistant county attorney, he would be unable to represent anyone in a criminal prose- cution, but that he would call several other attorneys in order to secure counsel for the boy.

Hogle was unable, however, in the middle of the night, to enlist another attorney for Wyley, and called Vivian Gates to tell her so. As a favor, however, he promised to do what he could to ascertain Wyley's whereabouts, and, when he found out where the boy was, he would go down there to be with him and to attempt to protect his rights. He added that he could do that only so long as Wyley was not under arrest.

By this time, Shook and Cozzolino, with Wyley in tow, had arrived at the Chatham Police Station, located in a municipal building on the town's main street. They depos- ited Wyley in the Veterans Affairs Office, across the hall from the police station, and offered him some newspapers as well as a cup of coffee, hot chocolate, and sweet rolls. At that point, a radio transmission informed the officers that an attorney for Wyley Gates had been obtained. Cozzolino immediately called Hogle, who announced that he would be coming there directly.

Upon his arrival, Hogle asked Cozzolino if Wyley Gates was under arrest, and he was told that he was not. Hogle asked if Wyley was in custody; the answer was that they were "in the investigative stage." Hogle's first order of business was to request a copy of Wyley's deposition. He was then taken to see his client, who remained, unhand- cuffed, in the Veterans Affairs Office, the door to which had been kept ajar. As he entered, Hogle closed the door behind him, and he and Wyley conferred for approximately an hour, during which time Cozzolino provided them with refreshments. As to Wyley's demeanor during this interview,

Hogle recalled, "He didn't seem a whole lot different to me than when I had interviewed him [regarding the custody of Jason]."

The police wanted Wyley to take a polygraph examination, to turn his clothing over for analysis, and to submit to palm scrapings. But when Hogle emerged from their conference, he told the authorities that they would agree only to the polygraph examination. At this, Cozzolino is alleged to have said to Hogle, "I hope you don't intend to hold his hand during the polygraph." Hogle replied, "I'd at least want to watch through the glass," to which Cozzolino responded, "What glass?" (In a later interview, Hogle told me that he had known Cozzolino from high school football days and had always enjoyed a cordial relationship with him; but he would ultimately testify that he did not regard Cozzolino's remarks as a "joke.") And so, as night moved toward dawn, Shook, Hogle, and Wyley set off for Troop K Barracks in Poughkeepsie. Before long, the fatigue of the evening caught up with Wyley. The seventeen-year-old boy, who had been up for nearly twenty-four hours, was soon catnapping in the front seat beside Shook, as Hogle sat behind him in the backseat, on the long drive down the Taconic Parkway.

At 4:45 A.M., Thomas Francis Salmon, of the New York State Police, was awakened at his home in Rhinebeck with the news that there had been a quadruple murder in Canaan, and that a suspect was being brought in by the Columbia County Sheriff's Department for a polygraph examination. Salmon, a thin, narrow-faced, intense man in his forties, late of Manhattan, who had been a sergeant with the Bureau of Criminal Investigation of the New York State Police for more than twenty years, got dressed and made his way over to headquarters.

By the time Salmon arrived at Troop K Barracks, Wyley, Hogle, and Shook were already seated in the waiting room. Its floor covered with green tweed industrial carpeting and its long conference table surrounded by chrome-and-orange-vinyl chairs, the waiting room is pleasant but completely anonymous, comparable to a conference room at any modern industrial plant or a lounge in any student center at any university across the country. The only idiosyncratic elements in the room—the only things that detract from the absolute anonymity—are two large blown-up period photographs showing state troopers on mountain duty, dressed in fur hats and accompanied by husky dogs, an elegiac nod to an heroic history. As they sat there waiting, under the gaze of these heroic figures from long ago, Hogle and Shook made conversation that touched desultorily on deer hunting and real estate. Wyley, for his part, maintained his calm demeanor; according to Hogle, the youth's behavior was "no different."

Officer Salmon arrived at the barracks at approximately 6:30 A.M. and went directly to the polygraph room, to prepare it for the examination. From there he went to the waiting room and introduced himself to Shook, Hogle, and Wyley as the "polygraph operator." Shook and Salmon went into the back room to discuss the facts of the case, and Shook showed Salmon Wyley's five-page deposition. Shook also pointed out to Salmon the discrepancies between Wyley's and Damian Rossney's stories concerning the Band-Aid and the phone call home from the Joseph residence. Salmon then directed Shook to a small room behind the polygraph examination room, where, through a one-way mirror, Shook could observe the procedure.

Salmon then returned to the waiting room and presented Hogle and Wyley with several documents. The first of these was the Polygraph Examination Agreement and Release Form (BCI-II), which is required to be executed before a polygraph test. A signature at the bottom of the form verifies that the subject has agreed to take a polygraph test without threats, duress, coercion, force, promises of immunity or reward; that anything he may say can be used against him in any court of law; that the subject may first consult with an attorney or anyone he wishes to before either signing this form or taking the examination; that he may have an attorney present and, if he cannot afford an attorney and desires one, an attorney will be appointed for him prior to any questioning; that the subject is in good mental and physical condition and knows of no mental or physical ailment that might be impaired by the examination; and that the subject has been well treated and has submitted himself freely to the examination knowing that he can stop at any time if he so desires by merely saying that he wishes to stop or that he wishes to consult an attorney or any other person.

Salmon also left for Wyley and Hogle a blue plastic folder containing an article from *The Journal of Polygraph Studies*. Among the points the article makes is that the polygraph machine should not be called a "lie detector" but, rather, a "truth verifier," since statistics show that in the vast majority of instances, the instrument verifies an innocent person's truthfulness. The article goes on to quell some natural anxieties related to the taking of the examination— no, it does not hurt; yes, the operator will be able to distinguish between nervousness and lying; no, you cannot be forced to take a polygraph examination—and it also states, reassuringly, that the subject will know beforehand the content of the test questions and that there will be no "trick questions."

Most people who come for a polygraph examination, according to Salmon, do so unaccompanied by an attorney and sign the permission form in the polygraph room. Of the approximately five hundred polygraph examinations Salmon has administered since he began doing this work in 1981, approximately forty of these have been subjects who were accompanied by attorneys. Salmon has gone on record as saying that out of all of the polygraph examinations he has given, no attorney has ever actually witnessed the polygraph procedure, nor has he ever videotaped, tape-recorded, or had a stenographer present for a polygraph examination. When attorneys are present, a slightly different procedure is followed, with the attorney and client being led to the waiting room and given time to confer over the form and the information that Salmon provides. When the subject has signed the form, Salmon usually asks the attorney to sign as a witness; the attorney will sometimes ask Salmon

to sign as the witness instead. Once the form has been
signed, Salmon asks the subject to tell him, in the presence
of the attorney, that he or she is willing to take the test.
Salmon always offers a glass of water or a cup of coffee; if
the subjects are intoxicated or otherwise evidence impairment of their faculties, he will not proceed with the examination.

At this point in the early morning of December fourteenth, Wyley Gates reiterated to Investigator Salmon, in
the presence of attorney Hogle, that he had no problem
with taking the examination and that he had nothing to do
with the four murders. Salmon told him how the polygraph
examination would be administered, and assured him that
he would give him all of the questions in their entirety
before asking them on the polygraph. He then left the
waiting room.

Trooper Bernard Keller, a young state trooper with five
years of experience, was off-duty when he was approached
by Investigator Salmon, who suggested that, given the fact
that they were dealing with a quadruple murder, Keller
should join Shook as a backup witness. Keller agreed and
went to the observation room.

Around 7:30 A.M., Salmon returned to the waiting room
to see if Wyley and Hogle had read the contents of the two
documents he had left with them. They told him they had.
Salmon asked Wyley to sign the permission form, which he
did, and then Salmon asked Hogle to witness it. Hogle told
Salmon he would prefer that Salmon witness it, which he
did. Salmon then offered coffee, which Hogle accepted and
Wyley declined. At this point, Salmon told Hogle that he
was going to take Wyley down the hall to administer the
test. Hogle asked how long it would take, and Salmon said
he didn't know. In his experience, he said, you can never
tell; sometimes the tests take ninety minutes, sometimes
four hours.

Salmon later maintained that he asked Wyley to leave
his jacket in the waiting room, as it would be impossible to
administer the test to someone wearing a jacket. Whether

Wyley actually did leave the jacket in the waiting room, or whether it was taken to the examination room, was a question that would be of much interest to Wyley's defense attorney. The other question that arose around this specific bridge of time concerned the interaction that next occurred between Investigator Salmon and Richard Hogle, for it was this interaction that was to prove a pivotal point in the subsequent defense of Wyley Gates. According to Hogle's account, he rose in the expectation of accompanying his client back to the polygraph examination room, and it was at this point that Investigator Salmon raised his hand—fingers splayed with a staying gesture—in his direction. Hogle sat back down and watched his client, Wyley Gates, pass through the door and into the back recesses of Troop K Barracks. It would be quite some time before Hogle would see the strange and distant young man again.

The polygraph examination room is approximately eight feet by eight feet in dimension, its floor covered in the same green industrial carpeting found in the waiting room, and is furnished only with a table on which sits the polygraph machine, an ordinary chair, and, for the subject, what looks like a school chair with outsized arms. On one wall, paneled with Masonite board, a four-foot-by-three-foot mirror has been sunk, subdivided by shelves that hold bric-a-brac: a sort of imitation Staffordshire thatched cottage; a pottery sombrero; an old bottle or two. This bric-a-brac, one supposes, is meant to distract from what is obviously a mirror set there for observation purposes.

Salmon ushered Wyley into the room and showed him where to sit. He then sat down across the table from Wyley and they began to talk. The standard procedure that Investigator Salmon observes with his prospective polygraph subjects is, first of all, to tell his subjects that they are free to use the telephone at any time. During this part of the examination, which is referred to as the "pretest," the subject is advised of his rights and is assured that the door is not locked and that he or she is free to go. Specifically now, to Wyley, Salmon emphasized that he was free to leave, that the door was closed but was not locked, and that his attorney was in the building. According to Investigator Salmon's subsequent testimony, Wyley said he understood. Salmon told Wyley that he never tested people against their will and asked Wyley if anyone was forcing him to take the test, whether it was the police or his attorney. According to Salmon, Wyley assured him that no one was. Salmon then informed Wyley that he had had two discussions with the police regarding last night's events and asked Wyley if he had anything he wanted to tell him.

Wyley essentially recapitulated the chronology of events as he had given them to Shook, at which point Salmon gave him the *Miranda* rights sheet. On this sheet a number of questions were posed. Can you have an attorney anytime you want to? What will happen if you cannot afford an attorney? Can you use the telephone to call an attorney anytime you want to? Certification of the examinee was requested to indicate that the examinee understood the questions, wished to continue without an attorney present, was here of his own free will, and understood that he could leave the room by merely telling the investigator that he wished to leave. Investigator Salmon then told Wyley that for him to do well in here today, he needed Wyley's cooperation. According to Salmon, Wyley assured him that that cooperation would be forthcoming.

Salmon next asked Wyley a series of short questions. What was his favorite hobby? Wyley replied, "Computers." What was the best thing in his life? Wyley didn't know. What was the worst thing in his life? Wyley didn't know. What was his ambition? To go to college. Had he ever been falsely accused of anything in his life? He had not. Why was he taking this polygraph examination? To find out the truth.

Salmon excused himself for a moment, and went briefly to the observation room to confer with Shook and Keller. When he returned, he continued with the "pretest." He explained the basic science of the examination, and showed Wyley the different parts of the machine. There was the galvanic skin response attachment, which is attached to any two fingers on the same hand; there were the pneumograph tubes, two of them, one placed above and one placed below the heart; and the cardiocuff, which is placed around the arm and gauges blood pressure. All of these are easily attached with Velcro tabs.

He told Wyley he was going to calibrate the machine, and he put the attachments on Wyley's arm, chest, and fingers. Salmon then constructed three semicircles out of looseleaf paper for use in a trial-run questioning, and he then questioned Wyley, asking him to use the semicircles to indicate the answers. After that, he unhooked all the attachments from Wyley except for the cardiocuff on his arm. He then brought his chair around to face Wyley; he said that when he asked questions of any significance, he would be able to determine, through the machine, if Wyley was telling the truth. He told Wyley that as we get older, we become more sophisticated and we can lie to people. But we can't lie to ourselves and our involuntary systems. The only way to beat the test is to not take the test. He said the function of a polygraph examination depends on the person taking the test. If that person is telling the truth, it will be a truth verifier. If untruths are being told, the machine will function as a lie detector.

At this point, according to the later testimony of Walter Shook, Wyley said, "I can't figure out how it would be to my advantage to tell the truth." Wyley then admitted that he believed he was partially schizophrenic and that 95 percent of his stress was caused by three people—Bob, Bobby, and Cheryl. He added that he had three personalities and could program himself like a computer and had no emotions. He allegedly said at this point that the only thing he was sorry about was that this was going to hurt his grandmother's feelings.

"Nobody can do anything about that unless they know what the truth is," Salmon is said to have replied, and he went on to suggest that people make mistakes.

"I didn't make a mistake," Wyley is alleged to have replied. "I planned it and I killed them."

According to Walter Shook's later testimony, Wyley

then made a series of fragmented admissions. He said that the previous weekend he had fired the gun three or four times for practice; that he had made only one mistake in that he should have changed his pants; and that he had originally planned to just kill his father and brother and that his brother was "worthless."

He is then said to have related the following events of the evening in a chronological order. At 6:30 P.M., he left the log cabin. As he left, his brother was in the room over the garage playing the drums. He left in Cheryl's car, which he had taken with her permission, and with him he had a .380 semi-automatic pistol, which was one of the weapons that he and two of his friends had stolen from his father. One of the friends, he is alleged to have said, was Damian Rossney. Salmon asked him the identity of the third person, but Wyley said that he didn't want to say who it was. Continuing the recitation of events, Wyley said he drove a short distance, parked the car, and walked through a field with the specific intention of shooting and killing his father, Cheryl, and his brother. Did he intend to kill Jason? he was asked. He wasn't sure at that time, but Wyley is alleged to have explained that Jason was about to be adopted by the family and would thus share in the inheritance. Before December thirteenth, Wyley is said to have admitted, he had twice gone down to the garage on Route 295, alone, with the gun, to kill his father and his brother, but "that did not work out."

He went back to the house, to the vicinity of the stairs that led down to the rec room. As he entered the house, he thought he heard his father on the phone but wasn't sure. Then he confirmed that his father was, in fact, in the middle of a phone conversation and he waited until his father got off, not wanting anyone on the outside to hear the shots. He entered the rec room; present were his father, Cheryl, and Jason. He shot his father approximately three times. While he was shooting at his father, he observed him trying to reach for the telephone. He then turned and shot Cheryl three times. At this point in the reconstruction, Wyley allegedly told Salmon that he was "not sure if he shot Jason then or not." He went into the kitchen, thinking that his brother would have heard the gunshots and would be on his way to investigate, but he was surprised to hear that the drums were still being played. He then saw Cheryl making her way up the stairs, and he shot her another time. Once again he went back downstairs, but again he was not sure if he shot Jason at that time. And still, throughout all of this, his brother was playing the drums, and so he headed for the weight room. Opening the door, Wyley, armed, stood before his brother, separated by perhaps six feet. Just before or just after Wyley fired—again, he was not sure—his brother cried, "You stupid fool." Wyley added, according to Salmon, that Robert used to say that to him all the time and it always made him mad. After shooting Robert once or twice, the gun jammed. He cleared it, and fired once or twice more.

"What does it mean 'to clear the gun'?" Salmon said he asked Wyley at that point.

Wyley explained that when two bullets attempt to enter the chamber at the same time, the gun jams, so he removed one of the bullets with his finger. While clearing the gun, he allegedly told Salmon, he dropped one or two live rounds, which he believed would still be where he had left them.

According to Salmon's account, Wyley then said he went back into the house and downstairs and found Jason framed against the flickering light of the television screen. "Jason was crying," Wyley is said to have reported. "No," he corrected himself, "he was screaming." He said he shot Jason at least once, and he believed he shot his father and Cheryl one more time each. Salmon then asked him where he shot Jason and Wyley allegedly replied that he shot him in the torso—"he was a small target," Wyley reportedly volunteered, gesturing to show his cousin's diminutive size. Salmon asked why he had shot Jason, and Wyley allegedly explained that the little boy was a witness and would have been able to tell everybody just who had shot Bob and Cheryl.

Wyley is then alleged to have said he left the residence and drove to Damian's house. He told his friend that he had murdered four people. Salmon asked whether Damian had been shocked or surprised and Wyley said he had not been.

He deposited the gun with Damian, trusting him with it because Damian was "safe." He treated the wound that he had earlier said he had gotten by slamming his hand in the car door but that, in fact, he had gotten from the slide action of the pistol when he had incorrectly held the Walther in the two-fisted grip. He added that he had been wearing rubber gloves at the time of the shooting.

Salmon asked about three cuts on Wyley's hand. One prominent one in the center had been sustained in last night's shooting; another cut, toward the index finger, came from a source that Wyley reputedly could not recall; and a third cut on the opposite side resulted from the same mishandling of the gun a week earlier during target practice at John Bailey's grandfather's farm. Continuing with his story, Wyley allegedly said that Damian left the gun at the Joseph house and they went to the movie. Leaving the theater after the movie, Damian chatted with a mutual friend whom Wyley would not identify. When Wyley asked Damian what the conversation had been about, Damian replied, "I just told that fellow you murdered four people."

"Did that make you mad?" asked Salmon.

No, Wyley allegedly replied, explaining that the "fellow" to whom Damian had spoken was a very good friend of theirs.

Wyley and Damian then returned to the Joseph residence, where Wyley made a phone call home, with the intention of seeing whether the police had been to the house yet. When he got a busy signal, he deduced that the phone was as he had left it—lying just out of reach of his father's hand—and that the police had not been there. That disappointed him, for it meant he would have to go back to the log house and pretend to "discover" the bodies.

And so he left the Joseph home and drove back to the log cabin. Salmon asked him what he would have done had he found one or more of the victims alive, and Wyley replied that he didn't know. In any event, it was not a contingency about which he had to be worried, as he found them all dead, in the same positions in which he had left them. Putting his fingerprints on the door to show the Bureau of Criminal Investigation that he had been there and found the bodies, he went to his grandmother's to tell her what he had found.

Salmon then drew up a list of questions on two separate pieces of paper. The questions were:

Did you intentionally kill your father?
Did you intentionally kill Robert Gates, Jr.?
Did you intentionally kill Cheryl Brahm?
Did you intentionally kill Jason Gates?
Did you plan to kill these people?
While you were shooting your brother, did your
    gun jam?
Did you tell Damian Rossney that you killed these
    people?
After you cleared your gun, did you shoot your
    brother at least one more time?

According to Salmon's account, after constructing these questions, he then proposed reading them to Wyley to see if it would be all right to use them on the polygraph examination. Wyley agreed and so Salmon read him the questions. To the question "Did you intentionally kill your father?" Wyley replied affirmatively, but, as this was still not the official test, Salmon did not record this. The same affirmative answer was given to every other question, except for the question of whether he told Damian Rossney that he killed these people. Wyley said that he did not want to answer that question. Salmon then asked Wyley to put his initials next to that question, and Wyley did so.

Salmon asked Wyley if he was telling the truth. Wyley allegedly replied that he was, that he hated these people, and that he had made only one mistake in that he had not changed his clothes. Salmon allegedly pointed in the direction of the waiting room and asked him if that was the jacket he had worn last night. Wyley is said to have replied that it was and that he was concerned that there might be powder burns on the jacket.

Salmon then asked if Wyley agreed to answer the prescribed questions on the actual polygraph examination itself. Wyley is reported to have said, "If I do, it would be bad. If I don't, I might have a chance." According to Walter Shook's later testimony, when Salmon asked if he could begin the test, Wyley said, "What do you think my attorney would say?" According to Salmon, Wyley then said that he would like Salmon to tell his attorney that he had confessed to the four murders. He was becoming increasingly concerned that there were powder burns on the jacket and said he wanted his attorney to tell him if he should continue. At that, Salmon left the room, went over to Shook, and said, "Well, that's it."

When Dick Hogle finally agreed to speak with me, we had already had a nodding acquaintance. We had met at the trial and I, like many others, had repeatedly asked to interview him about his role in this event. But Hogle had not wanted to talk to anyone. Not only had he been personally wounded by all the publicity, but he resented the idea of further negative publicity being trained on the town. And yet, as anyone who has ever lived in a small town knows, and as I was beginning to learn, there is no escaping one's neighbors, and so I would run into Hogle regularly, at the general store in East Chatham, at the solid-waste station, and at the home of the baby-sitter who took care of my son and his daughter. Some measure of familiarity was thus engendered, and so, one night we spoke, at last, in his one-man office in a "downtown" Chatham building.

What had brought Hogle so much unwanted attention, and what would in time become the crux of the issue regarding the protection of Wyley Gates's constitutional rights, was the fact that Hogle claimed to have risen to accompany his client but, on the weight of Salmon's hand gesture, which he interpreted as a barring gesture, he sat back down and remained seated for over two hours.

"I didn't like going down for the polygraph at all," he

told me, adding that "any attorney, even a green one, would say, 'Don't do this.' " With little criminal-law background—he referred to himself in this regard as "green, green, green"—he found himself in an extreme situation and was led to his decision—in his account, a thought-out decision—to sit there for the entire time Wyley was in the back room, by his conviction that this would be the best course of action for his client. "Once Mr. Salmon barred me from the room," he said, "I knew what the New York law was—anybody out of law school had better—and I sat and thought it through and the best thing for me to do for my client at the time, as an attorney, was to sit there." Part of his decision had to do with the nature of Wyley's personality. "I . . . figured that I could probably stop it," he said of the polygraph, "but Wyley didn't want me to stop it. That was my impression." Wyley only knew Hogle as his father's attorney and didn't have any reason to trust him. "People can fire their attorneys," said Hogle, who, in his dealings with the strange young man that night, was convinced that this might have been an eventuality. In any event, it was a "strange, strange position" in which Hogle found himself. "I thought long and hard about screaming and yelling and going back there," he said, "and then I went through an analysis and said, 'If I'm right—and I hope I am; I'm green as hell and I haven't been doing criminal law; I've been doing real-estate closings—if I'm right they can't use anything and the best possible approach, as hard as it is, is to sit here.' " Furthermore, in Hogle's mind, Salmon's hand gesture was not a benign, harmless one. "I was scared as hell, frankly," Hogle confessed.

And so he remained where he was, and there he was sitting when Investigator Salmon emerged. Salmon informed Hogle of the situation, and told him that his client was concerned regarding the powder burns on his jacket. "I'm sure you don't want me to continue with the polygraph," Hogle remembered Salmon saying, to which Hogle replied, "By all means not."

At exactly 10:33 A.M. on December 14, Walter Shook placed Wyley Gates under arrest for homicide and took him

into another room where he was read his rights again. At
that point, Shook called in the arrest to the D.A.'s office,
then frisked Wyley, found a pair of rubber gloves in his
pocket, and put them in a plastic bag. At approximately
10:45 A.M., Hogle and Wyley parted ways, and Shook took
the now handcuffed youth for photographing, with particular attention to be paid to his cut thumb, and from there
to his arraignment in Greenport. It had been a long night,
but, in the end, not a fruitless one for the law-enforcement
agencies of Columbia County.

10

Back at Vivian Gates's house, there had been no word of Wyley through the night, but, according to Evelyn Prescott, there were no special efforts to track his whereabouts. "I think we all walked around like zombies, to tell you the truth," said Mrs. Prescott. "Drank coffee and walked around." Around five o'clock in the morning, the police seized Cheryl's car and, at that point, Viki Hatch recalled, "I kind of surmised that they really suspected Wyley." Shortly after that, around daybreak, Howard Hatch answered a knock at the front door and found a reporter who asked him what the family thought of Wyley's having been arrested. It was the first he, or anyone in the family, had heard of it.

"Howard said, 'I have something to tell you, so come on, everybody, into the living room,'" Mrs. Prescott remembered. "So we all went into the living room, where Viv was by herself, and he told us that Wyley had confessed." The news was received by Mrs. Gates at the same time everyone else was hearing it, and Mrs. Prescott recalled her sister-in-law's reaction. "She never blinked an eye," said Mrs. Prescott.

"It was like somebody had hit her across the face." But there were no emotional outbursts that Mrs. Prescott could remember. "Just shock all the way through," she said. Mrs. Gates went upstairs to try to get some sleep, but for Viki Hatch, exhausted by the middle-of-the-night ride from Canajoharie as well as from the inordinate emotional strain, a restorative sleep was out of reach. "I had a dream," she recalled. "I guess I screamed or something. And Howard said, 'What is it?' and I said, 'I'm scared.' "

In a small town like Chatham, it doesn't take long for word to spread. The chief clearinghouse for information is The Bakery, a venerable institution in the heart of town whose great seasonal specialty is a pumpkin doughnut of such melting moistness that mention of it has been made in *The New York Times*. On the morning of December 14, however, no one at The Bakery was talking about the meltingly moist pumpkin doughnuts.

"I went down for coffee," recalled Dick Klingler, "and they said, 'Did you hear about the tragedy?' I said, 'What tragedy?' Well, they said the Gates had all been murdered." Klingler returned home immediately, and found his yard filled with Bob's friends. "We discussed it for a while," said Klingler. "At first I thought it was a hit job. Bob did salt piles in some of the worst sections of Brooklyn and Baltimore, down on the docks, which are notoriously crime-ridden, and I thought maybe he'd been in some kind of disagreement down there and somebody had knocked him off." On second thought, Klingler decided that professional killers wouldn't have killed the whole family. On third thought, he reminded himself of the conversation he had had with Bob the previous evening and he decided that he had better call the sheriff. "By this time Wyley was starting to come up in the back of my mind," he said, not knowing if Wyley had been one of the victims. "I called the sheriff's department and I told them about the conversation and I asked him who was killed." When he learned, in fact, that Wyley was a survivor, everything just clicked in his mind. "I said, 'Oh boy,' " he remembered. "I knew right then what had happened. No qualms in my mind about who done it."

Around that time too, the Brahms were being notified of Wyley's arrest. Their initial reaction to the news was that it was, in the words of Mame Brahm, "believable."

For Dennis Gawron, who, at the time of the murders, was working five days a week with Paul Groudas as a carpenter's apprentice and on Saturdays down at the Gates garage, Sunday was his one day of the week to sleep late. But not this Sunday. This Sunday there was an early morning phone call from Deloras Groudas. "My mother answered the phone," he recalled. "I woke up 'cause I heard the phone ring but I didn't think it was any real big deal, but then I heard my mother start to cry. I picked up the phone and she told me about it. And at that time I thought it was just Bob, Cheryl, and Jason. I thought maybe Bobby and Wyley were out. And then I heard it was Bobby too and then my first instinct was, Oh, poor Wyley."

For Skip Huvar and Dorothy Donnelley, the news came in a succession of strange, eerie twists and turns. They had been to a Christmas party and hadn't gotten home until two in the morning. Shortly thereafter, the phone rang and, as Dorothy heard Skip talking, she could only make out, from his end, some strange-sounding story about a mutual friend of Bob and Skip's being arrested for breaking into Bob's house. "I said, 'That's bizarre,' " she remembered. "I said, 'I don't believe that' . . . and I went back to bed."

The information Huvar had been given turned out to be entirely mistaken, but still Dorothy couldn't sleep. "I just felt that there was something wrong for our phone to ring and somebody was trying to tell us something," she said. The next day, still feeling uneasy, she got up by 6:30 or 7:00 A.M. to call Cheryl. "And this man answered and he said, 'What do you want?' " she recalled. "And I said, 'I'm calling Robert and Cheryl.' He said, 'Well, who are you?' And I told him. And he said, 'Well, what do you have to do with them?' And I said, 'Is there a problem? Who might this be?' And he said, 'This is Sheriff Proper.' And I said, 'Oh dear, I guess I rang the wrong number.' So he said, 'No, you didn't.' And I said, 'Well, could I please speak to

Cheryl?' He wanted to know what it was about. And I said,
'We're friends and we got a phone call in the night and I
think something is wrong.' And he said, 'Yes, something is
wrong.' He said, 'Something is very wrong.' "

That morning, the sense that something was wrong was
already being deeply felt at the residence of Stanley and
Sally Joseph. At approximately 9:00 A.M., Stan Joseph found
state police investigators Richard Nesbit and John Holt at
his door. They asked him to awaken Damian, and, after a
hasty breakfast, Damian left with the investigators for questioning over at the State Police Barracks in nearby New
Lebanon. As soon as they left, Joseph, who had stayed
behind to feed his dogs, began to think that perhaps he
should have accompanied his nephew.

    "I thought to myself, Maybe I'm really putting Damian
in a somewhat precarious position there, with the cops alone
in that vehicle, and I thought perhaps I really should have
been there with him," said Joseph, who had viewed the
investigators' deportment as "low-keyed," although he added
that he saw their low-keyed way as being as much a ploy as
anything. And so, within ten minutes of Damian's departure,
he got into his car and headed for the barracks to be with
him. When he arrived, he was in for a shock. "Investigator
Nesbit called us in and told us that Wyley had confessed,"
recalled Joseph, "and had implicated Miles and Damian in
the burglary." Nesbit suggested that perhaps Joseph and
Damian would like to talk about it; Joseph replied that
indeed he would.

    Meanwhile, Sally Joseph was throwing together some
'unch to take down to Stan and Damian when she received
. call. It was Miles McDonald calling from his grandmother's
house, where he had gone that morning after church. He
told her that he had heard Wyley's family had been killed,
and Mrs. Joseph confirmed this for him and told him, as
well, that Damian had just gone over to the police barracks
to talk about it because he had been to the movies with
Wyley. "Miles was saying, 'Oh, that's really terrible, that's

awful, I better go home,' " recalled Mrs. Joseph, "and I said, 'Well, you *better* go home cause they might want to talk to you too, Miles.' "

At the barracks, Damian began to tell his uncle the whole story. "And I probably said, 'Oh God, how'd you get yourself involved in that?' " Joseph recalled. Although Damian seemed quite eager to talk, Joseph discouraged him from doing so. "I said, 'Whoa, hold on, this is really quite serious and I don't feel competent to represent you,' " he remembered. " 'Let's see what we can do about getting a lawyer.' "

This, however, was easier said than done. On a Sunday just eleven shopping days away from Christmas, it promised to be a long afternoon as Stan Joseph set about making calls, looking for an attorney to protect the rights of this nephew who had always seemed so capable of taking care of himself.

With regard to Miles McDonald, Mrs. Joseph had been right. That Sunday, Officer Butch Harrison, a friend of the McDonald family, was dispatched to the McDonald home to interview Miles.

Although Wyley's defense attorney would later cast in a negative light the decision to send a family friend to interview a suspect, this decision, in the opinion of Gene Keeler, the district attorney, represented good practice. "Butch Harrison knows everybody," Keeler explained. "When you sit around and you try to interview people, the name of the game is to get whatever the truth is from the individual . . . if the cops are sitting around, each one has the responsibility if somebody knows somebody and is a friend and you can get the truth from them, then, you know, it makes sense to assign somebody to go and check them out. . . . That's only reasonable."

Harrison brought McDonald to see Keeler sometime between six and eight o'clock on the morning of the fourteenth. "He told us that morning about the burglary and Damian Rossney," said Keeler. McDonald would, on the

occasion of testifying before the grand jury, be granted total
immunity in the case in exchange for his cooperation with
the prosecutors.

Also on Sunday, the bodies of the four victims were
transferred to the Bender Hygienic Laboratory in Albany,
where autopsies were performed on them by Dr. Roberto
Benitez. Dr. Benitez, who had been in practice for over
forty years and had performed thousands of autopsies,
began the procedures at noon on Sunday in the presence
of Coroner Angelo Nero and various representatives of the
sheriff's department and the police of Columbia County. It
took six hours to complete the procedure.

Dr. Benitez began with the body of Robert Gates, fully
clothed in Levi's, white socks, checkered shirt, and blue
undershirt. After the clothing was removed, evidence of
four distinct gunshot wounds was visible. The first wound
had lacerated the diaphragm and traveled down toward the
liver. The second wound entered the right arm, exited above
the elbow, continued into the chest, perforated the lung,
and lacerated the left ventricle of the heart. A third wound
entered through the right wrist and exited above the wrist,
producing a large wound that caused tissue to protrude. A
fourth wound was to the chest, entering through the fourth
rib and perforating the right lung. An examination of the
contents of the stomach indicated the ingestion of a spaghetti
dinner that showed only the beginnings of having been
digested. The state of digestion suggested that death had
occurred very soon after the meal, roughly within an hour.

The examination of the body of Robert Gates, Jr.,
similarly clothed, in Levi's, a blue shirt, white socks, and tan
boots, also disclosed four distinct gunshot wounds. One was
to the right shoulder, causing numerous splinters and soft-
tissue injury and the fracture of the clavicle. A second
gunshot entered the right chest, near the right nipple,
fracturing the fourth rib and perforating the heart. The
third entered the left upper arm, passed into the chest, split
the third rib, and ended in the lung. The fourth entered
the left arm, fractured the humerus, exited the arm, entered the chest, perforated the heart, and ended in the right

thorax. An examination of the stomach contents of Robert Gates, Jr., paralleled exactly the findings of the stomach contents of his father. The cause of death, as in the case of his father, was hemorrhage and shock.

Turning to Cheryl Brahm, Dr. Benitez found rips and bloodstains on her clothing. Some of the tears were consistent with the gunshot wounds, others were not, particularly a tear to her shirt collar. Again, there were four gunshot wounds. The first showed entry into the back, below the right scapula, or shoulder blade, fracturing the seventh rib, perforating the right lung, and exiting the body. The second also entered the back, fracturing the tenth vertebra, and hitting the pericardium. The third wound was a perforation of the left breast, with complete entry and exit thereof. The fourth was a complex wound, really a cluster of four wounds in a group together, located on the left thigh. It was difficult to determine the entry and exit pattern, but the entry appeared to be at midthigh, where it completely shattered the femur. Many fragments at high speed created other wounds. An examination of stomach contents agreed with the findings of the other two victims, and the cause of death, again, was hemorrhagic shock.

An examination of three-year-old Jason Gates disclosed two wounds. One was close to the left armpit, grazing the chest wall, entering and exiting at the left arm. The second was a close-range shot, so indicated by a brownish discoloration of the skin, that entered the left chest above the nipple, fracturing the third rib, missing the left lung, entering the heart, lacerating the right lung and liver, and fracturing a rib as it exited. There were some superficial bruises, as well, at the tip of the nose and on the cheeks. Stomach contents and cause of death were identical to those of the other three victims.

After the booking of Wyley Gates, Investigator Walter Shook went to the district attorney's office and assisted in filling out several warrants for items he hoped to retrieve at the residence of Damian Rossney. Damian, meanwhile, had acquired counsel. After making a series of calls, Stan Joseph had narrowed the field of criminal lawyers down to two names: Charles Wilcox, who would later represent Wyley Gates; and Robert Adams, who, before establishing his own practice, had served as assistant D.A. under Wilcox during Wilcox's term as Rensselaer County district attorney. Joseph opted for Adams, and so, arriving as soon as he could in New Lebanon, Adams sat down with Damian and the Josephs. After a while, Adams asked Damian if there was anything he would like to talk to him about alone. "Damian said, 'No, my aunt and uncle know everything,' " recalled Mrs. Joseph. "Rob said, 'Well, why don't we just talk alone anyway?' And apparently at that time Damian told him about the stolen computers. And Rob went in and talked to the police and they were on the phone with the D.A. for quite some time."

The Josephs and Damian returned to Colane Road that afternoon, to be present at a controlled search that had been arranged by Adams. At 4:00 P.M., investigators Shook and Cozzolino, in the company of other law-enforcement officials, arrived at the Joseph residence, armed with a search warrant, which they did not need to have executed. A consent to search had been granted, signed by the Josephs, in exchange for the district attorney's granting Damian Rossney total immunity from prosecution relative to any charges involving burglary at the Gates residence. With the immunity guarantee in hand, attorney Adams and Sally and Stanley Joseph led investigators Shook and Cozzolino down the hallway on the first floor of the two-story structure to a bedroom located across the hall from Damian's room and used mostly for storage, ironing, and sewing. Adams pointed to a quilt on the bed in this room, and said, "I think what you're looking for is under there." While another police officer photographed him, Shook lifted the quilt and uncovered the Walther pistol, which he then picked up with a Baggie, placing it in an evidence bag held by Investigator Cozzolino. Adams then took the investigators on a tour of the house, pointing out items that he felt might be of significance to them, ranging from books stolen from Chatham High School to a twelve-gauge shotgun, a seven-millimeter Remington rifle, handguns and shoulder holster, and a box of .380-caliber ammunition.

Much later, the Josephs would recall the search as an unreal experience. While the authorities were pleasant and eminently human—Sheriff Proper talked to them about how affected he had been by the murder scene as Investigator Nesbitt had an allergic attack triggered by the household cat—the Josephs could not help but feel invaded. And then, in the quickly fading light, they began to see the stolen objects parade past them. "We didn't know about the computers till we saw them going past us, and I saw on the back of it, 'Chatham High School,' " said Mrs. Joseph. "It was flabbergasting," added her husband.

The search had taken about an hour. Rob Adams stayed a few moments after the police departed, and then, for the first time since early morning, the Josephs were alone with their nephew. "Damian went into his room and he was crying—it was the first; we hadn't seen him cry or anything before," recalled Sally Joseph—"And I said, 'Do you want to call your parents or do you want me to?' And he said, 'You.' And so I called and . . . and my brother just couldn't believe what I was saying."

The Gates family, too, found themselves suspended in an attitude of disbelief. The mechanics of the justice system having been swiftly set into motion, Wyley was arraigned and charged with four counts of second-degree murder. He entered a plea of not guilty and was ordered held in the county jail without bail to await a preliminary hearing scheduled for December 18 at the town court in Canaan. But for the family a dreamlike state—or, rather, a nightmarelike state—prevailed in which they pondered the imponderable.

"First of all, one of our own could not do something like that," Viki Hatch said, recalling her feelings at the time. "We were brought up to help each other, not to hurt each other." Mrs. Hatch could not come to terms with the idea that her nephew was the assassin of her brother and two of her other nephews. For one thing, she felt that he was simply not up to the task. "Wyley had never shot a gun before," she said. "My husband and I target-practice and we had our girls as well learn to use a gun . . . and any time Wyley would come up and we were doing it, he wanted no part of it." Beyond this, she felt that his essential character prevented him from committing such violence. "We lived right next door to him for a number of years, and growing up he was a very sensitive child, caring in many ways and generous," she said. "Oh, he hoarded his money and all that, but to give an example, one time we all went shopping together in Pittsfield, my girls and Wyley, and on the way back we stopped at Friendly's to get some ice cream and I gave him the money to pay and when he came back he threw the money back at me and said, 'Ha, ha, this is my treat.' Now, if this was a person that was mean, he wouldn't have done something like that."

Howard Hatch, acting at the time as a family spokesman, said the family was angered by suggestions that inheritance money was a motivation for the murders. "Things have gotten twisted around and these reports are just not correct," Hatch said. Furthermore, Hatch dismissed the speculation that Wyley was led to murder because of his father's attempts to instill macho values in him and denied that there was anything unusually bitter or hostile going on in their relationship. Arguments between the two of them were limited, as far as he knew, to subjects that were typical of generational clashes, such as minor tensions over chores. "In the fifteen years I knew him," Hatch said of Bob Gates, "I never saw him give either one of [his sons] a spanking. His way of punishing was to ground them . . . not to let them go see their friends." In fact, Hatch thought that his brother-in-law did a good deal to support Wyley. "I know from personal experience that Bob was extremely proud of what Wyley had accomplished. Wyley was a gifted child," Hatch said. "His father purchased things to develop those gifts and he would always attend things like school concerts."

Vivian's son Bill, who worked as a store manager in upstate New York and who would, in the months ahead, move himself and his family into his mother's house, shared the family's sense of loyalty to one of their own. "You just don't desert family . . . you just don't," he said, adding, of Wyley, "It's not like he was hated. He was loved."

In one of her only public statements, Vivian Gates told reporters of her intention to assist her grandson in his defense. "We have to get Wyley help," she said. "I am his grandmother and I still love him." To some degree, as Mrs. Gates indicated to me after her grandson's trial had concluded, part of her reason for standing by Wyley was out of loyalty to her son Bob. "Bob really cared for Wyley—I don't think Wyley realized that," she said. "I felt, after it happened, that Bob would have done anything to prevent Wyley from doing this and that he would want me to help Wyley." Mrs. Gates confessed that "some people don't understand why I helped Wyley," adding that a fellow shopkeeper told her "how the town couldn't understand."

The bottom line, however, of the family's decision to support Wyley may have been best stated by Howard Hatch. "We don't want anything bad to happen to Wyley," he said. "It would be like the loss of another member of the family."

In a family that had been stalked and haunted by violence, the loss of another member of the family, even one who would be standing trial for murdering one of their own, was more than they could bear.

11

*These thoughts take expression in the
following:*
Isolation.
Insulated from the press of crowds
Their happiness o'erflows.
*And no one knows how this one goes
about his day.*
He's not okay!
He's hurt and sad.
His heart NOT glad.
The season? Bad to feel so . . .
All aloof, alone.
Outside is one side.
Inside—numb.
What can be done?
Oh, what will help?
No help, no hope.
*No one to see the hurt, the hopeless
unending day*
Of pain. Of question:
What is life?

Why should discord
End in strife?
Why this coldness,
Numbing pain,
Causing grief,
Yet no real gain.
Will someone help?
Will someone care
To reach and tell him
Someone's there?

—Jacqueline Rhind, Excerpt from "A Tragedy at Christmastide," as printed in the Chatham *Courier*.

Chatham is not a storybook village, like nearby Stockbridge, shrine of Norman Rockwell, or even neighboring Kinderhook, with its elegant brick homes that once belonged to Dutch patroons. Rather, its history is tied up with the railroad, whose tracks bisect the village and whose freight trains still hold up traffic with their long, loud, and frequent passage through the heart of town. There are a number of fine and distinctive shops in Chatham, but the feeling in town, despite the recent addition of a fancy *patisserie* and an ambitious restaurant where one can order warm *chèvre* over salad greens, is decidedly not an elegant one. It is, in fact, a no-nonsense town, where lawyers are as likely as contractors to drive pickup trucks, and where the reigning department store still does a lively business in notions and duty shoes and string mops.

For all of its brisk utilitarianism, however, Chatham revels two times a year. One occasion is the Chatham Fair, the other is Christmas. Promptly after Thanksgiving, the holiday decorations and lights go up along Main Street and a cardboard crèche is erected alongside the railroad station, which has been abandoned since the termination of passenger service. For those who are interested, there is an endless round of fairs and bazaars in the weeks before Christmas; the delicious aromas of clove and ginger emanate from the ovens of church ladies busy with bake sales, and industrious hands all over town are constructing angels and reindeer from pipe cleaners and pinecones. It is a rare Christmas when there isn't a blanket of snow on the ground, and driving along the back roads one might encounter a horse-drawn sleigh, its tintinnabulation echoing in the frigid air as it makes its way over the hills. As Christmas Day approaches, some of the local hamlets have caroling on their greens, and on frosty mornings, if you get up early enough, you might glimpse children en route to their school pageants, dressed as magi or snowflakes. As you watch them hurry along, in groups of three or four, unmolested and unthreatened, you can't help but feel that this is a very fine place to live.

But in the eleven days before Christmas, in that December of 1986, there was an unfamiliar and unwelcome feeling in the air. Suddenly the traditional comfort and joy of the season had been savagely purloined, and in its place was a very large, very dark shadow cast by this heinous multiple murder.

On that Sunday morning of December fourteenth, Louise Lincoln, Wyley's English teacher, had the radio on and caught the tail end of a report on a murder in East Chatham. "I thought to myself, Well, it's those damn New York City people. There they are, at it again, and just went on my merry way, didn't give it too much thought, obviously it wasn't going to be anybody I knew," she recalled. Later that day, Mrs. Lincoln, on her way to Albany for Christmas shopping, heard the news come over her car radio that Wyley Gates had been arrested for murder. "I pulled off the road and stopped the car and cried," she said. "I couldn't believe it, I couldn't accept it, I was furious that they had arrested my student. You have very much an ownership sometimes of these children and you think you know them well. What were they doing to him? How horrible this must be for him . . . I just could not believe it."

Linda Renken, in whose computer lab the conspiracy was later shown to have been hatched, arrived home late on Sunday night and turned on the news in order to find out how the Giants had done that day. But she never got past the lead story. "I was totally blown away," she recalled.

"I was just in total shock. I mean, that was the last person I would have thought could have done something like that. He never seemed even to react crossly to anybody."

Gordon Ringer, back from playing at a wedding, was sitting down to supper when the telephone rang. "It was my mom saying something about some kid killing somebody," he remembered. "By the time I had the TV on, getting bits and pieces of it, some of the teachers were calling. At first I thought Wyley had been shot, then later on, and of course the next day when I went to school, I was very shocked by it. Disbelief, I would say, was my first reaction."

Zachary Gobel, president of the student senate, got a call from a friend late on that Sunday afternoon. "My friend called me and said that Wyley's family had been killed and that Wyley had survived, that he was still alive," Gobel recalled. "I said, 'What are you talking about?' Then, on the news, it said he'd been arrested. My first impression was like there was no way. The guy I knew . . . he always seemed in control. He always gave the image, to me at least, that he was in control."

Friend and classmate Desiree Kelleher was at the bowling lanes in East Chatham when she heard the news of Wyley's arrest. It struck her as "crazy" and "stupid," a feeling that was widespread among Wyley's high school community.

For a town like Chatham, an event of this magnitude was unprecedented, and the question of how it would be dealt with in the high school was the first order of business for those on the faculty and in the administration. Principal Wesley Brown called an emergency session of the faculty for early Monday morning to discuss how this trauma would be handled. Brown advised the faculty to allow their students to talk if they needed to talk. He also told them that the mental-health agencies had offered their services.

Louise Lincoln vividly remembered going into her first-period class that day, which was, in fact, Wyley's advanced-placement English class, a small group, from which one student was now conspicuously absent. "I was behind the desk and they weren't saying anything," she recalled. "And the thing is, do you go on with the lesson and pretend nothing has happened and give them a sense of normalcy, which is one strategy, or do you just look them in the eye and say, 'OK, this horrible thing has happened, do you want to talk about it?' " Initially, Mrs. Lincoln opted for the first strategy. "I got the book and had it in my hand and was, I think, about three-quarters of the way decided to go on with the lesson and have a little normalcy in the world and I looked at my students and I couldn't do that, I couldn't," she said. "So I put the book down and said, 'Do you want to talk?' And they did. They were still in shock. They weren't going to say too much, except they had to look at each other and feel that everybody was shocked, and we cried, we uttered our disbeliefs, we had no real factual knowledge of anything, and so we shared our ignorance, and then the bell rang and they left."

Mrs. Lincoln spent the rest of the day in a state of total numbness. "I remember sitting at my desk in between periods," she said, "and the total silence of the school just washed over me."

In Doris Gearing's criminal-justice class, however, the reaction of the students was more violent than benumbed. "It was a horrible mixed reaction," she said. "Some of intense anger—'I'll kill him if he ever gets out'—to, 'Well, what are they going to do for him? If he's not all right, what are they going to do for him?' "

While some of the students were experiencing a deep sadness, others were gripped by fear. "There were many kids who felt, 'What if he snapped here at school?' " said one teacher who was involved in counseling. "What if whatever drove him to do this to his family, he had done here at school? There was enormous fear that this could possibly happen. That somebody could be that hurting inside that they could do something so horrendous. And there was another group of kids that felt guilty! Why didn't we know? Why didn't we help him? Couldn't we do something for this person who was just incredibly hurt?"

Feelings of shock and fear were by no means specific to the students. "It was probably the worst day that I ever had at the high school," recalled Linda Renken. "Everybody was totally in shock, extremely upset. I got no work done in any classes." Miss Renken had a particularly unsettling moment the next day as she was alone in her homeroom. "I was setting up something or other, and I turned around and Miles was sitting there and that kind of threw me," she remembered. Miles, whose involvement was already known at the school, opened up a bit to Miss Renken. "He explained to me that he had been talked to," she said, "that he hadn't had any sleep and was really uptight, and it was not a lot of fun, being talked to by the state troopers," she said. "He seemed real nervous. This was something that had obviously upset him."

In one class, an envelope pasted to the bulletin board in front of the room was made available for anybody who wanted to send Wyley a note. Zachary Gobel read some of those letters. "Some people put things in that envelope that just weren't appropriate," he said, "and that angered me greatly. I can think of a guy who wrote in there, 'I hope you fry in the chair.' This guy happened to be a friend of mine and I jumped down his throat about it. Because I was still thinking maybe the trial would come and he'd be acquitted or whatever."

But, over the next few weeks, not many letters would find their way into the envelope. "I think they just didn't know what to say," said the teacher responsible for the idea. "It was such a horrendous act." In this teacher's opinion, there were a few students who were willing to consider the degree of pain that Wyley must have been experiencing to lead him to such an act. Otherwise, most of the students were angry, especially as time went on, and especially the boys. "And there were a group of students who felt it was almost a suicide," the teacher remarked. "It was a suicide in that he did destroy his life. He didn't take his own life, but he could have, he probably should have, they felt at that point."

■   ■   ■

Dear Wyley,
I don't really know what to say, except that I care,

and that I'm worried, and that it hurts me and a
lot of other people at Chatham High to see you go
through this tragedy. . . . Maybe we—your friends
at CHS—never showed you enough how much
we care—and a lot of us feel real guilty about
that. . . . You are part of us and you will always be
part of us.

Wylie,
I wish I had walked up to you several days or a
week ago. . . . I wish I had just taken your hand &
said "let's talk." I wish *lots* of people had done that.
. . . I have cried for you since Saturday. . . . I want
you to know that I can hate what you did, but I
can't hate you. . . . You had earned our respect a
long time ago.

Dear Wiley,
. . . I know you must feel very alone right now,
and maybe not just now, maybe you have always
felt that way. . . . but you're not. You're not at all.
. . . A lot of caring friends are thinking about you
and *loving* you. . . . You are a very special person,
don't *ever* forget that or let anybody else tell you
differently.

Wyley,
Others may condemn you but Jesus Christ will
forgive you of everything that you have done. I
will continue to pray for your salvation.

Everyone had his own reaction to the events of December
thirteenth and everywhere, in the halls and the classrooms
and in the schoolyard, were tight knots of people trying to
make some sense of it or simply grieving or reeling in shock.
"The thing that upset me the most," said Jim Andrews,
Wyley's fellow trumpeter, "was all these people that all of a
sudden decided that they were Wyley's friends and now
they're all upset because of this happening. But if this hadn't

happened they wouldn't even give him the time of day. It just bothered me. In fact, I left school halfway through the day because I just couldn't handle it."

For others who couldn't "handle" it, there was crisis intervention from mental-health personnel. The position taken by the school administration was that there should be adequate time allowed for the full expression of grief and bewilderment, and that the faculty should provide students with the opportunity to discuss the incident as long as they needed to. The situation was further complicated by the invasion by media. "It was off the wall with media people," said Doris Gearing. "Kids running out so they could be on TV. It was more, 'Oh, I'm gonna be on "News at Six" or "News at Seven" ' than grief that four people were gone." Louise Lincoln also found the media attention to be an undue strain. "When the media people would be standing at the end of the school driveway, those students who were ignorant enough to seek publicity for whatever purpose would talk to them," she said. "Those students who had a degree of maturity and sensitivity ignored them. When some media tried to come to the front door and come into the building, students pushed the door shut and said, 'Stay away.' "

Over the next few weeks, the expressions of anger would continue to flash. "One kid said, 'Boy, if he comes back to the school, I won't sit in the classroom with him,' " Doris Gearing remembered. "In other words, 'I'm not going to sit in a classroom with someone who's killed.' " Part of this reaction may have had to do with a widespread fear that Wyley would be let out. "I don't think they realized that he would be kept in jail," said Mrs. Gearing. "What kids see is that when kids get in trouble, they're released. Because they're juveniles, they're arraigned and then they're released in their parents' custody or on their own recognizance. They think people can get out easy." In the opinion of another teacher, the fear went beyond that of Wyley's being "let out" and, in fact, touched a deeper root fear in these children. "After the first week, a sense of fear seemed to take over," said the teacher. "They were saying, in effect,

'If this could happen to someone like Wyley, could it happen to me?' In other words, 'Could I "catch" it from him?' "

Some students had more reason to be upset than others. One teacher witnessed a student named Ben Cooper becoming particularly shaken. "He, I remember being extremely upset," said the teacher. "Because we had a meeting after school for anybody who just wanted to stay around and talk, and Ben was in tears. He was very, very upset." Ben Cooper would go on to testify at both the trials of Wyley Gates and Damian Rossney that Damian had put questions to him regarding the ethicality of being a contract killer.

Louise Lincoln specifically recalled John Bailey's reaction to the events. Bailey had missed quite a number of school days and, as a disciplinary measure, was made to take Mrs. Lincoln's night-school high school equivalency class. "In the break period . . . John was talking with a couple of high school dropouts and registering surprise at all of this," said Mrs. Lincoln. "This was before we knew how involved he was. He was truly taking on an innocent-onlooker, golly-gee-I-didn't-know-that-about-them attitude."

Some teachers felt that John Bailey was not the only student adopting a see-no-evil, hear-no-evil approach. "What surprised me more than anything else after the whole incident is the code of silence," said Mrs. Gearing. "Kids would not 'rat' on a fellow classmate." The first question that was asked of Mrs. Gearing on Monday morning after the murders was, "If you know something about the murders, do you have to report it?" "And that surprised me," she said. "There were a lot of things I think the kids knew and covered up for a long time . . . I think a lot of kids were aware of what was going on. A *lot* of kids." In fact, Mrs. Gearing cited incidents of privileged information beyond those concerning the core group of kids who were involved in the burglaries and the kids who had heard about the plans while sitting around the cafeteria table. "Someone said to me—one of the kids in the class—well, they called the father a few weeks before and tried to warn the father that he was going to do it and the father laughed it off," she said.

Gordon Ringer also sensed this attitude of silence. "As things started to snowball . . . it became apparent that there were a lot more people involved than even I think the authorities have been able to uncover," he said. "And I think that's the thing that probably scared me the most, to be honest with you." For Ringer, things were suddenly very different. "The thing that really hit me was when I walked down the hall, I looked at the kids differently," he said. "Before I would say something, I was analyzing what I was saying as to how something can be interpreted or misinterpreted." As information came out, there were more and more reasons to feel uneasy. "Finding out how many kids were involved, and the fact that these kids are back in the school—that was a big thing for myself and a lot of other colleagues to deal with," said Ringer. "I was very uncomfortable with everything that was going on, seeing these people walking around and having them in my class."

The following Sunday a group therapy session, open to the public, was held in Chatham. The session, entitled "Community Under Stress," had been instituted as a joint venture between the Columbia County Mental Health Service and Family Survival, a support organization for parents.

"No sooner did the murders happen than my phone started ringing off the hook," said Clair Winans, who operates a twenty-four-hour hot line as a service of Family Survival. "Parents were quite upset. They were getting questions from their kids in school. . . . And then other people in the community kept calling. 'I'm afraid to speak to my child!' 'What have I done with my children?' " Mrs. Winans, sensing the mounting community unrest, felt it necessary to enlist the aid of the County Mental Health resources. Michael O'Leary, deputy director of the Columbia County Mental Health Service, worked with Mrs. Winans to set up the crisis intervention groups, and he and staff members of the Mental Health Service spent Thursday,

December 18, at Chatham High School, for an all-day outreach program. "The timing seemed to be right. The numbness had worn off," O'Leary recalled. "It took no prompting. They needed no priming to talk." O'Leary remembered the prevailing feeling he encountered at the school as being one of guilt, that this could have been prevented if they had been better friends or better teachers. Moreover, the emotional trauma was intensified because of the proximity of the holidays. "It's a period of time when you're supposed to be happy," O'Leary said. "People didn't know how to react . . . it's like looking out the window and seeing a foot of snow. Then you go outside and it's ninety degrees. The scene doesn't fit the feeling."

At the forum, people talked about parental and school responsibility; how to recognize when a child was "at risk"; the power of computer games and television. "There were one or two teenagers and the others were parents, ministers, teachers, parents of small children," Mrs. Winans said. "One parent said her child was waking up having nightmares . . . a teenage girl who had known Wyley and had been in school with him and had been hospitalized herself for emotional illness was trying to deal with the whole thing. She kept saying, 'It could have been me.' "

The feeling that one could have been either perpetrator or victim extended even to the counselors themselves. O'Leary, arriving home that night, pulled into a dark driveway, unaware that there had been a power outage. "The first thing I thought was, Somebody killed my family," he recalled.

Before the murders, the residents of this small town felt they had a degree of safety and distance from crime and other big urban problems. But, suddenly, that safety and distance had vanished and people were asking: Why? Why did it happen here? "The conclusion is that there's nothing wrong here," O'Leary said. "The focus was on the school system—that was the scapegoat—but as we talked about it more people realized it could have happened anywhere, any city anywhere. In other words, it wasn't unique to Chatham." Despite this, the impact of the murders, as expressed by the people who voiced their concerns at the forum, was closely connected to an image of what the town and the county had been and what it was now, in the wake of this violence. "Everyone could identify with someone— the victims, the survivors, or the perpetrators," said O'Leary. "In that way it touched everybody." O'Leary also described the event and its impact as "a loss of innocence." People moved to Columbia County looking for peace, quiet, and family life. "And what was expressed at these meetings was that this is lost now, this is gone, you can never have that back," he said. "That something so terrible has happened here it has shattered the ideal image of why I came here in the first place." Of course people realized that such safety and distance was a pipe dream anyway—there's no place like that anywhere—but it was brought home in such a sudden, acute, dramatic way. "I think people can overlook an occasional car accident, even with drunken driving and people killed," said O'Leary. "People can overlook hunting accidents. People can overlook suicides. People can overlook murders. But people can't overlook an entire family killed."

12

On the Wednesday following the murders, services for Bob Gates, Bobby, Jr., and Jason were held at St. Luke's Episcopal Church in Chatham. The bearers of Jason's small white casket included three of his Groudas uncles and his uncle Bill Gates. Bob Gates's gray metal casket was borne by his brother Lou, his brother-in-law Howard, and his friends Dave Frick, Dick Klingler, Ronald Paulsey, and Skip Huvar. Bob's son and namesake, in an identical casket, was borne by his friends Dennis Gawron and Patrick O'Neil, by Peter Groudas, by his father's friends Don DeLapp and Ronald MacFarlane, and by his mother's brother, Gary Holcomb. Some 120 people came to the church; Wyley was not among them. Nor was there any allusion to the crime itself in the services, which included readings from Isaiah and the Twenty-third Psalm. A choir sang the children's hymn "Fairest Lord Jesus" and the Reverend Clinton Dugger, rector of the Church of the Redeemer in Rensselaer, who had known the Gates family from the days when he had served as vicar at St. Luke's, drew on the themes of hope and resurrection.

It was Deloras Groudas who had thought of contacting a lawyer for Wyley on the night of the murders, and now, according to Evelyn Prescott, she had another singular thought. "Jason was buried and that's another thing that Mrs. Groudas thought of that we didn't think of," she said. "To have him baptized . . . I don't think he had been. He couldn't have been. And she thought enough to call a priest and have him come up and baptize him."

The Brahms, meanwhile, were dealing with the arrangements for Cheryl. Their contact with the Gates family, in the days following the murders, had been, in their mind, distinctly one-sided. "We had to call everyone. They just left us alone. We were nonexisting people," said Mame Brahm. "We were even going to include Cheryl in the entourage of the caskets. But it just became too emotionally distressing." Instead, the Brahm family held services for Cheryl in Valatie, also on Wednesday morning.

The Gates funeral promised to be a media event, but the family closed ranks successfully, and the media were kept to the other side of the street, across from the church. As for Vivian Gates, she maintained her stoic posture at the funeral. "You could see that she was suffering," said Mrs. Prescott. "But she was keeping her chin up. She always does. An amazing person. We can't figure out how she does it."

On that same Wednesday, December seventeenth, Damian Rossney, charged with hindering prosecution in the first degree, was arraigned and a bail of $50,000 was set. The youth was remanded to the Columbia County Jail, where his friend Wyley was incarcerated, but by 7:30 that evening bail had been made and Damian was released into the custody of his parents.

Scheduled for Thursday morning was the preliminary hearing in Canaan in the case of Wyley Gates. Columbia County Public Defender Paul Czajka, appearing before Town Justice George Lee (who later, as a realtor, would undertake the selling of the Gates log house), said that his client had waived his right for a personal appearance at the scheduled hearing. Czajka requested, and was granted, a postponement of the hearing to allow more time to prepare the case. Rumors that threats on Wyley's life had led to the postponement of the hearing were not directly addressed by Sheriff Proper, but on Friday, a sheriff's department source confirmed that a threat against Wyley's life had been received sometime Wednesday night or early Thursday morning. In this small county, where violent crime was decidedly an aberration, this pale, bespectacled youth who had not shown any ostensible grief or remorse, and who might well have been involved in the murder of an orphaned child just before Christmas, was the cause of great anguish and the object of intense rage, and the need for increased protection and scrutiny became apparent. A suicide watch was ordered for Wyley as well—"anybody with this magnitude of charges is watched closely," Sheriff Proper explained—although nothing in the boy's behavior thus far suggested that the idea of suicide was present in his mind.

What precisely was on the mind of Wyley Gates became the subject of intense speculation in the media. Particular attention was focused on the computer discs that had been seized and on the Dungeons and Dragons connection. Classmates and family members told reporters that Wyley kept to himself, but that he loved to play with computers. "He was playing the game like a CIA agent," one source was quoted as saying. "The money was part of the payoff, but the real payoff was just playing the game . . . the thrill of it. He was into thrills and taking risks."

Wyley's fellow students at Chatham High alerted the investigators to the possibility that a blueprint for the murders might be found on the computer discs. "It was a consensus of the kids from school that if plans were made, they were made on computers," a source said. Approximately three hundred floppy discs were seized from the homes of Wyley, Damian, and Miles, and a special team of computer operators was recruited to review them. The review proved fruitless, to the irritation of the operators, one of whom wrote, "I can't believe these guys cut a notch in the original APPLE system discs and used them for blank discs. Seems they care very little about the property of other people. What a bunch of assholes!"

Around this time, too, Wyley's uncle, Louis Gates, discovered two plastic containers of odorless liquid while looking through a closet in the log house. He notified the police, who removed the containers to a field behind the Gates residence. The sheriff's department called in the Bomb Detachment of the U.S. Army, who sent three people to the scene. Explosives were placed around the containers. According to a police report, "when the containers were detonated no unusual circumstances arose from the explosion."

Meanwhile, from the confines of the Columbia County Jail, Wyley observed these goings-on with a bemused detachment. In what later became known as the "Black Maxx" letter—an intercepted communication that Wyley sent Damian from the jail—Wyley wrote:

Black Maxx [his nickname for Damian]:

I am sorry, not that that probably matters to you at this point.

You cannot make prime computations without the necessary data, so please don't try. I didn't break down when I confessed. I had no choice, and I was under extreme conditions at the time. Please reserve judgment until you have enough data.

Remember the three gallons of liquid paper glue ("slime") that I had? I put it in my closet and my uncle found it. No one could figure out what it was, so the police called in the bomb squad. They apparently thought that it might be nitroglycerin, as if I would leave 3 gallons of it lying around my room. Anyway, they took it up into the field behind my house and tried to blow it up with some explosives. My grandmother said that they even had a helicopter. So far I haven't heard anything about it in the media. I wonder why? Would you

happen to know how all of the hype about the
video game called "Infierno" evolved? I sure as hell
don't. The police will probably spend a lot of money
making fools out of themselves. They will probably hire a computer specialist to review all of our
discs. . . .

   Jail is fun (just kidding). Please contact me.
                                        The Coyote

"The Coyote" was Wyley's nickname for himself, after Wile
E. Coyote, a cartoon character. In Damian, Wyley had found
someone with whom he could kid about his given name, a
name whose origin he had never understood and that he
had come to hate.

On December 16, Dr. Anthony Marchionne, a clinical
psychologist in private practice and an associate professor
at the Albany Medical College, received a call from Wyley's
attorney, Paul Czajka. A few days later, the psychologist
met with Wyley, and thereafter he would meet with him
once a week for the first month, once every two weeks after
that, accumulating over forty hours of direct contact by the
time the trial took place the following summer. Dr. Marchionne administered a battery of psychological tests and
conducted a series of clinical interviews.

   "This boy was cagey," the psychologist recalled, "and I
was very reluctant to jump to any conclusions about him. I
really, really felt that I had to weigh every damned thing
he said. I didn't really believe him for, I would say, a good
fifteen hours of the time I spent with him. There are many
things that he had told me about his personal development
that just did not fit. It was like he was throwing me off."

   In the beginning, Marchionne made himself available
to Wyley with the idea that counseling would be needed
when the momentousness of the events hit home. "I would
say for the first fifteen hours or so I felt that I should keep
myself at his disposal for one reason: I thought that he
would decompensate more than he had," said Marchionne.
Despite the fact that when Marchionne asked Wyley if he

entertained suicidal thoughts and Wyley described a bizarre
method he felt still available to him in which he could gouge
his brain by putting his finger through his eye, the psychologist found that Wyley was primarily and inappro-
priately concerned with trivialities that had nothing to do
with the realities of his situation. For instance, when Dr.
Marchionne met with Wyley on the day after his arraignment, Wyley asked him to describe the shirt he was wearing.
The shirt was, in his mind, a nice sports shirt and he was
indignant that the media had described it as a "work shirt."
He was also very concerned about not being able to go back
to Chatham High School. "That was another eerie thing,"
said Dr. Marchionne. "In the early stages I saw him, he
thought he would just go back to Chatham High and
continue on living in that house there." Indeed, a cousin
with whom Wyley corresponded also saw evidence of this
inappropriateness. When Wyley wrote this cousin that
"spending five or six more months in [jail] is not my idea
of a vacation," she wrote back, "Wyley, what did you expect?
If you commit a crime, you don't go on any kind of a
vacation, you go to jail."

"My first immediate response to him was that this boy
has not integrated this experience," recalled the psychologist. "He's presenting it to me . . . like something he read
in the paper, there's no emotional connection there." In
fact, no sign of emotional connectedness would emerge until
March, when Wyley "shed a tear" over the loss of Bobby.
"And that's all," said Dr. Marchionne of that demonstrative
moment. "He recovered very rapidly."

Conducting a clinical interview with Wyley was inordinately difficult, for Wyley was "parsimonious" when it came
to dispensing information, so much so that Dr. Marchionne
was forced to revise his original expectations of who Wyley
Gates really was. "I kept thinking that this kid's got to be
really one of the most complex kids I've ever run into," he
said, "and he's not. He's very barren inside."

One place where Marchionne witnessed the barrenness
that characterized all of Wyley's relationships was in the
boy's relationship with his mother. This was an idealized

relationship on Wyley's part; he described her as "intellectual" and "creative" and, throughout his internment in the Columbia County Jail, he kept up a correspondence with her. But to Dr. Marchionne, the relationship appeared to be a sterile one. He happened to be seeing Wyley on the day when Wyley's mother had her first visit with him. The correctional officers told him that Kristi Gates would be coming at one o'clock, and so the psychologist decided to go out for lunch and see Wyley afterward. "I saw him right after he'd left her," Marchionne said. "You would never know that was his mother. Or that he had any deep affection for her. It just blew my mind because this was days after the murder, but he spent all this time telling her she had to go to that band concert in Chatham, that the Chatham High School band was playing and he wanted her impressions of the band and how it sounded without his being there. And I thought this was just absurd! Here was this woman just come in to bury her other son and this was what they talked about."

On only one front did the psychologist detect a sloughing off of that barrenness and parsimony. "He maintained this extraordinary protectiveness of Damian Rossney, as if he would shut down if I tried to explore the role of Damian," Marchionne said. "He would tell me quite frankly that he would perjure himself on the witness stand if he was being called in any way." Some of that willingness to take on all the blame was, in the psychologist's opinion, tied into Wyley's special brand of narcissism. "That was another eerie thing," he said. "Up to the middle twenty hours, he had this almost incredible need to get up on the witness stand and explain what was happening to him. . . . It wasn't as if he was trying to appeal for sympathy. It was like 'This is my day.' "

Then again the protectiveness could be traced to Wyley's deep feelings for the boy who had been his only friend. Indeed, the relationship between Damian and Wyley had provided for Wyley a spiritual succor that extended right up to the very night of the crime. Marchionne described Wyley's recollections of going back to Damian's house after the movies on the night of the murders. "He is feeling empty and in despair and Damian is just playing video games," recalled the psychologist, "and I asked him how Damian was feeling and he said, 'Damian's cool on the outside but on the inside he's worrying about whether I'll confess.' He mentions also being touched by the fact that Damian puts his hand on his shoulder and says something like, 'Are you all right?' He's touched by that, as if Damian's able to give him something emotionally that he hasn't been given before. That's pretty sad."

And, as if the relationship were not complicated enough, there existed between the two boys a fierce competitiveness that Dr. Marchionne felt was yet another reason for Wyley's veiling of Damian's role in the murders. In fact, the psychologist felt that if he had directly asked whether the murder schemes were of Damian's devising, this would have elicited a defense from Wyley that would essentially have been based on the conviction that "you're saying that Damian's smarter than I am, more able to come up with unique things to do, and I will not concede that at this point in time."

For all the intense feelings directed toward Damian, however, there was no suggestion, in all of Dr. Marchionne's interviews of Wyley, of sexual interaction between the two boys. But, in spite of the barren quality that characterized most of Wyley's relationships with other people, there was an occasional exhibition of the strong, powerful feelings that coursed within him, as evidenced by a letter he wrote from jail to a high school classmate, a boy whom he regarded with an ardor that he had hitherto suppressed. To this boy he wrote:

> I love you . . . I have no way of knowing what you will think when you read this, but I can only hope that you realize how much it means. I would give my life for you without thinking. I would suffer eternally for you. I hope that this doesn't sound too flowery, but I can't possibly begin to describe how I feel towards you . . . I can't possibly expect you to understand this, but can only hope that you

will try. I may very well never have the chance to
see you again, which is why I'm writing this letter.
I only hope that I'm not too late, or too early.

Perhaps the letter was a call for help from a boy
imprisoned in a county jail. Perhaps an act of violence had
released in this boy a passion that had been repressed by
years of living in an atmosphere of emotional sterility and
distance. Whatever the motivation or the catalyst for releasing these feelings, the letter was regarded by Dr. Marchionne
as further evidence of what he called Wyley's "inappropriateness."

"To me, he's totally inappropriate in the way he ex-
presses his anger and his affections," said the psychologist.
"There was absolutely no reason for him to write that letter.
No reason whatsoever. To me, it was another indication of
how inappropriate this youngster was that here he is, in jail,
indicted for the murders of four people, well aware that
the whole community is falling apart because of this, and
he writes this letter to this boy who, I'm told, at the time
that he got it, went white as a sheet."

In the course of his sessions with Wyley, Marchionne
collected enough material, he felt, to at least offer Wyley's
attorney the option of an insanity plea. The material included Wyley's admission that he had a long-standing goal
and aspiration to achieve a significant historical standing.
He told the psychologist that he wanted to be the head of
a corporation that would establish a military base in Antarctica, one that would patrol the environment and find
and punish people who polluted the atmosphere and hunted
animals. He spoke to Dr. Marchionne about an hallucination
he had experienced when he was twelve years old, in which
Christ told him to protect the plant and animal worlds. But,
through it all, Marchionne was not seeing the sort of material
he had expected to see. He recalled that when Paul Czajka
first called him and asked him to go down to the jail, he
said to himself, "I'm sure that I'm going to find that if he
did it, he was almost surely brutalized as a child or that he'd
been sexually molested or something." But none of these

typical conditions showed themselves—not a trace of them, to be exact. It was, in fact, a great shock for Dr. Marchionne to hear what Wyley's issues with his father were—"that his father wanted him to mow the lawn, take the garbage out, come down and watch TV, and 'God damn it, I'm gonna break that computer you're sitting in front of'—that these were the issues that Wyley was trying to convince me were the justifications for his hatred, which he knows he's never convinced me of." To the question of whether or not Wyley was hiding some dark secrets about his family, the psychologist replied, "I can't find it. I've pushed and pulled and pulled and pushed."

The conclusion that Dr. Marchionne reached, as stated in his clinical report, was that over a long period of time a psychotic process had been developing within Wyley and that what had begun as a lack of emotional involvement was developing into a delusional relief system. In a synopsis of his report based on his psychological evaluation, Dr. Marchionne cited among the salient points: the absence of any significant positive emotional attachment to family, peers, or significant others, resulting in an impairment of his emotional, social, and psychological development; a pervasive sense of being "unique" and "different"; a possible childhood hallucinatory experience coinciding with the development of a delusional belief system characterized by grandiosity and self-aggrandisement; a marked disassociation from angry, hostile, aggressive feelings and behaviors; ego resources so deficient that he was unable to empathize and identify with others, leading him to engage in a pathological empathy and identification with violent, aggressive, and emotionally disturbed peers; a contamination of his basic cognitive intellectual functioning, with an interference to his ability to engage in logical rational thought; and an absence of pathological parent-child interaction, with no evidence of psychological, physical, or sexual abuse. The normal responses of depression, apprehension, agitation or anxiety one would be expected to experience in a catastrophic life event were also absent. In its place he manifested a psychotic process of denial and emotional detachment.

Aside from the clinical report, the prognosis that Dr. Marchionne offered, some months after the trial, was a grim one. "The unfortunate thing about this kid," he told me, "is that he's in the process of going to paranoid schizophrenia but he's not there yet."

Shortly after Dr. Marchionne came on board, the Gates family resolved to hire an attorney for Wyley. It was in late December that Charles Wilcox, former district attorney of Rensselaer County and now one year into a private practice in Troy, received a referral from Nelson Alford, of the Chatham law firm of Connor, Connor and Schram, which was handling the estate of Robert Gates.

Wilcox, born and raised in Lake George in upstate New York, had graduated from St. Lawrence University and Albany Law School. While at Albany, he had become interested in the office of district attorney in Troy, having admired the incumbent D.A. for his honesty and diligence. Upon his graduation from law school, he served a stint with the army reserves, rising to the rank of captain, and, once discharged, he returned to the Albany area, where he held a counselor's position with the state legislature, but still had his eye trained on the district attorney's office. At first he was told that available positions were being filled by people with experience in trying felony cases, but, with a tenacious spirit, Wilcox wound up "essentially camping out on the steps of the courthouse" until he was hired.

Wilcox started as a part-time assistant district attorney and swiftly moved into the position of full-time assistant district attorney. But it was with the arrival of a new D.A., elderly and "on the downside of his career as a trial attorney," that Wilcox found himself in a position to accrue some significant trial experience. The new D.A. let Wilcox try just about any case that came up and, as a result, Wilcox became the chief assistant district attorney and tried all the homicide and murder cases that came up, as well as many of the major felony cases.

By the time his superior vacated his position, Wilcox had tried nearly thirty homicide cases and was in the position to run for the office of district attorney. He did so successfully and on January 1, 1978, began the first of his two terms as district attorney of Rensselaer County. His tenure in the district attorney's office was an impressive one. He had under his belt victories in thirty-six of the thirty-eight murder cases he had personally tried in Rensselaer County. Among his signal achievements was the county's first jury conviction ever in a fatal child-abuse death case. But there were setbacks as well, most notably in his handling—or mishandling—of a witness in a Hell's Angels murder case. The case involved an execution of one Hell's Angel by another, with two teenage girls giving statements to the police that they had witnessed the murder. According to Wilcox, the girls thereafter asked for protection, which was provided, and then one of the girls, Becky Redcross, said that, instead of being protected as a witness, she had been held against her will. A federal lawsuit ensued, with a jury finding Wilcox in violation of Redcross's civil rights. The resulting monetary settlement personally cost Wilcox $10,000 and a great deal of anguish. "It was probably the most disappointing experience in my legal career to date in terms of the system not working," said Wilcox, who believed that the jurors, some of whom wore "denim and cut-offs and sandals," had identified with Redcross and had viewed Wilcox as an establishment figure who should be brought down. The criticism of Wilcox—specifically that he had not obtained a court order allowing him to detain the witness—was, some speculated, injurious to his reelection bid as well. Shortly after his defeat, he established a private practice in Troy.

Assisting him in his practice was Joan Yowe, a paralegal who had started working with Wilcox in 1980 in the D.A.'s office. A mother of two grown children and the wife of a school principal, Joan, petite and fashionable, not only managed Wilcox's office but participated in investigative aspects of the homicide cases as well. The work was demanding, even consuming at times, and Joan was looking forward to some well-earned relaxation. "I hadn't had a vacation in years," Joan recalled, "and I had said I was taking off the last week in December. Nothing, absolutely nothing, was going to stop me." The week before her planned vacation, Joan caught the evening news on television and heard an account of the capital crime committed in Columbia County. "I saw the boy," she said, "and I thought at the time, What a sweet-looking boy. That was my first impression." She didn't give the case any further thought, however, until the end of the week, as her long-awaited vacation was coming into view. But the vacation was not meant to be. "Chuck came into my office and said, 'Well, I'll see you on Monday,' " she remembered. "I said, 'No, I told you *absolutely not*.' He said, 'Well, I think you'll want to make a change.' " Wilcox told Joan that they had been called by the Gates family for an initial meeting to discuss the possibility of their being retained as counsel for Wyley; Joan made the change.

A few days later, Wilcox and Joan met with Vivian Gates, her son Louis, in from California, her daughter Viki Hatch, and the referring attorney Nelson Alford. "My impression is that their approach to the whole thing was that they wanted to get to the bottom of it," Wilcox recalled. "They had reservations about [Wyley's] ability or capability to do what he was accused of doing, and I think they approached it from the standpoint of they wanted to get to the bottom of it in terms of making a final decision, maybe in their own minds, as to who did it. I think they felt it well could be somebody else or other persons, and that bothered them."

Joan Yowe recalled their particular concern about the confession Wyley was alleged to have given. "I think it was either Lou or Viki who said the reason they thought they should get a private attorney is that they saw that statement from Investigator Salmon and said, 'This isn't the way Wyley talks,' " said Joan.

The tone of the meeting, in Joan Yowe's memory, was "odd" rather than somber or strained. Viki Hatch and Louis Gates struck Joan as being totally perplexed and not understanding what had happened, whereas Vivian Gates seemed numb. But beneath the perplexed, benumbed exteriors, there seemed to be a whole other layer of unasked questions and answers. Joan described Louis Gates as very nervous and hyper, pacing back and forth. "I felt at the time that there was so much he wanted to say," Joan remarked. She felt that what Wyley's aunt and uncle were thinking was that if this boy had done something like this, then what had been their role in it and what could they have done to stop what had happened?

Both Wilcox and Joan Yowe felt, however, that the family didn't really know Wyley Gates well at all. In Wilcox's opinion, since Wyley was essentially a very quiet person, it would have taken an expert to determine, before a manifest sign such as the murders, that there was, in fact, something drastically wrong with him. "He never opened up," said Wilcox. "And [the family] probably took the approach that as long as he's performing ostensibly in the real world, like good grades, not doing anything totally bizarre that they were aware of or anything, then we won't poke and prod into his quietude." In Joan Yowe's opinion, although the family was "up front," there was an obvious gulf between Wyley and them. "It would be my personal opinion," she stated, "that they had no idea what was going on in Wyley Gates's mind" nor were they "able to evaluate Wyley Gates."

After the initial meeting, the family took several weeks to make their decision as to representation and then ended up hiring Wilcox. Shortly thereafter, Wilcox and Joan Yowe traveled down to the jail in Hudson to have their first meeting with their new client.

"That was an experience," recalled Joan. "We sat in a room—in the prison library, pretty ghastly—and I thought, Now, in a moment, I'm going to see a boy who possibly killed four people." But all of her expectations of the type of boy she was about to meet were beside the point when Wyley walked through the door. "I had seen a lot of criminals, some I liked, some I didn't like," said Joan. "But when this boy walked in, it was nothing, nothing, that I had expected." Here was a boy who was cooperative as he answered their questions, but within himself, so much so that he wouldn't look at either one of them. "My very first

thought when I saw him was, This child is a broken vessel,"
she said. "I looked at him and I just said, 'He's broken.'"
Joan recorded in her notes that Wyley was trembling; she
couldn't say if that was due to the room's being cold but
she strongly suspected otherwise.

"First impressions were really very difficult because
Wyley was essentially noncommunicative," remembered Wilcox. "Very flat, very seemingly unconcerned, unaware, not
in touch with what the allegations were, what the accusations
were, and what it all involved in terms of the magnitude of
the situation." Wilcox had the impression that Wyley was
living comfortably in the jail, seeming to have adjusted to
it. "Many people are very, very uptight, nervous, can't wait
to get out," said Wilcox. "Wyley didn't really stress that or
really mention that very much at all and anytime it was
brought up, which was only on one occasion I remember,
he never really pursued it. It was more like he was bringing
it up as an abstract concept as opposed to *I want to be out*. It
was almost like it was a query in terms of this thing called
bail and how does it work and how do people get out, as
opposed to *me*."

This first impression indicated to Wilcox that he was
dealing with a youth who was, in fact, deeply disturbed.
"[He] struck me as someone who was totally out of touch
with reality in terms of the situation he found himself in,"
Wilcox said. If his client had simply been unconcerned,
Wilcox might have interpreted that as a kind of acceptance
of his responsibility for the incident. But the fact that Wyley
seemed totally out of touch with the magnitude of the
charges and the nature of the crime he was alleged to have
committed led Wilcox to contemplate options that would
otherwise have been unavailable to him, namely an insanity
defense.

Wyley never discussed the loss of his family with his
attorney—in fact, Wilcox felt that Wyley never seemed to
be aware they were gone—and the family who visited him
in jail never discussed it with him either. Wyley wanted to
see his grandmother and other members of his family,
Wilcox said, but when he did see them he didn't expect

from them any sign of disfavor or any dissatisfaction with
him or any feelings of anger toward him as a result of what
he was accused of. "Whether he'd done it or not, he expected
them to come in and it would be a visit to someone who
was like in the hospital," said Wilcox. " 'How you doing?'
'Hope you're doing okay.' If they had not shown up, I think
he would have been very upset because again he just wasn't
in touch with why he was there."

Dr. Marchionne, too, detected this code of silence that
existed between Wyley and his family, particularly with
regard to Vivian Gates. "She was totally intimidated by even
mentioning simple things to him," Dr. Marchionne said of
Mrs. Gates. He recalled being especially stunned by her
reaction when he told her that he felt Wyley was emotionally
disturbed enough for him to offer Wilcox the option of an
insanity defense. "She became very upset," the psychologist
remembered, "and said, 'Who's going to tell him that you're
going to plead the insanity defense?' This stunned me
because she wouldn't tell him. And I said, 'Well, I've
essentially been talking to Wyley about this,' and of course
the oddity was that this was no problem for Wyley. And it
was not this protectiveness that 'We don't want to hurt this
boy.' It was just that 'We don't talk that way in our family.' "

Meetings between Wyley and his counsel were held
weekly from January until July. For Joan Yowe, the process
of establishing contact with this client continued to be an
arduous one. She sat beside him many hours, as he under-
went psychiatric evaluations, and still there was no significant
contact between them. Usually he would come in and sit
with his hands in his lap and his head down. He might look
up but his eyes would always be averted. If he was spoken
to, he would say yes or no.

The parsimony that Dr. Marchionne found was also
the experience of Wilcox and Joan Yowe as they attempted
to get the facts in the case. Joan had the strong feeling that
she was not hearing the whole story and, by her own
admission, she started to get tough. "He and Chuck would
be talking and I'd say, 'I don't think so,' " she recalled. "He'd
look at me and he might not answer me. He'd continue and

I might take a defensive posture, fold my arms, let him know I'm not pleased. I'm not pleased with this, this is bullshit, I'm not buying this." As their relationship progressed, heading into March and April, Joan would alert Wyley to the inconsistencies between what Wyley told them and the material submitted to them by their own forensic people. When Wyley saw that Joan instinctively knew that something was wrong with some aspect of the story, he began to respond to her and their relationship deepened. "He wanted me to know what I knew without being told," said Joan. "Because, as I found out later, this is how he operates. . . . Like, 'If this is what you believe then believe it. If you're smart, you'll read between the lines and between the lines and between the lines.' He's in layers."

As she probed over the next few months, Joan broke through some of those layers. Both Wilcox and Joan could see that Wyley was beginning to relax and, at a certain point, Joan resolved to achieve a physical contact with this unapproachable boy. "I wanted to feel his thumb where they said there was some kind of injury," she remembered. "I wanted to just see if there was a raised scar or whatever, so I took his hand and I really expected he was going to pull it back, because at this point, other than shaking hands, which was rather limp, there had been no physical contact with this boy. There was never a physical contact. He was so into himself. You could feel that this boy did not touch or was touched. I took his hand and he didn't move his hand, and for that second I was surprised. . . . And I sat rubbing his thumb and I felt him leave his hand in my hand and I felt that we had connected."

On January sixth, Wyley appeared at the Canaan Town Hall for the hearing that had previously been postponed at the request of Public Defender Paul Czajka. Spectators were asked to sign an attendance sheet and submit to a search by a metal detector on their way into the Quonset hut–type building that served as the Town Hall. A special roped-off section was created in the courtroom for the public, and paper was taped over the room's window; stringent security measures—unique in the history of this building customarily used for assessor's meetings and as a polling place—were the call of the day. Among the spectators were the Brahm family, who watched as Wyley, suddenly the most famous, or at least notorious, citizen in the annals of Canaan history, was driven, under heavy guard, directly into a garage adjoining the courtroom. He entered the courtroom looking straight ahead and sat next to his attorney. Clad in a black parka worn over a bullet-proof vest, in jeans and the sport shirt that was to be so irritatingly referred to in the press as a "work shirt," he lacked his signature necktie and had a wispy little beard he had been cultivating for the last few weeks. He was not handcuffed.

One of the first motions Charles Wilcox made on behalf of his new client was to call for the hearing to be closed to the public. Because Canaan was a "relatively small community" in a "relatively small county," he argued, it was likely that the airing of even a minimal amount of evidence would create an impression in the minds of potential jurors in the case, which would damage the defendant's right to a fair trial. While conceding that only a small amount of information was expected to come out of the hearing, Wilcox said that news media reports about the testimony would cause "irreparable, irrevocable, and irreversible" damage to his client's chances for a fair trial in the future. District Attorney Eugene Keeler assented to the motion. The assembled news corps, which numbered close to twenty, argued in opposition to the closing of the hearing and requested a short adjournment so that their attorneys could appear. Judge Lee adjourned the hearing for approximately five minutes, and, upon his return, announced that he was closing the hearing, citing a section of the criminal code which allows the court to close proceedings when the likelihood of disclosure might harm a defendant's right to a fair trial.

Testifying during the hour-long proceeding were Investigator Walter Shook and Coroner Angelo Nero. After an hour behind closed doors, Judge Lee emerged with the statement that he had determined that there was sufficient evidence to hold the case over for grand-jury consideration. The grand-jury investigation began the following day.

After the hearing, Wyley was returned to the Columbia County Jail, and Wilcox stated to the press that it was quite premature to comment on the line of defense he might take but indicated that he had reserved the right to enter an insanity defense and that a psychiatric examination of his client had been ordered. Wilcox also commented that the amount of information leaked to the news media thus far was "very disconcerting" and that he might eventually ask for a change of venue in the case. His client, he reported, was "very subdued" and it would be left to the psychiatric examination to determine whether or not he was competent to stand trial.

The psychiatric examinations of Wyley deemed him mentally competent to stand trial, however, and the grand-jury findings led to indictments of both Wyley and Damian. Both boys were charged with eight counts of second-degree murder—a class-A felony that carries a maximum prison sentence of twenty-five years to life—in the deaths of Robert Gates, Robert Gates, Jr., Jason Gates, and Cheryl Brahm. In addition to the eight murder charges, Damian was indicted for first-degree hindering prosecution, second-degree criminal facilitation, and second-degree conspiracy. Wyley was charged additionally with second-degree criminal possession of a weapon and second-degree conspiracy. Both boys were charged with two different counts of murder for each of the victims, one for acting "with the intent to cause the death of another person" and the other for "evincing a depraved indifference to human life." According to the murder charges, Damian was not at the log house when the murders were committed but "aided and abetted and acted in concert" with Wyley to cause the deaths of the victims. With regard to the conspiracy charge, the indictment further specified that Wyley and Damian planned the murders, knowing such planning was a felony, on "numerous and various days during the months of October, November, and December 1986, at numerous locations within the County of Columbia, State of New York."

On January thirtieth, Wyley and Damian were arraigned at separate hearings. No bail was requested for Wyley in his short hearing before Judge John G. Leaman, although Wilcox, who stated at the time that a request for bail would have been "premature," reserved the right to request it at a later date. Beyond the fact of its alleged prematurity, there were obvious questions concerning into whose custody Wyley could be released. With emotions high in his own community, and with his family stretched to the limits of their loyalty, it seemed that the county jail was, at the moment, the most suitable location for the boy.

As for Damian, who had been released on $50,000 bail since his arraignment on charges of hindering prosecution, he was enrolled as a student in the junior class at Ossining High School. Now, despite the arguments of his attorney, Robert Adams, bail for Damian was set by Judge Warren E. Zittell at $650,000. In arguing against the increased bail, Adams maintained that Damian had known for a week before his indictment that he would be charged with murder and had made no attempt to flee. Furthermore, he argued, the Rossneys, who had accompanied their son to the arraignment, had put up their Ossining home as collateral to raise the $5,000 cash necessary to post the $50,000 bond that had been set at his earlier arraignment on the hindering prosecution charge, and to precipitously raise the bail now would create strain that was not only undue but perhaps impossible. District Attorney Keeler, for his part, requested that bail be set at $1 million because of the "serious nature" of the charges. Zittell remained unmoved by Adams's arguments, and Damian, pleading not guilty, was remanded to the county jail until bail was posted. As he walked off, in the company of guards, the then-delicate-looking young boy, his face unfortunately distinguished by what many saw as a "smirk," carried one of the paperback sci-fi novels that he and Wyley so enjoyed reading.

By the time Damian arrived at the Columbia County Jail, Wyley had been incarcerated there for over a month. In that time, he wrote some letters and personal jottings that the district attorney would later present as self-incriminating evidence.

Two of his outgoing letters from jail were sent to a schoolmate named Cameron Price. Cameron, several years Wyley's junior, was a fellow member of the brass section of the band who would go on to achieve distinction as the first National Merit scholar from Chatham High School in over a decade. Despite Wyley's interest in this boy whose intelligence was obviously as superior as his own, there was no reason to think that Cameron was in any way involved in the conspiracy, nor has any suspicion ever been cast in his direction. Indeed, the relationship of Wyley and Cameron was a decidedly casual one, which never extended to socializing outside of school. The first of the letters that Cameron received was dated December 25, 1986:

> Dear Cameron,
>
> Feliz Navidad! y un alegre ano nuevo. I realize that you probably won't get this until either Saturday or Monday, but I thought that I would express the proper sentiments anyway. I have come to a point in my life where I need to know who my friends really are. I would appreciate knowing one way or the other how you feel about me, so please write a note or a letter and send it to the address I will indicate.
>
> I hope that you did well with the Youth Orchestra. I don't know at this point wether [sic] I will have the chance to watch the performance. The Canadian Brass are playing on Channel 13 Saturday at 8 pm. How did the school concert go, or did it go at all? I heard that it was cancelled for Thursday but I didn't hear that it was rescheduled. I certainly hope that you did well and I regret beyond expression my not being there. The thing I miss most about being in here is, believe it or not, my not being able to play my trumpet. I think that I must be addicted.

If you write to me, please send me your full address since I don't have it.

I regret that most of my life has been destroyed in one ill thought out moment, but I must go on from here. I'm afraid that our friendship will suffer from this, but I certainly hope that this is not the case. I'm afraid that I've lost Damian and Miles, perhaps forever. If you write, please mention something about current events concerning them. I would not want to try and contact either of them now, even if I could. They will probably be advised by their lawyers to help build a case against me, not that this would be necessary, in order to gain favour upon themselves. I can't blame them, but I really do hope that they don't blame me, especially Miles.

If you do see either of them, please tell them that I am sorry, for all of the good that it will do.

I gave my lawyer, Paul Czajka (pronounced Chaika) your name as a close friend of mine; I hope that you *don't* mind. Essentially the only route I have left is the insanity plea, which, considering my intelligence and self-control, will be interesting to prove (support).

I'm afraid that I won't make NYSSMA [the state music competition] this year. I'd appreciate it a great deal if you would play Carnival of Venice for me. Tell Gordy [Gordon Ringer] that I'm sorry. Please play for me. Please write.

Semper Fidelis,
Wyley.

Cameron did not reply, and on January eighth, Wyley sent him a second letter:

Cameron:

I haven't received a reply from you concerning my previous letter. I hope that this was not intentional. If it was, then please seal the envelope which

I have included and mail it. If it isn't intentional, then please write to me.

I read in the Register Star today about the arrests concerning the imitation drug dealings within the school. Any information concerning this? I met with a psychiatrist today who plays with the Ghent concert band. I can't remember what his name is though. Orchestra must be a real blast without me there. Not that it really matters, but Jerad must be getting bored by now. What the hell are they doing with the Student Senate? I really can't imagine Zachary running the meetings.

Have you read the *Dune* series by Frank Herbert? If you haven't then you should. I've read all six of the books. Where is Damian? I really can't imagine him going back to school, but I suppose that he might have to.

Please write. Being in here is understandably boring.

                                                  Wyley.

Again, Cameron didn't reply—instead he alerted his parents, who hired counsel and turned the letters over to the D.A.—but in another few weeks Wyley would have his answer to the cardinal question of Damian's whereabouts, as his friend joined the jailhouse community.

Also figuring significantly in Wyley's new world was a fellow inmate and contemporary by the name of Charles Keith Argyle II. Argyle was incarcerated on a number of charges, including unauthorized use of a motor vehicle and burglary. Argyle and Wyley spent five months in the Columbia County Jail together, from December to May, passing most of that time as cellmates. Argyle allegedly found on the floor of their cell several pages of jottings in Wyley's handwriting, which he turned over to the district attorney and which would become an important building block in the D.A.'s case against Wyley Gates. The jottings read:

*Miles was willing to help kill my father and my brother with Damian for half of what Damian would get. Damian *was willing* [deleted] didn't want him to actually help kill them, so that he would have to pay Miles 15% of what Damian himself would get.

Preguntas y puntas

What's the minimum sentence for 2nd degree homocide [sic]

What type of prison would I most likely be placed in?

If I were to go to an institution, for how long?

Damian has no way of proving that he was not in fact at the scene of the crime.

I lie better than Damian does.

Almost anything Damian could reveal/say about me would hurt him more or almost as much as myself.

Damian was willing to kill for money.

Damian "helped" me only because I was going to pay him. ($3000)

Damian destroyed evidence—the plastic gloves.

Damian *provided me* with the murder weapon and ammunition *knowing* exactly what I was planning on doing with them.

After Miles and Damian both backed out of the contract, Damian talked to me and offered to help me, at a reduced *cost* [deleted] fee. (15%)

At no time did he ever even suggest to me not committing the crime, nor did he ever refuse to be involved in it.

Damian and Miles have been in many more burglaries/incidents than I have.

Damian occasionally uses drugs and drinks alcohol.

Damian thoroughly believes himself superior to almost everyone (super ego).

One or more times when I mentioned that Skip Huvar might be around my father and brother, Damian said that he didn't care, he'd kill him too.

Personal

I abhor senseless violence (contradiction?)
I cannot stand hunting
I cannot understand hunting/killing innocent living creatures.

Self-Hypnosis—theories on relativity

If a person possesses strong inhibitions against doing something, often under hypnosis that person will not do that thing. If, under hypnosis, that person was relieved of said inhibitions by convincing himself that the inhibitions were false or unnecessary, would that person then be willing/ capable of committing that act under hypnosis? while conscious?

In addition to providing the authorities with this extraordinary document, Argyle would later testify to Wyley's authorship of another intercepted piece of writing that appeared in a paperback edition of the Stephen King novel *Cujo*, which Wyley had taken out of the jail's circulating library. According to Argyle, Wyley penned a note to Damian in the book. Dated February 5, 1987 (just a few weeks before Chatham High School announced that Wyley Gates was one of its thirteen regents scholarship winners), the note read:

Howdy, partner! Long time no hablo. Both of my cellmates play chess, cards, UNO, & monopoly. I'm going to try and have my grandmother bring one [Monopoly game] in. Isn't jail a blast? Some of the guards are all right, but some are real assholes, i.e. Tim Davis. Smoking isn't a very good habit. As far

as I see it, the prosecution's case against you is
based upon highly circumstantial evidence & speculation. You must try to convince the jury that you
did not believe that I was serious and that you
severed all *tie* [deleted] connections when you realized the true situation. You might be able to do
this. Honor demands that I do everything possible
to assist you, including perjury. We should meet
minds. Two mentals are better than one. I will try
to convince my lawyer to contact yours.

One additional communication passed between the two boys
when Wyley ripped a page from a jail library copy of George
Bernard Shaw's *Caesar and Cleopatra* and sent it as a missive
to Damian. Circling a portion of dialogue—a speech to the
Sphinx, in which the speaker states, "My way hither was
the way of destiny; for I am he of whose genius you are the
symbol: part brute, part woman, and part god—nothing of
man in me at all"—Wyley jotted down, "When I read that
I say, 'That's how I feel.' "

For Wyley, however, the relative security of having Damian
nearby would soon come to an end. In April, State Supreme
Court Justice George Cobb handed down a ruling that
allowed Joan O'Rourke, a Nyack schoolteacher and family
friend of the Rossneys, to use blue chip stocks in lieu of bail
for the release of Damian from the Columbia County Jail
after a three-month incarceration. (Judge Warren Zittell
had, some weeks earlier, ruled that he was unwilling to
accept stock as surety.) O'Rourke, who said that she believed
Damian should be allowed to pursue his education while he
awaited trial, guaranteed $212,000 worth of stocks, while
Damian's parents guaranteed $100,000 worth of real estate,
represented by their Ossining home. Damian returned to
Ossining, where he resumed his high school education.

But Wyley remained in jail, the issue of bail never
surfacing, and filled his days with reading, letter writing,
and visits from his grandmother and, infrequently, from an
aunt, cousin, or school friend. Efforts by D.A. Gene Keeler

to negotiate an arrangement regarding Wyley's plea got nowhere. "As in any criminal case, day one you start negotiating a plea sentencing arrangement," Keeler said, "if at all possible. From day one, we discussed it with Mr. Wilcox but it never came to fruition. . . . We couldn't come to terms." And so, the county, hitherto perhaps best known for its apple orchards, was now going to be put on the map with the help of the biggest murder trial in its history.

Wyley's legal defense promised to be costly, and the Gates family, who continued to stick by the boy despite some internal rumblings—"I was ready to let him rot in jail; I was very angry," said an aunt—arranged for an auction at Bob Gates's garage on the morning of Saturday, June 20, 1987.

All manner of tools, equipment, and vehicles were listed among the contents of the sale, held outside the metal pole barn that Bob and his friends had erected, some years earlier, as the first installment in the vision they half-jokingly referred to as "Gatesmall." On this bright morning, the air so warmed that the memory of another morning, frigid and foreboding, seemed momentarily remote, the auctioneer began to call out the items of sale. A road grader; a snowplow; a John Deere diesel #729 tractor with power steering; a ten-foot brush hog; a Lincoln 225 Welder; a Dewalt 250 Radial arm saw; an ATEC battery charger; a bench grinder; a two-ton floor jack; an air impact wrench, air tire changer, tire balance, gauges, and weights; a Syhil chain saw; hydraulic jacks; a twenty-ton shop press; a hydraulic ram and controls; a Pittsburgh two-ton chain hoist; a sand blaster; a Rosebud torch; a rivet gun; a brazen torch; a soldering set; an Ingersoll brake-bleeding kit; bolt cutters; drill sets; an Ingersoll chisel set; Lawson fittings; a pneumatic air wrench; an acetylene torch, cart, helmet, gauges, and hoses; an Allied air hammer; miscellaneous tires; miscellaneous glass and chrome; miscellaneous bolts and nuts. These were the machines and the parts of machines for which Robert Gates had a deep reverential love that he had hoped to pass on to his sons; these were the machines and the parts of the machines that Wyley Gates hated entirely.

And then there were the cars—the 1980 LeBaron, the 1974 Ford Gran Torino, the 1969 Plymouth Barracuda, the 1963 Pontiac LeMans. These were the cars Bob and his friends labored over, saving from oblivion, bringing back to life, shining them and oiling them and running them in the stock-car races where he had hoped to see his sons rise to glory. Finally there were the motorbikes. The three Harley-Davidsons. The 1941 Flathead. The 1942 Knuckle-head. The 1985 FXRS. He had ridden those motorbikes on the roads of Columbia County, with Skip Huvar and Don DeLapp, sometimes with Cheryl on the back, the wind blowing through her hair. "He used to buy old Harley-Davidsons and he had an old Triumph in the cellar and he took them all apart and they were all scratched up and banged up and he used to rebuild them, put them all back together, paint 'em up nice, and ride 'em," Don DeLapp recalled of his friend. "But Bob wasn't crazy. He didn't do anything that any other kid didn't do. I mean, he didn't live dangerously or anything. He just liked to have fun."

But now Bob was gone and the Harleys were on the block. Jim Klingler, having worked for Kelgate under Bob, went to the auction and talked with Flagg Herrick, who worked for Hudson Handling in Schenectady and for whom Bob was something of a mentor. "I think Flagg said it best," Jim remembered. "He said, 'You know, you got somebody who works as hard as he did all his life and it just comes down to this.' "

PART

THREE

13

Hudson, the county seat of Columbia County, lays claim to being the first city chartered in the United States after independence was declared. But, despite this significance, the history of Hudson has been one marked by inexorable decline. Founded by Nantucket sea captains as a center for the manufacture of sperm-whale oil, Hudson began to fall on hard times in the middle of the nineteenth century, when the growing use of petroleum eclipsed the whale-oil industry. Today, over two hundred years since it received its charter, Hudson has become a city whose past interfaces rudely with its present. One end of Warren Street, the main thoroughfare of the city, is taken up with cheap convenience shops, moribund department stores, and dingy luncheonettes, while the other end is lined with handsome restored town houses, many of which are listed on the National Registry of Historic Places. It is the restoration of these dwellings that has merited, at least in the hyperbolic language of real-estate agents, advertisement of the area as "SoHo North." This, however, is stretching reality to the breaking point, as the restoration, along with the influx of several stylish new stores and restaurants, has actually made little impact thus far on the essentially forlorn nature of the street. Traditionally, the poor of Columbia County have congregated in three locations: the main street of Valatie; Philmont, now celebrated as the birthplace of Ollie North; and Warren Street. And, despite the coming of antique stores peddling pricey wicker and boutiques redolent of Crabtree & Evelyn, the poor still linger here in doorways and vestibules or languidly push overpopulated baby carriages up and down the avenue. The doorways of boarded-up taverns like The Tarnished Lady still offer shelter to winos, and the grocery stores' stock in trade remains Dinty Moore stew and Vienna sausages rather than radicchio or arugula or shiitake mushrooms.

The one part of town that rises above this shabbiness and obvious decline is the courthouse square, where many of the Warren Street poor will eventually make their way, summoned there by family court. The courthouse itself is appropriately imposing, its columns topped by acanthus leaves, its oxidized copper dome overhanging crooning colonies of pigeons. On the opposite side of the square is a red brick Federalist post office, and bordering the square on its other two sides are splendid Victorian brownstones that largely house Hudson's law firms. A rustic wooden gazebo sits, cordoned off, in one green quadrant of the square. On it a plaque celebrates such Century Club donors as DinoSaw and Daisy Hill Poultry, Dunkin Donuts and Judge and Mrs. Warren Zittell, the judge who would eventually preside over the trial of Damian Rossney. Another sign, bowing to the tenor of the city as it is today, declares a curfew in the square between 9:00 P.M. and 8:00 A.M.

Generally, the square is quiet and uncongested, but on the morning of July 20, 1987, it was crowded with prospective jurors who had arrived in response to the summons that had gone out to four hundred of Columbia County's citizens. On this stiflingly humid day, with the temperature heading into the nineties and only a feeble promise of rain, the women, dressed in flowered shifts and pastel pantsuits, and the men, in sleeveless white shirts or, in the event they'd come over from their jobs as electricians or roadmen or tree surgeons, green twill work suits, headed into the courtroom.

The air was heavy in this room packed with bodies and buzzing with anticipation, but fortunately the ceiling was high and the walls were painted a light cool chartreuse, just a shade off "government green." An enormous mural on the rear wall depicting a colonial judge arriving at the old courthouse in Claverack was a pleasant escape for the imagination. Standing floor fans whirred noisily as the prospective jurors chatted with each other. Most everyone knew someone—it is a small county. The smallness of the county, in fact, was on the minds of many, particularly Charles Wilcox, Wyley's attorney, who had still not ruled out making a motion for a change of venue.

Sixteen of Columbia County's citizens were to be selected for a jury panel—twelve jurors and four alternates. For their service, they would be paid six dollars a day. The prospective jurors were getting their first look this morning at the attorneys and their assistants. Charles Wilcox, the defense attorney, forty, tall, dark-haired, tinted aviator glasses, dressed for success, cadet posture, aloof. Gene Keeler, the district attorney, thirty-seven, heavyset, ginger-haired, ambling, accessible. Joan Yowe, Wilcox's assistant, tiny, close-cropped blond hair, chicly gamine in peasant blouse and skirt. Assistant District Attorney Nancy Snyder, early thirties, tall, massed curly dark hair, severely tailored. The commissioner of jurors announced that the judge would be hearing excuses today and, moments later, Judge John G. Leaman entered the courtroom. Leaman, in his early forties, had fine features and a shock of thick reddish-brown hair that made him look almost Kennedyesque, an impression mitigated only by a slight tendency toward portliness. Leaman had grown up in New York City, but his mother's family lived in Columbia County and as a result of that family connection he had spent every summer of his life in Canaan. A graduate of Columbia University Law School, class of 1972, he had served a one-year clerkship with the appeals court in Albany. He then became associated with the Manhattan law firm of Chadwick and Park and, in 1975,

became a full-time resident of Columbia County, first practicing with the Conner law firm in Hudson and then, in
1977, establishing his own practice. He continued in his
private practice until he assumed, on January 1, 1984, his
elected position as county judge with responsibilities in
criminal, family, and surrogate courts.

Judge Leaman alerted the prospective jurors that the
trial could take between four and six weeks. He further
warned them from reflecting on the matter in such a way
that they might have any fixed, formed views that would
prevent them from being open to hearing evidence. The
jurors, he reminded them, are no more and no less than
the judgers of the facts of the case, and they must be
impartial. He further cautioned them against coming into
contact with any media accounts of the events, although he
acknowledged that many of them had probably already had
exposure. "We're not going to find people who have been
hibernating or are cave dwellers," he said. "People are going
to have heard things. What we have to find are people who
will make a decision based on the evidence presented in this
courtroom." With that, a mass oath was administered to the
prospective jurors. The trial process had begun.

For District Attorney Eugene Keeler, the trial was an event
that loomed so large it threatened to overwhelm him and
his staff. Technically, he was a part-time D.A. with a part-
time staff. The part-time D.A. had traditionally been a
common figure in small rural counties, but, according to
Keeler, "that's all going by the boards." Indeed, in Columbia
County, where Keeler's term expired on December 31,
1987, he was succeeded by a full-time district attorney, Paul
Czajka.

Born and raised in the county, which had been home
to five generations of Keelers, a big Irish political family
such as one might encounter in the pages of an Edwin
O'Connor novel, Keeler "played out in front of the courthouse all my life." Graduating from Hudson High School,
he went on to get his bachelor's degree in history from St.
Lawrence University in 1972 and then turned to the field

The Robert Gates log house, Maple Drive, East Chatham
(scene of the murders).

ABOVE: The Vivian Gates residence, Maple Drive, East Chatham. BELOW: Flag at half-mast over the Gates residence.

Vivian Gates *(foreground)* leaving the funeral of her son and grandsons. *ROBERT RAGAINI*

Miles McDonald, being escorted to the courtroom in the trial of Wyley Gates. *ROBERT RAGAINI*

Wyley at his murder trial. THE INDEPENDENT/*DIANE BOICE YORCK*

ABOVE: John Bailey holding the Walther automatic pistol at the Rossney trial. *ROBERT RAGAINI*

OPPOSITE: Wyley Gates leaving the Columbia County Jail enroute to Elmira Correctional Facility. *ROBERT RAGAINI*

Damian Rossney, after his conviction on conspiracy. At left, Undersheriff James Bertram. *ROBERT RAGAINI*

of social work, receiving his master's in science and social work from the University of Tennessee School of Social Work in 1976. "I'm a frustrated priest from way back," Keeler said, explaining what led him to social work. "For many years I was going to go to the seminary but a serious service orientation with my Irish-Catholic Democratic background is what developed my personality. I was raised to think that public service was one of the highest goods. So social work and democratic politics with that human-service orientation were all tied up together."

Upon his graduation from social-work school, in search of something interdisciplinary and functional, he turned to law school and graduated from Memphis State University School of Law in 1978. While awaiting the results of the New York State bar examination, he worked for six months as a social worker at Wilton Development Center, a facility in Saratoga County, New York, for the mentally retarded and developmentally disabled. Upon passing the bar, he returned to Columbia County, dividing his time between a private practice and the Columbia County chapter of the New York State Association for Retarded Children, for which he served as a client advocate.

Keeler ran for the office of district attorney in 1983, the same year that Judge Leaman campaigned for his position. They were the first countywide Democrats elected in almost twenty years in Columbia County and among the handful of Democrats elected to those offices in the past century. By the time the Gates trial rolled around, Keeler, who had once enjoyed a stint as a semipro football player and had formerly tipped the scales at 340 pounds, had had four turbulent years as D.A. that featured a history of friction with the Republican-controlled board of supervisors and a public argument with a police chief whom he labeled a "thug." He also saw, during the course of his tenure as D.A., a significant increase in the amount of violent crime in his county. "We've had in the last four years maybe six, seven murders," Keeler said, not counting criminally negligent homicides in that figure. "The amount of work it takes for one homicide case is so ungodly that it's mind-boggling. Judge Conners, who was the D.A. prior to us in 1963, the last Democrat countywide person elected, told me one day that they only had one murder his whole term. We're light-years away from that today."

Of those homicides perpetrated during Keeler's tenure as D.A., the only case that came to trial was the one that involved Wyley Gates. "The other ones either pled guilty and we had one fellow who hung himself in the jail before we indicted him," Keeler explained. The case of *The People of New York* v. *Wyley Gates* would be the first criminal case Keeler had brought before a jury in approximately two years. It would be a difficult undertaking for the D.A.'s modest operation. Keeler himself was paid only $26,500 a year for the part-time position and supplemented this income through his own private practice, his social-work activities, and a sideline insurance business. He publicly declared that "this is not a career position. It's not like Albany or Rensselaer County, where you have full-time assistants and full-time investigators. I'm concerned about putting my kids through college in a few years." In fact, Keeler felt the need to request the appointment of special assistant counsel to help with the Gates and Rossney trials, citing county law, which states that, with written approval of the county judge, the district attorney can appoint an assistant counsel for a capital crime which presents unusual difficulty. The request was denied, even though Keeler stated that he had been assured of financial backing from the county finance and legal committees if the court was to grant his request.

"The bottom line was that Mr. Keeler was concerned that in preparing for this case and prosecuting it, the business of the district attorney's office in other courts might suffer because he and an assistant would be busy in this court," explained Judge Leaman in a later interview. But Leaman further noted that the section that Keeler had put forward dealt with a situation where a district attorney felt unequal to the task of prosecuting a specific case and therefore wished to have trial counsel. Leaman recalled that he specifically asked Keeler if he felt that he was able to handle the case and Keeler "unequivocally stated on various occasions that he was absolutely equal to the task and that was not the reason why he was going under that section." The fact that Keeler was a part-time D.A. did not mean that he could request additional assistants, said Leaman, because "part-time," as it is used in reference to the district attorney, means only that he or she, as a public official, may have a private practice while in office. And so, with the appeal for assistance turned down, Keeler and his staff started working overtime to get the case together. The following spring, some six months after the conclusion of the Gates trial, Keeler would confess that prosecuting the Gates trial had impeded his processing of other Columbia County cases. "I had to devote one hundred percent of my time," he said. "It was difficult to keep tabs on what was going on in the office."

One of the first decisions that had to be made in this case was whether Wyley and Damian should be tried together or separately. It was the D.A.'s opinion that they had to be tried separately, and it was his conviction that if he attempted to try the two boys together, their attorneys would call for a severance, meaning separate trials. "I figured if they were together, either one of them would have made a motion for a severance," said Keeler. "I mean, they would have been crazy not to. Wilcox would have been asking for a motion for severance saying that Damian was the actual shooter and Damian's attorney would have been making a motion for severance." Keeler also believed that in pursuing separate trials for the two boys, there was more of a chance that Damian would help the state's case against Wyley. "I was trying to get Rossney to throw in Wyley," said Keeler, explaining his strategy. "The thing I was betting on was I was trying to turn Rossney against Wyley, which never really happened, so that the indictment would enter into a plea bargain or something." Keeler, in fact, was not looking forward to the massive trial that awaited him, but defense attorney Wilcox continued to evince no interest in plea bargaining for his client.

The grand jury had handed down separate indictments

for the two boys, which necessitated separate trials so long as the D.A. did not move for a joinder, or union, of the indictments, which he chose not to do. One person who was surprised by the decision not to try the two boys together was, in fact, Wyley's attorney, whose initial impression was that they would be tried together in a single indictment. As a former D.A. himself, Wilcox felt that the only real obstacle against such a joint trial was the possibility that the statement Wyley allegedly gave at Poughkeepsie might have incriminated a co-defendant. If this was the case, then the two boys could not be tried together because Wyley's statement would be judged inadmissible on the grounds that an admission by Wyley of someone else's guilt would constitute hearsay in regard to a co-defendant or co-conspirator. Wilcox pointed out, however, that such was not the case with the statement that Wyley allegedly made at Poughkeepsie. "As you recall from his statement, he was very protective of anybody else," said Wilcox. "Given the nature of his statement, I don't think it would have required a severance of any other possible defendant." Indeed, Wilcox stated that he does not believe he would have made a motion for severance, feeling that it might well have been to his advantage to have the boys tried together. He did admit, however, that if he had been Damian's lawyer, he would have moved for severance because it would have served his client to have Wyley tried first, in terms of getting a preview of police theory as to who had committed the crime. As Damian's lawyer, he would also have pushed for severance to forestall any "railroad mentality" on the part of the jury—not in terms of "railroading" someone, he explained, but in case the jury felt "here goes Wyley, let's put this guy on the train too, because we've got them both here."

Whether the motion for severance would have been granted had Damian's attorney made it is highly questionable in Wilcox's mind. "In the interest of economy, probably most judges, unless you've got a very considerate, thinking judge who's solely and exclusively interested in ultimately fair trials . . . would have said no," Wilcox remarked.

One can only speculate how a joint trial would have

affected the outcome. "There might have been a little bit more of a shakedown of evidence," said Wilcox, "but it would have been interesting to see what Damian Rossney did in terms of defense. Whether or not he decided to take the stand and, if he did, it would have been interesting to see what he would have done in terms of defending himself and what he had to say about Wyley to save his skin."

A second area where the district attorney had to make a crucial decision was regarding the theory of the actual commission of the crime. From the beginning, the D.A. set out to prove that Wyley was the shooter. "The whole theory against Wyley was the fact that he was the shooter," Keeler later explained. "We didn't have any evidence to show that anybody else but Wyley was the shooter." Single-mindedly pursuing this theory, Keeler never put forth an alternate theory of Wyley acting "in concert," meaning together with other parties. Keeler issued a statement in his bill of particulars that he would not be relying on Section 20 of the Penal Law of New York State, the section which essentially states that a person who has solicited, requested, commanded, importuned, or intentionally aided in committing an offense is just as criminally liable as the person who committed the offense.

Why the district attorney did not choose to plead in the alternative was a mystery to defense attorney Wilcox. "My approach to the whole thing would be to plead it both ways. You have nothing to lose. He could have pled in the alternative," said Wilcox of the D.A. "He could have pled him as a principal or [under] Section 20." Wilcox speculated that the reason the D.A. did not do so was because of his conviction as to the merits of his case. "I think he felt that his case was so strong that he was not going to attempt to possibly dilute his approach by saying, 'Oh, maybe he was just an aide or abettor,'" said Wilcox. Keeler, in fact, did feel that pleading an alternative under Section 20 would dilute his case. "Then who's the principal? Who's actually the shooter? Wyley? Damian? Somebody else?" he demanded at a later point. "I had to come up with a theory. I had to have a theory to present to the jury. And over and over again, we thought about this, and the only theory we had was that Wyley was the shooter. I mean, we didn't have any evidence to show that anybody else was the shooter."

Wilcox recognized that there was significant evidence in the case that would endanger his client in the event that a plea of acting "in concert" was entered. Consequently, he was vigilant in doing what he could to keep Section 20 out of the case altogether. "Strategically we moved right away to pin the district attorney down in terms of his reliance on such a point, and he issued a statement in his bill of particulars and discovery responses that the prosecution was not relying on Section Twenty," Wilcox recalled. "Having pinned him down on that, we didn't give him any opportunity to rethink it or reconsider it or have it pop up in his recollection that it might be advantageous to do it otherwise." Wilcox made sure to be not only vigilant but expeditious. "One of the reasons I wanted to go to trial very quickly," he explained, "was the fact that I had this strategic thing tucked away and I wanted to take advantage of it before it was found out or it was discovered by someone who'd say, 'Let's amend our papers and replead.' And during the trial, when it got down to the point of the trial going in and the pleadings being firm, I always did have the feeling that there would be a last-minute motion to amend." As it turned out, however, there never was, even though the key piece of evidence that the D.A. had to work with, which was Wyley's alleged confession in Poughkeepsie, was clearly vulnerable to attack.

Before the trial itself there was a protracted series of suppression hearings. Typically, in a suppression hearing, the defense attempts to have certain evidence suppressed on grounds it was obtained illegally. The judge ultimately decides which evidence will be brought to court. Among the most common subjects discussed in a suppression hearing are confessions, and the confession of Wyley Gates, allegedly proffered while Wyley was in the company of polygraph examiner Thomas Salmon, promised to be a particularly thorny problem.

Keeler felt that the confession was unblemished. "The positive argument for the confession is that the lawyer, Hogle, Salmon, and Wyley Gates were in one room together after full knowledge and full consent on their part to take the polygraph exam. They knew what the subject of inquiry was going to be, about the homicide deaths. . . . To me, that's waiver of right of counsel in presence of counsel. Counsel was there in that room and I think that's all you needed. To ask for more than that is, I think, being really restrictive, overly restrictive. I mean, counsel was there, client was there, Salmon was there—all in one room. They talked about what they were going to do. Polygrapher said, 'I'm going to ask you about these deaths. You said you had nothing to do with it.' And the lawyer stayed in there. They walked out and went in and sat down. I just don't see what more you need."

To Wilcox, however, the legitimacy of the alleged confession was very much in question. "I think what happened was when Wyley agreed to take the polygraph and was coming down [to Poughkeepsie], that was the perfect scenario for the police," he speculated. "If Wyley had said no polygraph, it might have been the best thing that could have happened to the police because they would have had to go out and build a case without his statement, which they should have been doing anyway. Once he agreed to take the polygraph, then the case slowed down immeasurably, because they felt, 'Well, Tommy [Investigator Salmon] always comes through.' "

The perfect scenario, in Wilcox's imagining of the night's events, took a wrong turn when attorney Richard Hogle entered the picture. "I think they would immediately see this as a big problem," said Wilcox. " 'What the hell are we going to do now? There's no way this attorney is going to let the kid talk to us. This is a worthless trip.' " But it was Wilcox's suspicion that Salmon, who had been through this sort of thing many times before, probably urged them to come down anyway, feeling that as long as they had a confession, even if it was in violation of the suspect's constitutional rights, it could, conceivably, be of some potential use. For, even though the law maintains that a statement taken in violation of a person's constitutional rights cannot be offered in evidence against that individual, there are certain limited ways in which that confession can still be of use. Principally, if the person takes the stand and testifies that he or she is innocent, under certain limited circumstances the statement can then be used to impeach the defendant. "So the thinking might have been 'Go for it anyway,'" Wilcox speculated. "'If he takes the stand, maybe we can get it into cross-examination.' You've got nothing to lose. The most the judge can do is suppress the statement. . . . They might even get a judge who isn't going to suppress it. Which they got."

The confession survived the suppression hearings, and Wilcox had his own theories as to why this was so. "The only real evidence they had as to the actual murders was this alleged oral statement by Wyley Gates," said Wilcox. "And I think the judge saw immediately that this statement was the focal point of the prosecution's entire case and I think, frankly, that's one of the reasons the judge didn't suppress it." Bluntly put, Wilcox ascribed the judge's admission of the confession to political motives. "I think the judge felt—he being an elected official and possibly running for [state] supreme court—he was not going to take it upon himself to knock it out, whether it was constitutionally required or not," said Wilcox. "And this is a cynicism you develop about the system after you see it work for a while; you see why people do things they do and the hell with the law. He wasn't going to take it upon himself to go out and suppress this statement which obviously, in my opinion, had definite, definite problems, because he couldn't get a sufficient forum in the media to get to the people of his county that he had to do this because there was a constitutional problem . . . he felt that it would be misconstrued and he wouldn't be able to explain that well enough to the public and then they would hate him for having done that."

Judge Leaman, in a later interview, disavowed this interpretation entirely. "This is the first I've heard it ever said that I would make a so-called political decision," he said. "The reality is that in order for an alleged commission or confession to be suppressed there has to be an application on the part of the defendant to have it suppressed. And that then triggers what is known as a suppression hearing." The procedures of a suppression hearing, he explained, are specified by statute and essentially it is the burden of a defendant to prove that the alleged confession should be suppressed. The initial burden at a suppression hearing is on the prosecution to set forth what is called a *prima facie* case for admissibility. Once the prosecution has done that, the burden shifts to the defendant to prove by clear and convincing evidence that there are grounds to suppress the alleged confession. And that burden was never discharged, Judge Leaman held, by the defendant at the suppression hearing, so, as a matter of law, he had to uphold the admissibility of the alleged confession. "It is always a matter of Monday morning quarterbacking," said Judge Leaman of the defendant's—and, by extension, Wilcox's—failure to discharge that responsibility. But he acknowledged, at the same time, that this "failure" may in fact have been a tactic. "Who can say—who can second-guess—what a defense lawyer has in mind?" he wondered.

The aspect of the Poughkeepsie episode that would eventually pose the biggest problem for the jury—the alleged barring of Hogle from accompanying Wyley to the polygraph examination area—was, in fact, presented at the suppression hearing, but was not presented in a way sufficient, in the judge's opinion, to warrant holding the confession inadmissible. "There were no words spoken, no statements by any law-enforcement officers that the lawyer could not go into the room with Wyley Gates," said Judge Leaman, "and it strained credulity for me to think that any lawyer would be deterred by a supposed gesture—a hand going up. At the very least, it seems to me, a lawyer would say, 'Do you mean to say I can't go in with you?' And elicit an answer. And if the answer was, 'That's what I mean, counsellor,' than the lawyer would say, 'Then my client will not go with you.'"

■   ■   ■

On August 3—hot, hazy, and humid at daybreak—the
process known as *voir dire*, or the interviewing of prospective
jurors by the attorneys, began. The selection of twelve men
and women to compose the jury in the case of Wyley Gates
would prove an arduous process, and, before such a jury
was empaneled, the pool would be extended to include a
brother of Cheryl Brahm and Vivian Gates herself.

Coming into the courtroom that first day of *voir dire*,
the prospective jurors saw three women seated in a box on
the other side of a wrought-iron gate that served as the line
of demarcation between spectators and principals. The three
women were Vivian Gates, her thick gray hair close-cropped,
looking tired but well groomed in a blue moiré-patterned
dress; her sister Jackie Simoneaux, a social worker with a
private practice, in from California; and a woman whose
appearance seemed strangely disharmonious with that of
the two older women. Kristi Gates, also in from California,
looked considerably older than her years. Her long, blond,
tousled hair suggested a California golden girl, but the face
beneath the hair was puffy and her dress, a low-cut, black-
and-white zebra print, was, by all accounts, a notably poor
choice for the mother of a defendant in a murder trial. A
few friendly smiles passed between Vivian and Kristi, leading
one to wonder what they could possibly have had to smile
about, and then, a bit later, the smiles blossomed into quiet
laughter that one had to assume was an expression of
giddiness brought on either by the momentousness and
solemnity of the occasion or by their anticipation as they
awaited this son and grandson who must always have been
something of a stranger to them.

They didn't have to wait long. Moments later, Wyley
was ushered into the room, bringing it to a momentary
silence. He looked very different from the pictures that had
been printed during the period of his arrest and arraignment. Jail had not been kind to his appearance—he had the
proverbial jailhouse pallor and a bad haircut that made his
head look, from the back at least, Howdy Doodyish. Which
is not to imply that there was anything comic or ingenuous
about him as he sat down at the defendant's table. Indeed,

with his rigid posture, his lack of eye contact with any other human being, and his look of stern asceticism, he projected an almost clammy presence. And yet, from another angle, there was a kind of unimpeachable dignity to him and, for some, a touching fragility. The two women guards who escorted him to his place seemed sympathetic toward him, almost maternal. And a number of women in the room, including, it later turned out, some of the jurors, were inclined to regard his rigidity as a deerlike stance of fear and the lack of color in his complexion as a sign of vulnerability rather than bloodlessness.

To the prospective jurors now seated in the jury box, the judge went down the line addressing questions: Married? Single? Place of work? Has anyone ever had a bad experience with the criminal court system? A unanimous no greeted the last question, a reminder that this was Columbia County, where things have remained perhaps more innocent than in other parts of the world. The judge asked if anyone had seen or read media accounts of the crime and all hands went up, another reminder that this was a small county faced with a large crime.

The judge read the indictment and then went down the line again to field any specific problems people felt they had. One woman said that she had a sister who was "close" to Sheriff Proper and that she had heard described how the sheriff had looked after he had seen the crime scene. Another woman haltingly confessed that she could not stop thinking about "the tragedy of the child," referring to little Jason. Still another woman said that she was a friend of Vivian Gates's and that she felt their friendship would affect her impartiality. An elementary school teacher on the panel had taught both Wyley and Bobby, Jr., in her classes. One of the men had worked with one of Cheryl Brahm's brothers. One of the men had had business dealings with Bob Gates. The smallness of the county became apparent at almost every turn.

When the D.A. rose to face the panel, he made a point of coming across warm and folksy. Anybody with a hearing problem? he asked. Anyone with a connection to the D.A.'s office, the Columbia County chapter of the New York State Association for Retarded Children, or the Francis Keeler Insurance Agency? No hands went up, and so Keeler moved on to questions about individual experiences with crime. One woman had had some jewelry stolen; another woman's parents had been burglarized. But no muggings, no assaults, no rapes.

When Keeler concluded, Defense Attorney Wilcox rose, crisp and purposeful. In preparing for this moment, he had not relied on what is known as "jury science"—"the jury selection was really an experience in instinct between me and Joan," he later admitted—but he seemed to be quite clear about who it was he wanted. He had in mind jurors who were "constitutional-minded," jurors who were on the younger or older end of the spectrum, and particularly those who had had "a rough dose somewhere in their life and who had dealt with the system, so that they could see the system in some respects is not all the time honest and can be perverted." The prototype of the juror he was ideally seeking, he later explained, was "a female juror with teenage children and preferably one whose children had had trouble with the law." Before the jury selection was over, just such a woman would be found and would become, in the opinion of many, a bellwether of the jury. But there were many prospects to be interviewed before such a "constitutional-minded" juror could be found.

Wilcox started with the simple questions: Did anyone know the Groudas family? Did anyone have any friends, neighbors, or associates in the law-enforcement area? Staring each potential juror in the eye, he asked them if they thought that they possessed the ability to be unswayed by others in the jury room. He also asked them if they could accept the notion that the police can be wrong. Moving on to the subject of Wyley's alleged confession, he asked them if they accepted the proposition that certain statements made under certain conditions might not be reliable. With the insanity defense in mind, he asked them if they believed that a person could suffer from mental disease without manifesting any sort of overt symptoms. Then he canvassed the group to see how many hunted—the overwhelming majority did—and he asked if anyone had bumper stickers on their cars, obviously looking for the NRA types. In conclusion, he posed one more question: "If you were sitting where Wyley Gates is sitting, would you want yourself as a juror?" Four people raised their hands to answer in the negative.

Two men were chosen the first day: Frederick Stonner, a research scientist for Sterling Labs in Rensselaer, and Robert Jensen, a service manager for 3M Corporation. No progress was made on the similarly sweltering second day, but, by the following day, the weather had cooled off considerably and a third juror, Walter Bikowitz, a state employee, was selected. The fourth day saw two young women chosen. One, Patricia O'Neill, a twenty-three-year-old mother, hailed from Niverville, home of the Brahms, and knew them slightly. The other juror who was picked, Debbie Seeley, also a young mother, worked for the New York State Thruway and also came from Niverville. She had intersected with several of the potential witnesses in the case. In addition to having known Cheryl from around town, she was also a first cousin by marriage to Investigator William Vick, who had been responsible for securing evidence from the crime scene, and she "thought" she had dated Investigator John Cozzolino some years ago. A sixth juror, Robert Lewis, middle-aged, burly, employed by the State Department of Transportation, was chosen as well.

Day five yielded Ruth Gregory, a working mother of three; Helen Janes, a mother who worked in Niverville and who also knew some of the Brahms; and Bradley Kelsey, who worked for IBM, was the father of three children, and who confessed that he felt he had once been dealt with unfairly in a traffic dispute.

The following day provided no new jurors, leading into day seven. The sun was out again after some wet and gloomy weather, and Wyley was in summer colors, a pink striped shirt and khaki slacks. He could be seen chatting with Joan Yowe, sloughing off some of the rigidity of posture that had made him appear an object in the room, Exhibit A. Two jurors were selected. One, Arthur Wade, was retired from hospital work and had a son who was a correctional officer at Sing Sing. The other was Mary Meyer, a bright and articulate woman in her forties, married to a farmer and retired from a successful beauty salon operation that she had started. She had known Cheryl Brahm as a customer— although she "never personally worked on her." In fact, the Brahm family—maintaining that on a number of occasions Meyer and her husband had come into contact with Cheryl and other Brahm family members and that, in fact, Meyer had attended Cheryl's wedding—alerted Keeler to this ac- quaintanceship. Meyer, however, claimed that she had no recollection of having been to Cheryl's wedding and that the only remote memory she had of the event was that she may have run over to see how Cheryl's hairdo, styled in her salon, had turned out. During the *voir dire*, Meyer excused herself from the jury box to have a private conversation at the bench, where she informed the judge and attorneys that she had had an involvement with the Bureau of Criminal Investigations resulting from a legal problem involving a member of her family. It was decided that this involvement would not compromise her ability to fairly weigh the evi- dence in the case, and so she was empaneled. In fact, it was Mary Meyer who so closely fit the prototype of the desired juror that Wilcox had sought—"a female juror with teenage children and preferably one whose children had had trouble with the law."

The next few days yielded no selections, but Friday, August 14, saw the process come to its conclusion. The last member chosen for the panel was Patricia Overly from Canaan, who lived closest of all the jurors to the crime scene. Mrs. Overly, the mother of grown children, was a bookkeeper and business manager for *The Echo*, the local Canaan newspaper. The judge cautioned the jury against any internal discussion and any contact with the media, and he set the starting date of the trial for the coming Monday at 10:00 A.M.

The languor of the last ten days, sultry and slow-moving, swiftly gave way to a stark sense of mission and inevitability. Wyley, so intent on not exhibiting emotion, let down his guard momentarily as his hand went nervously to touch his eyeglasses. Joan Yowe, who had worked so hard to develop a physical contact with this unapproachable boy, took Wyley's hand in her own, but his expression remained remote as he lingered in the private world of his secret thoughts. There was much to think about. The boy who had harbored for so long the dream of acquiring a place in history now had his best shot. An event of significant local history—the trial of Wyley Gates—was about to begin.

14

The weather continued to be hot on Monday, August seventeenth—hot enough for there to be ladies with fans in the spectator section of the courtroom. Something about ladies with fans and men with baseball caps in a hot dusty courtroom brought to mind the very essence of small-town justice. The mood of the courtroom was lively, almost convivial. Some people had even taken the morning off from work to have a look at the closest thing to notoriety this county had ever experienced.

As she sat on the other side of the gate that separated the spectators from the principals, Vivian Gates looked no different from any of the neat matrons in the audience. A colleague from her teaching days came over, teary-eyed, to kiss her and wish her luck. She accepted the good wishes and then turned to whisper something to her sister Jackie, her constant companion, who would be gone tomorrow on a trip to New Orleans in celebration of their mother's ninetieth birthday. It was a watershed event that Vivian had been looking forward to, but she would have to forgo attending the festivities. Right now, and for weeks to come, Vivian Gates had a watershed event all her own.

At 11:00 A.M., her grandson was ushered into the courtroom. In his white shirt, red striped tie, and dark blue slacks, Wyley could have been mistaken for any eighteen-year-old on his way to an interview for college or a summer job. But clearly, as the court artist sketched his impassive face and lank torso, he wasn't anything of the sort.

Moments later, the judge entered. As promised, he had ordered the transcript of the suppression hearings made public upon the opening of the trial, and now it could be seen that nearly all of Charles Wilcox's efforts to suppress material had been unsuccessful. The confession—the state's primary piece of evidence—had been admitted, as well as evidence furnished by Charles Argyle, Wyley's cellmate. Wilcox had attempted to show that Argyle had obtained the information, which was potentially incriminating to Wyley, while acting as an agent for the police, but Judge Leaman had not supported that theory. Other items that Wilcox had unsuccessfully tried to suppress were the letters written by Wyley to schoolmate Cameron Price, which could be interpreted as being self-incriminating; a video of Wyley at the time of his admission to jail; a picture of the thumb and fingers of Wyley's hand and of the Band-Aid he was wearing; a pair of seized gloves; the five-page statement written by Wyley while he was at his grandmother's house on the night of December thirteenth; and evidence of a bank transfer from Wyley's account in the sum of $200, given by Wyley to Chuck Argyle ostensibly as a loan but perhaps, as the D.A. hoped to suggest, as hush money to keep his talkative cellmate quiet. With all of this evidence remaining unsuppressed, the D.A. was going into the trial with about as much ammunition as he could have hoped for.

Before hearing opening remarks from the attorneys, Judge Leaman reiterated to the jury the need for a basic presumption of innocence. "No defendant has to prove that he is innocent in any criminal trial," he reminded them. "Rather, it is the burden of the prosecution to establish guilt of a particular crime and every element thereof by proof

beyond a reasonable doubt." With that, District Attorney
Eugene Keeler rose and, in a manner that managed to be
at once amiable and somber, restrained but hortatory, he
began to put forth his case.

"Back in October and November of 1986," Keeler said,
"Mr. Gates started thinking of hatred, murder, and money,
and back in October, November 1986, Mr. Gates started
talking to his friends." Wyley, who, Keeler said, had an
extreme hatred for his father, his brother, and Cheryl,
collaborated on a plan with Damian to "off" Bob Gates, a
plan in which he also attempted to enlist the help of Miles
McDonald. What was the motivation? For Wyley, it was
sheer hatred but also a desire for money. For Damian, the
motivation was the excitement of the act itself along with
the promise of monetary compensation.

Keeler presented to the jury an account of the night of
December thirteenth, and promised testimony from Miles
McDonald regarding the burglary of the log house and the
theft of the murder weapon; from John Bailey, regarding
the target practice during which Wyley fired the Walther
pistol, the eventual murder weapon; and from Chuck Argyle, Wyley's cellmate, to whom Wyley had allegedly confessed not only his hatred of his family but the fact that
he had shot each and every one of them. "Listen well to the
evidence and listen well to what is being testified to in the
chair," Keeler exhorted the jury. "It is important that you
listen very carefully and at the end of the trial you are going
to go back and deliberate, and it is important for you to
make sure that you have the evidence registered in your
mind because at the end of the trial I'm going to ask you
to convict Mr. Gates."

Now it was defense attorney Wilcox's turn to face the
jury, and when he spoke to them, it was in quiet, almost
confidential tones. "When all is said and done," he assured
them, "you will have many and deep reasonable doubts
about who shot Robert Gates, Sr., Robert Gates, Jr., Jason
Gates, and Cheryl Brahm. You might have a good idea but
that's as far as it will go. You won't be able to go any further
than that, and that good idea, I submit, will not be Wyley

Gates." Wilcox pointed to the insanity defense that he intended to argue. "He couldn't have done it," Wilcox asserted, "despite a psychotic and insane effort to admit it, and to try to convince everyone with statements and alleged writings of his own that he did do it. . . . Whatever part he played, whether it was talk only, discussions only, or otherwise, was the product of a sick and diseased mind or an extreme emotional disturbance."

As Wyley sat there—motionless, seemingly emotionless—Wilcox suggested that the boys with whom Wyley surrounded himself, his alleged friends, played viciously on Wyley's mind with full knowledge of what they were doing and what they were up to. Whatever this boy did, claimed Wilcox, was a result of an extreme mental or emotional disturbance, nourished, promoted, and prompted by none other than those who he thought, in his deluded mind, were his friends.

"You will feel very right, I submit to you, when it's all done," Wilcox told the jury, "in performing your duty of coming into this courtroom with a verdict of other than guilty, and you will continue to feel very right in performing your duty as you await, I submit to you, thereafter the hopeful and eventual prosecution of the murderer."

The prosecution's first witness was Officer James Sweet, deputy sheriff and communications officer for the Columbia County Sheriff's Department, who had taken the initial call from Vivian Gates on the night of December thirteenth. Officer Sweet testified that he received a phone call at 10:56 P.M. from Vivian Gates, who said there had been a shooting at the home of her son Robert Gates, who lived down the road from her, and that her grandson was the one who had discovered, in Sweet's words, "the problem at the residence." Sweet asked to speak directly with Wyley, who stated that he had arrived at the residence at "approximately 10:42 P.M." and found all four dead, and had then gone to his grandmother's, arriving there at "approximately 10:45 P.M." Sweet added that Wyley had been "coherent" in his speech.

Under cross-examination, Officer Sweet was asked

whether he had received a phone call from a resident of
Maple Drive by the name of Alan Gelb, concerning information Gelb was offering to the authorities. Sweet replied
that that information would have been given to the officer
whose shift came after his.

Hearing my name come up during the cross-examination of the first witness in the murder trial about which I
was writing reinforced, for me, the strange multilayering of
my involvement with this story. I knew immediately that my
name had come up in connection with the report I had filed
with the police on the morning after the murders, concerning a suspicious pickup truck I had seen on the road the
previous morning. Now, as Wilcox questioned Officer Sweet
about my call, I wondered whether he had further information regarding the suspicious pickup truck or whether,
in fact, my call to the police would serve as a kind of red
herring for Wyley's defense.

In any event, hearing my name actually entered into
the proceedings was a jarring moment. I realized that there
were, and would continue to be, many points of juncture
between me and Wyley and his family and his story. There
was that first glancing acquaintanceship, when we asked
Wyley to mow our lawn and as we thought about asking
him to baby-sit for us. There was the call I had received
from Wyley's grandmother in the month before the trial. I
was working in our yard and my wife summoned me inside
with the bulletin that Vivian Gates was on the phone. I don't
know what I had expected—an invitation to leave town
crossed my mind, as I had anticipated that Mrs. Gates and
her children, like anyone in their position, would look warily
upon a writer who was engaged in an unauthorized exploration of their family. But nothing of the kind occurred.
When I picked up the phone, Mrs. Gates, in a voice laden
with tentativeness, told me that she had been meaning to
call because Wyley had left a gas weed-trimmer up at our
place.

Moments later, I was bringing the trimmer over to the
big white house on the hill. Mrs. Gates was there, and her
daughter Viki and her son Bill and his wife Mary, and I

was received with a guarded politeness. They knew that I knew some of their secrets; they knew that I would be looking for more secrets; they knew that I would be writing about those secrets, and they had to judge who I was and what I would do to them. Eventually, I formally interviewed several of them, before they withdrew again, not wanting, they said, to be involved in anything that would "publicize" the tragedy, but perhaps, more to the point, not wanting to release any more family material than they had already, and perhaps regretfully, released.

Through it all, however, and continuing up to the present, the points of juncture have remained there in many odd ways. Waiting for my son's schoolbus, I park in their driveway. Around town, be it at the supermarket, at The Bakery, or just passing by them as they work in their yard, they are always a presence, as, I imagine, I am a presence to them. And there have been times when the points of juncture have become almost absurd. During a freak October blizzard that occurred during the jury's deliberation, I was the only one on the road to undertake the journey down to Hudson. And therefore it was I who was asked by Mrs. Gates to take a sweater down to the defendant. It had suddenly gotten very cold, Mrs. Gates explained, and she was worried that Wyley might not have any warm clothes.

The remainder of that first trial day was taken up by testimony from Undersheriff James Bertram and by Coroner Angelo Nero. Bertram, who would successfully run for sheriff two years after the Gates trial had concluded, described for the D.A. his arrival at the house and his ascertainment that there were four dead within, and his discovery of gun casings.

With his cross-examination of Bertram, defense attorney Wilcox began his chipping away at the credibility of the sheriff's department, an offensive that would continue throughout the trial.

"With regard to this particular matter, as undersheriff of Columbia County, did you file any official reports?" Wilcox asked.

"What kind of reports?" replied Bertram, seeming more genuinely confused than elusive.

Wilcox, clarifying the question, asked Bertram if he had made any official reports pertaining to what he did, what his duties were, where he went, or what he had observed in each room. Bertram said he didn't know if he had made any such reports.

"How about notes?" Wilcox pressed. "During that time you were going from room to room making observations, did you record any of your observations?"

"When I was going from room to room, I had a flashlight and a weapon in my hand. I didn't record any notes, no," Bertram replied acidly.

Wilcox moved on to the securing of evidence from the other boys in the case, starting with the question of whether any clothing had been seized from Damian Rossney.

"The only evidence that I remember personally taking with Rossney was some weapons that was in the house," said Bertram.

"Did you have occasion to request that any examination be done of Damian Rossney's hands?" asked Wilcox.

Bertram replied that he had not.

Wilcox asked the same questions regarding Miles McDonald and got the same answers. Having nailed down this point, Wilcox moved on to another area of evidence whose existence—or lack of it—was important to the case, and this was the bag of sweaters that Wyley said he had gone to Cheryl's car to remove. In Wyley's initial statements to authorities, he said that in retrieving the bag of sweaters he had closed the car door on his thumb, thereby causing the injury that was later traced to his mishandling of the Walther pistol. Wilcox now asked Bertram if he had secured a bag of sweaters from the log house, and Bertram replied that he thought he might have seen a bag of sweaters but he did not take it and did not know if it had been taken.

Finally, Wilcox focused on another item, small but suggestive of a physical struggle, which could contribute to the overall portrait of "reasonable doubt" he hoped to paint.

"Can you tell us whether or not, in your two times

through the residence, did you have any occasion to observe," asked Wilcox, "what appeared to be a broken button on the floor of the room you referred to as the rec room?"

"A broken what?" demanded an exasperated Bertram.

"Button," Wilcox repeated.

Bertram said he had not. Wilcox inquired whether, at any time, Bertram or any member of his department had occasion to compare any broken button with any article of clothing belonging to Wyley Gates, Damian Rossney, Miles McDonald, or Matthew Rueckheim, a friend of Miles's who had accompanied him to the movie that night, and Bertram said that he had not.

It was a two-pronged defense that Wilcox had planned for the case of Wyley Gates. He would, on the one hand, show that his client was insanely under the influence of nefarious-minded and skillfully manipulative boys, and, on the other, suggest that Wyley himself was incapable of committing murder. As far as Wilcox was concerned, the only substantial piece of evidence that the prosecution had was the confession, and that smelled of trouble.

"I learned early in my career as a prosecutor that the worst case you can have is where the primary piece of evidence you've got is an alleged confession by the suspect," said Wilcox, who believes that the public, weaned on television detective programs that show undue reliance on forensic evidence, are always on the outlook for "the hair that proves the whole thing." In Wilcox's experience as a D.A., he found that confessions are particularly vulnerable to attack. "You want to amass all of the corroborative evidence that you can amass to show that the confession is reliable," he said, "because you know that you're going to be faced with an attack on the confession with, one, its probably being unreliable and, two, coerced."

It was Wilcox's plan to undermine the alleged confession of Wyley Gates by, one, suggesting that all the information given in the confession was information that the police could well have gathered on their own, regardless of Wyley's cooperation and, two, by showing that there was forensic

material that did *not* gibe with Wyley's alleged account of
the event. Specifically, he would present forensic material
that would suggest the evidence of a struggle, pointing to
the ripped collar of Cheryl Brahm's blouse, gouge marks
on her finger, broken buttons, and other bits and pieces.
Wilcox believed if there was a struggle, which in his opinion
forensic evidence pointed to, then Wyley would certainly
have mentioned this in his confession. "Probably if he was
involved and did this, he would have said something about
the struggle and how it happened," Wilcox suggested. "He
was . . . giving them all that evidence that he hated these
people. . . . And if that were the case, if he hated Cheryl
Brahm like they claimed he said he did or whatever, he
might have gotten a sort of satisfaction in telling them about
the struggle with her. But it wasn't in there. It wasn't in
there at all. And they didn't know it at all. And I thought
that was a very important thing."

It was therefore Wilcox's position that the statement
given in Poughkeepsie had not, in fact, been made by Wyley
at all but, rather, was a reconstruction created through
a collaborative effort on the part of the various law-
enforcement agencies. And the struggle was not in the
statement, despite the forensic material that supported the
occurrence of such a struggle, because the authorities had
not bothered to talk with Dr. Baruch Davis, the coroner's
physician. "They were just talking to Investigator Gagliardi
[of the state I.D. team] and whoever else was on that scene
and 'What've you got up there?' " Wilcox said, offering his
version of police talk that night. " 'Oh, we've got two live
rounds in the garage. We've got live extended rounds
everywhere, blood on the stairs, looks like she fell down the
stairs.' I mean, they put these things together pretty much.
They reconstructed, which is not overly difficult to do until
you get to the finite areas." In fact, Wyley, in the statement
he allegedly gave in Poughkeepsie that night, merely *omitted*
mention of a struggle rather than presented material that
conflicted with such forensic evidence, and this could be
rationalized as a form of self-censorship or even the result
of a defense mechanism. But Wilcox was banking on the

notion that he could persuade a jury that the omission of any mention of a struggle actually threw the entire confession into grave doubt.

In addition to highlighting the discrepancies between the alleged confession and the crime-scene forensics, Wilcox also set out to attack the work of the sheriff's department. In Gene Keeler's stated opinion, this work was without fault. "I think the police did a fine job," Keeler said. "People . . . have absolutely no idea of what it takes to investigate a case. I mean, to prosecute a case. They see all these TV shows and everything else and they expect it to be like that. Well, life is not like that. It's not even close. There's no such thing as a perfect case . . . there are factual problems, there are legal problems," said Keeler, who compared the process of investigating and prosecuting a murder to putting together little bits and pieces of a big puzzle. The accumulation of these bits and pieces was effected, in Columbia County, by an egalitarian system in which the D.A. is one department head, the sheriff another, the state troopers a separate entity, and there is no central governor. The idea, however, that the law-enforcement agencies might not have adequately assembled these bits and pieces was met with fierce denial, as in the case of the failure to fingerprint the murder weapon. "The fingerprinting of the gun!" Keeler said, exploding. "What makes absolutely no sense to me is to fingerprint some lousy gun that came from the house that everybody had access to and you knew that everybody was shooting. It would mean nothing, OK? And when it came down to the choice between doing that and finding out if it had any blood on it, I'd rather [test for] blood on it."

In Wilcox's view, as he took on the Wyley Gates case, there had been, in fact, a breakdown in the system and the necessary forensic evidence had not been collected. "We laid everything out," said Wilcox. "What we had, what they had, what they didn't have, the lab reports that we had. We obviously expected some more results from the lab reports. They tested the weapon for blood, but they ascertained it was human blood and that's it. But they weren't telling the truth when they said they had to make priority decisions on what they did. Sometimes you have to do that, but in this case you could have protected the gun for fingerprints and done the blood test. You certainly could have tested the fibers that you took off the gun and attempted to match them with the clothing that Wyley Gates wore, or someone else. They didn't do that."

"Inexplicable" was what Wilcox termed the failure to carry out these tests. "If I was D.A. and I got those reports back, I'd call the lab immediately and say, 'What about those damned fibers? What about fingerprints on the gun?' " said Wilcox. As far as he could see, Keeler's justification for not running a fingerprint examination was that the gun came out of Wyley's house and so Wyley's fingerprints might well have been on the weapon. But Wilcox wasn't buying this. "You'd want the newer fingerprints in terms of who touched and handled the gun," he insisted. "The trigger housing of the gun—possibly the handle of the gun. Who cares if it was in the house? Assumedly it was used in a murder and therefore we have to assume that the person who committed the murder had his hand on the gun. I think that they devised this argument later—this priority-of-tests argument—as a way of explaining why they didn't do it, but it wasn't a good explanation."

As to the fact that evidence had not been gathered from the person of Damian Rossney, Wilcox called that "outrageous . . . this was just a collection of them deciding that they had their man. They were convinced it was Wyley Gates, and they were trying to go out and sink him as quickly as possible."

No statement had been taken from Damian Rossney on either the night of the murders or the following day, but the D.A. saw nothing irregular in that either. "You're assuming you'd have a tape recorder, you're assuming you'd have a written statement. In ninety percent of your criminal cases, you don't have that," Keeler maintained. "As soon as you bring out a piece of paper and a pen and start writing, people clam up. As soon as you start tape-recording, people clam up." It is Keeler's belief that people make confessions or admissions spontaneously. They respond to questions and they start saying things before they realize they're in trouble. "If you expect all of that to occur," said Keeler, referring to the idea that the taking of statements might actually lead to confessions, "then the criminal-justice system is in real trouble."

It was this feeling—that the criminal-justice system was in real trouble and that the source of the trouble was irregularities on the part of the sheriff's department and the New York State Police, both in their collection and processing of evidence and in their procedures with particular regard to the taking of a confession—that Charles Wilcox intended to explore, and, some came to feel, exploit, in his defense of Wyley Gates.

The last witness of the day was Angelo Nero, who had served as county coroner at the time of the Gates murders. Nero told Keeler that he had been called to the Maple Drive residence at approximately 11:40 P.M., that he had identified the residents thereof, and had contacted Dr. Baruch Davis, the coroner's physician. He helped in the tagging of the bodies and made arrangements to have the bodies sent to Albany Medical Center, for the autopsies performed by Dr. Roberto Benitez.

In the cross-examination, Wilcox began with a broad question.

"Mr. Nero, did you have occasion to make other observations at the scene, other than a preliminary examination, as you indicated, of the people?" asked Wilcox.

"I made a lot of observations," Nero replied. "I don't know which one you're referring to."

"Did you have occasion to notice a particle of what appeared to be a broken button on the floor?" asked Wilcox.

"No, sir. I did not."

"Can you tell us whether or not you made any observations in terms of your preliminary examination of Robert Gates, Sr., pertaining to a buttonhole on his shirt being torn?"

"No, sir. I did not."

"Can you tell us whether or not in terms of your

preliminary examination you made any observations concerning Cheryl Brahm's collar being torn?"

"That I did notice," Nero allowed.

Wilcox inquired whether the coroner had observed any bullet wounds or hole-type wounds in the wrist of Robert Gates, Sr., and Nero said that he had. He did not, however, recall scratch marks in the vicinity of Jason Gates's face nor any wounds, lacerations, or abrasions on Cheryl Brahm's wrist or hand, and could only be vague about gouge marks or puncture marks in a digit on her right hand. Wilcox handed him a photograph of Cheryl Brahm's hand and wanted to know if that depiction represented fair and accurate evidence in Nero's opinion. After scrutinizing the photograph for several moments, Nero said that it did.

The first day had concluded. The jury, having passed a long, hot time of it, and having had their first exposure to the photographs of the victims that had been entered into evidence, looked wilted. Considerably more so than Wyley, still crisp in the starched white shirt, the laundering of which had been undertaken by Joan Yowe, who understood that when Wyley appeared in public he wanted to look a certain way. Joan, who saw Wyley frequently from January to August, had been charting subtle but definite changes in his personality. "I think I saw the first change during suppression hearings in July," she remembered. "I called it to Chuck's attention and I called it to his doctor's attention because if it was anyone else, you wouldn't notice it, but with him it was very noticeable. The movement of his hands and arms went from a position of not moving to being now very expressive. He was very up and I thought, He's manic. He's going into another stage." When the actual trial started, and Wyley resumed his posture of rigidity, it wasn't at the suggestion of his attorney. "That was him," she affirmed. "In the first place, you never told Wyley what to do. Wyley was Wyley always. That was him. . . . He sat erect. I was always amazed. He could leave the room at five o'clock, looking exactly as he had when he came in at nine. Not a wrinkle. Never wilted. Incredible. Absolutely incredible."

Asked where, in her opinion, he found the wherewithal to achieve this, she replied, "It's Wyley. . . . It's just his way of coping with the world. Total discipline." In fact, the persona of Wyley Gates was a great mystery to this woman who shared a unique intimacy with him over a considerable length of time. "I would say he's not like any other criminal I've seen," she reflected. "There was something psychiatrically amiss even while you could relate. I always felt six months from now he could wake up and not even remember that he'd ever met any one of us."

15

On the second day of the trial, the courtroom was still packed with reporters, retirees, high school kids filling up their summer time, and those spectators who had a real stake in what was going on there. Chief among the latter were the Brahms, whose pained, bristling surveillance would become a fixture of the proceedings, and, of course, Vivian Gates, now in the company of her daughter Viki, who looked strained and uncomfortable in a high teased hairdo and ruffled blouse. Today, however, Mrs. Gates was present not only to provide moral support for her grandson but, as well, to provide testimony, for it was she who was called by the D.A. as his first witness of the day. As she walked to the stand, a sibilant outbreak of murmuring followed her, but this gave way, as she seated herself, to absolute silence in the courtroom.

"Now, ma'am," began Keeler, after Mrs. Gates had pointed out, for the record, her grandson at the defendant's table. "Do you recall the day of December 13, 1986?"

"On that day, my grandson, Jason, was supposed to come to my house, where he lived, at eight," she responded, in a small, faltering voice. "And he didn't get there at eight and I thought maybe my son and Cheryl had gone out and they didn't realize the time, and then I started calling my son's house and there was a busy signal, and I thought probably Wyley was on the phone talking." (The phone had been off the cradle since the shooting of Bob Gates.) Mrs. Gates described how she continued to wait, all the while getting "pretty nervous," and then finally she heard a car coming up the driveway. She assumed it would be Cheryl, but when she opened the door, there was Wyley. "He said, 'They're all dead,' " she testified, "and I thought they were in a car accident. My son and daughter-in-law and my granddaughter and her boyfriend were in an accident just fifteen months before and my son and daughter-in-law and my granddaughter's boyfriend were killed in that accident, and so I was pretty upset; and Wyley came in and I asked him where was the accident, and he told me that they were shot and afterwards he told me Bob, Jr., was shot too. After a while, I said to Wyley, 'We better tell the police,' and so I called the police."

As I listened to Mrs. Gates, I couldn't help but think of Dr. Marchionne's opinion of her affect, which he had found to be as flat as Wyley's, for, as she gave testimony, that flatness was again conveyed. She was "pretty upset." She called the police "after a while." I tried to project myself into her situation, being told by one grandson that my son and his girlfriend and my two other grandsons had been killed, and all I could think was that I would be screaming at him. "How do you know? Are they breathing? Call a doctor!" What she described instead was sitting on a sofa, consoling her surviving grandson with the reminder that it was "just you and me now, Wyley." It seemed an incomprehensible reaction, but then again we were listening to a woman who had suffered so much loss and so much shock. How fair was it to project oneself into her situation, to gauge her reactions by one's own?

Keeler was eager to get to the subject of Charles Argyle, Wyley's cellmate, and he asked Mrs. Gates if she had ever heard of him. She said she had, that Wyley had mentioned him and had told her that he used to play chess with him. Keeler asked if she had ever had a conversation with Wyley regarding his loan of money to Argyle and she acknowledged that she had. Wyley said Argyle was going to get out of jail and his mother and father didn't want him to move back in with them, but Argyle had a job and needed money to set himself up in an apartment. Wyley had asked her to take $200 from his bank account to give to Argyle. "I hesitated and I told Wyley I didn't think he would ever get it back and Wyley said, 'Don't worry. I can trust him,'" said Mrs. Gates. "And so I thought, Well, how could it hurt, you know, I thought, if he helped somebody else to get started? And so I did it. I transferred the money from Wyley's account to Chuck Argyle's account."

Keeler was obviously hoping that the jury would regard this bank transfer not as a sudden burst of generosity (and an uncharacteristic one, if we keep in mind that Wyley charged his brother interest on small loans) but as a kind of hush money to keep Argyle from talking to the authorities. The D.A. then moved on to an item that could serve as a far more powerful indictment of the defendant. He asked Vivian Gates how often she visited Wyley in jail, and she estimated at least twice a week.

"Did there come a time, ma'am, between December 13, 1986, and today while in the Columbia County Jail that you had a conversation with Wyley concerning the death of Jason Gates?" Keeler questioned.

She said there had been such a conversation.

"During that time, ma'am, did there come a time that you made a statement to him, when you were discussing the death of Jason Gates," asked Keeler, "that you didn't believe he did it?"

"I said I couldn't believe that he would shoot Jason," Mrs. Gates replied after a moment.

"In response to that question, ma'am, what did Wyley Gates say?"

Mrs. Gates looked toward Wyley, who stared straight ahead. "Well, I think that he was trying to cover up," she began.

"Ma'am, please, I asked you a question," Keeler pressed. "Would you just answer what he said?"

She took a breath before replying. "Well, I believe he said after some hesitation that I better believe it," she said in her small voice. "I believe that's what he said. He mumbled it, but I think that's what he said."

Keeler stared at her, his look not uncompassionate. "Ma'am, and I realize this has been difficult for you, but you love Wyley Gates very much, don't you?" he asked gently.

"Yes," said Mrs. Gates, looking down at the floor. "I do."

In his cross-examination, Wilcox established that Wyley Gates had never said, at least in the presence of his grandmother, that he wanted to go to Poughkeepsie. Nor had he been read any *Miranda* warnings in the presence of his family, inside Vivian Gates's house, where it was warm and brightly lit; instead investigators Cozzolino and Shook had chosen to read him his rights outside, where it was dark and frigid. As for the "you'd better believe it" comment, Wilcox asked Mrs. Gates whether she was testifying that it was her belief that Wyley was trying to cover up for someone, and, over strenuous but overruled objections from the D.A., Mrs. Gates replied that she felt "he had to keep up his role, whatever it may be."

Wilcox then moved into the area of Wyley's interaction with family members, seeking to portray a warmth that few had witnessed. Had she ever seen Wyley play with Jason? he asked, and Mrs. Gates said that her two grandsons used to play blocks together. Furthermore, Wyley had already shopped for Christmas presents for the family, including a set of glasses for his father that were engraved "Gates Bar," a sampler pillow for Cheryl, a deer-embossed platter for his Aunt Viki, and a denim vest for Bobby, Jr.

"Do you know whether or not he had ordered any type of gift," Wilcox asked, "for Miles McDonald?"

Mrs. Gates replied that she had seen in Wyley's checkbook that he had ordered a magazine subscription for Miles. "One of those survival-type magazines," she added.

"Mrs. Gates, you said you loved Wyley Gates," Wilcox said in tones that were almost reverential.

"Yes," she said.

"Did you love Robert Gates, Sr.?"

"Yes."

"Did you love Robert Gates, Jr.?"

"Yes."

"Did you love Jason?"

"Yes," she said. "And I loved Cheryl too," she added, with a hint of defiance in her voice that made the Brahms stir in the back row.

Mrs. Gates was followed onto the stand by Dr. Roberto Benitez, who testified to having performed the autopsies on the victims. He had found that all four died of hemorrhagic shock as a result of massive bleeding from gunshot wounds. Additionally, each had consumed a spaghetti dinner and had died roughly within an hour thereafter, although, Dr. Benitez said, it was the duty of the coroner, not the pathologist, to provide the estimated time of death. As Dr. Benitez gave details on the number and trajectories of gunshot wounds in the case of each victim, Keeler submitted into evidence color photographs of the bodies, which were passed among the somber jurors. The photographs were deeply disturbing, but, among the photographs that had thus far been entered into evidence, some of the jurors were most disturbed by the ones that seemed to indicate that bodies may have been moved or tampered with before the arrival of the police. "I think the bodies had been moved," one juror later told me. "There were three or four pictures of Jason on the floor and at one point there was something white on his elbow and in another picture it wasn't there. Now, whether it was a flash from the camera or whatever, I don't know, but it looked more like a piece of paper stuck to his elbow. Blood, too, didn't seem to match up, with Cheryl in particular." The photograph that struck many people as particularly disturbing and mysterious was the one of a slain Bobby, Jr., with his head resting on a jacket that appeared to have been placed underneath him, almost in a cradling sort of gesture.

Wilcox began his cross-examination by asking Dr. Benitez if he was certified as a forensic pathologist, and Dr. Benitez admitted that he was not. Wilcox then asked Dr. Benitez if he had gone to the crime scene; Dr. Benitez replied that he hadn't. Regarding the tears in the buttonhole area of Robert Gates's shirt and Cheryl Brahm's torn collar, Dr. Benitez acknowledged that he had observed these, but he had not observed a gouge wound on the second digit of Cheryl's hand nor any abrasions to her left wrist. Dr. Benitez further testified that he had not observed scratches near Jason's eye, which, Wilcox pointed out, were listed in the observations recorded by Dr. Baruch Davis, the coroner's physician who had made the initial identification of Jason's body; but, Dr. Benitez stated, it had been his exclusive concern to determine the cause of death, and these factors were not, in his opinion, contributory to the deaths. Concluding his cross-examination by establishing that no wounds had been excised from the bodies for further lab work, Wilcox successfully cast further doubt on the competency with which the authorities had collected forensic evidence in the case.

Vivian Gates's appearance on the stand had fatigued her and thus Wyley found himself, on the following morning, with no family supporters on hand. It would, in fact, be a long, trying day, a good day for emotional support, as Keeler's procession of witnesses attempted to build the case against this teenage boy who, even now, as he stood trial for the murder of his family, would not condescend to or, perhaps, was not able to exhibit any sign of emotion.

Richard Klingler, the tall and garrulous Canaan town supervisor and crony of Bob Gates, was the first witness of the day, testifying to the ten-minute conversation he had had with Gates at approximately 6:30 on the evening of December 13, the last contact Gates, or any of the four victims, had with anyone outside the home that night.

Klingler was followed by Ralph Marcucio, a forensic scientist with the New York State Police Crime Laboratory, who told the court that the tests he had run on the Walther automatic pistol established the presence of human bloodstains on the right front area by the sight and by the slide. But, under cross-examination, Marcucio admitted that the tests for blood had not enabled him to determine the age of the bloodstains or to tell whose blood it was. The witness stated as well that blue-colored fibers were found along the serial number, in the safety area, and by the slide, and maroon fibers were found in the slide area, but that further tests on the fibers had never been executed.

One of the most significant witnesses in the case—in some ways, perhaps, the single most significant witness—was up next, and his name was Richard Hogle. Hogle told the court of his arrival at the Chatham police station and the trip to Poughkeepsie. Keeler asked Hogle if Wyley's speech had been coherent at the time, if Wyley had appeared agitated or hysterical, or if there had been any odor of alcohol on his breath. Hogle replied that Wyley had been fully coherent, and that he appeared to be neither agitated, hysterical, nor inebriated.

When it came to the moment of Wyley's going off to the examination room with Investigator Salmon, Keeler demanded to know if Hogle had asked to go with them, and Hogle replied that he had not.

"When Mr. Salmon appeared to have Mr. Gates go with him, did you make any protest about Mr. Gates going with Mr. Salmon?"

"No, I did not," said Hogle.

"After Mr. Gates left the room, again, sir, what did you do?" Keeler questioned.

"I told you," Hogle replied testily. "I sat back down during this interim."

"And, sir, how long did you sit there for?"

"I was in the waiting room for a period of about two hours."

"What were you doing in the waiting room during those two hours?" Keeler wished to know.

"Sitting," said Hogle, as the strained credulity in the room grew thick as a fog.

"Did there come a time during those two hours that you had any conversation with anybody else?"

"An officer came in roughly about nine, I would guess, with a cup of coffee," recalled Hogle. "If there was a conversation, it was 'thank you' or something along those lines."

"Did you ever have any conversation with [the officer] concerning Mr. Gates going with Mr. Salmon?" asked Keeler.

"No, sir."

"Did you protest to that officer or ask that officer to help you to see Mr. Gates or Mr. Salmon?"

"No, sir."

"During that time period, sir, did you go to the communications desk and ask any officer at or near or about the communications desk that you wanted to talk to your client?"

"No, sir," said Hogle, shifting uncomfortably in his seat.

"At any time did you go to that communications desk, which was from your testimony approximately twenty-five or thirty feet away, and ask to see your client?"

"No, sir."

"Sir, did you during that period of time when you were waiting for approximately two hours make any movement," Keeler demanded, in a rising voice, "or say anything to anybody or do anything in an attempt to see Mr. Gates?"

"No, sir," Hogle replied, his hand going nervously to his beard.

"During that period of time, did you make any attempt or make any requests to get a hold of Mr. Salmon or any other police officers concerning Mr. Gates?"

"No, sir," Richard Hogle said quietly.

In his cross-examination, Wilcox asked Hogle to describe what he had done physically when Salmon announced that it was time to commence the polygraph examination.

". . . I stood up, I picked up my jacket, placed it over my arm, and picked up my briefcase and turned to go through the door to accompany Mr. Gates," said Hogle. "As

I turned, Officer Salmon raised his left hand, palm extended, fingers splayed, and made a pushing action directed toward me." This then was the alleged barring gesture that would prove so utterly pivotal to the case, but even now Hogle added that there had been no physical contact between him and Salmon and that, in fact, they had been some six to eight feet away from each other at that point.

"What did you interpret him to be doing?" asked Wilcox.

"My interpretation," said Hogle, "was that was an order for me to stop."

Keeler rose once more for the redirect examination. "You were Mr. Gates's attorney, were you not?" asked the D.A. in an increasingly judgmental tone.

Hogle agreed that he had been.

"And you testified you were there to protect his rights, is that correct?"

Hogle agreed it was so.

"You testified, sir, that while at the Tracy Memorial Building you had at least an hour to talk with your client in private, did you not?"

Hogle confirmed this.

"When you went down to Poughkeepsie with Mr. Gates, you testified that you had an opportunity of at least fifty minutes to discuss the issues with Mr. Gates, is that not correct?"

"That is correct."

"You sat there for two hours?"

"Correct," Hogle said, staring straight ahead.

There were no more questions and so, finally, the witness was allowed to step down. The small-town lawyer, whose stock in trade was wills, closings, and assorted legal tasks far removed from what he had been called upon to perform on the morning of December fourteenth, passed by Wyley Gates at the defendant's table, offering him a small nod, and exited the room.

The testimony of Richard Hogle, which caused not only credulity to be strained but jaws to drop among the spectators in the courtroom, was a hard act to follow, and certainly Criminal Investigator William Vick, a phlegmatic, pie-faced man who had served with the department for fourteen years, would not compel anyone's attention. Nor was he a figure who would reflect distinction on the Columbia County Sheriff's Department, as he detailed his duties with regard to this case. Vick had been the primary custodian of the evidence gathered from the log house, and it was through his testimony that Keeler was able to enter into evidence the bullets removed from the bodies of the victims, the lead fragments found at the log house, and the Walther pistol and clips.

Under cross-examination, Vick was asked if he had requested a fingerprint examination of the Walther, and Vick replied that he had. Wilcox asked if that examination had been performed by the sheriff's department, and Vick admitted that it had not been, although, he stated, the sheriff's department did, on occasion, perform fingerprint dusting. In this case, however, the sheriff's department had not performed the fingerprint examination because of "the degree of the crime," and they enlisted the aid of a more expert agency to carry it out. But, under further questioning, the fact emerged that the fingerprint dusting had never been done. By way of explanation—or justification—Vick told the court that he had requested the state police crime lab to conduct such a test but had been told that the lab did not perform that process. Furthermore, he had learned that dusting the weapon for prints might result in the loss of a blood sample from the gun, and he viewed the latter evidence as worthier of preservation. Contributing also to the decision to forgo the fingerprint dusting was the fact that Wyley Gates had confessed to wearing rubber gloves at the time of the shooting. Consequently, it was Vick's belief that no fingerprints would be found, and so it made even less sense to possibly jeopardize the securing of blood samples from the weapon.

"When you heard about gloves, you formed an opinion and closed off all other avenues of investigation?" Wilcox said accusingly, as Vick looked increasingly unhappy.

It was this theory—that the sheriff's department had

felt, from the start, that they had "gotten their man" and singlemindedly, if not blindly, pursued the case from that supposition—that Wilcox hoped to promulgate for the jury's benefit. But Wilcox's interrogation also brought out the fact that only one doorknob from the log house had been submitted for fingerprint analysis and that Vick did not know the results of that test; that Vick had not taken fingerprints from Damian Rossney, Miles McDonald, or Matthew Rueckheim ("I don't even know who he is," Vick said, frowning, in regard to the boy who had been Mc-Donald's companion to the movies on the night of December 13 and, by extension, his alibi); and that as far as Vick knew no tests had been made on Wyley Gates's clothing for gunshot residue, nor on the clothing of Damian Rossney or Miles McDonald. Finally, there were no further questions, and Investigator William Vick was allowed to step down.

Having had their luster already tarnished by Wilcox's aggressive attacks, the Columbia County Sheriff's Department offered up their next witness, Walter Shook, who, more than anyone, had really been at the center of things on the long night of December 13.

   "Shooky," who started out what was to be a lengthy stint on the stand with a ready smile and an immediate rapport with the jury, described for the D.A. the events of the night of December 13 and the morning of December 14. Keeler then set out to clarify Shook's relationship with a forthcoming witness, Wyley's cellmate, Chuck Argyle. Shook testified that he had arrested Argyle for the burglary of a Nice 'n Easy convenience store in Kinderhook, New York, in the early part of December 1986. On January 2, Shook was notified by Investigator Cozzolino that one of the jailers had received from Argyle a letter pertaining to the Gates homicides. Shook picked up the letter—the letter having been written inside a paperback edition of the Stephen King novel *Cujo*—and put it into the Gates file. On January 5, Shook went to the jail to speak with Argyle "relevant to why [Argyle] had turned it over" and Argyle told Shook that "he thought it was the thing to do."

Another interview with Argyle took place on March 12, when Argyle presented Shook and Assistant District Attorney Nancy Snyder with what was allegedly a three-page self-incriminating letter written by Wyley, which Argyle claimed to have found on the floor of the cell they shared.

It was this "Argyle Connection" that Wilcox set out to sully as he began his cross-examination of the witness. He immediately established that charges had been pending against Argyle on several counts of burglary, and that, despite the fact that the authorities had what Wilcox characterized as "a good case" against him, there had not been, at least until the point of Shook's appearance in court this August 21, any preliminary hearing in the case of Charles Argyle, nor had Shook ever been summoned to appear before the grand jury on charges that he had filed against the young man. As to why Argyle chose to help the police in the matter of the Wyley Gates case, Shook confessed, under questioning by Wilcox, that he "was just as amazed as you are at the fact that he came forward with this information."

"You're amazed at that?" Wilcox asked, his voice laced with incredulity and sarcasm.

"Yes, I am," said Shook earnestly, as he glanced at the jury. "I see no reason why he did it."

"You, who were the officer charging him with six felonies, he had four more hanging over his head," Wilcox continued, "does that *amaze* you that he turned over this information?"

As Shook was forming a reply Keeler objected. The objection was sustained and so Wilcox turned to the fact that the felony charge that Argyle was facing had been reduced to a misdemeanor and that Argyle had been granted youthful-offender status. Shook replied that as far as he knew all that Argyle received for a sentence was time served, which amounted to six months. He also had no knowledge of how or why the youthful-offender status had been granted.

Having cast doubt on Argyle's sudden civic-mindedness, a theme that would be played again when Argyle himself assumed the stand, Wilcox now sought to further disparage the investigative work of the Columbia County Sheriff's Department. He asked Shook why no tire-track molds had been taken in the field behind the log house where Wyley had allegedly parked Cheryl's car before walking back to the house with the gun. Shook explained that the site had not been checked until a day or two after the shootings and by then it had snowed, making an exact location of the tire tracks, and any moldings thereof, an impossibility. He also stated that, although Cheryl's car had been secured and he himself had looked it over for blood, he was not sure if the New York State Police crime lab had performed any tests on the car's interior to ascertain whether there was blood from where Wyley said he had closed the car door on his thumb. As to the possibility of a struggle before the murders—a possibility that Wilcox was assiduously promoting whenever he could—Shook told Wilcox that, although he had not personally visited the crime scene, he had been told there had been no struggle. Wilcox asked if he had not seen, in the crime photographs, that Cheryl's hands had been bloodied.

"I did not look at the pictures closely," Shook replied with distaste. "To be frank with you, they were not nice to look at."

"Well, now, wait a minute now," said Wilcox, swooping down. "You are the lead or mainly involved investigator in this case. Did you look at the photographs or discuss the scene with your fellow investigators during the time that you were investigating this?"

"I was not involved as far as securing physical evidence or taking of photographs relevant to that scene," Shook said, obviously realizing that it might have been less than judicious to have been so "frank" with the defense attorney.

"In terms of Wyley Gates having a white tie on," asked Wilcox, "would it have been important to you or would you have inquired as to whether or not any of the deceased appeared to have been involved in a struggle with any assailant?"

"I was told that there was no struggle," Shook replied, in an attempt to stonewall Wilcox.

"You did not know, as you sit here, that Cheryl Brahm's hands were bloody, correct?"

"Not of my own knowledge, no," Shook allowed.

"Well, I mean any knowledge," Wilcox cried. "Did anybody communicate that to you?"

"The pictures that I glanced through, she had blood on her. I didn't go over them with a microscope or anything like that," Shook snapped.

"You have no recollection as you sit here of ever being advised by anyone that Cheryl Brahm had injuries to her hands or that they were bloody?" Wilcox persisted.

"Today," Shook replied cryptically.

"Pardon me?" said Wilcox.

"Today," Shook repeated.

"Today is the first time?" Wilcox asked, with his practiced tone of incredulity.

"That's correct," said Shook, staring ahead.

Moving along, so as to flesh out the portrayal of deficiencies in the investigation on the night of December 13, Wilcox established that Shook had not taken statements from Vivian Gates or Paul Groudas, Jason's uncle, regarding their activities. More significantly, Wilcox brought out the fact that no written statements or depositions had been taken from Damian Rossney that night either.

"Did you proceed to the Damian Rossney residence to ask Damian Rossney whether or not he changed his clothes that evening?" asked Wilcox.

"I did not," replied Shook.

"Did you proceed to the Damian Rossney residence to ask Damian Rossney whether or not he had washed his hands that evening?"

"I did not," said Shook.

"Did you or anyone else at your direction ask Damian Rossney at that point in time whether or not he would give you his clothes?"

"I did not," Shook replied, in his staunch refrain that,

he must have hoped, would lend him some measure of dignity.

"Did you yourself go to Damian Rossney, or any other person, to ask Damian Rossney if he would take a polygraph examination?"

"I did not."

"Did you ever say to Damian Rossney, 'I would appreciate it if you wouldn't wash your hands?' " Wilcox asked, making pointed reference to that very request Shook had made earlier that evening to Wyley, but Keeler objected.

Wilcox then turned to the sequence of events at Vivian Gates's house, focusing on Wyley's departure from the house that night. "Do you recall [Mrs. Gates] saying, 'Oh, no, he's been through too much already. Don't take him'?" asked Wilcox.

"I do not recall that at all," Shook said.

"If she testified to that, she would be in error?"

"She didn't say it in my presence," Shook insisted.

". . . Did you not tell her," Wilcox continued, "that you were taking Wyley to Poughkeepsie for a lie detector test and you would have him back in an hour?"

"That's ridiculous!" Shook returned. "I did not say that."

"Was it your testimony on direct examination that you left Vivian Gates's residence, went to your car outside, and got into the car and read *Miranda* warnings to Wyley Gates in the police car?"

Shook suggested that there was more to it than that.

"Well, is it fair to say that the car was parked at the Vivian Gates residence?" Wilcox probed.

"That is fair to say," Shook agreed.

"And is it fair to say that you left the Vivian Gates residence and you didn't administer any rights to Wyley Gates until you were in the police car?"

"That is correct."

"We can agree it's December?" asked Wilcox.

"We can," replied Shook.

"We can agree it is cold outside?"

"We can."

"We can agree it is dark outside?"

"It was."

"Can we agree that there were lights on in Vivian Gates's residence?"

"We can."

"Can we agree that there was heat on in Vivian Gates's residence?"

"We can."

"But you proceeded to take him out of the residence with light, with heat, in December to a car that had been sitting in the driveway for a period of time, put him in the car, and give him his *Miranda* rights then?" Wilcox cried.

"That is correct," replied Shook, digging in.

"Was he seventeen years old then?"

"He was," said Shook, with a hint of dismissiveness.

From there, Wilcox moved into the crucial area of attorney Richard Hogle's access to his client on the morning of December 14. Shook acknowledged that Hogle had gone down to Poughkeepsie to accompany his client for the purpose of a polygraph examination, but somehow the attorney had not made it into the observation room where Shook sat with Trooper Bernard Keller.

"Can we agree that this is the same attorney Hogle who got up at four in the morning, went to the Chatham station, was there with you for a period of time, rode down from Chatham to Poughkeepsie, and waited in the waiting room for the polygraph examination?" Wilcox demanded.

"That is correct," said Shook evenly.

"Did you at any time rap on the window or go around and say to Investigator Salmon, 'Hey, where's Hogle?' " Wilcox demanded.

"I did not," said Shook, who, it should be noted, was not legally compelled to do so.

Wilcox moved into the polygraph room itself. "Investigator Salmon, sir, came around from his operating position, did he not, and placed his chair in front of Wyley Gates at that point in time?" asked Wilcox.

Shook allowed that Salmon had brought the chair around to face Wyley.

"They were sitting right in front of each other, weren't they?" asked Wilcox.

"Yes."

"Knee to knee?"

"They weren't touching, I don't believe."

"But right in front of him?"

"That's correct."

"And there is no doubt at this period in time he was not administering a polygraph examination?"

"Not on the machine," said Shook. "That is correct."

"Isn't it a fact that at this time Investigator Salmon was leaning over in close proximity to . . . Wyley Gates?" Wilcox demanded to know.

"I don't know if it was at that time, but there did come a time when he did do that," said Shook.

"Wyley Gates wasn't hooked up to that machine then, was he, except for the arm cuff?"

"That's correct."

"Did Salmon put his hands on Wyley Gates's legs?" asked Wilcox.

"I remember seeing him put his hands on Wyley Gates's arms," Shook allowed.

Finally, as the grueling cross-examination drew to a close, Wilcox returned to one of his central leitmotivs: the failure of the sheriff's department to collect evidence.

"Pertaining to the gun, can you tell us whether or not you yourself conducted or instituted or directed fingerprint examination of the gun?" asked Wilcox.

"I did not," Shook replied.

"Would it not, sir, have been advantageous to request that a fingerprint test be done on the gun recovered at Damian Rossney's?" inquired Wilcox.

"We discussed the pros and cons and it was decided that the dusting for the prints might ruin other evidence that was on the weapon," Shook explained. "So it was not dusted. I believe we also came to the conclusion that Wyley had confessed to the crime and his prints would be on it anyway or they could be on it anyway, let's put it that way, because he had access to the weapon at his parents' house before it was stolen."

"Wouldn't you want to have information or conduct an investigation to determine whether or not any third person's prints could be on that gun?" asked Wilcox.

"Not if it were going to destroy other evidence that's more valuable," Shook replied.

"Sir, you were asked that question about why prints weren't taken on that gun before the Columbia County grand jury, were you not?"

Shook agreed that he had been.

"And you didn't say anything about destroying other evidence," Wilcox pointed out.

"I probably didn't think about it," Shook explained. "But I'm telling you that is the reason."

Wilcox read a passage from the grand-jury transcript in which Shook was asked by a grand juror if a fingerprint test had been performed and Shook replied that it had not been because Wyley had been wearing rubber gloves and, moreover, the gun was found in his house and he had had access to it.

"Can you tell us whether or not you were asked by the Columbia County grand jury whether or not any gloves were recovered in this matter?" Wilcox questioned Shook.

Shook said that he had been.

Wilcox read another portion from the grand-jury transcript in which the D.A. asked Shook if any gloves had been recovered and Shook replied that a search for gloves had been made but that they were not recovered.

"You took a pair of gloves off the very person of Wyley Gates, did you not?" asked Wilcox.

Shook admitted that he had. The issue regarding the rubber gloves was that no torn pair had ever been found, and, if Wyley had been wearing rubber gloves during the commission of the crime, and if it was assumed that he had cut his thumb through the mishandling of the Walther automatic pistol, then, consequently, any gloves he had been wearing would have been torn. Shook said he found a pair

of untorn rubber gloves in Wyley's jacket pocket upon
Wyley's arrest. By any standards, it would have been curious
for Wyley to have disposed of the torn gloves—the gloves
that really would have implicated him—and yet have kept
the untorn pair. On the other hand, the possession of *any*
pair of rubber gloves could have been construed as suspect
for a boy in this situation. The whole glove issue became
even more mysterious when Investigator Salmon denied
that any rubber gloves had been recovered, thus conflicting
with the story that Investigator Shook told.

Wilcox then read another grand-jury passage, in which
the D.A. asked Shook who had been present at the polygraph
examination and Shook replied himself, Salmon, and
Trooper Bernard Keller. One of the grand jurors then
asked if an attorney had been present and Shook replied
that, in fact, there had been an attorney there. His voice
now rising to a censorious shout, Wilcox demanded to know
of Shook whether he had given those answers. Shook, pale
but composed, replied that he had. Wilcox concluded his
questioning, hoping that, in his last exchange, he had entirely
discredited the witness before a jury who had already heard
that Wyley's attorney, Richard Hogle, had not been present
for the polygraph examination, nor, in fact, had any other
attorney been present.

The following day, Walter Shook returned for one more
go-round on the witness stand. Gone was his easy and
confident smile and in its place was a distinct unrest.

Laboriously, Gene Keeler set out to repair the damage
that Wilcox had done the previous day. He started with the
issue of the tire tracks, having Shook explain the impossibility
of taking tire tracks on frozen ground. Next he moved on
to the issues that Wilcox had raised in his reading of the
grand-jury excerpts, with particular attention to Shook's
reply to a grand juror that there had been an attorney
present at the polygraph examination.

"It's not a discrepancy the way I answered the question,"
Shook replied, justifying himself. "His attorney accompanied us to Poughkeepsie. His attorney gave him permis-

sion to take the polygraph. His attorney was with him in Poughkeepsie. His attorney was available to him any time he wanted him."

Keeler moved on to the response Shook had made before the grand jury regarding the rubber gloves. "What gloves were you referring to?" asked the district attorney.

"I was referring to the gloves that Wyley was wearing during the commission of the crime," said Shook. "They were not recovered."

Keeler showed him a pair of gloves that had been entered into evidence. Shook identified them as gloves he had taken off Wyley Gates at Troop K Barracks—*not* the gloves he was referring to before the grand jury.

It is Charles Wilcox's contention that the doubt he had hoped to cast on the procedures of the sheriff's department and the State Police was not his own creation in the service of his client, but, rather, the outgrowth of what he viewed as untoward actions, irregularities, and inconsistencies throughout the investigation. One such inconsistency, in his mind at least, was Wyley's alleged admission that the only mistake he made was not changing his clothes. Wilcox never believed that Wyley had made that statement. "Here's a kid who really doesn't talk," said Wilcox, in a posttrial conversation, "a kid who's very reticent, and Salmon would have you believe he volunteers stuff all over the place." Furthermore, the jacket, which would have constituted a key piece of evidence if, in fact, there had been gunpowder residue on it, was never tested for such residue. Wilcox speculated that perhaps the authorities were "afraid of themselves," that they didn't want to have the jacket tested because if it came back without gunpowder residue, then it would have cast doubt on Salmon's whole account, particularly with reference to Wyley's admission to the polygraph examiner about his "one big mistake."

The other inconsistency that Wilcox plumbed had to do with the rubber gloves, about whose existence Salmon and Shook disagreed. "I found it a very interesting thing that Salmon deep-sixed those gloves immediately because he saw those gloves as a real problem," charged Wilcox, who also contended that the other witness to the scene in the polygraph room, Trooper Bernard Keller, followed the "company line" by disavowing any knowledge of such gloves. But Shook, according to Wilcox, was not a company man. Essentially then, in Wilcox's opinion, Shook and Salmon mixed up their stories. "Shook said there were rubber gloves; Salmon said, 'What rubber gloves?' He saw them as a problem," Wilcox believed, "because he probably was still there when Shook patted down Wyley and took the rubber gloves out of his pocket. Which obviously didn't have any cuts or blood on them or anything else. And there was no evidence anywhere to establish that there was another pair of rubber gloves. So all we could assume is if the shooter used rubber gloves, then there was another shooter who had rubber gloves, because we don't know why Wyley would [have carried] two pairs of rubber gloves. If he was going to destroy one, why would he keep an extra pair in his pocket?" What Wilcox didn't address was the possibility that the rubber gloves found in Wyley's pocket were left over from the batch that the boys had used during the robbery of the log house, or even that Wyley had brought along an extra pair on the night of the murders, disposed of the ones he had used during the commission of the crime, and kept a pair in his pocket for the very reason of wanting himself to be found out. The confessional mode of a teenage boy who may have committed a ghastly crime was not an option that Wilcox ever spent a lot of time considering.

Instead, Wilcox continued to pursue those aspects of the case that he felt the authorities had been deficient in investigating. The reputed bag of sweaters, which Wyley allegedly went to retrieve from Cheryl's car, in the process of which, he initially claimed, he cut his thumb, was a case in point. "As a former D.A., in corroborating this cut-of-the-hand scenario, you would want to wipe out any other explanation of the cut of his hand," he said. "If I looked at the deposition and saw what he said in the deposition, I would say, 'Oh, my God, this is a problem' right away. 'This is a definite problem. Get that bag of sweaters—I want to see if there's any blood on the bag of sweaters—and get this kid to a doctor so we can get a professional opinion as to the nature of this cut while it's still fresh, as to whether it's a close-in-the-door cut or a sharp-piece-of-metal cut.' " As to why this was not done, Wilcox offered a theory. "Sometimes the police take the attitude 'We don't want to know anything bad,' " he said. " 'We don't want any negative readings that could be misconstrued.' Well, you'd better have them right away because they're going to be brought up anyway. You might as well get them up front and deal with them, if they can be dealt with."

The following day, Investigator Thomas Salmon would take the stand and offer his version of what had happened on the morning of December 14, 1986, at Troop K Barracks in Poughkeepsie. Essentially, it would boil down to his story against the story of Richard Hogle, the portrait of the police as they and the D.A. painted it against the portrait of the police as Charles Wilcox represented it. The big question was would the jury—those average citizens of this small, close-knit county—buy the story of the police, those home-town boys whose lives intersected with their own, or would they get behind this strange, pale, and forbiddingly remote youth who might well be feeling the same sort of contempt for them as he had felt for his own family?

One would have to say that, armed with all the evidence that had gone unsuppressed by the judge, the hometown team was regarded as the favorites.

16

The "company line" that Charles Wilcox talked about was further eroded with the appearance on the witness stand of the young state trooper Bernard Keller. Under questioning by the D.A., Keller corroborated Walter Shook's account of Wyley's alleged confession in the polygraph examination room, but, under cross-examination, Keller found himself facing questions regarding Investigator Salmon's physical contact with Wyley on the morning of December 14, questions he could not avoid answering. Wilcox asked Keller if Salmon had left the position of operator to come around and sit in front of Wyley Gates, and Keller confirmed that he had.

"And we can agree, can we not, that from that position he could not run the polygraph machine?" asked Wilcox.

"That is correct," said Keller.

"During the time Investigator Salmon was in that room with Wyley Gates, he had physical contact with Wyley Gates, did he not?"

"Yes," Keller allowed. "He touched him."

The word lingered in the courtroom, as Wilcox let it

sink in. "In fact, sir," Wilcox said, resuming his questioning, "he touched Wyley Gates's legs, didn't he?"

Keller appeared to hesitate for a moment before answering. "Yes," he said. "His legs were touched."

And so, Keller, the company man, had now provided a detail about the polygraph episode that was far more damaging than anything Walter Shook had offered. "And as you sit here, can you tell us how many times Investigator Salmon touched Wyley Gates's legs?" Wilcox asked.

"No, I wasn't keeping count," Keller replied sarcastically, in an effort to regain some of the police's lost position.

Wilcox, undeterred, asked if there were any attachments to the polygraph machine that would require attaching to the subject's legs, and Keller said that there were not. With no further questions, the witness was allowed to step down.

The next and much-awaited witness was Thomas Francis Salmon. Forty-eight years old, physically trim, neatly dressed, with close-cropped hair and a clipped nasal delivery, Salmon was the very image of a "regulation man," conveying a kind of reassuring Elliot Ness–like solidity. To Charles Wilcox, however, there was nothing reassuring about Investigator Salmon. He was, in fact, quite convinced that Salmon had been the engineer of a sly scheme that had backfired on the morning of December 14.

"I think when Hogle showed up, Salmon devised a routine to try to dance around Hogle and get Hogle to agree to let Wyley go in the back room and just go for it," Wilcox conjectured. In Wilcox's opinion, Salmon's "dance around Hogle" involved setting up Hogle comfortably with coffee and a magazine and then walking Wyley back. "I think he even thought about the fact ahead of time, that 'If Hogle gets up to come, what will I do then?'" said Wilcox. "And he devised a hand routine as a nonverbal communication, hopeful that Hogle would interpret it as Hogle did." Wilcox, in fact, had half expected Salmon, in the suppression hearings, to maintain that he had turned around as he went toward the examination room so as to wave to Hogle, rather than to deny altogether that he had put his hand up.

Wilcox believed that it had never been Salmon's intention to actually perform the polygraph examination on Wyley. "They went back there to intimidate a confession out of him, using the machine as an intimidator . . . and they expected him to confess or, if he didn't, pry him to confess by coming around, facing him, touching him," Wilcox theorized. The problem came, Wilcox believed, when Salmon grew utterly baffled by Wyley's continued agreement to take the test after he saw how the machine worked. "I think after a couple of hours Salmon finally deduced in his own mind, 'Jesus, maybe this kid didn't do it. He's too anxious to take this test!' " said Wilcox. Wilcox felt that Salmon should certainly have changed his tactics when he said to Wyley "If you didn't do it but think you know who did," and got the first balk of the evening. "That should have put [Salmon] on notice right there that 'We've got a little problem here,' " said Wilcox. "I would have been on the horn back to Shook and Cozzolino and said, 'You'd better keep investigating this matter because, one, this kid is a little off-centered and, two, he wants to take this test badly, and, three, he just balked, for the first time, only when I said if you didn't do it but might know who did.' "

The fact that Wyley wanted to take the test as badly as he did could conceivably be viewed as a manifestation of a guilty teenager's compulsion to confess, but Wilcox rejected outright that possibility. "If he wanted to take that test, that means one of two things to me only," he said. "One, that he thought he could beat it, which I don't feel he did when he saw how it worked, or, two, he wanted to take the test because he felt he'd be found out as not doing it and then the police would have to look for somebody else and he was not going to rat on anyone else, so the police would have to go out investigating again."

Indeed, Wilcox speculates that it was the sheriff's department's reluctance to continue their investigation that led them to the polygraphist in the first place. "They usually save the polygraph for the last resort," said Wilcox. "They don't usually jump on it immediately. Some do. But the ones that do basically consider it a time-saving device. 'Hey, it's cold outside. Why beat the bushes and walk around? Let's send him down to Tom and see if Tom can work his magic.' " Wilcox saw Salmon as a man intent on displaying his magic. In his experience as district attorney in Rensselaer County, Wilcox had encountered polygraph examiners who were regarded as "miracle men" who could turn around an otherwise stalled investigation. "When the police bring in these people who have been absolutely denying, suddenly they go back in the polygraph room and by magic the guy comes out and says, 'Got your man, guys,' and he becomes a hero," said Wilcox. "And if he comes out and says, 'He's not your guy and it's not going good,' his status is diminished. So these polygraphers go in there with the idea that they have to work their magic to keep their standing in the law-enforcement community . . . and I ran into cases where there was no doubt in my mind that the polygraphist made up certain things."

But, whatever the truth was regarding the events at Troop K Barracks on the morning of December 14, it was clearly evident, as Investigator Salmon took the stand, that Wyley Gates, pivoting his chair slightly and looking with intense interest at this witness, was manifesting more emotion than he had at any other point in the trial.

With a frequent, tense smile, Tom Salmon offered his version of events on the morning of December 14, which, up to the point where he asked Wyley to accompany him to the polygraph examination room, closely matched the accounts of Richard Hogle and Walter Shook.

"Just prior to leaving the room," asked the D.A., nearing the pivotal moment of that morning, "did Mr. Gates express any comment at all about not wanting to go with you?"

"Absolutely none," said Salmon firmly.

"Did Mr. Hogle express any comment at all about his not wanting Mr. Gates to go with you?" Keeler pressed.

"Absolutely not," replied Salmon.

"At any time did you physically touch Mr. Hogle to prevent him from going with you?"

"No," said Salmon. "When you say 'touch' him, I shook

hands with him initially. To prevent him from coming with me, absolutely not."

"Did Mr. Hogle express any verbal comments that he wanted to accompany you with Mr. Gates?"

"Absolutely not."

"At any time," said Keeler, lighting on the critical moment, "did you raise your hand in a motion to prevent Mr. Hogle from accompanying you with Mr. Gates?"

"I did not," Salmon replied, with evident anger.

Under Keeler's questioning, they moved into the polygraph examination room, where, again, Salmon's account closely matched the accounts of Shook and Bernard Keller. Only one piece of new material emerged from Keeler's examination of the witness. Keeler asked Salmon if there had come a time when he asked Wyley why he had not shot his grandmother, and Salmon said such a time had come. "This was after he admitted the four murders," Salmon testified, "and he went over to his grandmother's house to tell her he had found the bodies and to call the police. I said to him, 'Why didn't you shoot her?' and he said to me, 'Because I like her.'"

It wasn't until the following morning that Charles Wilcox began his cross-examination of Investigator Salmon. Wyley, taut with anticipation, was wearing a white shirt and a white tie, the latter perhaps in some kind of unconscious recollection of what he had worn in the early morning hours of December fourteenth, when he and Salmon had shared the anonymous little room with its pottery bric-a-brac and two-way mirror.

Wilcox began by asking Salmon if, upon his arrival at the barracks and after his briefing, he had classified Wyley, in his own mind, as a suspect, and Salmon said he had. Salmon confirmed for Wilcox that Wyley had admitted to nothing at that time nor was there any physical evidence incriminating Wyley, but, having classified him as a suspect, he opened up the polygraph room and prepared it. Wilcox then began to discuss the apparatus and functioning of the polygraph machine. "When you're asking questions on the polygraph machine, the paper is running?"

"Sometimes," Salmon allowed.

Wilcox, looking quizzical, asked if there were times when the machine was hooked up, the person was hooked up, questions were asked, but the paper was not running, and Salmon said that there were such times.

"You just hook them up for the pure heck of it, is that what you're saying, Investigator?" Wilcox charged, his little lancet of a question causing Salmon's cheekbones to clench. "Isn't it supposed to measure involuntary response?" Wilcox asked, attempting to suggest that Salmon had used the machine for purposes of intimidation rather than for measuring involuntary response, and he demanded to know as well if there was any other reason to hook up a person to the machine beyond measuring that involuntary response. Salmon agreed that this was the machine's purpose, but added that his first purpose in putting the cuff on a subject was to get the subject used to having the attachment on while questions were being asked. Wilcox, pressing the point, demanded to know if there was any other reason for a person being hooked up while the machine was not running, and Salmon, turning more bureaucratic by the moment, cited as a reason that this was "accepted procedure" that he followed on every polygraph he conducted.

"What does that mean?" Wilcox wondered aloud. "After the person is comfortable with the cuff on, sir, is it your testimony that you leave him with that cuff on for two hours, or two and a half hours, with no other purpose than as your, Thomas Salmon's, usual procedure? Is that your testimony?"

"That is not my testimony," Salmon said angrily.

"What other reason is there, sir, for leaving the cardio-cuff on after you have made sure they're comfortable with it, other than to measure an involuntary response?" Wilcox persisted.

"Procedure as taught to me by the National Training Center of Polygraph Science in 1981," Salmon said, bristling.

"I have followed that procedure through each and every polygraph examination that I have conducted since that time, including the polygraph examination of Mr. Gates."

The defense attorney's line of questioning grew increasingly aggressive. "We can agree as we sit here today in August of 1987 that you never gave Wyley Gates a polygraph examination, correct, sir?" said Wilcox.

"We can agree that I never completed the test," Salmon said.

". . . Wyley Gates said to you when he got there that he was there to take the polygraph examination test, correct?" asked Wilcox.

"That is correct."

"Is it a fair statement in accordance with your testimony that at least on seven occasions in your . . . litany, you kept saying to Wyley Gates 'No one can force you to take this test, you don't have to take this test.' Is that correct, sir?"

"You use the figure seven," said Salmon. "I imagine that's a fair estimate."

"And on each occasion when you went through this litany . . . Wyley Gates said to you, in words or substance, at that point in time, 'Bring on the test,' did he not, sir?" Wilcox demanded in a near shout now. "And there is no doubt about the fact that you were in that room at least two and a half hours with Wyley Gates, correct?"

"That is true."

"At no time," said Wilcox, "during say the first hour being in that room with Wyley Gates, did you ask him, hooked up to all the attachments on that machine with the chart running, did you ask, 'Did you kill Robert Gates, Sr.,' did you?"

"I did not do that," Salmon admitted.

"And we can expand that to the first hour and a half, couldn't we?"

"Yes," Salmon said evenly. "We can expand that right through the entire time he was in the room with me."

Having laid open the serious inconsistency in Salmon's hooking up Wyley to the machine without performing the test, Wilcox moved on to the all-important point of Hogle's absence from the observation room.

". . . You testified yesterday that you felt someone should observe, is that correct?" Wilcox asked.

"Yes."

"And of course you had Mr. Hogle in the waiting room," said Wilcox, "and you were going to be giving an examination or a test to his client, correct?"

"That is correct."

"Did you invite Mr. Hogle into the room where he could observe Wyley?" Wilcox demanded.

"I did not," said Salmon.

"But you did invite Investigator Shook," charged Wilcox, "and you did search out a trooper in the barracks who happened to be on duty on that particular night but was going off duty and you invited him, didn't you?"

"Yes, I did," said Salmon, who was not compelled to invite Wyley's attorney to observe, but was compelled to have the attorney present if Wyley or the attorney had so requested.

"Did you think that when Mr. Hogle picked up his briefcase and put his coat over his arm and started to go with you that he was not interested in going with you?" Wilcox challenged.

"I believe that I had testified that I did not see him do what you just described," Salmon maintained.

"It is your testimony to the jury here that you didn't see him do that?" asked Wilcox, incredulous once again. "You were leading his client out of the room where he was and you didn't make any observations about what Mr. Hogle was doing?"

Salmon faltered. "I didn't testify to that at all."

"Did you see him take his coat and put it over his arm, take his briefcase, and walk toward where you were and where Wyley and you were going?"

"I did not see that," Salmon said.

"In terms of Mr. Hogle, sir, can you tell us what you meant," asked Wilcox, "when he got up and walked to go into the polygraph area with you and you put up your hand, splayed your fingers, and made a pushing motion with them?"

"I did not do that!" Salmon cried, his eyes flashing. "I testified to that in the hearing. I did not do that."

Wilcox concluded with a series of questions related to the physical contact between Officer Salmon and Wyley Gates on the morning of December 14—the "touching" that both Shook and Keller had now testified to.

"We can certainly agree that there did come a time when you were in the front of Wyley Gates seated in a chair very close to him and you were touching, had your hands on his legs, correct?" Wilcox asked.

"That is incorrect," said Salmon furiously. "I have given that great thought since we went through this point in the hearing. At no time whatsoever did I place my hands on Wyley Gates's knee or leg. I touched his arms in that vicinity as they were placed on the polygraph chair. That is my total recollection at this time."

"And Trooper Keller would be mistaken if he indicated that you touched his legs, would he not?"

"Anybody would be mistaken or lying if they said I touched his thighs or his knees."

"And we would have to include in that Mr. Shook?" Wilcox asked, with a touch of wryness.

"We would have to include in that anybody," said Salmon.

Wilcox asked Salmon if it was his testimony that Wyley Gates had been free to leave the polygraph examination room on the morning of December 14; Salmon said that it was. Wilcox stared at him for a moment, and then asked him if he knew how old Wyley had been at the time of their contact.

"I believe he was seventeen at that time," Salmon said, with a deliberate blandness.

"How old were you, sir?"

"I'm forty-eight years old," Salmon replied.

Before Salmon was allowed to step down, Wilcox had one more issue that he wished the witness to address. He asked Salmon if it was in fact his testimony that he had no recollection regarding the rubber gloves.

"That is my testimony," replied Salmon. "I have no recollection of gloves being mentioned."

"He indicated to you that he had cut his hand," said Wilcox, "supposedly during the course of one of these shootings, correct?"

"That is correct."

"The gloves represented a problem to you, didn't they, Investigator?" Wilcox sneered.

"There were no gloves as far as my recollection goes. I have testified to that," Salmon maintained.

Having concluded his testimony, Salmon stepped down and crossed the courtroom to the exit. As he walked past the defendant's table, Wyley, now eighteen, grown taller and more mature, blinked rapidly behind his glasses—again, a display of emotion that would have been minimalist in anyone else, but that some on the jury later claimed to have noticed, as they watched this boy for any signs of emotion, no matter how minimal they may have been.

Before Keeler could get to Charles Argyle, Wyley's former cellmate and the next big building block of his case, he had some lesser business to attend to. Called to the stand was sixteen-year-old Cameron Price, in jeans, rugby shirt, and sneakers. Cameron had found himself the recipient of two letters that Wyley had sent him from the Columbia County Jail, the ostensible point of which was to get Cameron to declare his friendship. But, for the prosecution's purposes, the letters could also help to incriminate Wyley in the crimes. Cameron's testimony did not cast new light on the enigma called Wyley Gates, although it did offer, at Wilcox's behest, a characterization of the defendant as a "peaceful" person. But what was especially distinctive about Cameron's appearance was the fact that he had been accompanied to the trial by his parents and by an attorney, even though he clearly was not criminally implicated in the matter. In the days ahead, a series of Chatham High School youths would testify without the accompaniment or moral support of

anyone but each other. Evidently, the Price family did not
regard their son's subpoena to a murder trial as a negligible
matter. What was also noteworthy about the youth's appearance was the crimson flush it brought to Wyley's cheeks.
One could only speculate on the reasons for this emotional
reaction—ardor, shame, guilt, or any combination thereof.
In any event, between Salmon and now Cameron, Wyley's
sphinxlike posture was crumbling.

The next two witnesses of the day were a former and
a current assistant district attorney, both of whom Keeler
was calling in order to lay the foundation for—or, more to
the point, in order to lend credence to—the eventual
appearance of Chuck Argyle. William Lally, who had left
the Columbia County D.A.'s office in July 1987, had been
responsible for the prosecution of Argyle on criminal
charges pending against him in Valatie. Keeler established
that Lally had never had any contact with Argyle or his
attorney regarding the case of *The People of New York* v. *Wyley
Gates* and that he had never offered any deal to Argyle for
his help with the Gates case. In his cross-examination, Wilcox
asked if, in fact, Lally had notated a suggested prison term
of "one to three" on the flap of the file that the D.A.'s office
kept on Argyle, and Lally said that he had. Lally also
"seemed to recall" that he had agreed to release Argyle
from jail on his own recognizance in January 1987.

"Do you have any recollection of Judge Williams [of
Kinderhook, the site of Argyle's burglary] nixing that idea
or refusing to go along with that recommendation of
releasing Mr. Argyle in his own recognizance?" Wilcox
asked.

"Only from your calling that to my attention in the
previous proceeding," retorted Lally. "I do not have an
independent recollection of it."

"In terms of charges pending against Argyle," asked
Wilcox, "isn't it a fact that there was also pending against
him a criminal-mischief charge?"

Lally said there had been.

"In the month of March, and more specifically on or

about March 3, 1987, his case was disposed of in the Town of Kinderhook?"

"Yes," Lally acknowledged, "as I was refreshed from the previous proceeding."

Lally stepped down and the second of the A.D.A.s, Thomas J. Donahue, took the stand. Donahue, an A.D.A. only since October 1986, told Keeler that he had been familiar with the Valatie charges against Argyle for unauthorized use of a motor vehicle and that Argyle had pled guilty in the late winter of 1987 and was sentenced to time served. Echoing Lally, Donahue told Keeler that he had never offered Argyle any help or leniency in return for his assistance with the Gates case.

By the time Charles Keith Argyle II—a.k.a "Chuck," a.k.a "Chucky"—appeared in court on August 26, he had already staged his own little media blitz. Granting interviews to print and TV media, he alleged that Wyley had told him details of the murders. It would be Wilcox's approach to this key prosecution witness to suggest that the sudden civic-mindedness of this previously corruptible young man was the result of a deal he had struck with the authorities.

"I think the deals were made and that Argyle set out to make the deal," said Wilcox, who pointed out, as well, that Argyle himself had been betrayed in exactly the same scenario when he supposedly made some kind of admission in jail to his cellmate, who got immunity testifying against him. "I think Argyle learned that game very quickly," charged Wilcox, "and I think he found himself in the fortuitous situation of being the cellmate of Wyley Gates." Wilcox also found it highly unlikely that Wyley would have chosen Argyle as a confidante. "I didn't believe it for a minute that Wyley sat down and stated to Charles Argyle, who would be a real Dumbo and nobody that Wyley Gates would be interested in associating with, all these grand, inculpatory facts and evidence," said Wilcox. "I just can't see him talking to Argyle. They were two fully different kinds of individuals."

The documents that Argyle had submitted, however, did sound authentically like Wyley's voice, and his afternoon appearance followed a morning that the jurors had passed considering the Cameron Price letters. Taken together, these documents must have struck the jury as significantly incriminating evidence.

Appearing in the witness docket, Argyle, who was now living in Schenectady with his mother, had obviously made no special effort to look clean-cut. Stout, moon-faced, with a small smile and small eyes, a shadow of a mustache, and long filmy blond hair, he swaggered up to the stand. He evidently knew his way around a courtroom. It was hard to remember that he was just a year or two older than the boyish Cameron Price.

Argyle told Keeler that he had spent five months in jail with Wyley, from December 17 until the end of May, and that they had shared the same cell for most of that time. He had never met Robert Gates, Sr., he told Keeler, but had known Cheryl Brahm. She had gone to school with his father and would sometimes stop in for gas at his father's service station. Argyle added that he had been in school with some of Cheryl's nephews.

"Did you ever tell Mr. Gates or any other prisoners that Cheryl Brahm was your godmother?" Keeler asked.

"I said it, but it's not true," Argyle replied, explaining that he had told this untruth as a way of justifying to the other inmates why he was testifying against Wyley.

He went on to tell Keeler that he had been in jail because he had taken a car from his father's garage and because he had robbed a Nice 'n Easy store. In the Town of Valatie, he had faced charges of burglary, unauthorized use of a motor vehicle, and criminal mischief. In the Town of Kinderhook, he had faced a charge of burglary.

"Did there come a time that your charges . . . were disposed of?" Keeler asked.

Argyle replied that they were "packaged together"— time served for unauthorized use, six months in jail for petty larceny.

"Are you presently employed?" Keeler asked.

"Right now, no," replied Argyle. "I quit work so I could play football at Mount Pleasant High School."

Keeler showed him a paperback copy of the Stephen King novel *Cujo* and asked if he had ever seen the book. Argyle replied that Wyley had taken it out of the jail library, and had given it to him to read. Wyley had then written a note in it for Damian Rossney but it never reached Damian because a guard intercepted it during a strip search. Argyle confirmed that the writing in it was Wyley's—he said he was familiar with it on account of having been in school in the jail with Wyley—and that he had, in fact, seen Wyley writing in it. Keeler entered the copy of *Cujo* into evidence.

Keeler next showed Argyle the three-page document in which Wyley posed a series of hypothetical questions about his guilt and the legal ramifications thereof. Argyle told Keeler that he had found the document on the floor of their cell. "I figured somebody should know about it," Argyle explained, "so I handed it to the next guard on duty."

"Did there ever come a time that you ever had conversations with Wyley Gates concerning the charges that were pending against him?" Keeler asked.

"Yes. I asked him about how it happened and why he did it," said Argyle. "I asked why he killed the people and he said he didn't get along with them, they expected more out of him, that he was never really a part of the family, like he went to school, came home, played with his computer and he played trumpet and I guess they wanted more of a son out of him than they got." Argyle testified that Wyley had told him that he shot the four, but that it wasn't supposed to happen the way it had. It was supposed to happen at his father's garage and it was supposed to look like a burglary, and the only two people who were supposed to die were his father and his brother. But each day that he went to the garage, he kept getting scared, so finally he waited until they were home and then he went in and shot them, and he said they never knew what hit them.

"What else did he say?" Keeler urged.

"He told me that he wanted Cheryl to suffer because

him and her didn't get along well," he recalled. "He said she was the last to die."

"What else did he say?" Keeler pressed, making the most of his witness.

"He told me that Damian and Miles McDonald were supposed to help but at the last minute Miles chickened out and told him that his mom wouldn't let him use the car, so he canceled," Argyle continued. "When Damian found out about that, Damian said he wanted twenty-five percent of Wyley's estate to do it; and Wyley said, no, he said he could hire a professional killer to do it far cheaper, so he said he'd do it himself, and they staged a burglary at his house a few weeks earlier and stole a bunch of guns and ammunition and trashed the house."

As Wyley sat, his rigid hauteur back under control, Argyle went on with his testimony. "He told me that he had forgot about the gunpowder that was left on his clothes," Argyle said, details pouring out of him. "He said he was planning on getting away with it, but he forgot about that. He told me he got rid of the plastic gloves that he had. He also made a remark that he didn't like one of the jail guards that was there and he said that he was going to trash his house and kill him. He also mentioned that he saw his father's will and said that most everything was left to him and his brother, and I mentioned how I would like to see what was on my own father's will because I just wanted to see it, and I told him about my father kicked me out of the house and stuff that went on, and he told me if I ever wanted to get rid of my father and mother and find out what was in the will, he'd help me."

Concluding the direct examination, Argyle said that Wyley had told him "he wished he had told his parents and Cheryl Brahm and his brother to go to hell before they died." He added that Wyley had told him "that he was sane when he did it and could somehow get his psychiatrist to prove otherwise at the time."

Wilcox began his cross-examination bluntly. "There's no question that in this particular matter you have, in fact, told lies?" he said.

Argyle agreed, not seeming particularly remorseful when it came to telling untruths.

"You stole a large and substantial sum of money from your father?" he asked.

"That has nothing to do with this case," Argyle replied.

"Is it a fact?"

"Maybe."

"Maybe," echoed Wilcox. ". . . As a result of the money you stole from your father . . . he advised you . . . that you were not welcome to go back to his house?"

"Wrong," said Argyle. "That's not why I was kicked out."

Wilcox then suggested that Argyle's mother had kicked him out because he had physically abused his handicapped brother.

"It's a kid that's eleven years old that weighs two hundred and thirty pounds," said Argyle sullenly. "I'm not going to sit there and you wouldn't either and let somebody hit on you."

From that Pinteresque moment, Wilcox returned to the suggestions of a deal struck between Argyle and the law-enforcement officials. He wondered why Argyle had held on to the notes from February 19, the date when he allegedly found them on the floor of the cell, until March 12, when he handed them over to the authorities, some nine days after his sentencing and after additional charges against him had been dropped. "Can we agree you didn't like it in jail?" Wilcox asked.

"You could assume that," young Argyle replied, in perfect legalspeak.

"And you didn't give them those notes pertaining to the conversations with Wyley Gates, as you would allege, until after you had been sentenced?"

"I don't remember which day it was exactly," said Argyle.

Finally, Wilcox tore into him with a series of questions that were designed to portray the essential dishonesty of this witness. Once again he brought up the lies that Argyle had told other prisoners about Cheryl Brahm being his godmother, and lies he had told these same men about his sentencing.

"There is no question that you did make up things in jail, is that correct?" Wilcox said once again.

Argyle admitted that was true.

Wilcox withdrew a document. "Is that a letter of several pages?" he asked the witness.

"Yes, it is."

"It was certainly written by you, wasn't it?"

"Yes, it was."

"And it's all pure fabrication, isn't it?"

"Yup."

"You made it all up, didn't you?"

"Yes, I did," said Argyle, with a grin that did little to veil his discomfort.

With that, Wilcox submitted into evidence a "fantasy" letter that Argyle had written to *Hustler* magazine and that Wyley had intercepted and forwarded by legal mail after learning of his cellmate's decision to testify against him. At the judge's request, the public filed out to leave the jurors alone as they read the letter. Their laughter, bordering on hysteria, as it represented the only real "comic relief" in the otherwise relentlessly grim proceedings, could be heard in the corridors. Joan Yowe characterized Argyle to the press as having "quite an imagination—he's creative" and said that the letter was "just an example of his creativity."

When the public was admitted back inside, the D.A. conducted his redirect examination of the witness, asking Argyle if anyone had offered him any deals in exchange for testimony in the Wyley Gates trial regarding charges pending in Rensselaer County, to which Argyle replied that no one had. But the titters evoked by the *Hustler* letter were still reverberating and, in the wake of this derision, another of the D.A.'s central building blocks in his case had collapsed around his feet.

17

The following day, August 27, began with the reappearance of Vivian Gates, called back briefly to the stand for the purpose of identifying, for the record, her son as Robert Gates, her grandsons as Robert Gates, Jr., and Jason Gates, and Cheryl Brahm as her son's girlfriend. The day would present far greater challenges to Mrs. Gates, however, and to the jurors as well, for the next witness was Investigator William Vick, also called back to the stand, and this time he carried with him plastic trash bags containing the clothing removed from the four victims at the morgue.

People's Exhibit 44 was a plastic trash bag containing the clothing that Jason Gates had been wearing on December 13. Investigator Vick withdrew a pair of poignantly mismatched socks. Suddenly there was the feeling of a crypt having been opened—a disturbance of the dead, nothing less. Mrs. Gates closed her eyes and lowered her head, surrendering to a kind of narcoleptic state and, with a hurried conference following at the bench, Investigator Vick's withdrawal of the bag's contents was suspended.

"Is that all of the clothing that was recovered from the body of Jason Gates?" Keeler asked.

Vick said that it was, and that it had been in his custody since its recovery.

He then turned to the plastic bag containing the clothing of Robert Gates, Jr., exhibiting a blue flannel shirt. Mrs. Gates's eyes remained shut; her sister Jackie dabbed away tears. The shirt was passed among the jurors, some of whom obviously did not wish to handle it but forced themselves to do so. Investigator Vick next withdrew a green striped sweater worn by Cheryl Brahm at the time of her death. Overcome by the sight of it, Gretchen and Mame Brahm— Cheryl's sisters-in-law—bolted from the courtroom. The sweater made its way along the line of jurors, until Juror #4—delicately pretty Patricia O'Neill—quietly informed the court officer that she preferred not to handle it. The judge instructed the court officer to place the garment, bloodied and torn, on a table for the jurors' viewing.

The afternoon witness was another of the key building blocks in the D.A.'s case, one that he had set in place early on with promises of immunity, and his name was Miles Edward McDonald. Seventeen years old, Miles made a dramatic presence in the courtroom. He was a handsome youth, dark, sleek, chiseled-featured, strong, and compact. All that darkness and sleekness and compactness, together with his closely cropped haircut, brought to mind the teen idol of the day, Tom Cruise, specifically as he appeared in *Top Gun*. Now, as Miles sat in the docket, awaiting his turn, in his jeans and blue oxford shirt that seemed to fit him so comfortably, his eyes made no contact with Wyley's. The defendant looked inordinately pale and gangling by contrast and stared with a burning intensity at this boy whom he had once included in his small circle of friends.

Assuming the witness stand, Miles told the court that he had lived in the Chatham area for fourteen years, that he was a senior at Chatham High, and that he served as a sexton at St. James Church in Chatham. He had been acquainted with Wyley for three years, with contact in classes, the concert band, and the jazz band. He knew of Robert Gates but had never met him, and he had only a passing familiarity with Bobby and Cheryl, having been introduced to them in the course of several visits to the log house.

Under questioning by Keeler, Miles re-created the sequence of conversations that had laid the groundwork for the burglary and, perhaps, for the murders that followed. He gave, as well, an accounting of the actual burglary and the target-practice session that followed at John Bailey's residence. Turning to December 13, he testified that Wyley and Damian had invited him to join them at the Crandell Theater that night, but he had already made plans for the evening with Matt Rueckheim, who had been "his best friend since sixth grade." Matt picked him up between 5:00 and 5:30 that night, Miles testified, and drove to Matt's brother's house in East Chatham to drop off a power saw that Matt had borrowed. They stayed there through dinner and left just in time to get to the nine o'clock movie in Chatham. As they waited in line to get in, they ran into Damian and Wyley, who were exiting. Miles asked Damian about the movie and Damian said it was all right. Then, gesturing with his thumb toward Wyley, whom Miles described as having had his back to them, looking toward the village landmark known as The Clocktower, Damian said, "He did it." When they left, Matt asked Miles what Wyley had done and Miles replied that Wyley had smashed up Cheryl's car. Neither Keeler nor Wilcox in his cross-examination would trace the mysterious logic of Miles's deduction.

When Miles and Matt got out onto the street, they heard that there had been an accident on Route 295 in East Chatham and they decided to check it out. Following a sheriff's car down Frisbie Street, they lost sight of the patrol car and so turned around, heading back to Matt's house, where Miles spent the night, leaving at approximately 8:15 the next morning.

Keeler now questioned Miles about early phone conversations with Damian that concerned the plot to kill Robert Gates. As he spoke, Miles's eyes began to dart nervously and irresistibly in the direction of Wyley, who continued to stare at him.

"It would be toward the end of November," Miles began. Damian had called him and somehow, within the context of a conversation about a proposed ski trip, Damian mentioned that Wyley had proposed paying him to kill his father. Damian added that Miles could also get paid, but he did not, according to Miles, elaborate at this point. Miles then went on to describe a second phone conversation he had with Damian. "He had called and we were just talking again," said Miles, "and he told me what percentage of Wyley's inheritance he would get by killing Wyley's father, but I don't remember the percentage that I would get, I believe twenty percent of whatever Damian got, for driving him there." Miles explained that they were "just joking around," that he was "haggling" with him, joking with him about how much he wanted, and that Damian said that the only way he could get more was if he had to "cover" him and that way he would get half of whatever Damian got. Keeler did not probe into the linkage between these conversations, or how the dialogue progressed from one plateau to another. Instead, he concluded his questioning by establishing that Miles had been interviewed immediately after the homicides by the McDonalds' family friend Detective Butch Harrison. Miles told Harrison that he knew nothing about the killings, but later corrected that, on the following Tuesday, during a second interview with Harrison. For the record, Keeler asked Miles if he knew that he was testifying with immunity.

"I believe so," said the ingenuous witness, his eye wandering once more to the tall, rigid young man at the defendant's table.

For many in the community, the granting of immunity to Miles McDonald was troubling, but the prosecution felt they had no other choice. "Immunity is a tough issue," acknowledged Assistant D.A. Nancy Snyder, "because you don't like to see someone who's involved in a case get off scot-free, but immunity exists as a tool because sometimes if you don't give it to an individual, there is no incentive for that individual to talk to you." Without giving immunity to Miles, Snyder maintained, they would not have been able to charge Damian, for Wyley had not inculpated Damian.

One of the people who was troubled by this granting of total immunity was the defense attorney, Charles Wilcox. "They could have provided him with immunity in the burglary case," said Wilcox, in a posttrial conversation wherein he discussed the D.A.'s options, "[but] once he got an attorney, the deal was he had something to offer; in exchange for which he wants the total immunity." In Wilcox's opinion, the D.A. found himself in the position of having to decide just how important this information was, and he evidently decided it was very important indeed, in light of the problems that he might have down the road with Wyley's statement. "On the other hand, I think Miles McDonald didn't give the whole story when the investigator went to his house—his, quote, friend, the investigator," said Wilcox. "I think Miles McDonald basically gave him the burglary. He didn't tell him he didn't know anything about the murder. It was only after the immunity was exchanged that he came forward and gave him what he claimed was information he had on the underlying plan of conspiracy and murder. So I think he held out. I think he was cute."

In terms of what the authorities knew from Miles, the offer of total immunity could be seen as a reasonable action, but what troubled Wilcox was that they offered immunity before they really knew Miles's exact participation, essentially accepting his representation of what his involvement was. "Again it goes back to that Section Twenty idea," said Wilcox. "They're focusing on Wyley Gates and their focus is so intent on him and [they have] such tunnel vision in regard to him, they're just trying to get witnesses that will testify against Wyley and they're presuming that Wyley did the shooting. They were very willing to accept Miles McDonald's claim that he on the night in question wasn't there but was with someone else. They probably developed an immediate 'Oh goody' mentality—'this will help'—without really searching it out."

And so Wilcox began his cross-examination, intent on ripping apart Miles McDonald's credibility. But Miles, it turned out, had a good share of Teflon in his composition.

Wilcox, having reviewed the sequence of conversations and the testimony regarding the burglary, now turned to the target practice at John Bailey's, specifically the .380 pistol they had fired there.

"You mentioned that Damian had it," said Wilcox. "You have referred to that as 'Damian's little toy,' haven't you?"

"Yes," Miles answered forthrightly.

"And isn't it a fact that when Wyley got there, that Damian Rossney and John Bailey had to show Wyley Gates how to put the bullets in a gun?"

"I have no idea," Miles said.

"Isn't it a fact that John Bailey and Damian Rossney had to show Wyley Gates what the safety does and what the safety is?"

"I don't know," Miles said.

"And isn't it a fact that at any time Wyley Gates pulled the trigger of that gun, he was very timid with that gun?"

"I don't recall," said Miles.

"Would it be fair to describe Damian Rossney's demeanor during these discussions that you were involved in as 'gung-ho'?" asked Wilcox.

"Yes, that's what I testified," Miles coolly replied.

"Incidentally, did you sell a magnum pistol to Matt Rueckheim?" asked Wilcox.

"No," said Miles.

"Did you attempt to sell a pistol to Matt Rueckheim?" Miles repeated that he had not.

"Did you see or have knowledge of Damian Rossney trying to give or sell guns, including handguns, to John Bailey?"

"I don't recall," Miles said.

Wilcox next questioned the witness about materials that the police had collected at his home, naming book titles that had to do with terrorism and illicit forces. Miles, disavowing knowledge of such books, was asked what titles he did recall.

"I remember *Best of Creative Computing. Doonesbury. L. L. Bean's Guide to the Outdoors*," Miles replied craftily.

"Are you a reader of survivalist periodicals or literature?" Wilcox wanted to know.

"I received a gift subscription from Wyley Gates for Christmas," said Miles, "which was canceled immediately."

"Your testimony is that you don't do any reading in that particular area?" Wilcox pressed.

"No, that is not true. I am an avid hiker and camper," Miles avowed.

"I'm talking about survivalists, war games–type periodicals," Wilcox pressed.

"I don't receive any, and I don't have any home to my knowledge," said Miles, as if offended by the idea.

Wilcox was making no progress with this witness. He asked him a few more questions, verifying that Miles had never had a polygraph examination or had his fingerprints tested, and then the witness was allowed to step down. He walked hurriedly to the door past Wyley, who shifted in his chair so as to follow the departure of his friend from the courtroom.

August 31 began with brief appearances by pale, beefy Matt Rueckheim and Matt's sister-in-law, Mary Rueckheim, both of whom corroborated Miles's whereabouts on the evening of December 13. The rest of the day was taken up by what would register, in the end, as a chilling procession of Chatham youths who had been, in one way or another, privy to knowledge of what Wyley had been up to in the autumn of 1986.

Assuming the stand was Michael Swen Lofgren, a stout soon-to-be college lad with an Amway air of confidence and a smile that could, under the circumstances, be described as smarmy, especially when he directed it at Wyley, his former luncheon companion at Chatham High School.

Lofgren informed the court that he had known Wyley for seven or eight years, and that they had often sat together at the same cafeteria table. Once, Lofgren recalled, about a

month before the killings, Wyley had come to the table with
a book entitled *Improvised Munitions*, which contained instructions on how to produce your own armaments. "We shared
it around the table," Lofgren remembered. "We said, 'Wow,
this is pretty weird stuff.' " At another time, Lofgren asked
Wyley how he and his brother got along and Wyley said,
"Oh, we never got along." Regarding the burglary, Lofgren,
having read about it in the newspaper, approached Wyley
at band practice. "So, Wyley, you got two thousand dollars,"
Lofgren testified he had said to Wyley, but Wyley replied
that he had only gotten $1,000. As for Damian, Lofgren
said he knew him as a fellow classmate and had once had a
conversation with him in the computer room, wherein
Damian told him he was going to be getting twin nickel-
plated .44-caliber handguns from Wyley's house.

In cross-examination, Wilcox elicited from Lofgren the
information that both Damian and Miles had told him in
advance that they were going to break into the log house
and that Miles had told him afterward that he had taken
several handguns. Lofgren also stated, however, that he had
never seen Wyley Gates exhibit aggression or violence and
that his lunchtime companion was always "kind and cour-
teous." (As contrasted with Damian, whom Lofgren had
described in a deposition as "solid mischief" and "out of
whack".) With the questioning concluded, the witness
stepped down, crossed the courtroom, and gave Wyley a
cordial nod before exiting.

The third Chatham High witness of the day was Benjamin Cooper, a slight, long-haired boy who limped badly.
With his physical infirmity, his barely audible responses,
and his look of trauma, he had about him a victimized air.
Indeed, if Tom Cruise were to play Miles McDonald, then
a young Elisha Cook, Jr., would be needed for the role of
Benjamin Cooper.

Asked if he was familiar with Wyley Gates, Cooper
replied that Wyley was a friend from school. They never
socialized outside of school, but they often talked in the
halls and in the by now legendary computer room.

"Are you familiar with Damian Rossney?" Keeler asked.

"Yes. A friend from school," said Cooper. "The same way."

In fact, moments later, under cross-examination, Cooper would identify Damian as "a good friend," whereas Wyley was "basically an acquaintance." It wasn't until many months later, in Damian's own trial, that the glue of the Rossney/Cooper relationship would become evident, when Damian testified that Cooper, who was "interested in ninjas and other assassination cults," had attempted to enlist him to type and proofread for him a book he wanted to write on the subject.

"Did there ever come a time that you had conversation with Damian Rossney?" Keeler asked.

Cooper said that he had. Two weeks before the murders, Damian had told him that he had been offered a "contract" on two people. In the stricken mumble that caused the judge to more than once sternly but ineffectually request that he speak up, Cooper elaborated. "Damian asked me if it was all right to 'off' someone for the right amount of money," he said, and Cooper suggested to his friend that it was *not* all right to do so.

In a subsequent conversation, in the hallway near his locker, Cooper asked Damian to describe what kind of person he was talking about. A sleaze? A drug pusher? An awful person? Damian went so far as to tell him that the person in question didn't push drugs but smoked a joint now and then.

In yet another conversation, Cooper made a guess as to who was involved, extrapolated from conversations he had been party to in the computer room, during which Bob Gates was described as a "biker type." He asked Damian why Wyley wanted his father killed, but Damian wouldn't say why. And in still another conversation, Damian assured Cooper that he wasn't going to do it, but "wasn't above getting the gun" . . . the type of gun, Cooper remembered Damian boasting, that James Bond uses.

As the day progressed, the procession of one boy after another created a portrait of a certain dining table in a

certain cafeteria in a certain small-town school where talk
of murder, munitions, and blood money was presented in
a stunningly numbed fashion, wedged in amid the trivia of
teenage life. The cars, the games, the girls, the burglaries,
the music, the beer and pretzels, the murders. What had
Hannah Arendt written of Eichmann's trial? "In those last
minutes," she wrote, "he was summing up the lessons that
this long course in human wickedness had taught us—the
lesson of the fearsome, word-and-thought-defying banality
of evil." Here, on so much smaller a scale, the same lesson
seemed to be presenting itself, still fearsome, still thought-
defying. The banality and the absence of feeling sent a
distinct chill into the courtroom. The initial response of
moral outrage—Why didn't they tell anyone? Why didn't
they stop it?—felt simplistic and naïve in the context of what
was being said. Rather, those who were watching and
listening in the courtroom felt that they were encountering
a breed of kids who were not so much immoral as amoral
in a particularly bored, soulless, even mutant way. I remembered Wyley's English teacher, Louise Lincoln, telling me
that when she found out about the conspiracy aspect of the
crime, she recalled "being surprised . . . probably hurt
because my own ignorance had been ripped . . . and really
not truly accepting that these children were cognizant of
what they were about." She remembered thinking as well
about the Arthur Miller play *The Crucible*, about how those
girls could declare somebody a witch and put on a little
performance and adults believed those girls enough to have
people actually killed. "You kind of wonder what these high
school students got into and how much they really knew
and how much was kid stuff that had gone out of control,"
she said. I thought too of what Dr. Marchionne had told
me about the "pseudo-community" that had sprung up
between Wyley and Damian and Miles and John Bailey and
one or two other kids, how Wyley had sacrificed his family
for the friendship of and membership in a peer group to
which he had never before been admitted; of how Dr.
Marchionne believed that Wyley had conceived of these
murders and then brought it to these other boys as a kind

of gift, and these other boys bought into it. But the question was Why? Money? It wasn't enough money, not even by their standards. Blood lust? Kicks? Boredom? Any or all of the above, but maybe something more profound . . . or more profoundly shallow. As these boys came and went on the stand, the thought came to mind that maybe, just maybe, the deed had been done for no good reason whatsoever, or, at least, no reason that could be connected to recognizable human emotions.

The afternoon witness was John Bailey, the boy who had hosted the target practice. Martial-looking despite his magenta alligator shirt, he exhibited on the stand an earnestness that would have done Ollie North proud.

Bailey told the court that he was eighteen years old and had been in the U.S. Army for one year and eight months. Wyley, whom he had known for three years, was a "friend" from school. Actually, they were just acquaintances, he amended, as everyone before him had amended. He and Wyley had "socialized" on "just one occasion," by which he meant the target practice. Damian, on the other hand, was more of a friend. They often sat together at lunch and in chemistry class.

"Did there ever come a time, sir, when you had a conversation with Wyley Gates concerning an alleged burglary at his father's residence?" Keeler asked Bailey.

Bailey testified that this conversation had taken place at a lunch table in the school cafeteria. "Damian and Miles told me already that they broke into the house," he said. "I wanted to know why he would break into his father's house, and he said that he resented his father and he didn't like the fact that the girl was living there and that he would get away with it, and he also said that he could kill his father." He added that Wyley particularly resented the way his father was "just needling him." Bailey went on to detail the target-practice session and to characterize Wyley's participation in it. Wyley was unsure of how to use the Walther, so he and Damian loaded the magazines for him and showed him how the safety worked. Wyley shot into the trees, into the ground, and into Bailey's grandfather's tractor, and then, at the end of this session, Wyley and Damian talked for a moment by themselves. Wyley then left with the pistol, four loaded magazines, and a box of ammunition.

Bailey also mentioned that he had suffered a minor injury on the day of the target practice. "When we were shooting, because the gun was so small and my hand was too big for it and it had a big recoil because it was so light," he explained, "I cut my hand in the meaty portion through my index finger and thumb, just like gouged out the skin." He added that Wyley had suffered an identical injury that day.

Bailey told Keeler that both Damian and Wyley had asked him what weapons he could obtain for them. "He knew I was in the army," said Bailey of Wyley. "He wanted to know if it was possible if I could get him any types of weapons or ammunition . . . hand grenades or whatever."

Keeler then asked Bailey if, on the day before the murders, Wyley Gates had been, in his considered opinion, coherent.

"He was just the same, just plain old Wyley, no different," Bailey said, grinning. "Had his tie on, whatever, and was just like any normal day at school."

Wilcox began his cross-examination of Bailey by asking him if he had graduated from Chatham High, and Bailey said that he had not on account of failing math.

"In terms of Damian Rossney," Wilcox continued, "has he shown you books pertaining to killing or torturing people?"

"Yes. He had all the different books on how to torture people and stuff on how to kill people, like how you want to interrogate someone with torture and stuff like that," said Bailey. "It showed you you'd stick somebody inside a tub of water and throw in a radio or an electric radiator, stuff of that nature."

"Did Damian ever attempt to give you guns or have you take guns?" asked Wilcox.

"Yes, he tried to give me the guns from Wyley's house, but I told him I didn't want them because they were stolen," Bailey said, earnest again.

"Did he do that on more than one occasion?"

"Yes," said Bailey.

"Did Miles McDonald ever attempt to sell you or give you any handguns?"

"Yes," Bailey admitted, "he tried to sell me some of them but I said no, I didn't want them, they were stolen."

Wilcox turned his attention to his client's manner with the weapon. "Is it a fact that in terms of Wyley's shooting he was very timid with the gun, very awkward?" he asked.

"Yes," said Bailey. "I guess it was his first time using that particular gun there."

Wilcox reminded his witness that the district attorney had asked him questions about whether or not Wyley had been coherent. "Is it a fair statement," Wilcox asked, "that in terms of knowing Wyley, you never saw Wyley show any emotion?"

"No. Well, he laughed every now and again," Bailey allowed, "but he wouldn't be the kind like who'd joke in the halls, you know."

Finally, Wilcox turned to Bailey's whereabouts on the night of December 13. Bailey said that he had been at his mother's house in Farmingdale, Long Island—"just hanging out."

Wilcox asked him if he had had occasion to call Damian's house that night.

Bailey said he had. "I wanted to ask him about the chemistry test because he knew the answers for the test and I wanted to find out," Bailey testified, adding that he had called him up around 6:00 or 6:30 and his aunt answered the phone and said that Damian had gone to the movies with Wyley.

Finally, Keeler, following Wilcox, had Bailey repeat the fact that he had spoken with Damian's aunt—although Bailey said he did not know her name—and then the last Chatham High boy of the day stepped down, swaggered across the courtroom, stuck on his shades, and headed out, yet another Top Gun to be reckoned with.

18

Keeler's major witnesses had already been presented, but, in the remaining five days of the prosecution's case, amid much tying up of loose ends, there were some gritty exchanges. Investigator John Cozzolino spent a long and uncomfortable day on the stand, as Wilcox unleashed the same battery of questions he had used on Walter Shook, probing in particular "Shooky" and "Cozzy'"'s decision to read Wyley his rights in the unheated, dark car with the dome light going, rather than in the warm and illuminated house where they had been for the better part of the evening. A point of even more intense interest for Wilcox was Cozzolino's visit to the Joseph residence, first in the early morning hours of December 14 and then in the late afternoon. During that initial visit, Damian had volunteered to Cozzolino that it was not Wyley's habit to call home, as he had done that night, and that Wyley had not asked him for a Band-Aid, thus commencing, in Wilcox's words, the ride of Cozzolino's life. Now, dredging up what he hoped would convey further evidence of the investigator's naïveté, Wilcox inquired into the matter of the Band-Aid. Wilcox asked him if he had testified that, on his first visit to the Joseph residence, he had "asked Mr. Joseph to check to see if there was a Band-Aid?"

"That is correct; to see if there was any signs that a Band-Aid was used," Cozzolino confirmed.

"Is it your testimony that you delegated the looking for of that Band-Aid to Damian Rossney's relative?" Wilcox challenged.

Cozzolino acknowledged that this was true, and, even by the standards of this small town where doors go unlocked, this could perhaps be perceived as a bit too trusting. After all, Damian's uncle could, hypothetically, have confiscated an item that might, in some way, have been incriminating to his nephew.

"Now, is it a fair statement that the following day there was a Band-Aid wrapper and backing found at the Rossney residence?" Wilcox demanded.

Cozzolino said that it was.

"But that evening Mr. Damian told you that Wyley didn't get a Band-Aid or ask for a Band-Aid at his place, correct?" said Wilcox, whose new ploy was to address Wyley's alleged co-conspirator as "Mister" or, better yet, "Master" Damian.

Cozzolino admitted that this was so, and then Wilcox moved on to the controlled search of the Joseph residence on the afternoon of December 14, wherein Damian's attorney gave the authorities a "tour," taking them to specific locations that he thought might be of interest. "You did not search that house otherwise?" asked Wilcox.

"Basically the attorney pointed most of the items out," Cozzolino confirmed.

"Did he exhibit to you the books that Mr. Damian had concerning torturing people and killing people and the like?" Wilcox asked, his voice rising.

"I don't recall him pointing out books to us," Cozzolino replied evenly.

Wilcox continued, with his questioning, to drive home once more the fact that Wyley's jacket was never examined for gunpowder residue and that no clothing was recovered from Damian, Miles, or Matt Rueckheim. "In terms of seeing Wyley Gates that night," he charged, "you and Shook made an assessment that Wyley Gates was the perpetrator solely and exclusively because he acted strange to you?"

Keeler rose to object, and the objection was sustained, but the jury had heard Charles Wilcox's accusation.

"Did you fill out a search-warrant application wherein you indicated that Wyley Gates's conduct was unnatural and he showed no emotional response?" Wilcox asked.

"Yes, sir," replied Cozzolino.

"And isn't it a fact, Investigator, that that is why you and your department seized upon Wyley Gates as a suspect and the culprit in this particular case," said Wilcox, on the attack, "and he was in your custody from the moment you first talked to him throughout that entire evening and you put the blinders on and went straight out for Wyley Gates without checking anyone else out?"

Once again, Keeler objected and once again his objection was sustained, but, more significantly, once again the jury had received Wilcox's message, which was that in a case that proved to be so fraught with unknowns—a case where there were so many players playing roles that would remain, to the end, undefined—the authorities had proceeded as if the whole thing were a one-man show.

On the following day, Vivian Gates sat in the courtroom, carrying a copy of Willa Cather's aptly titled *Obscure Destinies*, waiting for this trial to come to an end. Keeler's first order of business was to clear up a confusion that lingered from yesterday's testimony. John Bailey had testified that he called the Joseph residence at approximately 6:00 or 6:30 P.M. and had spoken with Damian's aunt. Sally and Stanley Joseph, however, had given statements to the authorities that placed them out of the house at that time. The question, therefore, was to whom had Bailey spoken at that time? In fact, according to the Josephs' statement, it was Damian who had been in the house at that time. If Bailey had spoken to Damian, then why had he lied about it? Why had

Bailey covered up a conversation with Damian if, in fact, there was nothing to cover up?

Recognizing that this discrepancy could throw one of his key witnesses into a disreputable light, Keeler and his staff did their homework and came up with a remedy. Now Keeler called to the stand a young woman named Laura Sanford, a customer service specialist for MCI Telecommunications. Accompanied by MCI's house counsel, who popped up to the bench numerous times, Sanford appeared to be the most protected witness of the trial, particularly in contrast to the string of teenage boys who had gone it alone, without benefit of family or attorneys. Producing phone records, Sanford testified that a one-minute phone call had been direct-dialed from the Farmingdale, Long Island, home of John Bailey's mother to the Joseph phone number not at 6:00 or 6:30, but, rather, at 7:24 P.M. John Bailey made a return appearance immediately thereafter to look at the phone record. His memory thus refreshed, he confirmed that the time of his call was, in fact, 7:24 P.M.

With that confusion apparently rectified, the prosecution called Sally Joseph to the stand. The well-groomed, well-spoken Mrs. Joseph gave details of her activities and those of her husband on the afternoon and evening of December 13, which included errands in Chatham, a visit to her father-in-law, who lived in nearby Ghent in an adult-care home, and then, when it became apparent that Mr. Joseph's father was ill, a trip to a physician in nearby Valatie. Returning to Chatham, the Josephs stopped at a pharmacy to get the medication the doctor had prescribed (a cash-register receipt that Keeler entered into evidence showed the time of purchase as 6:21 P.M. on December 13) and then drove her father-in-law back to Ghent. In order to give Damian an update on their whereabouts, Mrs. Joseph called home again between 6:30 and 6:40, a time corroborated in the subsequent testimonies of both Stanley Joseph and Joanne Logan, the woman in whose home Mr. Joseph's father resided. During this conversation, Damian told his aunt that Wyley was going to pick him up in a few minutes and that they were going to the movies.

After they left Mr. Joseph's father, the Josephs did their grocery shopping and returned to Colane Road at either 7:25 or 7:30. Keeler asked his witness if she had any recollection at all of John Bailey having called that night, and Mrs. Joseph said she had not. This seemed a startlingly curious lapse of memory, indeed one of the many small mysteries that would continue to linger around the case, as Bailey's phone call had been placed at 7:24, almost the very moment that Sally Joseph would have been coming into the house. One would think that the coincidence of timing, coupled with the significance of the call, or, indeed, any call on the night that her nephew was implicated in a multiple murder, would have caused her to retain the conversation in her memory. Apparently, however, it did not. Or, more likely, perhaps John Bailey and Sally Joseph never, in fact, spoke on the evening of December 13. This gave rise once more to the question, If Bailey did not speak to Mrs. Joseph when he called her house at 7:24 P.M., to whom did he speak?

The remainder of Keeler's case was taken up with the testimony of Ralph Gagliardi, the New York State Police officer who had been responsible for processing the crime scene; with the forensics regarding the Walther pistol, provided by Dominic Denio, a police ballistics expert; and with the return to the stand of Undersheriff Bertram, who demonstrated, as a graduate of the FBI firearms school in Peekskill, New York, and a certified teacher of firearms, the wrong way to hold a Walther (he himself, he assured the D.A., had suffered cuts on his hand by gripping the Walther in an improper way).

Upon the conclusion of Bertram's testimony, the People rested. The D.A. had called thirty-three witnesses and had submitted dozens of pieces of evidence. Above all, he had the defendant's own stated admissions to the state police and to his cellmate, and the suggested admissions to his grandmother and in his own writings to his peers. All the material which had led Gene Keeler to feel that he had a strong case for conviction had been presented. Now it was Wilcox's turn. He had repeatedly told the media that Wyley was not the shooter, and that if his client had made any confession at all, he had done so because of an "insane and psychotic loyalty" to those whom he thought were his friends and whom he was compelled to protect by taking on their crimes as his own. Since the burden of proof in a criminal case is placed on the prosecution, Wilcox, in his defense, did not have to prove who actually did the shooting. All he had to do was raise doubt about Wyley's having done it—"reasonable" doubt—and he had thus far proven himself artful at this.

His first witness was Dr. Baruch J. Davis, who, in his capacity as coroner's physician, had been called to the log house in the early morning hours of December 14. Dr. Davis reviewed for the court the scratch marks near Jason's eyes, the gouge mark on the pad of Cheryl's right index finger, the parallel lacerations on her left wrist, and her torn collar. As elicited by Wilcox, these observations suggested the struggle that had been left out of Wyley's alleged confession in Poughkeepsie and whose omission from that statement would, Wilcox wagered, cast doubt upon the confession as a whole. But under questioning from Keeler, who sought to disconnect the scratches from the alleged struggle, Dr. Davis admitted that the scratches around Jason's eyes were of the type that could have been caused by a fingernail—conceivably, in fact, Jason's own fingernail, which, if that was the case, would have represented an extremely common injury, as children whose nails are not trimmed can often inflict scratch marks on themselves.

Dr. Davis was followed onto the stand by two of Wyley's teachers, Frank Shannon and Linda Renken, both of whom described Wyley as quiet, cooperative, amiable, likable, and peaceable. Wyley was particularly excited to see Linda Renken. Wanting to talk to her, he began to make his way toward the railing that separated them, and suddenly found himself entirely surrounded by guards. "I think for the first time he realized 'I can't even move. I can't turn around. I can't go to the right or to the left,' " said Joan Yowe, who recalled a haunted look on his face.

The following morning saw one of Wilcox's prime witnesses on the stand. His name was Dr. Jack Neville Phillips Davies, and he had testified in many of the most publicized murder cases in the Albany area. Just before his appearance at the Gates trial, he had made headlines testifying in the highly publicized case of Mary Beth Tinning, a woman accused of smothering her own child, a child who, Davies testified, had actually died from a rare genetic disease.

"He has a pedigree medically that takes about three-quarters of an hour to give," said Albany County District Attorney Sol Greenberg, who had worked frequently with Davies. This pedigree included studies at the University of Bristol, the University of Edinburgh, and Duke University and consultancies to many organizations, including the National Cancer Institute and the World Health Organization.

"He comes in wearing a dark business suit, a pair of glasses and carrying his briefcase," said Greenberg's chief assistant district attorney, Daniel Dwyer. "All experts come in carrying a briefcase, but some of them just have a ham-and-cheese sandwich inside. Davies comes in fully prepared with all his slides and everything he needs to back up his testimony. That makes him unique."

Because of his frequent appearances as an expert witness, Davies has had to counter charges of being a "hired gun" who will sell his medical expertise to the highest bidder. In public statements, he has said, however, that he turns down five of every seven cases referred to him because he can't say anything either useful, accurate, or of service. Dr. Michael Baden, the nationally known director of the New York State Police Forensic Science Unit and former chief medical examiner of New York City, had positive things to say about Dr. Davies, although Baden would later challenge the content of Davies's testimony in the Gates case. "Dr. Davies is very earnest, very sincere, and very concerned about what he does," said Dr. Baden. "What we're talking about here is second opinions. If you go to get a hernia repaired, most insurance plans require you to get a second opinion. Maybe there are some hired guns around, but by and large a second opinion in an autopsy is like a second opinion in surgery. Most times they agree. Sometimes they don't." Indeed, the fees for offering this second opinion are not exorbitant. In Dr. Davies's case, he usually charges $125 an hour. "Most pathologists can make two or three times as much as a hospital pathologist, running a lab, doing tests at their leisure, working Monday to Friday with Wednesdays off to play golf, and not getting any calls at night," pointed out Dr. Baden. "We're fortunate to have people like Dr. Davies around, because testifying in court is not a popular item among pathologists." Beyond this, Captain William Murray, chief of detectives for the Albany police, saluted Dr. Davies for his generosity in their regard. "He's always been a friend of law enforcement," said Captain Murray. "We don't have to pay him twenty-five dollars an hour to ask him a question."

This day, however, September 10, Dr. Davies was not on the side of the law-enforcement officials. This day, he was testifying for the defense of Wyley Gates. Accompanied into the courtroom by his assistants, Dr. Davies, seventy-two, cut an imposing figure, and, when he spoke in his mellifluous British accent, he seemed like nothing less than a character out of Graham Greene, one of those hoary colonial figures hanging on to civilization in some hot, ruined, pestilential outpost. As he entered he treated a somewhat startled Gene Keeler to a small but courtly bow, a gesture that he repeated, almost imperceptibly, in the direction of the jury box.

After running through an abbreviated version of that pedigree, and establishing that he had been performing autopsies since 1936, Dr. Davies turned to the Gates murders. Among the points he made in his testimony, which was interrupted with great frequency by Keeler's objections, was his belief that Jason had been shot not from a distance of several feet away, but, rather, from a distance of several inches away; that his body had been moved after death (a small child shot in the chest and heart would almost certainly be thrown backward, Davies argued, and yet Jason was found lying facedown with a trail of blood); that Cheryl had been moved; that Cheryl had, based on her gouged finger, her torn collar, and scratch marks at the wrist, been involved in a struggle just before her death; that her gouged finger was an injury that was consistent with one's grabbing the foresight of a pistol; and that the assailant who had committed these shootings would most likely have had quite a lot of blood on his clothing. Of perhaps greatest significance in his testimony, Dr. Davies maintained that the "enormous majority" of the fourteen bullets that struck the victims were directed to or angled toward the heart. This indication of marksmanship, Wilcox would later remind the jurors, was out of keeping with the timidity and awkwardness that Wyley had evinced with regard to guns, according to John Bailey's testimony.

Keeler's first objective, in his cross-examination, was to alert the jurors to the fact that Dr. Davies had not come to the case until late March or early April, and that he did not go to the crime scene until some weeks after that (the log house having already been substantially altered by the Gates family, who had been quick to remove carpeting, furniture, and other items). Keeler then concerned himself with the fact that, although Dr. Davies had been "responsible for" some fifty thousand autopsies, he had personally performed only seventeen thousand of them.

"Out of those seventeen thousand autopsies personally performed, have you had a lot of difficult cases trying to determine the cause of death?" Keeler asked.

"A great many," replied Dr. Davies, whose accent managed to make almost everything he said sound sage and everything anybody else said sound callow. "And sometimes I've been unable to find the cause of death."

"Doctor, is it a fair statement to say [that] out of seventeen thousand autopsies you performed where you have had to make determinations and where you have had to deal with some very difficult cases, that on occasion you might have been wrong in your determination?" Keeler inquired.

"Yes, sir," he said with a benign twinkle that would have done the Edmund Gwenn of *Miracle on 34th Street* proud. "We all make mistakes, and I have made many."

Although Keeler repeatedly hammered home the message that Dr. Davies's opinions were based on his years of clinical experience, and his viewing of photographs from the murder scenes and the autopsies, rather than on an actual inspection of the murder scene and the corpses, Dr. Davies was successful in making certain additional points. He said that he had very little doubt that Cheryl had been slapped across the face by her assailant, and he believed that Jason was grabbed and held by the killer, whose fingernails caused a bruise on the child's back. Dr. Davies did concede to Keeler that some of Cheryl's lip and eye bruises might have been caused by her falling from the shooting impact and hitting her face, but in general the venerable physician weathered the cross-examination handily and could be said to have contributed significantly to the web of doubt that Wilcox had set out to weave.

In fact, a little over a year later, in the wake of the Damian Rossney trial, Dr. Michael Baden issued a public statement repudiating the testimony Dr. Davies had given at the Gates trial. Baden, who had been hired as a potential rebuttal witness for the prosecution in the Rossney case, reviewed all of the evidence in the case, including the autopsy and ballistic reports, clothing, photographs, and drawings that Dr. Davies had created for his testimony. "I was prepared to testify at the Rossney trial," said Dr. Baden, "that after my evaluation of all the materials, the confession made by Wyley Gates was entirely consistent and uniquely matched the physical evidence at the scene. He stated things that only a person involved with the shooting would know."

Additionally, Baden said the trajectories of the bullets and the position of the bodies supported Gates's account of how the murders had occurred. Furthermore, Baden said that it had been his experience that it is nearly impossible for someone unfamiliar with a crime to provide details that are consistent with the crime scene. The cut on Wyley Gates's thumb was also consistent with the kind of cut that can be inflicted upon the improper firing of a Walther PPK. Finally, Baden said that he did not agree with Dr. Davies that the evidence of the bullet placements indicated a high degree of marksmanship. "I respect Dr. Davies very much," Baden said, "but I strongly disagree with him on this point. There is no evidence that the shooter required any extraordinary knowledge of firearms. Of the fourteen shots fired, I think only two or three struck the heart."

After several more character witnesses, Wilcox concluded the proceedings of that afternoon with what came across as a bombshell. Calling to the stand Pamela Agostino, a chemistry teacher at the high school, he was able to establish that John Bailey was not enrolled in her chemistry class on December 13; and that, in fact, he had dropped out on December 2. This fact seemed to give the lie to Bailey's story that he had called Damian's house on the night of the murders to ask Damian for the questions on the upcoming chemistry exam. If, in fact, he hadn't called about chemistry on December 13, then why had he called? In other words, here was a further mystery surrounding Bailey's phone call, and, by extension, a further discrepancy that the D.A. would now have to work overtime to remedy.

"I don't think [the police] ever checked on John Bailey," said Wilcox. "We questioned [his family] and the information they gave us was, 'Yeah, he was down on Long Island.' But it didn't take a lot of smarts for them to quickly realize that they'd better have him in place too, because when we started investigating this thing we started rousting up a lot of people. We started stirring up a lot of dust. And I think really that was the first time when people suddenly decided they had to have certain people in certain places because this could disintegrate." The crucial phone call that Bailey allegedly made raised particular doubt in Wilcox's mind. "It was never established to me that it was John Bailey at all who made that call," he said. "This could have been a preplanned thing. These kids, particularly Damian Rossney, were so cute and so into thinking about this whole thing that they well could have devised a scheme whereby someone would call so there would be a call to establish an alibi for John Bailey." In fact, before the trial was over, Wilcox would attempt to connect Bailey with the phantom truck on Maple Drive that I had reported on the day after the murders and that Wilcox would have Wyley's great-aunt, Dorothy Dooley, testify to having seen that day as well.

But, for Wilcox, the main order of business ahead was the psychiatric defense, a prospect about which he had been less than sanguine from the first. He felt that it would be difficult to get the jury to accept the insanity defense because Wyley had not manifested the signs of insanity that a jury would expect to see. In fact, in Wilcox's opinion, as much as you can *voir dire* a jury in terms of weeding out preconceptions about mental illness, jurors still expect to see what is referred to as "gross stigmata," or major manifestations of disturbance.

Beyond the problems of arguing an insanity defense for a client who lacked any really compelling manifestations, there was another central problem in pursuing this line of defense. On the one hand, he felt convinced that his client's mental status, with or without bizarre manifestations, called for an insanity defense, and he had psychotherapists lined up who would attest to the boy's psychosis; but, on the other hand, one of his goals was to demonstrate, through character witnesses, that Wyley was peaceful, equable, nonaggressive, and hence incapable of committing the violence of which he was accused. Essentially, then, Wilcox came to the decision that the insanity defense, while probably not strong enough to carry on its own, could, in his own words, "augment" the forensic case. He would convince the jury that the peculiar nature of Wyley's psychosis caused him to take on the blame for this crime out of an insane need to protect his so-called friends.

The idea of presenting two defenses is normally a daunting one, but this was a case that came with its own set of rules. "There's a textbook you go by and then each case

is different," Wilcox later reflected. "Like presenting two
defenses is a classic cardinal sin in defense. But this case
called out for it." The next day, the layers of Wyley Gates
would began to be unraveled; what would be found at the
core would prove to be one of the more mysterious aspects
of this unfathomable case.

19

If Charles Wilcox had his doubts about arguing an insanity defense of Wyley Gates, his hopes must have plummeted even further in light of the performance of his first witness, Dr. Dorothy Lewis. On September 15, Dr. Lewis began an appearance that would stretch out to three exhausting days on the stand, as she and Gene Keeler appeared to engage in a psychodrama of their very own.

Dr. Lewis, who would gain some publicity a year later with an article in *Vanity Fair* detailing how she had shared Ted Bundy's last hours, had impeccable credentials. Specializing in child psychiatry, particularly in the area of violence, she had been a co-founder of the first court clinic in New Haven, where, as clinical director, she had performed hundreds of psychiatric evaluations. She had received her baccalaureate degree from Radcliffe and her M.D. from Yale, where she also served her internship in pediatrics and her residency in adult psychology and child psychology. Her academic appointments included professor of psychiatry at

New York University School of Medicine, clinical professor
of child psychiatry at Yale University Child Study Center,
and associate attending physician at Bellevue. She had
chaired a committee on juveniles and the law for the
American Psychological Association and had published
many articles and books. Indeed, in research published that
year in the *American Journal of Psychiatry*, Dr. Lewis had
disclosed findings derived from her study of fourteen of
the thirty-seven U.S. males sent to death row as juveniles,
whose ages ranged from approximately sixteen to eighteen
years at the time of their crimes and who had been evaluated
by Dr. Lewis at ages that ranged from eighteen to twenty-
nine. She found that all of the fourteen young men had
suffered head injuries during childhood, most of which were
serious enough to result in hospitalization, indentation of
the skull, or loss of consciousness, and that neurological
abnormalities, including evidence of brain injury, abnormal
head circumference, and seizure disorders, were also discovered in the majority of cases. As well, severe psychiatric
disorders were evident in all the youths studied. Dr. Lewis
further discovered that brutal physical abuse had been
visited upon twelve of the boys and five had been sexually
assaulted by older male relatives. Twelve of the subjects had
I.Q. scores below the normal range, and ten had an impaired
ability to think abstractly. This hitherto undescribed and
unreported constellation of mental and physical problems
found among juvenile murderers was coined by Dr. Lewis
"limbic psychotic aggressive syndrome."

Beginning her testimony, which was based on two
interviews with Wyley, totaling four and a half hours; a two-
hour interview with Vivian Gates; and a review of Wyley's
writings, police reports, reports made by two of the prosecution psychiatrists, and records of Wyley's mother's psychiatric hospitalization, she told the court that, in her expert
opinion, Wyley was psychotic at the time she interviewed
him and as far as she could ascertain had probably been
psychotic for many years. Defining the term *psychotic* as
meaning "out of touch with reality" and "operating on

premises that the rest of us don't operate on," she added that Wyley himself did not believe that he was suffering from any psychiatric impairment and that it was difficult for her to be testifying in front of him because he was hearing things he did not believe to be true.

She began to sketch a portrait of Wyley's grandiosity and paranoia, fitting him into a family pattern of behavior that Dr. Lewis was convinced had been troubled for generations.

Wyley, Dr. Lewis reported, was secretive about his family. In fact, Wyley's discomfiture at the trial emerged mostly in relation to the family material that came out through the psychiatric testimonies. "He sat as stiffly those days, as stoically [as ever]," Joan Yowe recalled, "but I could hear him breathe sometimes during the testimony. I would occasionally turn around and look at him to see if he was all right. He did not like his grandmother referred to; he did not like his mother referred to."

Now his grandmother and mother were having their lives rawly exposed through Dr. Lewis's testimony. The history began with Wyley's grandfather, who, according to what Mrs. Gates allegedly told Dr. Lewis, was "probably schizophrenic." Mrs. Gates said of her late husband that "there were times when he was fine and times when he was violent." Asked if he had been an alcoholic, Dr. Lewis said he had not been, but, based on what Mrs. Gates had told her, was paranoid. "In the army he said that this officer was trying to get him," Dr. Lewis said. "Everywhere he went he thought somebody was out to get him." In addition, he was physically violent with his wife and children. "He beat her," Dr. Lewis said of Mrs. Gates, "threw a bottle at her, an artery in her foot was cut. He distrusted her, distrusted his son, stashed away secret bank accounts, was convinced that Louis [the eldest son] and she were out to kill him." His inclinations paralleled Wyley's own grandiosity, as well. "He'd go from grandiose to the bottom again," said Dr. Lewis, noting that he had tried to trace his lineage to European royalty.

For the purposes of Dr. Lewis's evaluation, Mrs. Gates
had also charted the behavioral disorders of her sons. Robert
was "a daredevil" who owned six motorcycles and who rode
along the highway standing on the handlebars of his bike.
Mrs. Gates also acknowledged, in Dr. Lewis's account, that
Robert picked on Wyley, whose introverted, self-involved
style was so different from his father's.

There were, as well, two uncles whom she labeled as
"seriously psychiatrically impaired." Uncle Dane had died
in the car crash—further evidence of the streak of violence
in the family—and Uncle Steven, who had been permanently
damaged in another automobile crash, was heavily on tranquilizers to control his paranoia. "He accuses you of doing
things," Dr. Lewis quoted Mrs. Gates saying of her impaired
son.

As for Wyley's mother, she also had a history of severe
psychiatric disturbance. There had been two serious suicide
attempts and many bouts with depression. Dr. Lewis quoted
Mrs. Gates as saying that Kristi was "very withdrawn at
times; at other times very attractive to men" and that at
these times she had "multiple relationships and was very
outgoing."

All of this family material pointed to a distinct vulnerability to serious mental illness, Dr. Lewis claimed, and she
claimed as well that there was ample evidence to indicate
that Wyley himself was already seriously disturbed. In the
beginning, she—like so many others—felt that Wyley presented himself as an "intelligent, coherent, logical" youngster, a bit guarded and withholding at first, but perfectly
normal and rational. But in terms of his affect—the way he
related his emotions—he was "sort of flat" and did not really
relate his feelings as most people do.

But Dr. Lewis went on to note far more serious mani-
festations of mental imbalance than this flat affect. "When
I asked him . . . whether he ever heard voices," she testified,
"Wyley at first absolutely denied ever having heard voices.
It was only actually later on in the interview that it became
clear that he had on occasions heard voices . . . and had

auditory hallucinations." The content of these hallucinations—these voices—was somewhat vague. "Sometimes I'm
thinking something to myself," she quoted Wyley as telling
her, "and 'IT' will cut in. I will tell 'IT' to shut up."

The diagnosis that Dr. Lewis arrived at was, in her own
assessment, a complicated one, because Wyley had symptoms
of two serious disorders. He showed signs of being a
paranoid schizophrenic, as evidenced by his delusions of
grandeur, his grandiosity, his auditory hallucinations, and
his peculiar writing (he had devised his own alphabet, a
"runic" alphabet that enabled him to write in code and that
he had been using since the ninth grade). His other major
disorder was a manic-depressive syndrome, with suicidal
periods alternating with manic periods. Wyley suffered from
a schizo-affective disorder, said Dr. Lewis, and her diagnosis
was that he was paranoid schizophrenic, with a mood
disorder.

As a result of that mental disorder, asked Wilcox, did
he lack "the substantial capacity to know or appreciate the
nature and consequences of any conduct that he engaged
in at that time?"

"Yes," she said. "I think he felt that he was doing what
he was meant to do and that this was the correct thing to
do."

The appearance of Dr. Lewis at the trial became a source
of great distress to those close to the Gates family, for they
felt sure that whatever Vivian Gates had said to this psychotherapist had been misrepresented and misused. In fact,
when she spoke with me after the trial, Mrs. Gates did not
deny the general thrust of what Dr. Lewis had told the
court with regard to the family history. Asked what she felt
had been the source of Wyley's problems, Mrs. Gates replied,
"As I told the therapist, I thought it was genetic. Wyley
inherited it from two sides." But most of Bob's friends were
particularly chagrined by this so-called family history because they felt it presented their friend as being unstable
and unreliable, which they believed to be totally inaccurate.

What Dr. Lewis called serious psychiatric disturbance—for example, standing up on a motorbike—they thought of as the sowing of wild oats. Indeed, there emanated from Dr. Lewis's testimony a definite cultural gulf. Part of this impression may have derived from Dr. Lewis's personal mannerisms, which had a faintly condescending air of "visiting the provinces," but part of it may have had to do with a failure to understand the cultural values and standards of the people whom she was evaluating. In any event, the Gates family was wounded and outraged at the fact of their private lives being picked apart this way in public. "Oh, she was a horror," said one of Wyley's aunts. "How she could take money for what she did—it was a disgrace!" In fact, this first witness would wind up costing the Gates family quite a bit of money, for it was Keeler's turn to cross-examine and he applied, from the start, a pit-bull grip on the witness that wouldn't let go.

With a series of questions that highlighted her ignorance of Robert, Jr., Dane, Steven, and Jason Gates, Keeler was successful in seriously rattling his witness from the first. As Keeler zeroed in on the paterfamilias whom she had portrayed as schizophrenic, Dr. Lewis was unable to remember when Lou Gates died, how old he was when he died, what he did for a living, or even what his name was. Similarly, although she characterized Mrs. Gates as a "coherent, intelligent, sensitive, caring woman," she could not recall anything of her occupation, referring to her as a "housewife." Regarding Wyley's mother, she was similarly unprepared. When Keeler requested her name, Dr. Lewis was unable to find it in her notes. But, under further questioning, she provided the information that Kristi Gates lived in California with a five-year-old out-of-wedlock daughter and a man who was not the father of the child, and that, in her suicide attempt at the age of nineteen, she had ingested approximately one hundred aspirin tablets and had been rushed to the hospital to have her stomach pumped.

"Ma'am, isn't it true that you have very little data about the whole family?" Keeler challenged.

"No," said Dr. Lewis defensively. "I have an extraordinary amount of data considering the amount of time allotted to do an evaluation. And I have data suggesting that there were several extremely disturbed individuals."

As the testimony dragged out over several days, necessitating Dr. Lewis's return to New York and then back to Hudson again, Keeler began an extensive questioning of the medical history she had taken from Wyley.

Dr. Lewis told the court she had taken a very careful history of any accidental nervous-system injuries, discovering that at the age of seven or eight, Wyley had fallen off an embankment and hit his head. He could not, however, recall the severity of the injury then or in any of the other head injuries he had sustained over the years, including those received from turning over in a car; from falling backward off a stool; and from falling off a bunk bed. As Keeler tried to pin her down to a specific date—or even year—for each of the injuries, she became increasingly distracted and unable to provide them. She then began to speak of his fainting spells and episodes of *déjà vu*, but Keeler got her to admit that neither of these could realistically be tied into any sort of seizure disorder nor were they indicative that Wyley was a paranoid schizophrenic.

Again and again, Keeler returned to the same attacks on Dr. Lewis's methods and findings. Some speculated that this was his revenge for all the time he had had to put into this case at the part-time D.A.'s salary he earned, and that he had perceived this occasion as his opportunity to make someone else pay. Indeed, in an appeal to the court, Wilcox, who said that Dr. Lewis's department at New York University was "chagrined" by her extended absence, noted this possible motivation on the D.A.'s part. "She is aware of certain comments made by the district attorney," said Wilcox of Dr. Lewis, "in terms of . . . [Keeler] losing financial resources or money as a result of this trial, and she feels she is paying the price in terms of punishment as a result of his having to be here against his will and losing his monetary resources, which she feels is being communicated to her in an extraordinarily repetitive and lengthy cross-examination." The judge advised that Wilcox instruct his witness to keep to the point, suggesting that "her wordiness is her desire to be precise in an imprecise science." As for Dr. Lewis herself, this was not what she had planned on and, in an irritable exchange during one of the breaks, after noticing Wyley smiling in the courtroom, she suggested to him that he wasn't helping his case any. The obvious question was whether she was either, at the *per diem* rate she was getting paid.

Keeler, who had questioned at length the issue of whether Wyley's writings, which she had put forth as evidence of his delusions, were "elicited signs" and examples of "self-reporting," carried the issue forward to the third day of testimony from Dr. Lewis. On this morning of September 17, she related that Wyley had told her a number of delusional things about himself, including that he felt as if he were a "sort of Messiah" and that in the fifteen seconds before he committed the shootings, his voices told him that he could still stop. But Keeler continued to focus on what he wished to portray as the inadequate methods Dr. Lewis used in gathering her information, including the fact that she did not know what Wyley's activities had been on December 13 both before and after the shootings. Dr. Lewis said that Wyley did tell her, however, that he was responsible for the shootings. "I asked him, 'Do you believe you did it?' " she told the court. "He said, 'I think so. I can't remember everything. Some of the things people say about where the bodies were don't seem right.' It's not the way he remembered it," Dr. Lewis explained. "He doesn't understand the discrepancy."

"When you interviewed him," Keeler asked, "would it be your opinion that he was in touch or out of touch with reality?" Keeler asked.

Dr. Lewis replied that in schizophrenics, delusions are present within a clear sense of orientation. Wyley, she said, knew the time, the place where they were located, who he was, and who she was.

He asked her if it was not true that the majority of her information had come from self-reporting in the case of

Wyley Gates, and she replied that it had. Asking her to define "malingering," as it was identified as a syndrome in the DSM-3 manual, which is used by psychiatrists and hospitals for coding diagnoses, she explained to the court that "malingering" meant pretending to have a disorder, feigning being crazy, pretending to hear voices.

Letting that settle in, Keeler, at long last, announced that he had no further questions.

During the course of this marathon cross-examination, there came a moment of brief respite when Judge Leaman interjected into the proceedings a celebratory note regarding the bicentennial of the Constitution. Announcing that this was the two hundredth anniversary of the adoption of the Constitution of the United States, he said that the chief judge had asked that courts throughout the state mark the occasion at eleven o'clock, which is when, legend has it, the signing of the Constitution and its actual adoption took place.

"I think to live the Constitution under certain circumstances—and a trial is, indeed, living the Constitution—outweighs on some occasions mere oratory concerning the Constitution," said the judge. "The Constitution was the culmination of a war and also the culmination of what's been declared by many as being the most incredible, marvelous piece of statesmanship in the history perhaps of political science and government. I certainly believe that, and I think the history of this country for two hundred years demonstrates that what was done two hundred years ago was a magnificent achievement. But it is an ongoing thing; it is not static at all. If it becomes static, it has a tendency to self-destruct."

While bells tolled on the courthouse square, the judge continued. "Just as we are the beneficiaries of a great legacy, we have the obligation to our descendants, if you will, to transmit to them the same freedoms that we ourselves have received. And that requires effort," he cautioned. "It is not something that we can simply take for granted, always taking and never giving. So I simply take note of the fact. I ask

you all to reflect, as I am reflecting, on what it is that we
have and celebrate this day as a great anniversary in the
history of our country."

The jury, who generally regarded the judge as a fine
gentleman and so well spoken, gave him their absolute
attention. After all, the weight of history was upon them,
not to mention the weight of the future.

20

Nothing that followed would match the to-the-mat tango that Keeler had danced with the first of Wilcox's psychiatric team, but the defense continued their case with the appearance on September 18 of Dr. Anthony Marchionne, the psychotherapist who had spent by far the greatest amount of time with Wyley and who had met with Wyley's grandmother and his cousin Tina Hatch as well.

Marchionne administered a wide assortment of psychological tests evaluating intellectual, memory, and psychomotor functions. His clinical interviews corroborated the findings of Dr. Lewis as to the grandiose nature of Wyley's fantasies. To Marchionne, Wyley confessed that he had committed the murders and gave as a reason the fact that his family criticized him and that he hated them. In Wyley's opinion, Robert and Cheryl were motivated, for devious if unspecified reasons, to interfere with his long-standing goal to achieve importance and intellectual distinction. "Come on down and join us for watching television" or "you're studying too hard" were two examples of this interference that Wyley cited for the psychotherapist. To Marchionne, these examples were simply evidence of what parents normally do with their youngsters to integrate them into the family, but to Wyley they were proof of his family's maliciousness, and his report of this plaintive, ordinary appeal— "Come on down and watch TV with us"—turned by Wyley into something that merited their assassination, became one of the most chilling and hollow moments of the trial.

Marchionne also hauntingly portrayed the specific moment when the murder plot was hatched. "It all comes together," he told the court, "at a football game. Wyley describes coming off the football field after having performed in the band and Damian Rossney is talking to a small group of people and he asks Damian to come over. Now, this is at half-time at the football game, and it's at that time, which I call 'inappropriate,' that he says to Damian, 'Will you kill my father?' Which Damian responds to: 'Call me later. We'll talk about it.' That's what happens. That's the beginning of this whole tragedy."

"On December 13," asked Wilcox, "was Wyley Gates suffering from mental illness or defect?"

"I feel quite certain he was," Marchionne replied.

Wilcox asked if that mental disease or defect would have substantially impaired his ability to know or appreciate the nature and consequences of his conduct, and Marchionne replied that Wyley felt it was right to remove these people, that he did not have a sense of the consequences of doing so, and that he lacked the "substantial capacity" to know that his conduct was wrong.

In his cross-examination, Keeler questioned Marchionne about Wyley's intelligence, and the psychotherapist told the court that Wyley had an I.Q. of 126 or 127. But, in Wyley's case, he felt, this relatively high I.Q. was deceiving. Indeed, Marchionne said that he had been surprised that, with Wyley's level of academic superiority, he was planning to go to Ithaca College or the University of Houston, which he characterized as fine schools but not the most demanding. The reason for this, he opined, was that Wyley's intelligence was a "reproductive" intelligence, meaning that he could learn something and reproduce it, but had very little creativity. Expanding on this, Marchionne said he felt that Wyley would have difficulty in thinking abstractly and that his intelligence would show up as less than superior in a more freely structured environment.

Keeler then delved into the subject of Wyley's hallucinations and the delusionary quality of his ambitions, including his plan to establish a military base in Antarctica. Rather desperately, the D.A. attempted to rationalize such an ambition. "Is it not true that some people do become presidents of multinational corporations . . . some people do actively fight for the environment?" he demanded, and even wound up referring to Antarctica as a "Third World area." Marchionne remained unswayed by such efforts and told the court that Wyley's responses on certain psychological tests evinced a very strong showing in the area of delusions.

At the outset of his cross-examination, Keeler had asked Marchionne to explain why he had felt it necessary to spend so much time with Wyley, to which the psychotherapist had replied that every time he met with Wyley, he would find out things that he felt required further exploration. Now, in concluding his questioning, Keeler returned to this issue, asking if, in fact, it was not true that Marchionne had asked Wyley to cooperate in an in-depth study of him that he hoped to then have published. Marchionne confirmed that he had made this request, and Keeler, convinced that he had exposed the psychotherapist's alleged ulterior motive for having spent this much time with the defendant, had no further questions.

Moments later, however, Wilcox asked Marchionne to explain why he had made that request of Wyley Gates and Marchionne replied that this particular case had enormous implications for understanding why people do enormously destructive things. "We don't have much information on youngsters who destroy their parents or people who they are close to," he stated. "This is an area that concerns many, many people and I felt a professional responsibility to

determine just what was going on here, which I could share
with other professional people somewhere along the way."

The remaining witness on Wilcox's psychiatric team was Dr.
Richard Felch, who had once been a student of Dr. Marchionne's and who had consulted with him on the case at
hand. The most salient characteristics that Wyley conveyed
to Dr. Felch were his lack of affect and his determination to
present himself as an articulate and intelligent fellow. But
Felch found Wyley to be "chronically anxious" and he
interpreted Wyley's lack of affect as a defense against the
youth's underlying intensity. "It's turning the volume control
down too far because inside the volume control is up too
high," he explained.

At Wilcox's request, Felch offered his theory as to the
genesis of the crime that Wyley had set out to commit. He
asserted that Wyley actually believed, in a very childish way,
that you can go ahead and erase somebody with a gun and
then step back into your life. Indeed, in Felch's opinion,
Wyley believed that he would somehow magically kill these
people, they would somehow be carried out the door, and
then he would move into the house and go back to school
and pick up with his life and his career. There was no sense
of being caught; there was no sense of loss; there was no
sense that there would be an investigation; there was no
sense that this was murder or that death had occurred. "It
was a kind of fantasy. You see these fantasies in eight-year-
old boys," said Felch. "They get together in their fort and
make up a plan. . . . Of course the plan is not realistic but
they have a lot of fun making this plan. They rarely take
steps in it because it's an unrealistic plan. It was the same
kind of plan for Wyley, but he took steps in it; and he had
to take steps. It was the only thing he had to hold him
together, and it didn't work."

It was Dr. Felch's diagnosis that Wyley suffered from
schizophrenia of the paranoid type. Wilcox asked if such a
diagnosis was compatible with an individual who was capable
of elaborate plans, and Felch said that it was. "When they're
decompensating," he said of such individuals, "they will

bring out pages and pages of writing. . . . Thought B doesn't follow Thought A . . . their thoughts are just scattered chaotically, like that moment of falling asleep, when you know you're not really awake, but not asleep, and you're about to be dreaming and your thoughts are starting to break up." Felch added that, with such a diagnosis, it could be said that the defendant lacked the ability to recognize the consequences of his actions or to distinguish right from wrong.

Keeler, in his cross-examination, asked if Wyley Gates had had the substantial capacity to know that bullets, if they hit people, could make them die. Felch replied that Wyley knew physics, but didn't have the mature understanding to know that he was taking another life.

"So he basically had the understanding, Doctor, is it not true, of the nature and consequences of his acts?" Keeler pressed.

"Yes, that he was making something dead," Felch gravely replied. "He knew that he was making something dead."

The jury had now heard from three different psychotherapists that Wyley had confessed to these murders in detail; they would hear four more accounts of Wyley's confession by the time the prosecution's team of psychotherapists had concluded. Many of the citizens of Columbia County cite this plethora of confession as being sufficient to have convicted Wyley, but they do so ignorant of the fact that the jury was instructed not to accept these confessions to psychiatrists as evidence of any actual commission of crime. The instruction to the jury was made in accordance with Section 60.55 of the Criminal Procedure Law, which stipulates that any statement made by the defendant to a psychiatrist or licensed psychologist during that psychiatrist's or psychologist's examination of the defendant was admissible in evidence only in regard to its use in what is known as the affirmative defense of lack of criminal responsibility by reason of mental disease or defect. Further, in accordance with Section 60.55, the court, upon receiving the statement into evidence, must then instruct the jury that the statement was to be considered only for the purposes of arguing an insanity defense and could not be considered by the jury in its determination of whether the defendant committed the act constituting the crime charged.

The idea that jurors can hear confessions of murders made to psychiatrists and then tuck that information away in some segregated pocket of their minds was a mystifying thing to the citizens of Columbia County, as it would be to people anywhere. Even the eminent jurist Judge Joseph W. Bellacosa of the New York Court of Appeals, addressed, in a practice commentary on Section 60.55, this almost inhuman thing that jurors are expected to do. Judge Bellacosa wrote that the practical impossibility of the jury's obeying, with any degree of intellectual honesty or sophistication, the admonition not to consider such evidence for anything other than the insanity defense, had to be, in his words, "blinked," or ignored. Judge Bellacosa went on to speculate that "one day reality and simplicity will intrude to stop these semantical games." Obviously, the judge had never anticipated the Gates jury, which was somehow able to "blink" the seven recitations of guilt that Wyley made to seven different psychotherapists.

The rebuttal team of psychotherapists that Keeler had assembled started with Dr. Kishor Sangani, director of community services for Mohawk Valley Psychiatric Center, who had met with Wyley on two occasions for a total of approximately three hours and who now reported that he had found Wyley to be coherent and fully in touch with reality on both occasions. In the course of their interviews, Wyley told Sangani that he felt he would have "self-destructed" if he had not rid himself of the negative feelings that were building within him before the murders; that he particularly hated Cheryl because she was "ignorant by choice"; and that he had felt that he would only be free from suffering when he saw his father dead. Sangani ascribed a schizoid personality disorder to Wyley, characterizing him as aloof, shy, and possessed of a difficulty in forming relationships. He explained that the difference between a

schizoid personality disorder and a psychosis is that in a
psychotic condition, the person loses contact with reality,
experiencing delusions and hallucinations or hearing voices,
and that his functioning is severely impaired, while in the
case of a schizoid personality disorder, the only thing other
people might notice is that the affect of the person with the
personality disorder is blank and flat. Sangani concluded
that Wyley, at the time of the murders, had understood the
nature of his act and appreciated right from wrong.

Keeler's second witness was Dr. Jay Thalmann, a co-
ordinator of forensic services at Albany County Mental
Health Clinic, who had examined Wyley on two separate
occasions for two hours each and had administered a battery
of psychological tests. On the Rorschach test, Wyley's responses "reflected an individual who was in good contact
with reality." On the Minnesota Multi-Phasic test, there were
indications of mild antisocial tendencies but the responses
were "essentially normal." In an objective drawings test,
Wyley was asked to draw his perception of a house, a tree,
and people; he drew a diagram of people "encased in a
triangle" in what Thalmann felt was an expression of his
being trapped in his family life. (In his cross-examination,
Wilcox wondered whether this "triad" might not, in fact,
represent Wyley, Damian, and Miles.) All together, however,
the tests indicated a schizoid personality disorder rather
than schizophrenia. Thalmann also reported that Wyley
had admitted the shootings to him, and he concurred with
Dr. Sangani that Wyley knew, when he had the gun in his
hand and pointed it at an individual and pulled the trigger,
that the individual could be killed, and that he had substantial capacity to understand that such behavior was wrong,
both morally and legally.

Keeler's parade of expert witnesses was interrupted by the
brief return to the witness stand of John Bailey. The mystery
surrounding Bailey's phone call to the Joseph residence on
the evening of December thirteenth had been exacerbated
by the testimony of Pamela Agostino, the Chatham High
chemistry teacher who had stated that Bailey had not been

registered in her class at the time of that call. As the alleged purpose of that call, as earlier stated by Bailey under oath, was to ask Damian about the chemistry exam, one had to wonder why the less than studious Bailey had chosen a Saturday night to inquire into a chemistry exam in a course in which he wasn't even enrolled. Now, to clear things up, Keeler recalled Bailey to the stand and asked him to review the purpose of his call to Damian on the night of December 13. Bailey reiterated his earlier explanation that he was calling for the questions on the chemistry exam. Keeler asked him if he was enrolled in the class at that time, and Bailey said that he had dropped the class about a week before, but didn't think he would have enough credits, so he thought he could get back into the class and, presumably to get a jump on the material, was calling Damian for information on the exam.

Wilcox rose to question the witness. "So, Mr. Bailey, the time you made this phone call pertaining to the test you weren't even in any chemistry class, were you?" he said.

"No, I wasn't," Bailey replied.

"You were talking about a test you weren't even in a course to take, correct?"

"Right."

"We can certainly agree, I assume, that Damian Rossney was not your guidance counselor, was he?" Wilcox demanded.

"No, he wasn't."

Wilcox did what he could to raise questions in the jurors' minds about what the intent of Bailey's phone call had been if it had not been to discuss chemistry. But he could go no further with the mysterious phone call nor could he make any real inroads when he asked Bailey whether he had a 1969 Chevrolet pickup truck registered to him in December 1986. If, in fact, Bailey had owned a pickup truck, then he might prove a likely candidate for the driver of that pickup truck that I had reported to the police on the morning following the murders and that Wyley's great-aunt Dorothy Dooley had testified to having been almost broadsided by on the evening of the murders.

But Bailey denied that he had had such a truck registered to him at that time, replying that he had had one registered to him the following February. And so the pickup truck would remain a red herring in the trial, just another of the elements that made up Wilcox's web of reasonable doubt.

Following Bailey onto the witness stand was Dr. Neil Borenstein, the clinical director of the Central New York Psychiatric Center. Dr. Borenstein specialized in forensic psychiatry, and was, in fact, one of only three hundred psychotherapists in the country board-certified in that field. In the course of two interviews with Wyley, he had developed a profile of the youth that he now shared with the court. Regarding his parents, Wyley had a "positive relationship" with his mother but was not "really close" to her, while his father inspired negative feelings on account of his "never being around" and being "stern and distancing."

Borenstein stated that, during these interviews, he had asked the youth to make certain associations. "I asked him to think about certain objects and how he would have described his father as that object," Borenstein said. "I asked him in terms of a truck, what kind of truck would he be, and his response was . . . that it was a large truck, a seventy-five-year-old pickup truck. What kind of animal he would have pictured his father as, and it was a jackass. What kind of food was meatloaf, and what kind of candy, a Granola bar."

To Dr. Borenstein, Wyley characterized his father as being "a boring individual" and "antipleasure." As for Cheryl, he told Dr. Borenstein that he had liked Cheryl initially for two or three years after he had returned home from California but that eventually she became too domineering, as if it were her house. He thought of her as a "bitch," and cited one or two instances in which she had pushed him physically. As for his brother Bobby, they had been close growing up but this had changed when Bobby became more like his father, working on cars, and being generally more physical.

Drawing from his sessions with Wyley, Borenstein began to set the stage for the shootings, describing first the difficult summer of '86, the disappointing return to school in the fall, and the decision to rid himself of his family. To this end, Wyley told Borenstein, he had spoken to Damian, offering him 25 percent of the inheritance he stood to receive. Borenstein found this relationship to be of great significance in making his ultimate diagnosis. He told the court that in all the evaluations he had made, he had yet to find a mentally disorganized person able to find nonpsychotics to help carry out a plan. "Most insanity is one person acting in a bizarre way," said Borenstein. "It doesn't involve other people."

Now, as he meticulously detailed the buildup that led to the murders, Borenstein reported that Wyley had told him of the difficult week he'd had before December thirteenth, a week in which all his plans had been foiled. "I became more and more frustrated as the people I wanted to kill weren't doing what I wanted them to do," Borenstein recalled Wyley telling him.

Wyley told Borenstein that Saturday, December thirteenth, "took on a momentum of its own . . . it just happened." He parked Cheryl's car a quarter-mile away, in a field down the road, and took a look at the clock: it was a quarter to seven. Donning white gardening gloves that he had bought several weeks before, he began to walk back to the log house. There was, inside of him at this point, a sense of struggle, but he could not stop himself. When he came to the top of the stairs that led down to the rec room, where Bob, Cheryl, and Jason were congregated, he stood with the gun in his hand, wanting to, not wanting to.

And then he descended the stairs, Wyley told Borenstein. His father looked up at him. "What are you doing here?" he asked. But he never heard the answer. Wyley fired three times and then, as Cheryl stood up, he fired four times at her. The clip was empty. He inserted a new clip. Standing there, amid the bodies, he listened for the sound of drums. And there they were: his brother, in the room over the garage, was still playing. He started up the stairs, and then caught Cheryl coming up after him. He fired at her twice more, then he went out the side door, pausing to see if his brother's drums could be heard and there they were, still, the drums in the dark night, and he went to where his brother was, and he fired twice, the gun jamming, and he fired again.

He put in a new clip, according to Borenstein's testimony. Heading back downstairs, he found Jason still in front of the TV, and the little boy was crying. Disavowing the idea that Jason's death was planned because of the possibility of his being an heir, Wyley told Borenstein that he was concerned mostly that the child could identify him and so he shot him.

Regarding what later transpired at Troop K Barracks in Poughkeepsie, Wyley told Borenstein that he had confessed because he felt "down" during the interview—another manifestation of the "letdown" feeling that he had described to Dr. Marchionne as having hit him after the movies, back at the Joseph residence, in the company of Damian—and, what's more, he couldn't stand what he described as the "buddy-buddy" routine. By this, he was presumably indicating that he had been aware of the manipulative ploys of the investigators down in Poughkeepsie and had confessed not because he had been skillfully manipulated but, rather, because he had decided, on his own steam, to do so.

To Dr. Borenstein, however, months after the shooting, Wyley could give no good reason or offer any real motive for why these murders had come to pass. He spoke about conditions of "warped logic." He had no particular reason to hate his brother, for instance. "I looked at life in the negative," admitted this sadder-but-wiser Wyley.

Dr. Borenstein did not see Wyley as suffering from a psychotic illness. Rather, in his opinion, Wyley had a severe personality disorder, long-term and ingrained. But he felt that Wyley was very much in contact with reality. There was a vast difference, he told the court, between a teenager who wishes to be in charge of a large corporation, or even in charge of the world, and a mental patient who can't think in any other way and is preaching that he is the head of the U.N. and is hiring and firing staff. Corroborating what Drs. Thalmann and Sangani had said, Borenstein was convinced

that Wyley Gates knew, on December 13, what was morally
and legally wrong and that he was capable of appreciating
the effects of his acts.

The last witness in the trial, Dr. Henry Camperlengo,
a forensic psychiatrist for Albany County, saw the same
"very shy, private, withdrawn young man" that the other
psychotherapists had seen, but saw no indication of clinical
depression that would require medication or hospitalization.
Wyley had told Camperlengo that he had been reared as a
Presbyterian but had given up religion because it was "a lot
of bunk," even though he acknowledged that the teachings
of Christ and the Ten Commandments might have "some
validity." He had his own utilitarian philosophy, and within
that construct saw death as a not very important thing—
"dead is dead," Wyley told Camperlengo. He further avowed
that if he had to do it all over, he would have sought
counseling or run away from home rather than resorted to
violence, although, in a second interview, he maintained
that if he hadn't committed the act, he would have committed
suicide or suffered a "mental breakdown." Again, as had
the other members of the prosecution team, Camperlengo
stressed that Wyley was not psychotic and that he had
substantial capacity to understand the consequences of his
act and to differentiate right from wrong.

The evidentiary portion of the longest trial in Columbia
County history was thereby concluded. It had lasted nine
weeks and had produced 49 witnesses and 230 pieces of
evidence. Now, on October 1, almost ten full months after
Bob, Cheryl, Bobby, and Jason were slain, it was time to
hear the closing remarks.

The courtroom was filled with those who had a personal
stake in the outcome—the Brahms; Stanley Joseph; Walter
Shook—and those who remained merely curious. One whose
personal stake was as great as anyone's was, however,
conspicuously absent. Vivian Gates, who had maintained a
presence at the trial that some found moving and others
inscrutable, was not in attendance this day nor would

she appear again during the long deliberation nor for the reading of the verdict. To fill the empty place behind the defendant's table reserved for family, Chuck Wilcox had asked his wife and his parents to be present. Surely it was their pleasure to be there, for his performance would prove to be a highly—some thought "overly"—dramatic one.

"It would have been very easy for me to come into this courtroom in this case and present to you solely an insanity or mental-disease or -defect defense," began Wilcox, addressing the jury, "but I could not. I could not because I looked at this case, I looked over everything . . . and it was my duty and my obligation to present to you as well a *factual* case on behalf of this boy, Wyley Gates, whose mind wouldn't allow him, can't allow him, to testify in his own behalf. I went over this case and I went over this case and I lived with this case for months, day and night," said Wilcox, "and I submit to you before we barely get started that I can think of thirty reasonable doubts . . . I think when all is said and done that you, yourselves, each of you and all of you, will have even more."

Painstakingly, but with rising swells of outrage and anguish, Wilcox delineated the reasonable doubts in the case. He began with the issue of Damian Rossney, Miles McDonald, and John Bailey. No clothing was ever secured from any of these boys, nor was a polygraph administered to any one of them. Damian Rossney had no alibi whatsoever; Miles McDonald's was shaky; and John Bailey—"Mr. Clean-Cut Appearance," as Wilcox now described him—had a shakier one still.

As for the gun, it was found in the home of Damian Rossney. "Remember how carefully it was picked up, how carefully it was retrieved, to preserve the possibility of obtaining, maintaining, and preserving fingerprints," Wilcox said, "which was never done, *never done*," he shouted. His voice fell to a whisper. "And why? Well, there was another test they wanted to do. One of the tests they wanted to do was a fiber test. Such an important test that [they] would forgo fingerprinting the very weapon they claim was used in the crime. Was there *ever* a fiber test? Never. Never. It wasn't done. That, ladies and gentlemen, I respectfully submit to you, is a reasonable doubt."

He moved on to other areas of reasonable doubt. The gloves that were found on Wyley's person had no cuts on them and no blood. The white tie that Wyley wore on the night of December 13 had no blood on it. "As the police will have you believe . . . as Salmon would have you believe," charged Wilcox, "[the defendant] said, 'I made one mistake. I didn't change my clothes, my jacket has gunpowder on it'—this is what Salmon alleges. With those statements, was there ever a gunpowder examination of those clothes? There was not!" Wilcox cried, pounding on the table. "There was not. My God, that's negligence; that's reasonable doubt."

Wilcox turned to those unexplained aspects of the crime that were inconsistent with details of Wyley's alleged confession: the scratches on Jason; the wounds on Cheryl's hands indicating a struggle; the broken button found in the rec room, which didn't fit the clothing of any of the deceased nor the clothing of Wyley Gates. Then there were the angled shots to the heart, indicating a degree of marksmanship that Wyley Gates—"Mr. Aesthetic, Nonmasculine, Nonaggressive, Nonconfrontational, Nonviolent, Never-Slams-a-Locker, Didn't-Know-Anything-About-Guns Gates"—would not have possessed. "A reasonable doubt?" asked Wilcox. "A deep reasonable doubt," he said.

The relationship of Damian and Wyley presented, in and of itself, a reasonable doubt, Wilcox suggested. "All the testimony you heard from anybody indicated that Damian was coming up with this plan . . . Master Rossney was doing this planning. Mr. Planner. 158 I.Q. Rossney was out there, planting little seeds, planting little statements to different people, taking care of himself, before and after. The same Damian Rossney that Miles McDonald and Wyley Gates wouldn't proceed with the burglary without," he reminded the jury. "They went to the house. They were there . . . ready to go, could have done it. But hold on—'We're missing Master Damian. We can't proceed in his absence.' And leave the house they did, drove over to Damian Rossney's house and back again. He would not miss that, ladies and gentle-men. Let Master Rossney miss the final scene . . . that he was leading up to, all the pumping and prompting and promoting? Miss it? No way. No way Master Rossney was going to miss it."

Wilcox returned to the inadequacy of the police work: the failure to take molds of the car tracks from the field where Wyley said he had parked; the failure to secure evidence from Cheryl Brahm's car; the failure to find or rule out the bag of sweaters that Wyley said he had taken from Cheryl's car just before he left for the movies.

As he had several times in the course of the trial, Wilcox brought up the mysterious pickup truck seen on Maple Drive. "Investigator Shook said yes, there was a call. . . . Alan Gelb called up and said there was a pickup truck on Maple Drive, he lives on Maple Drive, and it was scary. There was a couple of people in it, I think he said, a couple of people and it was scary. He called in to check it out; didn't hear another thing about it," charged Wilcox, who also reminded the jury that Wyley's aunt, Dorothy Dooley, had been "run off" the road by a pickup truck on December 13.

"And the biggest and deepest reasonable doubt of all is the alleged statement of Wyley Gates," Wilcox put forth. "This oral statement does not match the facts. The most glaring and biggest reasonable doubt. There is no way, ladies and gentlemen, I submit to you, there is no way that you can convict Wyley Gates of shooting these people and the weapons count as contained in that indictment on the proof that was submitted to you. You cannot find, but you must do that to convict, that he was the shooter, the person who pulled the trigger to cause these deaths. There are too many reasonable doubts.

"We have overzealous police, who want the right result but close their minds to the possibilities in this investigation," Wilcox declared. "Who seize upon Wyley Gates, who they think, and they are right, is strange because he acts different when they talk to him; because he's different; he's sick. And they say to themselves that because he's strange, this must be our guy, because he's emotionally not reacting the way we would expect. And they hone in and corner him and trample on the Constitution to get to Wyley Gates.

"That is why we have a constitution!" cried Wilcox. "That is why this is the United States of America, to encourage complete and legitimate investigation and police conduct." His voice dropped to a hush. "Don't, I beseech you, I implore you, compound this tragedy and the tragedy of the Gates family, including Vivian Gates, who sat here every day, almost every day, on his behalf, by convicting him on this evidence that has been submitted to you. It is wholly inadequate and unthorough."

Wilcox stared into the eyes of each and every juror. "You have a momentous decision," he told them. "His entire life is before you in this particular matter. I can only analogize this situation to making some decision concerning life-threatening surgery, amputation. Consider the magnitude of that decision and consider the magnitude of your decision here today."

With a finely honed sense of pacing, Wilcox turned to the pivotal point of the case: the Poughkeepsie interlude. "Mr. Hogle, searching for Wyley Gates, was told to go to Chatham," recalled Wilcox. "At Chatham, Wyley Gates agrees to take the polygraph test and Mr. Hogle comes out and says, 'My client will take the polygraph examination' and they wait. . . . Cozzolino says to him, 'Well, I hope you don't want to hold his hand.' . . . He said, 'No, I might not want to hold his hand but what about the one-way mirror?' This begins . . . the rape of the Constitution and the defrauding and scheme to defraud the attorney for Wyley Gates, which got the police in the trouble they got into because they tried to circumvent the Constitution!" he cried. "They find themselves alone with Wyley Gates, a boy whom even they in their minds say is strange, is sick; and as a result of that they get inaccurate, untruthful information. . . . It wouldn't have happened if they had done it right. Mr. Hogle goes all the way to Poughkeepsie . . . in the middle of the night. For what reason if he wasn't going to accompany his client for the polygraph test? So when he says to you from that chair under oath that he picked up his briefcase and put his jacket over his arm to follow his client into that room, that is what he was doing, that is what he was there for, and you can believe. I submit to you, without doubt that that hand came out, because he was an obstacle. . . . Mr. Salmon would tell you no, that didn't happen, but it is the same Mr. Salmon who says I don't remember if I touched his legs or not. But everybody else remembers."

Building on Judge Leaman's celebration of the Constitution just a few days before, Wilcox, in the climax of his speech, primed the pump.

"The Constitution is a magnificent document. We stopped the courtroom proceedings," he cried, his voice on the edge of tears. "We stopped for the bells to ring and I don't want those bells to be the death-knell of the constitution of this state and this country, because if what happened [in Poughkeepsie] is right, we might as well bring in that bugler, ladies and gentlemen, and sound 'Taps' for the United States Constitution!" Seven times, he reminded the jurors, Wyley Gates asked Thomas Salmon to give him the test, but it was never done, all the time the youth was "tethered" to the machine. "They knew they had a strange boy, a sick boy in that room. Salmon came out from behind that table and sat down next to him, I submit to you, knee-to-knee. A boy with his personality who's got his sexual identity problems; maybe starts touching his legs, doing everything else like that. Abominable!" he shouted. "It cannot be tolerated. It's that simple. I sat . . . for fifteen years at the prosecution table and I never saw anything like it in my life! It cannot be tolerated!

"I could go on and on, but I can't. But how can you sit down in a case like this? I can only say to you, look at everything closely, consider," implored Wilcox. "There are many deep and reasonable doubts." He took this moment to make eye contact again with each juror. "I spent a long time with you when we started out. . . . We have been together a long time. I have tried not to look at you during the case. I didn't want to invade your province. I can only go back to the time I spent with you in the very beginning and say I trusted you then and on behalf of Wyley Gates right now I trust you. Thank you."

Wilcox's closing remarks took just short of two hours to deliver. Gene Keeler's remarks fell short of Wilcox's by a half hour, but, more significantly, many felt it fell short in terms of organization and impact. In any event, it certainly lacked the kind of histrionics that caused some to accuse Wilcox of scenery chewing but whose effectiveness would soon become apparent.

He began with one of Wyley's letters to Cameron Price, with its signal line: "I regret that most of my life has been destroyed in one ill thought out moment."

"The only evidence in this case that you are to consider," Keeler told the jury, "is the evidence that comes from that chair and the other hard-core exhibits. . . . The only thing you are to listen to is what has been permitted by the court to go into evidence. . . . No matter what I say or Mr. Wilcox says, you have the job of analyzing it and making your own judgment."

He read on from the Cameron Price letter. "Essentially the only route I have left is the insanity plea, which, considering my intelligence and self-control, will be interesting to prove," quoted Keeler. "Cameron Price was a good friend," Keeler pointed out to the jury. "Miles McDonald was a good friend. Damian Rossney, a good friend. . . . How can you be so far out of touch with reality that you solicit out two friends and plan over a matter of months and weeks to do that?"

He read a portion from People's Exhibit 39, the "notes" to himself that Chuck Argyle had found on the floor of their cell. "Damian was willing to kill for money." "Miles was willing to help kill my father and my brother with Damian for half of what Damian would get." "I abhor senseless violence (contradiction?)." Is this out of touch with reality? Keeler demanded.

The "Cujo" letter to Damian. "Honor demands that I do everything possible to assist you, including perjury." Out of touch with reality? Keeler asked, sounding the refrain.

The "Black Maxx" letter to Damian. "I didn't break down when I confessed. I had no choice and I was under extreme conditions at the time. Please reserve judgment until you have enough data." Out of touch with reality? Keeler asked the jury. Makes sense?

Keeler began to attack the psychiatric defense that Wilcox had presented. Dr. Lewis had tied Wyley's problems to his "genetic vulnerability," said Keeler, but wouldn't you have to know more about someone's family history to make such a diagnosis? Dr. Marchionne, he reminded the jury, had publication on his mind, but still, with all the interviews he'd had with Wyley, there was no evidence of hallucinations. He saw delusions, said Keeler. Is it a delusion to be seventeen years old and want to run a major company? Is it unusual to want to live in Antarctica? he continued, this time overreaching.

On cross-examination, said Keeler, all three psycho-therapists had said that Wyley Gates operated on his own code of conduct, and that he knew that what he was doing was wrong from society's point of view. He knew that society would find it illegal and immoral. Keeler told the jurors that the judge was going to read them a definition of what *wrong* means in the law; he wanted the jurors to take that psychiatric testimony and match it against the legal definition.

Keeler put forth the theory that the root of what had happened could be found in an "ancient formula": anger, hatred, and money. Wyley had the hatred—for a father who never appreciated him and didn't pay him for his work; for a brother who was favored by his father. Why would Damian and Miles help Wyley? What would make them hate Bob and Cheryl and Bobby and Jason? Their motivation was money. In this whole case, Keeler stressed, who has the motive? Who is the one filled with anger and hatred?

Keeler turned to the alibis of each of the boys, beefing them up. He recalled Damian's aunt testifying to Damian having been at the house when she called around 6:30. He recalled John Bailey's verified phone call from Long Island.

He recalled the testimony of Matt Rueckheim's sister-in-law saying that Miles and Matt had been in her company from five to almost nine that evening. Keeler went over the charge that "marksmanship" was evident in the shootings. "How good a marksmanship person do you have to be to shoot a three-year-old in the chest at close range?" he demanded. With regard to Cheryl, he asked, "How good do you have to be to shoot somebody in the back if they are laying on the ground?"

In a summation that was mostly a rebuttal to Wilcox's remarks, he went down the list, asking what real significance the scratches on Jason's face had, scratches that could, after all, have come from his own fingernails; the broken button—that "piece of plastic;" the pickup truck whose sighting on the road by Wyley's great-aunt might actually have occurred earlier than she said it had.

Finally, he moved into a defense of police procedure. "We've had comments on the United States Constitution," he said. "Is it unreasonable for a police officer to take a statement from an individual? Is that overreaching?" As far as Poughkeepsie went, Keeler gave his own view of it. "They get to Poughkeepsie. Shook goes off. It's Dick Hogle, the lawyer; Wyley Gates; and out comes Investigator Salmon. They talk out there. They know what the subject matter of the test is going to be, what the questions are going to be. They know it's about the death of relatives. He comes out, gives him a journal to read and review. He gives them another form to sign. He asked them to read them all. He goes off and leaves them alone in private, an opportunity to confer. He comes back and says, 'You all read these documents that I gave you?' 'Yup. Affirmative.' Then [they] go into the back room where the polygraph machine was. Were any guns drawn? . . . Dick Hogle says that Tom Salmon put his hand up. That's all Dick Hogle says. . . . Dick Hogle sat right back down. Is that undue influence? . . . Dick Hogle said there was no body contact. . . . How far away was the communication desk? Was there an officer on duty? Were there windows there? The whole time you were there did you go to the police officer in charge and demand to see your client? Did you get up and go to the back room? Did you demand to see your client? Dick Hogle says no, no, no, no, no. . . . And when did Investigator Salmon stop talking with Wyley Gates? As soon as Wyley said, 'I wonder what my lawyer's going to think about this.' Tom said, 'Oh I can't talk to you anymore'; goes out to Dick Hogle and says, 'Your client wishes your attendance.' Is that improper police conduct?"

Keeler concluded with a recapitulation of the exchange between Wyley and Vivian Gates, during her visit to the jailhouse. "I can't believe you'd shoot Jason," he quoted Mrs. Gates as saying, to which Wyley replied, "You'd better believe it." He looked at the jury. "A crazy, insane admission out of touch with reality to his grandmother who loves him and he loves dearly?" he asked them. "Out of touch with reality?" he added, the question echoing after he sat down.

The last order of business was Judge Leaman's charge to the jury, which also took close to two hours to deliver. "This is the precise moment towards which the entire trial has been directed," the judge began. "You the jury are the sole judges of what the facts of this case are. You must accept the law as I give it to you," he instructed. "As I tell you the law, so you must accept it."

He reminded the jury that during the course of the trial, various witnesses had testified and that it would be important for the jurors to determine their credibility. To do so, they should use the same criteria to judge people that they used in everyday life, meaning they should take into account interest or lack of interest, bias, age, appearance, manner, probability or improbability. He also told the jury that a defendant in a criminal case is presumed to be innocent until proven not to be without reasonable doubt. What does the law mean by proof beyond a reasonable doubt? A doubt is deemed reasonable when, because of an insufficiency of evidence in the case, a reasonable person would be likely to entertain it. A doubt is not a reasonable doubt if it is based on "some guess or whim or speculation unrelated to the evidence in the case and also . . . if it is based merely on sympathy or from a desire on the part of any juror to avoid doing a disagreeable duty."

He then asked the jury to address six counts lodged against Wyley Gates in connection with the December 13, 1986, shooting deaths of Robert Gates, Robert Gates, Jr., Cheryl Brahm, and Jason Gates. Four of the counts were murder in the second degree—one charge for each death— claiming he "did intentionally cause the death of another person . . . by shooting with a pistol." The original indictment had also carried an additional four counts of second-degree murder, claiming the defendant caused the death of another person by "means of shooting a pistol under circumstances evincing a depraved indifference to human life," but those counts had been dismissed under a mutual agreement between the judge and the attorneys.

To find the defendant guilty of the murder charges, the judge charged the jury, three elements needed to be proven: that on or about December 13, 1986, the defendant caused the deaths; that he shot them with a pistol with the intent to cause the deaths; and that the act of shooting did cause the deaths. Judge Leaman went on to detail the elements that needed to be proven for the remaining two counts of criminal possession of a weapon in the second degree and conspiracy in the second degree.

In considering each count, Judge Leaman told the jurors, they had to first determine whether there was sufficient evidence to establish guilt. If they so found, then they must consider either the affirmative defense of not responsible by means of mental disease or defect, or, if mental disease or defect was not proven but extreme emotional disturbance was found, then they must consider the reduced charge of manslaughter. Citing Section 40.15 of the Penal Law, the judge discussed the issue of mental disease or defect. This meant, he said, that the defendant lacked substantial capacity to know the consequences of his actions; that the defendant lacked substantial capacity to appreciate the consequences of his actions; that the defendant lacked substantial capacity to know that his actions were wrong; or that the defendant lacked substantial capacity to appreciate that such conduct was wrong. He reviewed the psychiatric testimony, recalling that the three defense psychotherapists had testified that Wyley Gates lacked substantial capacity, and that the four members of the prosecution team had testified that he possessed substantial capacity. He also reminded the jurors that, in accordance with Section 60.55 of the Criminal Procedure Law, he was obliged to direct them not to consider any of the statements Wyley had made to psychiatrists or psychologists for any purpose other than weighing the insanity defense.

As for "extreme emotional disturbance," the judge told the jurors that they had to figuratively put themselves in the shoes of the defendant. The law does not specify a particular kind of emotion that results in extreme emotional disturbance, but anger, terror, passion, fright, and grief are some examples of emotions that can be extreme enough to have caused the defendant to lose self-control. The judge then gave instructions as to the possibility of a manslaughter finding, in the event that the second-degree-murder charges were dismissed.

He moved on to the subject of the confession, specifically in regard to its "voluntariness." Two elements had to be determined to establish voluntariness. "If a particular alleged statement by the defendant was the product of custodial interrogation," he said, meaning that if it came out of the defendant's having been questioned by the police while in their custody and when he was not free to come and go as he wished, "it must have been preceded by the so-called *Miranda* warnings and appropriate waiver in order to be voluntary." The judge reminded the jury that no *Miranda* warnings had been given while Wyley was in Vivian Gates's residence before he gave his statement, and none were required if the jury found that there was no custodial interrogation. The second aspect of voluntariness had to do with whether any particular alleged statement of the defendant had been influenced by certain factors that were present in the circumstance under which he offered his alleged statement. These factors include whether the setting

was familiar or unfamiliar to the defendant; whether the
police officers were respectful or overbearing, candid or
deceitful; the age of the defendant; his intelligence; and
the time of day or night when the statement was being
given.

Some of the head-shakers in Columbia County would
later maintain that if the judge had ruled the confession
admissible, it was not up to the jury to rule otherwise. This
is not true. The jury always has to decide whether the
defendant actually made the confession and whether its
contents were true—those are factual questions that bear
directly on guilt or innocence. In order to decide those
questions, the jury has to hear whether the defendant was
threatened, tricked, beaten up, and so on, for, as stated in
the landmark case *Miller* v. *Fenton*, "Certain interrogation
techniques . . . are so offensive to a civilized system of justice
that they must be condemned under the Due Process Clause
of the Fourteenth Amendment." To make sure that the
results of such techniques are never used to secure a
conviction, the landmark case of *Sims* v. *Georgia* further
stated that due process requires that a jury not hear a
confession unless and until the trial judge has determined
that it was freely and voluntarily given. The question
remains, however, that if the jury decides that the confession
was made and is true, should they nevertheless be instructed
to reject it if they decide that it was extracted from the
defendant in violation of the Fifth Amendment? *Jackson* v.
Denno left this decision to the states. New York decided in
People v. *Huntley* that the New York State constitution requires that this issue continue to be left to the jury. This
rule was then codified in Section 710.70 of the Criminal
Procedure Law, which essentially states that nothing pre-
cludes a defendant from attempting to establish at a trial
that the evidence introduced by the People, such as a
confession made by the defendant, was made involuntarily
and so should be disregarded by the jury. Even though the
issue of the admissibility of such evidence may not have
been submitted to the court, or may have been determined

adversely to the defendant, the defendant may otherwise contend that the statement was involuntarily made. In the case of a jury trial, the court must submit this issue to the jury with instructions to disregard such evidence upon a finding that the statement was involuntarily made.

New York is in a minority of states that give the defendant a "second bite" regarding the voluntariness issue with the jury, but it is a substantial minority. New York also follows a minority rule in that the prosecution has the burden of proving "beyond a reasonable doubt" that the confession is voluntary. *People* v. *Huntley* states, "The Judge must find voluntariness beyond a reasonable doubt before the confession can be submitted to the trial jury. The burden of proof as to voluntariness is on the People." The Supreme Court in *Lego* v. *Twomey* decided that the Constitution requires only that voluntariness be proved by a "preponderance of the evidence," a much easier standard. The federal courts and most states now use the preponderance standard.

Moving on from the matter of the confession, Judge Leaman then addressed the issue of the testimony of Charles Argyle and told the jury that they had to determine if Argyle was or was not an agent of the police. According to what is known as the *Massiah* rule, when an individual has been indicted, he has the right to counsel and the police cannot question that individual without counsel present. Hence, they cannot send in an agent of the police without counsel being present. This is to be differentiated from information received when an individual voluntarily passes it on to a cellmate, or one cellmate takes it upon himself, without direction from the police, to gather information from another individual in the hope of possibly benefiting from it by informing. In short, Judge Leaman was instructing the jury to determine whether Charles Argyle was really acting under instructions from the police, in which case his testimony must not be considered. Concluding his remarks, Judge Leaman reminded the jury that their decision had to be unanimous.

At last, after these many, many weeks, there was nothing

more to be said. It was up to the jury now. For lack of a jury room, the courtroom was cleared and turned over to the twelve men and women who would begin their deliberation. When they emerged, many lives, including their own, would be altered.

PART

FOUR

21

Deliberation on *The People of New York* v. *Wyley Gates* began at 5:00 P.M. on Thursday, October 1. Three days later, a state of emergency was declared in Columbia County. By the time the jurors returned their verdict on October 6, the state of emergency had become a state of disaster.

From the beginning, there were a great many strange things about this case. "I always had the feeling that there was something very cultish about this particular murder," one juror confided to me afterward. "The whole thing . . . the whole trial . . . just seemed strange." Now, in some kind of grotesque but fitting way, nature had provided as strange a twist as any when the cold rain that had fallen all day Saturday—which also happened to be Yom Kippur, the Jewish Day of Atonement—gave way to a dense, thick snow. By morning the entire county was devastated by eighteen inches of snow that had fallen on trees still heavily in leaf, snapping boughs and power lines everywhere, bringing all activity to a crippled halt. This was the earliest major snowstorm on record, the previous record for an early storm having been set on October 10, 1925, when a paltry two inches had fallen on the Albany area. This incredible eighteen-inch snowfall set another record, this one for interruption of electrical service, with some twenty-three thousand customers of Niagara Mohawk and New York State Electric and Gas left powerless, and the extent of telephone service interruption had yet to be calculated. Two fatalities were reported, of motorists hit by falling limbs, and Sheriff Proper imposed a dusk-to-dawn curfew to prevent looting during the disaster.

The jurors, who had been sequestered since Friday, were now, on this snowbound Sunday, under the intense strain of deliberating in an unheated courtroom; of not knowing the situations of their families during this crisis; and of having to return a verdict in a powder-keg case, the only genuine powder-keg case in the county's memory.

A long time had elapsed since midsummer, when these six men and six women were first called to appear for jury duty, and the length of time was made to seem much longer by the feeling that one season had too precipitously given way to another. What had begun in sweltering humidity was now adrift, in white-out conditions, with the end, as far as anyone could tell, nowhere in sight.

At the beginning, the jury, left alone in the courtroom that was now serving as the jury room, had taken a vote. The tally was seven not guilty, five guilty. One juror remembered the process as "fairly orderly," but another remembered instead "yelling, cursing, all talking at once." Robert Jensen, the service technician for 3M Corporation, recalled the focus of discussion repeatedly coming back to the issue of evidence not having been collected. "It always came back to the question: Why no fingerprints taken from the gun?" recalled Jensen. "So he said he wore gloves. So what? You take his word for it? Why not take [fingerprints]? Why was his clothing not tested for gunshot residue? Nobody else's clothes or hands were checked. None of these tests were done."

The call for readbacks from the testimony started on

Friday, when the jury asked to hear once again the testimony of Thomas Salmon. On Saturday, readbacks of the testimonies of Richard Hogle, Sally and Stanley Joseph, and John Cozzolino were requested. Saturday night, after their dinner break, the jury asked the judge for a further definition of "reasonable doubt," posing the specific question of whether there is any doubt that is *not* reasonable.

The atmosphere in the jury room had become quite tense by Saturday, portrayed by one juror as a "battle," with more yelling, more cursing, and now even some crying. There was also, in the opinion of one of the female jurors, a great deal of sexism, both overtly and subliminally expressed. To some extent, the battle lines here were being drawn between men and women over the fact that the men perceived the women as being too sentimental and yielding in Wyley's regard. Although all the jurors to whom I would speak described Wyley as "odd," "cold," and "distant," several of the women jurors had, in the course of the trial, studied him carefully for any evidence of underlying emotion. One woman juror, who remembered the defendant as "quiet," said, "I felt he had a lot of discipline just to be able to sit there and show no emotion. But then again, too, there are people like that. But he did show emotion. Sitting there in the jury box I could see him smile. He even cried. You could see him crying, sitting there. There were times when he would sit just at an angle and you could see his face and when something funny was said, and everyone would laugh, he'd smile. He was a young man who was . . . unusual." Another woman juror recalled seeing Wyley in tears when Jason Gates was mentioned and then again during the testimony of Thomas Salmon. "When Mr. Salmon was testifying," recalled the juror, "[Wyley] had moved his chair slightly so that he was angled and could have more of an eye-to-eye contact. I could feel that there were a lot of things hovering around inside of him. I watched his Adam's apple and the tears would start and you could almost sense it. From where I was sitting you could almost feel him inside saying, 'Oh no, I can't do this, I have to hold it together,' and almost this hard swallowing to keep it down." One of

the male jurors characterized the defendant differently. "I
think he's a pretty cool character," the juror said. "I think
he maintained a pretty good composure. The one thing that
kind of set it up, I guess, was one day we were returning to
the courtroom and he was back by the rail, talking to his
school friends, joking around, and then immediately, when
the jury sat down and there was a call for silence in the
courtroom, he sat down and the mask came on again. I
think he was a master at being calm and collected."

On Sunday, a few of the jurors, in need of spiritual
solace, trudged through the snowdrifts to church. Later that
morning, the jurors, wrapping themselves in blankets and
eating hot food delivered to them from the Columbia County
Jail, went to work, intent on breaking the deadlock. One of
the jurors came up with a plan. He suggested that they all
take an hour to review the evidence before them and then
take another hour to write down what they felt they did or
did not have evidence for. At the top of the sheet, each
juror should write their verdict.

One of the women jurors, who spent considerably more
than an hour on the assignment, remembered the other
jurors shouting viciously at her. "What do you think you're
writing? A book?" they cried. But the juror took her time,
unswayed, filling her sheets with "reasonable doubts":

NOT GUILTY
Wyley Gates was not the shooter:
(1) We have no quality evidence putting the
gun in his hand. We do have unwritten, unsigned,
untaped paper written up by Mr. Salmon. Wyley
Gates' attorney was not present.
(2) No testimony of State Police Officers working this case. Only technicians, BCI Investigators,
and [ballistics expert] Dominic Deneo.
(3) Testimony stating that Wyley Gates did not
know how to shoot a gun.
(4) Testimony making Walter Shook unbelievable.

(5) Testimony from Damian Rossney saying Wyley Gates never had the gun.

(6) Testimony from Miles McDonald saying they stole the gun.

(7) McDonald and Rossney shared the loot, not Wyley.

(8) Wyley Gates under extreme conditions when he confessed.

(9) No fingerprints taken from the gun.

(10) Do not have definite proof of whose blood was on the gun, only that it was human blood.

(11) No quality evidence showing Wyley Gates got a cut on his hand from the gun.

(12) Testimony stating there were no powder burns on the jacket.

(13) Testimony that Wyley Gates "didn't like killing."

(14) No blood on the jacket or cut on the gloves found in the jacket.

(15) No fibers on the gun that matched his clothes.

(16) Wyley Gates never changed his clothes after Investigator Shook arrived.

(17) Damian had the gun.

(18) Damian had a lawyer the very next day.

Regarding the confession:

(1) Shook's testimony about reading rights to Wyley in the car. He should have done it in his grandmother's house.

(2) Mr. Salmon touched and handled the legs of Wyley Gates and never did do the polygraph when that's what he was supposed to do.

(3) Lawyer not present in the room. Had been barred by Salmon's hand gesture.

(4) Letter to Damian stating Wyley would perjure himself to help Damian.

Regarding Damian Rossney:

(1) Damian was willing to do the killings according to Wyley's letter.

(2) Gun recovered from Damian's house.

(3) Wyley's letter saying Damian would even kill Skip Huvar.

(4) Damian had all the gloves.

(5) Damian had weapons that had been stolen.

(6) Damian had a motive according to Wyley's letter—that he would do it for money.

(7) Psychiatrists' testimony that Damian had high intelligence.

Regarding the crime scene:

(1) Helter-skelter pieces. No match-up. Bodies moved and cops not careful enough in that room.

(2) Expert testimony regarding evidence of marksmanship.

(3) Photos showing Cheryl Brahm to have been in a struggle, but no statement from Wyley confessing to that struggle.

(4) Plastic button proved never to have come from Gates or victims.

(5) Wyley and Damian planned to kill only Robert Gates and Bobby. Wyley knew Jason was at home.

(6) Phone call received from someone about two people parked in a field.

(7) Dorothy Dooley's report of a pick-up truck sighting.

(8) Mrs. Dooley told police about the truck, but nothing more was done.

When this juror had finally completed her assignment, one by one the jurors read their sheets. No one else was allowed to speak; no one was allowed to argue. When they got to the juror accused of "writing a book" the silence deepened as everyone—particularly, this juror recalled, the men—listened intently. The count, upon completion, was four for not guilty; four for guilty; four undecided. That meant that one of the original five "guilty" votes had dropped out.

There had been movement, but at an agonizingly slow pace. Several of the jurors were now in the grip of a flulike ailment, and the space heaters that were being used to warm the courtroom produced nauseating fumes that made the difficult work that much more difficult. Beyond these problems, there was a continuation of the emotional wear and tear that had started almost from the beginning. One woman juror recalled being spoken to "roughly and gruffly," being told by one of the male jurors that the only reason she was holding out for not guilty was because she was thinking of her own son, who'd had trouble with the law. An exchange between the two ended with the woman juror being called a "pussy" by the male juror. Finally, at the end of the day, the woman juror addressed the group at large. She declared that because her anatomy was different from that of the men, it did not mean that what we have in our heads is any better or worse. I am neither man nor woman in this room, she told them; I am a person and I will take no more disparaging remarks.

Through all of this, the jury kept calling for readbacks of testimony: Investigator Shook's; Undersheriff Bertram's; more of Cozzolino's.

The D.A. dealt with his own tensions by reading. Sitting in a chair in the courthouse library, he could be seen with books on sales—*How to Close*, one might guess—and with Dale Carnegie's classic *How to Win Friends and Influence People*. The assembled media and spectators, dazed to giddy with the long vigil in the blacked-out courthouse, burst into a rendition of "Happy Birthday" to an excruciatingly embarrassed Chuck Wilcox, whose plans to unwind up in Kennebunk had been jettisoned in the face of the lengthy and still-undecided deliberation.

No members of the Gates family could be found at the courthouse vigil. Wyley would soon ask to see his grandmother, and it was his attorney's unhappy duty to tell him that she had retreated to an elderhostel in the Adirondacks with her sister. Rumors spread that the Gates family was in turmoil over the possibility of Wyley's being found not guilty on all of the charges. What would happen in the event of his release? There were people in Columbia County who had done everything short of making official statements that they intended to resort to frontier justice if the courts failed at their version of it. It was rumored too that the family was looking into commitment for Wyley if, in fact, he was going to walk away from all this.

On Tuesday, October 6, the notes from the jury were coming at a fast clip. At 11:15 A.M., just fifteen minutes after they had reconvened for deliberation, the jury sent out a note requesting a definition of *voluntariness*. It was a clear indication that they were wrestling with the Poughkeepsie episode. In fact, the confession was the major stumbling block for most of the jurors. One juror felt that there was no question that Wyley's attorney had been banned from observing the polygraph examination and found it particularly troublesome that the attorney had had to search for Wyley as long as he did before finally finding him in Chatham. "I don't know what they were trying to do when they took him from the house," the juror said. "Why didn't they take him right down to Poughkeepsie? Why did they have to take him to Chatham? I have no idea. They could have phoned from the Gates place themselves, and gotten right on the parkway. Why did they have to do it in a roundabout way?"

Although they had qualms about how the police handled the polygraph episode, the jurors didn't hold Hogle blameless. "I think everybody agreed that [Hogle] was excluded from the questioning by their request," said another juror. "And the thought that went through my mind was How could he be so inept as to sit there and say nothing while they're doing this? Either he was inept enough to do this or shrewd enough to know that they were jeopardizing their case. I tend to think it was the first one, that he really didn't know."

But beyond the issue of whether or not Hogle had been barred, a number of jurors shared the feeling that Wyley himself had been mishandled and under extreme conditions down at Poughkeepsie. "Here's this boy who was willing to take this polygraph test seven times, and if he had had anything to hide I'm sure he would have known it would come out in this polygraph test," said a juror. "And if he had had anything to hide, would he have been that willing to take it? I mean, he went into the room with them. They had him all hooked up. They kept him sitting there for what? Two hours? Two and a half hours? Never gave him the test."

At 12:40 P.M., after lunch, the jury sent their fourteenth note, this time asking if the court could provide in written form what had been said earlier about custodial interrogation. The judge deemed that this would be inappropriate and, instead, reread the relevant portion from his charge. "Custodial interrogation is initiated by law-enforcement officers after a person is taken into custody and is no longer free to go," he explained. Within the next few hours, more notes would be sent out from the jury room on the issues of voluntariness and custodial interrogation. The jury also requested a visit to the crime scene, but this was denied on the basis of its having already been substantially altered.

The day dragged on. At five o'clock, there was a request from the jurors for fresh air, and they took their "constitutional," as it was quickly dubbed, around the courthouse square, looking like trapped deer as the media seized the photo opportunity. "You have to know what it's like to be locked up for six days and six nights, to have guards on you at all times, to know that you're with eleven other people who are not always going to be in agreement," said a juror. "You have to have, I think, a fairly strong character to be a juror and to be a good one."

At 5:40 P.M., upon their return from their walk, the jury sent out note #17, requesting a rereading of the elements in the second-degree-murder charge, in the conspiracy charge, and in the charge of criminal possession. Those who were waiting let out another big groan, but, in fact, much was happening in the jury room. One of the jurors had given what was described by another juror as "the most stupendous, marvelous oration about constitutional rights—like something you would see in a movie." But there were still more notes to come. The jury asked for instructions concerning the definitions of *wrong*, *preponderance*, and *mental disease or defect*.

What was holding up the process was the fact that many of the jurors were convinced that Wyley Gates was guilty of involvement with the murders, but they were having difficulty finding him guilty according to the charge given by the judge. "I was definitely sure he was involved," said Robert Jensen. "To what extent I couldn't be positive, but I knew that he had helped plan it, helped carry it out. Whether he actually shot the people or not, that I didn't know, but I do know he was part of it and helped plan it." Jensen recalled the uneasy feeling of being hemmed in at the moment that the judge read the charge to the jury. "The judge read the charges, and as he read the counts on the indictment and the specific elements that you had to find under each count," recalled Jensen, "this thought that I had made up in my mind, I just felt it slipping away. And I'm sitting in the jury box, saying to myself, 'Now wait. No, no, no, no—you can't do this! I don't want to go this way!' " Jensen believed that his feelings were shared by others in the jury. "I think with a great number," he said. "Oddly enough . . . I still really believe there were a couple who actually considered him completely innocent of anything. I don't know how they could come up with that but I really think they did." As far as Jensen was concerned, he would have wanted the charge to be otherwise presented. "I think it's too bad they couldn't have worded the counts differently," he said. "The elements common to all four counts of murder was that he had [to have had] the gun in his hand and he [had to have] pulled the trigger. Nowhere did we find anything that gave us that. Absolutely nothing. And think if they'd gone complicity or accomplice or anything along that line. This is how we easily came up with the conspiracy, because we were positive he was part of it, took part in it, planned it, but the act of taking the gun itself and doing the shooting we felt we could not prove." Jensen, in fact, did his own research after the trial was over to see how else the case might have been presented. "I made it my business to go and look it up, to find out where the elements of the counts come from," he said. "And it's all in the penal law. Depends on how it's written up. If it had been written up

—aiding and abetting—if they had used that, that would have opened the door."

Mary Meyer had the same feelings. She felt that there had been sufficient evidence presented at the trial to convince her that one of these boys had killed the family and that the murder had come out of the conspiracy, but she could not find Wyley Gates guilty of actually shooting the four individuals. "Time in and time out, we were told that it was the [prosecutor's] place to prove Wyley Gates shot the four individuals," said Meyer. "He had the burden of proof. If I were to have to make a statement, I would have to say that Mr. Keeler did not prove beyond a reasonable doubt that Wyley Gates killed those four people. That he had the gun in his hand, that he shot the four, that the four died because he shot them."

In the jury room, on the evening of October 6, the moment of truth was approaching. One of the jurors made a speech in which he stated that the only piece of evidence they could legitimately use was the alleged confession, and that they had searched through the testimony and had had numerous rereadings of the testimony and they had come to the conclusion that their one piece of evidence was not acceptable. "It just doesn't taste good and it just doesn't feel good," said the juror, who had been in the "guilty" bloc from the beginning. "The law is the law and it doesn't feel right. I have to go with not guilty."

There were tears at this point; a feeling of the tide having turned. The foreman, Frederick Stonner, called for another vote, this time asking for hands. For the first time in six days, all hands went up for the same vote. There was a certain sense of accomplishment, but it was a muted, ambivalent sense of accomplishment, accompanied by more tears. "We all knew we'd been handed a difficult task," one juror recalled. "We'd been handed a bag and we were going to be left holding it."

22

At 10:30 P.M., on October 6, the jury sent out note #22 indicating that they had reached a verdict. Within five minutes, the courtroom was filled with reporters, spectators, law-enforcement officials, attorneys, the defendant, the jury, and finally the judge. The court clerk took attendance, noting the presence of all jury members. The foreman rose, obviously nervous, his hands gripping the railing in front of him. At the defendant's table, Joan Yowe took Wyley's arm in her own firm grip; they had come a long way from the beginning, when he couldn't even bring himself to meet her eyes. She remembered, just before the jury went into deliberation, that he had actually allowed her to hug him. "I was never allowed to touch him," she recalled. "I mean, we couldn't touch him or anything. But at the end . . . I said to Chuck, 'I just want to give him a hug before he goes downstairs.' So we went around to the side and I said, 'Just give me a hug. Everything's going to be OK.' And he hugged me and he went. The next day, Chuck told me that when Wyley left me, he had tears in his eyes." She and Chuck had done their best to prepare him for the moment that he was now about to face. "By this time we'd gone through thirteen weeks," she said. "He was funny. He was brave; he was courageous. He came up and Chuck said, 'Now, Wyley, whatever happens, it's not the end of the road. There's all kinds of remedies. There's things we can do.' And he said he was fine. The more the kid said he was fine, the more broken up I would get because I thought, This is too much. He shouldn't have to be so brave. He shouldn't have to be so courageous. So he sat down and I took his hand." As she took his hand, Joan glimpsed an interaction between two women jurors that gave her a glimmer of hope. "When we walked in, I saw one of the jurors touch another juror, like 'Here he comes,'" she recalled. "And I thought, Oh, my God, is it possible that this is going to be all right?"

The judge addressed the foreman. On the first charge of the murder of Robert Gates, Sr., Judge Leaman asked Frederick Stonner how he found the defendant. In a quiet, almost diffident manner, the foreman replied, "Not guilty." The courtroom was absolutely silent; in fact, stunned. On the charge of the murder of Robert Gates, Jr., the response was "Not guilty." On the charge of the murder of Jason Gates, "Not guilty." The judge, urbane and unflappable all along, now seemed seriously rattled as he questioned the foreman as to whether the jury really knew, in so many words, what it was up to. (In a later interview, the judge disavowed any surprise. "There was no surprise if you will on the part of the court," he said. "A judge of experience and temperament is rarely surprised by anything in life when it comes to the way people act, what they say, any number of things.") "I ask you if the jury . . . perhaps wishes to reflect and reconsider before rendering its final verdict, and there is no problem or fatal flaw in that regard," said the judge to the foreman. "Sometimes a jury might render a verdict that appears to be based on a misapprehension, and once the court is aware of what that misapprehension is [then] it simply has to set the jury straight, if you will, as to what the verdicts and possible verdicts may be and ask the jury to resume its deliberations and decide and return a verdict in accordance with my legal instruction." The foreman and other members of the jury looked blank as the judge continued. "I wonder if before we continue with accepting the verdict," Leaman said, "I would ask if the jury might wish to discuss what we have just now said and make certain that the verdict that you are returning is a verdict that you truly wish to set forth, the one that you truly have arrived at."

"I don't think so," Mr. Stonner managed to say. "Could we move back to the first count, start out . . . ?"

"Yes, we can," said the judge.

Mr. Stonner began again, delivering the same decision, even as the jury felt the reverberations of the shock waves emanating from the audience. "Not guilty" on the charge of the murder of Robert Gates, Sr. "Not guilty" on the charge of the murder of Robert Gates, Jr. "Not guilty" on the charge of the murder of Jason Gates. "Not guilty" on the charge of the murder of Cheryl Brahm. "Not guilty" on the charge of criminal possession.

"I took his hand and as each 'not guilty' was read, he squeezed my hand," Joan Yowe remembered, "and I thought, Well, I was squeezing and he was squeezing. But in later times, since then, in conversation, I think somebody asked him and he said he had no reaction to the verdict and I said, 'You did too.' I said, 'You squeezed my hand.' He said, 'that was for you.' So I thought, you know, he was unbelievable."

It was all unbelievable. Strangenesses everywhere. At 10:54 P.M., as the verdict was being read, there was a partial eclipse. . . . Why not? There had been everything else swirling around this bizarre case. One last order of business was ahead—count 10, the conspiracy. "How do you find the defendant?" the foreman was asked, and at last the word *guilty* issued from between his lips.

A polling of the jury was requested and evidenced the necessary unanimity. Each juror, in tones that were almost defiant, corroborated the verdict that Mr. Stonner had given.

The judge, in his closing remarks, saluted the work of the jury. "I must express the profound sense of appreciation that I have for your patience, for your forbearance, and for your good will and good faith in undertaking your duties," he said. "Truly it is said that if there were not people of quality and ability and commitment willing to put into practice what everyone preaches about doing one's civic responsibility, if there weren't people like you to put into practice these high-sounding ideals, then the whole concept of justice would remain a light and airy nothing, always out of reach and never brought down to this life where it belongs. So I know that to be true, and I believe it, and I want you to know that I know just how large a contribution you have made to the justice system of which I'm proud to serve, and I hope that for you, while it has been difficult . . . I hope you leave the experience with a sense that as imperfect as the system is, populated by mere men and women, it is the best system that I believe in this world can exist."

While Keeler remained silent, Wilcox, too, offered his thanks to the jury, saluting them as "truly a perceptive, thorough, and just body." He and Wyley shook hands, Wilcox looking rigidly avuncular, Wyley appearing primly misty-eyed. But, in fact, on the occasion of his avoiding a conviction on four separate murder charges, the enigmatic young man showed not much more emotion than he had at any other point in the proceedings. "He was not different then than he was [throughout] the whole trial," recalled Joan Yowe. "Absolutely no change. Chuck said that he stood there with him and he was just the same, there was never any change."

As for Keeler, he had disappeared, some said into the bathroom, and made no public statement that evening whatsoever.

The police—Shook, Cozzolino, Bertram—left the courtroom in a mood that was two parts disgust, one part despair. Almost immediately they began to issue statements. "I still feel one hundred percent that we had the right person," said Undersheriff Bertram, insisting that the sheriff's department would not reopen the investigation of the case.

"We got the person who did it. We're not going to go out looking for Santa Claus. We have nothing to show anyone other than Gates killed the four."

Bertram also assailed Wilcox for courtroom theatrics and for trying his case in the media. "Whatever he couldn't get into the courtroom, he held conferences about in the hallway," claimed Bertram. For Wilcox, however, the case was clearly a triumph and also a sort of reversal of an earlier defeat. During his tenure as Rensselaer County district attorney, Wilcox had been on the losing end of a similar albeit far less notorious case, in which a teenage boy was accused of murdering an elderly man in Cherry Plain, New York, and was ultimately found not guilty even though he had allegedly confessed. Shoddy police work during the investigation was the turning point in that case, said members of the jury, who had been polled after that verdict. But Bertram denied that there was anything shoddy about the investigative work of the Columbia County Sheriff's Department in this case. "We did everything right," he declared angrily. "If we did it over again, we would do it the same way. We did it by the book. Nothing was done wrong. Nothing was improper."

Above all, however, Bertram assailed the jury. He told reporters that he believed the jury had been confused by legal points in the case. "I don't think they really understood. I believe in this system," he said, "but this time I feel it failed." The feeling of disillusionment took its toll on this law-enforcement official with eighteen years of experience. "When the jury came back, I was so shocked," he admitted. "I hadn't slept for three days, but I went home and I couldn't sleep. I got up and came back to work."

Despite Bertram's remarks, for many the verdict that the jury returned could only be read as a clear repudiation of police practices. "I think the police didn't do a good job. They did very sloppy, shoddy work, and I don't imagine I'm the only one who felt that," said one juror. "Don't get me wrong. I think they're good men, they have a lot of years experience, it's just I think they got sloppy. I think they got overconfident in what they were doing and they figured, well, they had an ironclad case. Why do this? Why do that? They didn't realize they had to convince twelve people."

"I think if the state police had handled this from the minute that Shook went in to talk to Wyley Gates, you might have seen a totally different picture in the courtroom," ventured another juror. "Experience-wise, they have everything at their beck and call. They're much more geared to getting information without frightening someone. I think they're better trained. Not that Mr. Shook hasn't been trained. I'm sure he has and Cozzolino and all of them. But it seemed to me that with a quadruple homicide you would think that this would be New York State Police–handled."

For the police, this repudiation could only have been both a mystery and a shock. In a county that experiences relatively little violence, a horrendous and highly atypical multiple murder had assaulted the senses of the decent folk who lived here. The alleged perpetrator of the crime, a strange, aloof young man, allegedly had offered confessions that had been heard by the jury, in one form or another, nearly a dozen times. Investigating the murder were law-enforcement officials who were, on the whole, local boys. They'd gone to school in the area, played football here, raised families here, hung out with everybody else at the Bakery. The people who were in contact with these men on the night of the murders—Vivian Gates, Sally and Stanley Joseph—reported that they handled themselves calmly and professionally. And yet, when it came down to the bottom line, the jury sent home a clear rejection of their conduct.

"I don't think Wyley was found not guilty," said a friend of Bob Gates's. "I think they found that there wasn't enough evidence to convict him. And I think there's a big difference. And I also think the biggest problem with the trial was it doesn't appear Wyley was on trial. It appears almost as if the sheriffs were on trial. I also think, on the other hand, the police deserve this. Something's got to be done with a police situation like that. First off, any fifth grader knows

that you (a) read the person their rights and (b) they have
the right to have a lawyer present. I don't think it takes any
genius to figure that out."

The jury, anticipating a public outcry, fortified themselves with a defensive posture. "I think the jury handled it
very well," said one member. "I think we handled it the
only way we could have and have it done in the proper
manner. I think everything that was horrendously wrong
was done before it got to us. I don't think the district
attorney did his job; and very possibly the judge didn't do
his. I don't know. Now who knows? A county judge is an
elected official and you don't want to make unpopular
decisions on something like this if you're an elected official
in the county," said the juror, alluding to the judge's having
admitted Wyley's alleged confession.

Another juror agreed, saying, "I was only chosen to
listen to the testimony and look at the evidence on Wyley
Gates, and I personally don't feel that he pulled the trigger.
Now, I could be all wrong, but I'm satisfied, and I feel I
can live with myself for the way I voted and the way I feel
about this. I could be proven wrong in the long run, but
right now this is how I feel."

Whether the jury was right or wrong is a subject that
will be discussed in these parts for many years. But now
was not the time to discuss the fine points of the law. Now,
for most of the local citizens, it was time for the shock,
revulsion, and anger that spread in a wave to cover the
county from north to south.

On the morning of October 7, reporters, canvassing opinion
on the verdict, roamed through the tiny hamlet of East
Chatham, still suffering from the effects of the freakish
storm that had deprived it of power for days now. But even
without phones or television, news from the courtroom had
crackled through the streets like a live wire, passing from
citizen to citizen, and leaving an acrid smell of disillusionment to mark its path.

"It just knocked everyone for a loop," said Betty Brorup,

who had succeeded Viki Hatch as Canaan town clerk after Mrs. Hatch moved away following the ghastly automobile accident on Peaceful Valley Road. "It's like a bad dream. I'm just in shock. I think the whole town feels the same way. Just shock that it happened."

"Nobody thought that he would get away with what he did," said Don Elsasser, who owns Slattery's General Store in East Chatham. "And nobody wants him back."

For Doris Gearing, there was no longer the possibility of wishing or hoping that her former star student was innocent of the crime. "Initially, when it started out, I hoped it wasn't Wyley. But the more I knew, the more I believe he did it," she said. "Whether he actually pulled the gun or not, he planned it. No kid carries plastic gloves in their pockets if they aren't going to attempt to do something wrong, a burglary or a robbery or whatever." In her criminal-justice class at Chatham High, Mrs. Gearing gauged the visceral impact of this perplexing verdict on her students. "I had a kid say to me, 'Well, I'm gonna steal, I'll get away with it,'" she recalled. "I think that's the impression—you can do anything. You can commit murders and get away with it. I honestly believe they think that." To a certain degree, Mrs. Gearing shared her students' disillusionment. "I call it a tragedy of errors," she said of the whole affair. "Not a comedy of errors, but a tragedy of errors, in the sense that, first of all, why didn't they let his attorney in, why didn't they follow through with a lie detector test, why didn't they get something in writing? I think the county's at fault," she added, "for not having a full-time D.A."

Again and again, the locals took aim at the police. "I think they should be brought up on charges," said one of Bobby, Jr.,'s closest friends. "Somebody should be out of a job—that's the way I feel about it. How can they be considered police officers when they screw up that badly?" A classmate of Wyley's offered a similar but more tempered view. "The sheriffs should have done a more thorough job with the investigation," said the East Chatham youth, who also, however, could not understand the jury's findings. "I

couldn't believe it when my cousin came over and told me,"
added the youth. "I thought at least they would find him
not guilty by reason of insanity."

Vivian Gates had the same expectation. Some weeks
after the trial, when we spoke, she told me that she had
been expecting a guilty verdict by reason of insanity. "But
now that it's over and I've thought about it, for Wyley it's
good," she said. "He'll have a better opportunity to accomplish something than [he would have] in a mental institution."

In fact, the jury had given scant attention to the insanity
defense. "I think we all agreed that he did have mental
problems of some type," said Robert Jensen. "But whether
or not those problems contributed directly to his actions to
the extent that he really didn't know what he was doing, we
felt that if seven professionals couldn't decide that issue, we
couldn't either." Mary Meyer had stronger feelings about
pursuing the insanity issue but essentially acquiesced in the
group feeling. "I really felt that it should have been discussed
and considered . . . kind of picked apart more than it was,"
said Meyer. "But I think at that point in time, you had
people who wanted to say guilty and people who felt not
guilty. So somewhere along the line, even though you never
verbalized it, you almost felt inside, Well, you've come down
to the wire, you're down to the last charge. Maybe it's just
as well that you kind of . . . go along. I think if I had felt
really, really vehement about it or very, very strongly like I
had felt about other things in that room, that I would have
said, 'I'm not moving. I'm staying here another night. I
don't care, you can notify the judge, whatever.' I would
have been that vehement about it. But I felt at that point
this is okay—I think everyone in that room wanted to say
guilty to something."

But "guilty to something" wasn't enough for most of
the citizens in the county. "I heard the verdict this morning,"
said Iliff Shatney, chief of the East Chatham Fire Department, for whom Bobby Gates had been such a promising
recruit. "I'm not happy with it. I don't think there is any
justice in Columbia County."

The Brahm family went directly to the media with their outrage. "I'm disgusted," said Diane Collins, Cheryl's sister. "I feel her death was meaningless. Her death was unjust and the law didn't do justice."

"It really hurts to think the justice system let this happen," said Cheryl's sister-in-law Gretchen Brahm. Far from blaming the police or the D.A., however, she commended them. "They did a fantastic job," she said, "and it's like a slap in the face. I don't think the [jurors] understood. I think they've made a terrible mistake. I don't think they understood the charges."

Pete Brahm, Cheryl's brother, also credited the police and the D.A. with having done "one heck of a job." Brahm pointed out that Gates confessed seven different times and once to his grandmother, and that his alleged confession was consistent with details of the crime scene. "I don't think there's a person in Columbia County who thinks he didn't do it, except those twelve people," he said.

"I'm hurt," Cheryl's brother Jim told reporters. "I've lost all faith in the judicial system." And Pete's wife, Mame, echoed her brother-in-law. "We feel awful; we feel shocked, stunned," she said. "How did this happen? It seems to me like a miscarriage of justice. . . . How do we digest this? How are we going to get to the end of this?"

"I want to know who is going to pay for this murder," demanded Gretchen Brahm. "Now four people are dead and nobody is going to pay for this. They said his constitutional rights were violated. Well, what about the four people who are dead? Their rights were violated also."

In fact, almost as soon as the verdict was in, the jurors began to "pay."

"We had a couple of phone calls the next day," recalled Robert Jensen. "One where somebody called and my wife answered the phone and they asked if this was my residence and they said, 'You tell him he's a no-good sonofabitch.'"

The juror who lived closest to the scene of the crime, Patricia Overly, had a similarly frightening experience. "I did get a death threat, over the phone," she said. "It sounded like a woman to me, I can't be sure of that, it could have been someone disguising his voice." The caller addressed the message to Mrs. Overly's husband, saying, "Your wife is dead, George, the bitch." Mrs. Overly, badly frightened, wanted the threat to go down on record, and one of her associates at *The Echo*, the Canaan town newspaper for which she was the business manager, called the sheriff's office to see if it was all right for Mrs. Overly to come down and report it. On account of the storm, it was very busy down there and they weren't sure whether the police could handle additional problems, but, beyond that, Mrs. Overly had her reservations about going at all. Knowing that she would be seeing Undersheriff Bertram, and not knowing what the feelings would be toward a juror in her situation, she hesitated but went down anyway. "It was his job to protect me," she stated. "Regardless."

For months after the return of the verdict, the harassment continued, in varying degrees of severity. One juror likened herself to a Vietnam veteran, called upon to do her duty only to be reviled upon her return to the community. The stress affected not only the jurors themselves but those around them. "It had a profound effect on our family," said Donald Meyer, a farmer and the husband of Mary Meyer, who, he said, continued to be plagued by nightmares. Robert Jensen's wife also felt an intolerable strain. "I'm always thinking, 'What next?'" she said. "It was hell. It was a nightmare. It still is!" But, for all the fear and the hate and the crank calls in the night, it was, in the minds of at least some of the jurors, worth it. "If it weren't for the negative parts, this would have been the high point of my life," Mary Meyer told a reporter. "It's a tremendous growth experience you go through." Indeed, Mrs. Meyer, who had crawled across her living room floor on the night she returned home from deliberation, fearful of being shot at through her picture window, would, months later, return to college to pursue a course of studies in the area of criminal justice.

Some of the town's citizens, not content to grumble around the general store, decided that they would pursue a more active course in trying to right what they perceived as a gross miscarriage of justice. Bob's pal and former town justice Dick Klingler was one of those who tried to spread the word that something was rotten in the state of Columbia County. "I got a call from a radio station in New York City," said Klingler. "They asked if I would go on a talk show to talk about the murders. My wife objects to my even discussing it—it's over, let's put it behind us—but I got to thinking it over and I said no. I said, 'I'm going to speak now.'" As far as Klingler was concerned, the murders had been committed and there was no way to bring back his friends, but there was one worthwhile thing that, in his mind, could come out of all this. "And that is to prevent or to work towards a solution which prevents another jury from making this kind of decision again," he stated. "I was town justice for eleven years, and the jury erred very seriously in this deliberation. They claimed how long they deliberated and all this and all that, but in their deliberation it's my contention that the jury violated the rights of the victims very, very severely."

Klingler appeared on "The Bob Grant Show" on WABC in New York, along with Jim Brahm. The show's producer had read about the verdict in *The New York Times* and had decided to bring what she called the "bizarre case" to greater public attention. After the airing of the show, a transcript was sent to New York Senator Alfonse D'Amato in the hopes of getting a "reversal" of the verdict. Senator D'Amato's office, not unexpectedly, did not choose to act on the matter. State Supreme Court Judge Edward Conway, contacted by the press regarding the possibility of overturning such a verdict, deemed the idea "ridiculous . . . [it's] never happened and probably never will, because of the unconstitutionality of trying an individual twice. . . . There's nothing a United States Senator could do or anyone else can do."

The town, which had been traumatized by the crime, was doubly traumatized now by what many saw as a breakdown in the justice system. Furthermore, there was a corrosive division of opinion as to whether the jurors were honorably right or perversely wrong. "The local citizenry continues to discuss the jury's verdict in the case of The People Against Wyley Gates," began the editorial in the Chatham *Courier*. The editorial went on to acknowledge the loopholes in our laws and commented on the irony of one lawyer's alleged mistake resulting in the defendant's acquittal, but it also maintained that laws with loopholes are far better than "angry lynch mobs." The editorial concluded with the statement that "we are bound to accept the verdict of twelve dedicated citizens who swore to carry out their duties as a juror to the best of their ability 'so help them God.' "

In that same issue ran an angry letter from one of the town's citizens:

To the Editor:

My wife and I were shocked at the verdict in the Gates trial almost as much as [by] the murders. The horror of that December midnight was felt anew. We lament what seems to be a terribly wrongful decision.

It is difficult to understand how the jury could dismiss the reality of Wyley's alleged multiple admissions of guilt and the honest efforts of the police and the District Attorney to piece together compelling factual evidence, yet so readily accept a fanciful tale woven by an artful attorney fighting his damnedest to get the best decision for his client. It would seem that a half-grown schoolboy could see through the latter as a mere illusion in the service of the client.

In contrast, the conscientious Mr. Keeler is to be commended for presenting his case as he did. He was direct and straightforward and made no attempt to play unduly on the jurors' emotions. Undoubtedly, he would have fared better with so pitiably impressionable a jury had he embellished his arguments and put on more of a show.

But not all the blame can be laid at the jury's

clay feet. I find myself disquieted that the jury may have been too confined by Judge Leaman or that they took the Judge's instructions too literally and boxed themselves into a corner. I am dismayed as well at Judge Leaman's denial of the jury's request to visit the site of the murders. What better, fairer opportunity for them to assess the physical particulars of the shootings?

Alas, the only opportunity to partially ameliorate this travesty will present itself on November 9. [Wyley's sentencing date]

The letter was signed Stanley Joseph, Canaan, New York. A few days before it appeared, he had gone to get it photocopied. The nearest service was at the town newspaper. He handed it to a woman who must have looked familiar to him. "He came into the office when I was there and gave it to me. I was the one that had to make copies on our copying machine," recalled juror Patricia Overly, with a sense of irony that was very close to pain.

23

Wyley now stood acquitted of the murder charges, although convicted of the conspiracy to commit murder. As the murder that he had been convicted of conspiring to commit had, in fact, been committed, it was not only a confusing verdict, but one that certainly did not provide solid ground for the prosecution of Damian Rossney. People immediately began to assume that Damian would get off altogether, since there was considerably less evidence to convict him than there had been in Wyley's case. And this made people angrier still, as the prevailing feeling was that Damian not only had been present at the scene of the crime but, many suspected, had been the shooter. This, of course, was speculation, based primarily on the fact that Damian, up from Ossining, was the "outsider" and that the murder weapon had been referred to by one of the other boys as "Damian's little toy." It was also based, to some extent at least, on the unfortunate choice of name Mr. and Mrs. Rossney had made for their last-born child, a name that brought to the minds of many the satanic child in the occult film *The Omen*.

In the weeks following the verdict, Robert Adams, Damian's attorney, let it be known that he would be pursuing a dismissal of his client's case. The eleven-count indictment against Damian included eight counts of second-degree murder, one count of second-degree conspiracy, one count of second-degree criminal facilitation, and one count of first-degree hindering prosecution. Before the Gates trial, Adams had made an omnibus motion to have all charges against his client dismissed. Now, based on the outcome of the Gates trial, he would be arguing for dismissal of charges with renewed vigor. "A prerequisite of the case against us was that Wyley committed four homicides," said Adams, referring to the fact that Damian was being tried on the grounds of acting in concert with Wyley, who had been regarded as the principal. "There is obviously a problem in proving that," Adams added. Judge Warren E. Zittell, who would be presiding over the Rossney case, granted Adams access to grand-jury testimony in order to supplement the attorney's motion for dismissal. Damian, meanwhile, remained free on $360,000 bail, continuing his senior year at Ossining High School.

While Wyley awaited his sentencing, the protagonists in the case were provided with a further vessel into which they could unburden themselves when the ABC news-magazine show "20/20" came to town. When the show aired in December, viewers heard Barbara Walters introduce the segment with the question "Was justice served in the case of Wyley Gates?" If nothing else, "20/20" was served in the case of Wyley Gates. Like extras in a Preston Sturges movie, the townspeople bent over backward and ran around in circles in order to accommodate correspondent Tom Jarriel and his producers. Vivian's son Bill, who now lived with her, opened up the log house to the media for the first time, allowing Undersheriff Jim Bertram to lead the televised tour, which was interspersed with graphic photos showing the corpses of Bob, Bobby, Jason, and, as she was described by Jarriel, "spry, cheerful" Cheryl Brahm. Dick Klingler was on hand too, telling Jarriel that "most people don't even lock their doors" in the area and adding that the community was "devastated and still in shock." Gene Keeler, who had offered no comment in the days following the return of the verdict, now conveyed his shock to the national audience. "I would probably have bet my soul, my kids' lives, and the family farm that that's one verdict they wouldn't have come back with," the ever folksy Keeler told Jarriel. On a bench outside the courthouse, Chuck Wilcox offered his own bromide. "God bless them, they had the courage to consider the Constitution," he commended the jurors, "and say 'This evidence is here but we can't consider it because it was taken in violation of his constitutional rights.' " Five of the jurors looked extremely uneasy as they sat together for an interview. "Is it possible Wyley Gates beat the system?" Jarriel asked them. Two of the women conceded that it was a possibility, but when Jarriel posed the question to Robert Jensen he got a different reply. "I think the system beat itself," Jensen gravely allowed.

But the centerpiece of the segment was the interview with Wyley himself. Looking puffy and twitchy, Wyley, attended by his attorney, who guarded against any indiscretions, answered Jarriel's questions. "Do *you* feel justice was done?" Jarriel asked.

Wyley thought about that for a moment. "*Justice* is a funny word," he said finally. "I feel that whenever the Constitution of our country is upheld, whenever the laws are upheld, justice in that aspect has been served."

Same old Wyley, to borrow a phrase from John Bailey. But there were more questions. About his father ("We never got along that well. We didn't have much in common. Basically I suppose I avoided him as much as possible"); his brother ("At times we could be the best of friends or we could be at each other's throats, so to speak"); and Jason ("a typical three-year-old; I like kids generally"). At last, Jarriel brought up the issue of remorse, as in, "Do you have any, Wyley?"

"It was a great tragedy and I'd give literally anything to reverse what happened but that's impossible," Wyley cryptically replied after a moment.

■ ■ ■

Two days before his November 9 sentencing, I met with Wyley at the jail. Wilcox and Joan Yowe were with us, and we sat at a picnic table in a vestibule adjacent to the cafeteria. I had never been in a jail before; it was about what I had expected. I was struck by the absolute absence of color as well as by the steam-table smell of the food, that inescapable redolence of industrial-strength chicken soup. As we sat across from each other, I examined Wyley. So this is what they call "jailhouse pallor," I thought. And his eyes, small and almond-colored, still darted in an effort to avoid anyone else's. We had, up to that point, only the most tangential history together. He had mowed our lawn and, for thirteen weeks, we had sat in the same courtroom. I had sent him a few books to read, and he had sent back word through his grandmother or Joan that he had enjoyed them. Now, as we sat here, I thought of this boy mowing my lawn and I tried to imagine him, on some early May day, when the fern are pushing through the warming earth, when the red-winged blackbirds have returned for nesting, and when there doesn't seem to be anything very wrong with the world at all, and I wondered what he had seen. I thought of him too waiting for the schoolbus at just the point in the road where my son now waits. Sometimes, in winter, as we wait for the bus to arrive, we spot a flock of three dozen wild turkeys in Wyley's grandmother's hills, survivors of the hunting season. Surely Wyley had seen them too, but I wondered, What had he thought when he had seen them? Had it given him any of the same gratification it had given us? And then I remembered what my neighbor's son had said about Wyley, how they rode on the bus together every day for years and Wyley never once said "hello" to him or "good morning" to him or "good-bye" to the bus driver at the end of the day. As we sat here now, I could believe it. A quality of isolation cloaked him thoroughly. From what I had been told, he had not found the confinement he'd been in for almost a year particularly onerous, but then why should he have? It occurred to me that for this boy the entire world must have seemed a jail.

I told him a few things about my book, and asked him
how he wished to be portrayed in it. He thought about that
for a moment before replying. "That's a tough question,"
he said with a smile, but went no further. He had an
interesting smile, I thought. Really half a smile—nothing
more than a little curve at the corner of his lips, wry, bitter,
self-effacing. And there were definite indications of a sense
of humor. That was something I found hard to reconcile,
humor and homicide. They seemed to me to represent two
irreconcilable worldviews. But then maybe that was just the
point: something had to give.

I tried another question. "How have you changed?" I
asked him. He told me that he had changed a lot. He was
more open. Joan had a lot to do with that, he said, blushing
as he looked at her. For a moment, I felt a surge of empathy
for him. Joan, warm and vital and affectionate, had touched
him—literally touched him. I thought back to something
Wyley's aunt, Evelyn Prescott, had told me. She had recalled
how she and her sister had gone to the big white house on
the hill after Mrs. Gates called them with the news of the
tragedy, and how when they got there they found Wyley
on the couch, with Deloras Groudas holding his hand. As
she told me this, a thought flashed through my mind—fair
or otherwise—that it had taken an outsider to touch him. I
thought too of Dr. Marchionne telling me how, upon
returning to the Joseph home after the movies that night,
Damian had touched Wyley on the shoulder and said, "Are
you all right?" And how moved Wyley had been by his
concern. Maybe he was hungry, I thought. Maybe he was
starved. Maybe he was absolutely crazed with starvation. I
had been told that when Wyley's mother came to see him
in jail, the guards had instructed her that there was to be
no contact between them . . . *and she obeyed.* The woman
who told me this was a mother herself, and said that if she
had been in that situation, nobody and nothing could have
kept her from reaching out to hug her son. But maybe that
too was unfair, I thought. No one had the answers; all we
had were the questions. Now, as we sat at the picnic table,
the question that was nagging at me was whether he had

become untouchable because he had not been touched enough, or whether he had not been touched enough because he had somehow been born untouchable.

But the time was limited, and so I moved quickly into the area of answerable questions. "Tell me about your father," I said. He characterized him as being bright, but not particularly intelligent, adding that he had had no special interests besides his work. His mother was "more creative and intellectual," but it was his perception that he had gotten his own cerebral nature from his father's parents. Regarding his grandfather, he had never heard anything of the abuse that Vivian Gates testified to, but wasn't surprised, for he didn't think she and his grandfather had enjoyed a great relationship. He attributed his grandmother's strength not to any religious conviction, but to the fact that she was simply the kind of person who "picks up the pieces." Asked if he was the same type of person, he replied, "Not in the process, but in the end result." At that point, I asked him who he would suggest I speak with to get further insights into him. He suggested his grandmother and his Aunt Viki. I told him I had already spoken with them, and that they didn't seem to have any insights into him whatsoever. There was a flicker of irritation, but it immediately gave way to his customary lack of affect. "I'm not really surprised by that," he said mildly.

"Did your father ever humiliate you?" I asked, looking for some of the pith that thus far had been thoroughly concealed. "I guess you could call it that," he replied. He revealed the humiliating insults: "All thumbs." "Computer hands."

They didn't sound that bad to me. Not wonderful, granted, but not exactly the sort of thing that would push someone over the edge. I tried to dig a little more. "Did anyone ever make efforts to deal with your being so withdrawn?" I asked.

His eyes darted and then returned to my own. "My father and brother used to tell me you can't live alone," he offered.

Now that, in fact, sounded pretty good to me. I knew

families who had struggled for years to get to that point of
open dialogue, and I told him so. "What else could they
have done?" I asked him. "I don't know," he said. "I guess
showed more interest in my interests."

I moved on to the subject of his friends. He told me
that he didn't know why people said Ben Cooper and
Michael Lofgren and John Bailey were his friends—more
"just acquaintances," he corrected. As for Damian and Miles,
they were *not* his friends, he said emphatically.

"You would choose different friends if you were to do
it all over?" I asked.

"Yes," he replied, with that crooked little half smile.

"Would you want to see Damian punished?" I asked.

He seemed surprised by the question. "Punished?" he
said. "I don't know about that. I'd like to see him helped, I
guess. I think he needs help."

I couldn't stand the diplomacy anymore. "I take that to
mean that Damian was involved in these crimes?" I asked,
but Wilcox intercepted, warning Wyley not to answer that
question.

I asked a few more questions, but by then Wyley was
beginning to disappear, as he tended to do when his stamina
for social intercourse had been exhausted, which tended to
happen very quickly. And so we took leave of each other,
and I headed home. Driving through Chatham, I decided
to stop at The Bakery. It was pumpkin doughnut season—
comfort food *extraordinaire*—and I was surely in need of
comfort food.

As I sat in a booth, drinking coffee and eating my
"meltingly moist" doughnut, I made notes. As I did, I
noticed in the booth directly ahead of me a husband and
wife and their two preteen sons. Nothing unusual—there
was no reason why anyone should have noticed them—but
I did, and it occurred to me, as I studied them, that their
every gesture was expressive of love and concern. As I
watched them, it affected me more and more, this tender
and beautiful thing, and I grew increasingly sad thinking
of Wyley's family, shattered when he was just the age these

boys were. What a terrible destructive system a family without that kind of love can be, I thought, and I thought too of what that kind of deprivation can lead to. What it can lead to, I thought, no longer with any appetite for the sugary doughnut or the coffee, is the loss of soul, and the loss of soul, in turn, can lead to acts of utter inhumanity.

Over the next year I was to see Wyley several more times and we would correspond. Working on this book, I went through an entire spectrum of feelings; actually I wove in and around and up and down an entire spectrum of feelings. There were times when I felt an empathy for him, when I could see that humor, that bracing sense of the absurd, and feel that there really was a dimension within him that was regrettably undeveloped but that, perhaps, I could actually help him to develop. And then sometimes there was a feeling of acute identification. I could think back to myself at that age, also depressed and isolated, and could easily retrieve the recurrent homicidal fantasy I had nurtured in my high school French class, my private nemesis, wherein I would remove that long wooden pole used for opening windows and crack heads with it, smiting my enemies with a fine merciless zeal. But there were many more times when that identification disappeared entirely, replaced by the realization that my adolescent homicidal fantasies had given way to an acceptance of the way life is, a recognition of the pleasures that coexist with the pain. This made me very different indeed from a boy who had never come to that realization, who had never made that passage, and who now probably never would; a boy who conveyed to me such a fundamental soullessness, such a basic lack of human fiber, that it seemed entirely possible to me that he was capable of committing a brutal murder. The utter waste of it all was profoundly sad, but it also made me angry, just as my fellow citizens in Chatham and Canaan felt angry, for in his not making that passage himself, he had denied the rights of others who might, in fact, have made it or who were working at making it, or who, at the very least, were born with the inalienable right to try to

make it. It wasn't his province to take that away. His
conviction that we all die anyway did not afford him the
license to kill.

That following Monday, November 9, the courtroom in the
Columbia County Courthouse was filled to capacity. The
sheriffs were represented by Investigators Shook and Vick.
Stanley Joseph was there. Also present were members of
the Brahm family and Deloras Groudas and her daughter-
in-law Laurie, who, once upon a time, had hoped to adopt
little Jason. No members of the Gates family, however, were
in attendance.

As required by law, Judge Leaman entertained remarks
from Keeler, Wilcox, and Wyley Gates. Keeler requested
the maximum sentence of eight and one-third to twenty-
five years, and strongly opposed the granting of youthful-
offender status to the defendant. Wilcox began his remarks
by drawing to the court's attention the fact that Kevin
McDonald, the uncle of Miles McDonald, ran the County
Probation Department and that he had continued to stay
involved through the process of preparing a presentencing
report on Wyley. With that in mind, Wilcox moved that the
sentencing be adjourned in order that a new report be made
up. Leaman rejected this motion, citing that the report
represented a combined effort of the State Probation Department and the County Probation Department. Wilcox
went on to address the matter of the sentencing. He charged
that there was an "overemphasis" on what the allegations
were in the case, rather than on the findings by a jury of
peers. Again, he evoked his inventory of reasonable doubts,
particularly in terms of the lack of forensic evidence, and
he maintained that there was no clear proof that any overt
act had ever been committed by Wyley. He felt, as well, that
the partiality of the report was manifest in that it did not
include any of the evidence that had been presented by
forensic pathologist Dr. Jack Davies. Beyond all this, there
was the issue of Wyley Gates's mental illness. Wilcox cited
Dr. Borenstein, testifying for the prosecution, who said that
Wyley was "very ill."

In a final appeal, Wilcox urged the court to consider a program of psychiatric counseling for Wyley so that when he was released—and it was Wilcox's belief that Wyley could become a functioning member of society—he would be ready. The only end a maximum sentence would accomplish would be to satisfy the "visceral, emotional reactions of the community." The most important thing that could be done for everyone—Wyley Gates and society at large—was to ensure that he got the treatment he needed. He added that one of the social workers who had prepared the presen-tencing report had told him that the facilities needed for Wyley Gates did not exist in the state prison system. Finally, in an unfortunate turn of phrase, Wilcox, alluding to the jury, referred to "profiles of courage."

Wilcox sat down, and then it was Wyley's turn to speak in his own behalf. Unsurprisingly, the pale young man, in his trademark button-down shirt and conservative dark tie, did not choose to exercise this right.

At last, Judge Leaman spoke. In tones that strove to sound alternately stern, compassionate, and, of course, just, he indicated that he had read the report and that he had, as Mr. Wilcox had pointed out, sat through the trial and heard all the evidence. Certainly then, he stated, he needed no help in that regard. Furthermore, he had been judge long enough to know what facilities were available.

It is a hard thing in any case, in any criminal case, to discharge a sentence that is appropriate to the crime, he continued, and that takes into account the particular de-fendant. In trying to put himself into the shoes of the defendant, as well as taking into account the public interest, Leaman said that he had thought long and hard to arrive at a sentence that was "reasonable and constitutes justice." He was not interested in labels, in "profiles of courage," or anything like that. He was interested in justice. Mindful of that, it was necessary to look at what the defendant was charged with. "The motivation for the conspiracy stemmed directly from this defendant's dissatisfaction, even to the point of hatred, for a member of his family, namely his father," Leaman said. "His hatred gave birth to this conspiracy which achieved its end, and I conclude that to a moral certainty." Furthermore, the actual consummation of the conspiracy was preceded by criminal conduct that achieved the theft of the necessary weapon.

As Wyley waited, paler perhaps than he had been, Judge Leaman turned to the question of Wyley's mental state. In terms of the mental state of the defendant, said Leaman, it became evident, through many witnesses, that there is some personality disorder and psychiatric disorders but this issue was presented to the jury, the triers of the facts, who found him still accountable in the eyes of the law. Leaman concluded that whatever personality disorders existed, they were not of a magnitude to relieve him of whatever culpability of crime he was charged with.

There is a time for mercy and a time for rigor, said Leaman. After much thought, he said, he would like to think that what the public wanted was not relevant. Instead, what he was offering was a product of his own conscience as to what was right. He could not live with himself, he said, if this was not so.

With that, Judge Leaman delivered the sentence: an indeterminate sentence of not less than eight and one-third and not more than twenty-five years in a state prison facility. It was his hope, he added, that the defendant would find whatever assistance in terms of psychiatry or psychology he needed within the state correctional system. He concluded by stating that the defendant was entitled to appeal, which had to be filed within thirty days, and he then remanded him without bail to the county jail until the state correctional system took him into custody.

With the sentencing concluded, a number of spectators—most notably, members of the Brahm family—burst into applause. As for Deloras and Laurie Groudas, their eyes gleamed with welled tears but their lips registered hard, triumphant smiles as they marched from the courtroom, their arms fiercely interlocked.

To the uninitiated, Wyley's face remained a mask of impassivity. But inveterate Wyley-watchers thought they could detect a slight shadow of uneasiness reflected in the youth's face. For the last time, he was led out of the Columbia County courtroom, which had become his home away from home. Wearing handcuffs for the first time in many months, with that pained, tight, disapproving look that had scarcely changed throughout the ordeal, he became the focus for dozens of flashing cameras, TV minicams, and questing reporters. "Wyley!" the photographers called. "Over here, Wyley!" The spectators, having come for reasons that were painfully personal or entirely recreational, struggled to get a last look, but, before you could say "salutatorian," he was gone, whisked down the back stairs to the confines of the jail.

"Justice at last," Jim Brahm declared to reporters.

"He made a statement to fellow inmates that the only regret he had was that he didn't tell Cheryl to go to hell before he killed her," said Jim's brother. "Now *he* can go to hell!"

Mame Brahm said she wasn't pleased at all. "But at least it makes the whole thing a little civil," she added. "Something solid has happened to him to make him understand the deaths. Three cheers for the judge."

At his station in the corridor, Wilcox told reporters that they had been hoping for something a little better. "But the judge did what he had to do with the community," Wilcox added acidly.

And then the principals were gone. For a long while, however, milling knots of people remained in the courthouse corridors, still discussing this boy whose crime had troubled them more than anything else in their memories. He was just no damned good and now he had gotten what he deserved, they said, their faces alive with a righteous sense of indignation and vindication that betrayed their knowledge that, maximum sentence aside, the queer boy had afforded the community only the most hollow of victories, if, in fact, you could call it a victory at all.

24

By the following morning, Wyley had been transferred from the Columbia County Jail to the Elmira Correctional Facility, in Elmira, New York, a maximum-security prison geared toward younger offenders. Upon his arrival, Wyley was held in the prison's reception center, where new arrivals generally reside for four to six weeks before being integrated into the prison's general-confinement area or transferred to another facility in the state.

A week after he got there, I received a letter from him. "I wasn't really surprised that I left so quickly; from what I overheard, at least half of the Sheriff's office had volunteered to drive me over on their days off," he wrote, his humor surfacing again. At another point in the letter, he expressed sympathy for the jurors. "I really feel badly for some of the jurors," he wrote. "They did their duty as citizens to the best of their abilities, and whether people agree with their results, they should at least respect them for their integrity. When ignorance and emotion mix, the result is always barbarism and chaos; perhaps Rousseau's *Social Contract* isn't all that people think it is." At the time I received the letter, I was interviewing members of his family, and he wrote, "I'm glad that you've been talking to family members, but I'm afraid that you're looking for answers where there are none. The people who were around me only knew a small part of me, the one that was obviously visible. There was always much more of me on the inside. If you really want to find answers, whether satisfactory ones or not (not all answers *are* satisfying), you will have to learn about who I really was then and am now, as well as what made me that way. . . . It is not a simple picture, but one that needs an open mind, patience, and unconventional wisdom to fully appreciate. Unfortunately, it's much easier to substitute a simple one in its place. There are some things which people simply don't want to believe."

Armed with this cryptic invitation to plumb his depths, I made my first visit to Elmira approximately a month after he was sent there. The Christmas decorations had already been erected on the broad sweep of lawn in front of a phalanx of ugly, red stone buildings. There was a cardboard grouping of Ye Olde Merry carolers; a crèche; and, most improbably, giant candy canes flanking the sentrylike booth where visitors were required to check in. But, for all of it, there was nothing jolly about the place.

We met in the commissary, a brightly lit room lined with vending machines, and all around us were men and women who could scarcely keep their hands off each other. Wyley was thinner than he had been at the trial and, sporting a wispy little beard, projected a fragility that rendered him, at least for the moment, a more sympathetic figure. We talked about his ambitions and he told me that he could finish college in here if he wanted, although he didn't know whether he'd be able to find sufficiently challenging courses. We talked a bit about his mother, who was back in California working for the phone company. "How many times did you see her after you returned from California?" I asked him. "Was it just two Christmases and one summer?" "Yes," he said. "That must have been rough for you," I offered. "Yes," he said.

We talked about the prison population. It was 80 percent black, 15 percent Hispanic, 5 percent white. There were, I imagined, very few salutatorians, and the ways in which he differed from the rest of the inmates seemed to be a sore point for him. As for his cell, there was almost nothing in it. Because he hadn't yet been processed into the general population, there were all kinds of restrictions as to what he could not have. But the fact was, he said, that he didn't really mind being alone in his cell. He could read, he could write, and he could think. "What do you think about?" I asked him, to which he just smiled his enigmatic smile.

Sooner than I had expected, there seemed nothing more to say. He began to withdraw, and I had the sense that the exertions of the visitors around us—their very human wants and needs—had made him uncomfortable. I told him it was a long trip back, which it was, and that I had left the white cheese popcorn he had asked me to bring at the visitor's station. He thanked me, and I wished him luck, and he walked off. I remember thinking, as he disappeared through a door, that his inviolable dignity was fully, strangely intact, even in the face of all that was foreign to him.

On December 28, 1987, slightly more than a year after the murders, Wyley filed documents in surrogate court in which he stated his wish to renounce his inheritance. "I think he's upset that he was cast in the light of a greedy person by the district attorney and the Brahms," Charles Wilcox explained. Robert Gates had died without a will and left an estate of $169,555, according to court records. Additionally, the log house was up for sale for an asking price of $175,000 (there was not a lot of activity, however, on a house on which four people had been brutally murdered).

A wrongful death suit filed in state supreme court by Jim and Donald Brahm, Cheryl's brothers and the administrators of her estate, named as defendants Viki Hatch, Bob Gates's sister and the administrator of his estate; Wyley Gates; Damian Rossney; and Damian's father, Paul Rossney of Ossining. The suit claimed that Wyley killed Cheryl by shooting her four times with a 9-millimeter Walther PPK pistol and that she had suffered "great pain" due to the shooting. It also charged that Cheryl's mother, Florence Brahm, had lost the companionship and support of her daughter. Furthermore, it alleged that Robert Gates, Sr., had been negligent in allowing his son to have possession of the murder weapon and bullets, and the suit made similar claims against Paul Rossney in regard to Damian. The suit included seven causes of action against Wyley totaling $1.355 million; three against the estate totaling $600,000; six against Damian totaling $1.350 million; three against Paul Rossney totaling $600,000; and three against Wyley and Damian together totaling $750,000.

Wyley's renouncement of the estate would leave him without any significant moneys, and hence the Brahms, in the event that their wrongful-death suit was successful, would have little to collect from him. Consequently, the Brahms, later in the year, were to maintain that Wyley Gates should inherit his father's estate despite his renouncement. Attorneys for the Robert Gates estate contended that the Brahms' legal actions could result in a retrial of Wyley in a civil court, where the burden of proof is considerably less onerous than in criminal court. In fact, attorneys for the Gates estate stated in their papers that "with a lesser burden of proof and without the constitutional limitations which apply to law enforcement officers in a criminal proceeding, including the alleged confession of Wyley Gates, it is likely that Wyley Gates will be found to have caused the murder of his father and other victims at the Robert Gates Sr. residence." To the Brahms, the idea that a civil court might be able to find Wyley guilty of crimes of which a criminal court had failed to convict him could only be a cheering prospect.

In a statement to the press, Jim Brahm said that he and his brother were challenging Wyley's renouncement not to further their own ends but because they were "taxpaying citizens" and did not think it right that the county was paying for Wyley's appeal and for his education. Brahm was referring to the fact that in February 1988, the state supreme court appellate division granted Wyley status as a poor person, which meant that the public would now be paying for the appeal that Wyley had already filed. The local papers had also run stories about the fact that Columbia County was funding Wyley's education while he was in prison. The Chatham *Courier* had stated that Wyley was the only Columbia County resident who was serving a prison sentence outside of the county but was attending college classes for which the county paid tuition, to the tune of $319 for two summer courses at Corning Community College near the prison. If he attended college full time through Corning's inmate education program, it could conceivably cost the county $1,396 per semester.

Galling the citizenry further were reports released later in 1988 that tabulated the cost to the county of the Gates trial. The fees for the prosecution's expert witnesses alone came to $22,459. The jurors' pay and mileage came to $15,000. Their sequestering at two different hotels, along with their food costs, came to $4,000. Transcripts of the Gates trial were promised to the prosecuting attorney in the Rossney trial and the attorney handling the Gates appeal, and each transcript was expected to run approximately 4,500 pages at a cost of $2.75 per page, amounting to $12,000 per transcript.

"This was not only the longest and most complex trial in the history of the county," said Gene Keeler. "I'm sure it is the most expensive matter ever considered in the courthouse in Hudson. Not only in terms of finance but in terms of emotional turmoil."

The trial of Damian Rossney promised to be nowhere near as long, but it was certainly very long in coming. Almost immediately after the verdict on the Gates trial came in, Robert Adams began the legal maneuvering that he hoped would lead to a dismissal of the case altogether.

In a motion filed December 31, 1987, Adams put forth a number of points in support of dismissal. He suggested that there was insufficient evidence to prosecute the case, as the grand-jury evidence did not include any admissions on

Damian's part regarding his alleged participation in the events of December 13, 1986, at the Gates residence. Furthermore, Adams maintained that statements by Wyley Gates should be eliminated because admissions by one defendant are not binding on another, and he also discounted statements made by Benjamin Cooper, John Bailey, and Miles McDonald. Cooper's statement, according to Adams, was insufficient because Cooper never stated that Damian mentioned the Gates family as the target of the "contract" he had been asked to carry out. With regard to John Bailey, nothing that Bailey said could actually link the murders to the burglarizing of the log house. As for McDonald's statements, they incriminated Damian only so far as Robert Gates and Robert Gates, Jr., were concerned, but that particular alleged plot, Adams wrote, bore no resemblance to the crime that was actually committed. Turning to the conspiracy charge, Adams suggested that the time, place, and manner of the homicides that Damian and Wyley had allegedly plotted according to the statements of the purported co-conspirators did not agree with the time, place, and manner of the actual homicides. "None of the witnesses are able to supply the necessary proof, whether circumstantial or direct, to show that there had been a meeting of the minds between Gates, Rossney, and McDonald," Adams wrote. As for the charge of criminal facilitation, Adams held that there was no proof that Damian had provided Wyley with the murder weapon. The count of hindering prosecution was also discounted by Adams, who said that Rossney had responded openly and forthrightly to the inquiries of Investigator Cozzolino.

A further ground for dismissal that Adams cited was the theory of collateral estoppel. Collateral estoppel is generally invoked with regard to civil matters, but it can have application as well to criminal law. It is, in a sense, a kind of cousin to the theory of double jeopardy, in that collateral estoppel is used to bar repeated and harassing litigation for recovery against a defendant. Essentially, the rule of collateral estoppel states that when an issue has been resolved legally by a jury or a trier of the facts, the identical issue with the identical parties cannot be litigated again. Adams wrote that collateral estoppel could be applied in the Rossney case because of the "inability to satisfy the jury of Gates's responsibility for the murders at the Gates residence."

But the bottom line of Adams's argument for dismissal of the Rossney case was that the prosecution's case was predicated on Damian's having assisted Wyley in the murders—the indictment specified that Damian had aided and abetted and acted in concert with Wyley, who was put forth as the shooter—and that the acquittal of Wyley on the murder charges made the case against Adams's client insufficient. The prosecutor would eventually agree with Adams's motion to dismiss the four murder counts against Damian that cited murder with depraved indifference; she did so because, she said, the murders were "as intentional as you can get." The original counts of murder in regard to Cheryl and Jason would also fall by the wayside, for lack of any evidence indicating that Damian had plotted or helped carry out their murders. But defense attorney Adams was not satisfied and argued that there was no reasonable basis for prosecuting the Rossney case in any way, shape, or form. "It is readily apparent that Rossney, under the pleadings herein, is only liable if the prosecution is able to prove that Wyley Gates committed the murders charged in the indictment," he wrote. "As this Court is aware, the trial of Wyley Gates resulted in an acquittal of Gates on the charges of murder which are the cornerstone of the first eight indictments of this indictment."

In a more informal vein, Adams aired his opinions to the press. "From day one I thought they would have a problem," he said, referring to the prosecution's chances of proving anew Wyley's guilt. "They didn't do it too well last time. The prosecution played all the cards in their hand last time. They have less proof to try my client than they had to try Wyley Gates."

To prosecute this case, presiding judge Warren E. Zittell appointed Nancy Snyder who, as assistant district attorney, had aided Gene Keeler in the Gates trial, had been responsible for compiling much of the evidence in the Rossney case, and had written the response to Adams's original omnibus motion. "A dismissal in this case would undermine the community's faith in the justice system," Snyder had written in December. "It would surely send the message that as long as an individual does not pull the trigger, no matter how much he may cajole, assist, aid, encourage, or otherwise assist in the plan and execution and cover-up of a murder, he will walk free. There will be no disincentive to the motives of greed and thrill seeking. In this instance a selfish and cold-blooded, greedy individual will be let loose to wreak more harm upon the community and perhaps will have been emboldened by the experience."

Regarding the motion citing collateral estoppel, Snyder maintained that Wyley's acquittal on murder charges should in no way prevent prosecution of co-defendant Damian Rossney. "The acquittal of one defendant would never be allowed to serve as a bar to the prosecution of another," she wrote, citing a Court of Appeals decision. Collateral estoppel applies only to parties who are identical or are related, she further maintained.

In March, Judge Zittell handed down a decision on Adams's motion for dismissal. He granted the attorney's request for oral arguments, which he scheduled for mid-April, on the charges of murder and hindering prosecution. He wrote, however, that the motion to dismiss the conspiracy and criminal-facilitation charges were denied. Enough evidence existed to charge Damian with conspiracy "based not only on the testimony of an unindicted co-conspirator" (by whom he meant Miles McDonald) but, he added, based on the testimony of "another boy to whom such characterization would not apply" (by whom he meant Ben Cooper).

At the April hearing, Nancy Snyder told Judge Zittell that she did not want to, in her words, "rehash" the Gates trial, but that she planned to prove that Wyley Gates was the murderer and Damian Rossney his accomplice. Adams, for his part, argued that there was an insufficiency of evidence, as there was no corroboration among witnesses to show that Damian had been an accomplice. "The witnesses' testimony isn't any good because it fails to show that Damian participated in carrying out the crime," he said, maintaining further that the witnesses had testified that they regarded discussions about the murder plot as a joke. Additionally, the actual murders differed from discussions about how Robert Gates should be killed. Snyder countered that Damian "did enter into a plan, shared the intent to commit the crime, and acted to assist in the crime. . . . He did not renounce the furtherance of the plan and that makes it necessary to try him on murder counts." Judge Zittell, in his subsequent decision, would agree with Snyder.

Snyder also told the press at that time that she would not ask Wyley to testify in the Rossney trial because he would probably plead the Fifth Amendment. Moreover, his alleged confession during the polygraph examination would not be used, as it would be considered hearsay, and the psychiatrists' testimonies would not be used. Snyder acknowledged that her task of convincing a jury that Wyley was the murderer would be a difficult one. "I'm not saying it's going to be easy," admitted the young Dartmouth and Albany Law School graduate, in a model of understatement.

The difficulty in preparing the massive Gates trial transcript held up the Rossney trial for many months, but, by November 1988, more than a year since the Gates verdict had come in, jury selection had begun. By then, those counts citing murder with depraved indifference and those implicating Damian in the deaths of Cheryl and Jason had been dropped, but the murder counts naming Robert Gates and Robert Gates, Jr., remained, as did the counts of conspiracy, criminal facilitation, and hindering prosecution. In a motion filed six days after jury selection had begun and with eleven jurors seated, Adams requested a change of venue for his client's trial, claiming that widespread publicity surrounding the case made it impossible to find a fair and impartial jury in this county of sixty thousand residents. "It cannot be overstated that the feelings in the Columbia County community run high on the subject of the Gates homicide," wrote Adams in his motion, "and that the overwhelming majority of persons expressing such opinions feel that [Wyley Gates] was the beneficiary of too lenient treatment by members of his jury. As this trial progresses it seems clear that there is a real risk and danger that the community attitudes will be passed on to sitting jurors."

The motion for change of venue was denied by the appellate division of the state supreme court, and jury selection continued. Trying another tactic, Adams filed a motion for dismissal of special prosecutor Nancy Snyder on the grounds that a special prosecutor must live in or maintain an office in the county in which the case is conducted. As far as he knew, Adams stated, Snyder did neither. Furthermore, Adams charged, Snyder had failed to file a timely oath of office. The oath, by which the special prosecutor swears to uphold the constitution of New York State, must be filed within thirty days of an appointment to a case. Snyder replied that she had filed after the thirty day stipulation but cited a July 1988 appellate-division case in which it was decided that such an oath of office can be filed retroactively. As for her county residency, she stated that she maintained a mailing address in the county and that, in connection with the Rossney case, she had been provided with office space in Hudson. Judge Zittell denied Adams's motion, and, by November 22, when the last of the alternate jurors had been selected, there were no further impediments to the process of dispensing justice in the case of *The People of New York* v. *Damian Rossney.*

As for Wyley, over the course of the year he had made an adjustment of sorts to life at Elmira. "You asked if I had been able to adapt to the prison environment," he wrote me in one letter. "A suitable response might be: 'Has the prison environment adjusted to me?' I am one of those fortunate people who carry their environs about them like a cloak. I can be at home wherever I happen to be (which isn't to say that I enjoy where I am.)"

He pursued his music and his studies with absolute diligence. "I had a 99 average for my math course (with a 99 on the final) and Biology is very discouraging," he wrote.

"The fact that I've taken all of this before is bad enough, but coupled with the intense stupidity of many (but not all) of my 'peers,' it really gets on my nerves. These people, I suspect, are not capable of doing high school work, let alone college level. Also, as can be expected, their attitude leaves something (!) to be desired. . . . These people aren't just ignorant, they're stupid (which I suppose is why they're here . . . and why most of them will be back). I was looking forward very much to the fall semester, when I should be taking some more challenging courses (at least the material will be new), but suddenly I realized that the same people (or ones like them) will be in all of my other classes! I'll survive, I suppose (I always do)."

The contemptuousness that had marked him for so many years now continued in full force, as did his sometimes eerie penchant for detachment. He wrote in April 1988:

> My major impressions of prison so far would probably be broken down into: bleak, cold, impersonal, with a constant (although mostly unseen) undercurrent of brutality and savageness (sounds sort of like a weather report).
>
> I am of the view that the prison environment does nearly nothing to rehabilitate inmates, and fails even in the officially unacknowledged task of punishing them (I say unofficially, but that's not taking Judge Leaman into consideration). This place is, I suspect, so much like what the typical inmate experiences in normal life (i.e., the aggression, violence, coldness, et alii), that they don't regard it as punishment (except, of course, that it prevents them from participating in many of the pleasures of life (e.g., drugs (although there are drugs in here), sex (and again, that does occur, although I think that the security here prevents that for the most part (at least involuntary sex)), and, of course, driving their brand-new Lincoln Continentals around New York (bought with drug money, of course, not to mention peoples' lives).

In short, these "people" are sickening, degenerate, emotionally unstable animals (for lack of a better word, although I would never put these scum (my favorite descriptive word for them) on the same level as animals). To all of the people who say that they're just misguided, troubled souls, I say . . . well, I really don't know what to say, other than that (in 99% of cases) they're horribly mistaken (for once my fabled eloquence escapes me).

The vast majority of these inmates will never reform, never stop (unless someone stops them), and *never* be sorry for *anything* that they've done.

One of the problems is that these people have learned how to play social workers, parole officers, et al, like finely tuned instruments. If those people knew what they were really like, then they'd give up their fantasies about "helping" them, and concentrate on keeping them away from decent people (that nebulous part of humanity), and to keeping young children from growing up to emulate their elders.

Crime and the criminal mentality are diseases of society, and they can only be fought successfully by society as a whole. But then, who am I to talk, I'm just an inmate.

25

When his trial began, on November 22, 1988, Damian Rossney, who had looked like a young boy at his arraignment almost two years earlier, unable then to suppress a smile that some described as a smirk, now presented a very different appearance. He had become a young man, tall, husky, dressed in a conservative gray suit, with a sober deportment emulating that of his father, Paul Rossney, who would be present throughout the trial with his wife, Geraldine. In the last year, Damian had graduated from Ossining High School and had been accepted for admission to college in Boston. Because of his legal entanglements, however, he had not been allowed to go out of state, and so was working at a warehouse near his home at the time that the trial began.

The atmosphere in the courtroom as the trial got under way contrasted sharply with that which had prevailed at Wyley's trial. There was no showboating; no grandstanding. It was all getting down to business, a posture reflected by the jury, who walked into court with an expression that many who were there that first day saw as grim.

Judge Zittell, one of the county's two multipurpose judges, handling criminal, surrogate, and family court cases, appointed to the bench in 1974 and elected that year and then again in 1984 to ten-year terms, was impeccably gracious as he greeted the jury and offered them his instructions. It was clear that he wished to have a civilized courtroom, and the attorneys, responding to this desire, gave their opening statements in a manner that was low-keyed and, at times, almost perfunctory.

Nancy Snyder's remarks were markedly brief. She told the jury that the case before them was about the murders of Robert Gates and Robert Gates, Jr., in Canaan, New York, almost two years ago. It was also about three teenage boys who plotted to kill Robert Gates, one of whom, Miles McDonald, would come forth to testify as to how he, Damian, and Wyley had devised a plan. Ben Cooper would also appear, Snyder said, and would tell how one day, at the Chatham High School, Damian approached him and asked if it was all right to "off" someone for money.

There would also be testimony regarding the burglary of the log house and the target practice at John Bailey's, as well as testimony from Investigator John Cozzolino, attesting to Damian's denial of any knowledge of the crimes when Cozzolino interviewed him in the early morning of December 14, and evidence from Investigator Walter Shook regarding the recovery of the murder weapon on the day following the murders.

Expressing her confidence that the jury would find the defendant guilty of murder, criminal facilitation, hindering prosecution, and conspiracy, Snyder concluded her remarks.

The opening statement of Robert Adams was just as brief and to the point. Proof would not show that Damian Rossney committed the murders, Adams assured the jury; proof would not show that Damian took a gun and fired it at anyone. One of the things they had heard Mrs. Snyder talk about very peripherally was the role of Wyley Gates, he said, and one of the things she must show was that Wyley Gates committed a murder. Furthermore, each and every count of the indictment required the prosecutor to show a particular frame of mind of Damian Rossney as to intent to commit murder. Adams reminded the jury that Damian was only sixteen at the time of the murders, and that he and the other boys regarded the conversations about Wyley's father's murder as a joke . . . "a sick joke," he allowed, "but a joke."

When they went over these events, he told them, they would be tempted to force them into a pattern but, he warned, no such pattern existed. Events in this case did not add up to conspiracy to commit murder, he insisted. As for hindering prosecution, he acknowledged that, like other individuals questioned on the night of the murders, Damian did not offer information. But what was a citizen's obligation to do so? he questioned. And he urged the jury to consider also that they had a sixteen-year-old boy facing something that was new and different. Their duty at the end of the case would be clear, he said. Their duty would be to say "Not guilty."

The first witness was Miles McDonald, who, like Damian, had put on some weight. With his hair longer and frizzier, in informal clothes, he had lost that sleek look that had characterized him at the Gates trial. Indeed, with his slightly splay-footed walk to the witness chair, he seemed almost vulnerable. The sense of vulnerability increased as he stammered through the beginning of his examination, causing Prosecutor Nancy Snyder to ask if he was nervous. Miles admitted that he was, and Snyder suggested that if he felt she was going too fast, he should tell her and she would slow down.

She began with a line of questioning regarding the series of conversations that Miles had had with Wyley and Damian in the fall of 1986. Miles testified as well about the burglary of the log house, the target practice at John Bailey's, and his encounter with Damian outside the Crandell Theater in Chatham, when Damian told Miles that "he did it," gesturing toward Wyley with his thumb.

Under cross-examination, Miles told the court that in that first conversation in the computer room, all Wyley had said was that he wanted to kill his father. Miles had taken this not necessarily as a joke, but as a statement "not meant to be taken seriously." He also said that he had not connected the burglary with the murder plot in any way, and that when Damian had said Wyley "did it," he thought that Damian meant that Wyley had totaled Cheryl's car. Again, as when he made this statement at the Gates trial, he was not asked how he arrived at this conclusion based on Damian's curt remark.

In her redirect examination of her most important witness, Nancy Snyder asked Miles whether anyone, in the course of any of these conversations, had said that this was all a joke or that they were just kidding. He replied that no one had. This was an important point for the prosecutor, who needed to convey the seriousness of the plotting. She concluded by asking Miles to describe his last conversation with Wyley in the computer room. Miles said that it had taken place one morning when he was typing something and Wyley came along and shut off the computer. Miles called him a name or two because he had lost work and, he added, he told Wyley at that time that he "wasn't going to do it." Again, that amorphous "it" lingered in the courtroom.

Miles's alibi as to his whereabouts on the evening of December 13 was corroborated by his buddy Matthew Rueckheim and by Rueckheim's sister-in-law Mary Rueckheim, as it had been in the Gates trial. The following day saw a reappearance by two other Chatham High classmates, Michael Lofgren, now a student at Daniel Webster College in New Hampshire, and Ben Cooper. Lofgren repeated exactly the story he had told at the Gates trial, about the cafeteria discussions of the robberies, and then it was Cooper's turn. With his hair in a ponytail this time, but dressed in a jacket and tie, Cooper still appeared to be terrified.

Now Cooper, who was the second most important witness for the prosecution, reviewed the conversations he had had with the defendant, with primary attention paid to Damian's asking him if it was all right to "off" someone for the right amount of money. Under cross-examination,

Cooper was asked whether Damian had ever said anything about killing, but Cooper replied that the meaning was implied in that first conversation about "offing." Now intent on defusing the damaging testimony of this witness, Adams asked Cooper if it was not true that throughout December 1986 Cooper had accepted all of these conversations as something like a game. "Did you not, in an earlier testimony, characterize these conversations as 'just like silly, just like talking,'" Adams demanded of Cooper. In his customary timid murmur, Cooper replied that this was true.

The third day of the trial marked the return of John Bailey, now with the 101st Airborne Division, stationed at Fort Campbell, Kentucky. Huskier now also, Bailey too sported a new hairstyle, one that would have been suitable, it could be said, for a low-budget exploitation movie about street gangs in Southern California. Shaved at the sides, it gave a disturbing edge to his appearance.

Repeating his testimony from the Gates trial, he discussed the target practice he had hosted on December 7, 1986, with special mention of the identical cuts that he and Wyley had sustained from the sharp recoil of the Walther automatic pistol. He further testified that Wyley had left that day with the gun and the ammunition.

Walter Shook, John Cozzolino, and William Vick also returned with abbreviated replays of their testimonies from the Gates trial, as did Dr. Roberto Benitez, who had performed the autopsies on Robert Gates and Bobby; Ralph Marcucio, the forensic scientist who had tested the Walther for blood; and ballistics expert Dominic Denio of the state police, testifying again as to the danger of improperly gripping a Walther automatic pistol.

The following day saw an appearance on the stand by Sally Joseph. Mrs. Joseph was the sister of Damian's father and they bore a strong familial resemblance to each other. Her brother, who often retreated to the corridor for a smoke, sold insurance for New York Life Insurance in Port Chester, New York, and had aspired to a political career. In 1986, he had run for state senate on the Right to Life party, and, in 1988, had run for town supervisor of Ossining. He lost both elections. Now Mrs. Joseph told the court how her nephew had come to live with them in Canaan in August 1984. She then detailed her whereabouts on December 13, as she and her husband attended to his ailing father, during which time she had several phone conversations with Damian. Later that night, she told the court, she had seen Damian and Wyley when they returned from the movies and she described as well the events of the following day, when Damian and Stanley Joseph went to the State Police Barracks in New Lebanon and then the police returned to the Joseph home in the afternoon.

With Sally Joseph's testimony, the People rested their case. The following day many of Damian's family members were in attendance, including his older brother and sister, for it was on this day that Damian himself was taking the stand.

Adams's decision to call Damian to the stand had been anticipated by Nancy Snyder. Snyder felt that there was a choice of one of two routes for Adams to take. Either he could attack the prosecution's contention that Wyley was the murderer, thus causing the murder charges and the criminal-facilitation charge against Damian to fall, or he could try to disprove that Damian was involved in the conspiracy and demonstrate that the youth had no intention of committing a crime at all, but, rather, that this was just a sick, perverted game they were playing. "To do that effectively," said Snyder, "you would really have to put Damian on the stand, to have him basically plead mercy to the jury, and say, 'Look, I was just a kid, I didn't know what was going on.' "

Now, in the witness chair, Damian, still in his conservative dark suit, told the court that he was eighteen years old, that he lived in Ossining and had been working up until three weeks ago. In the fall of 1984, he had moved to Canaan to live with his aunt and uncle because he had been doing badly in junior high school in Ossining and he and his parents had decided that a smaller school system might be better for him.

Adams asked if he knew Miles McDonald, and Damian described Miles as a good friend of his. They went skiing together; he spent time with Miles's family in Ghent and Miles would visit him down in Ossining. As for Ben Cooper, he was described by Damian as being interested in a lot of "fantasy stuff . . . like ninjas, other assassination cults." Damian added that Cooper had been attempting to write a book on these cults and had attempted to enlist him to proofread and type it for him. Regarding John Bailey, he had at first been a lunchtime companion but they had become friends when they discovered they lived just a mile away from each other.

When Adams asked about Damian's relationship with Wyley, Damian explained that they had only become friends when Damian found out that Wyley lived near him and had a car. "After he got his license, we became friends," said Damian, who added that Wyley gave him rides after school. This callow account of the genesis of the friendship—the only "real" friendship to which Wyley had ever been privy—sounded one more soulless note in a story that was already heavy on soullessness.

Damian continued his testimony with an account of the school burglaries, and then Adams asked him if he recalled December 3, 1986. Damian remembered that date as the last occasion on which he, Miles, and Wyley had penetrated the school. At that time, Wyley had suggested that it would be an "interesting thing" to do the same thing to his father's residence in East Chatham that they had done in the school, that is, to "go in and take stuff." Damian then provided testimony regarding the log house burglary. Aside from the firearms, he told the court, he and Miles had divvied up loot that included Walkmans, a camping hatchet, binoculars, a bottle of Crown Royal bourbon, and miscellaneous other items. Wyley had told Damian and Miles before the burglary that they could split up the loot as they chose; he didn't care. Damian was asked if he ever told anyone about the burglary after it had occurred, and he replied that "everyone who sat at the same table with us at lunch knew about it

. . . Lofgren, Bailey, four or five other kids who sat at the same table."

Adams focused on the sequence of conversations that Miles McDonald had earlier testified to. In the version that Damian was now offering, the first conversation took place in early October when he, Miles, and Wyley were in the computer room, waiting for school to start. Wyley mentioned, "just in passing," said Damian, the idea of burning down his house, but Damian testified that he and Miles had laughed, taking it for a joke. Two or three weeks later, Wyley had a fight with his father over using the car to drive to school and had only been allowed to take the car because he had promised a ride to Damian. Later that day, Damian testified, Wyley complained about his father and said if he did burn down the house, he wouldn't mind if his father was in it. But Miles suggested that if Wyley did burn down the house, it would be better to "fill the house with ether" first so that the people within would be put to sleep. Adams, aiming to convey the whimsical quality of all this, asked Damian if anyone had access to ether, and Damian replied that they had not.

In late October, Damian testified, there was a third conversation. Basically it was the "same stuff," with one new twist: this time Wyley mentioned the insurance money he would get from burning down the house. Damian said he had laughed because Wyley was quoting a number like $300,000 or $400,000.

Damian told the court that he had laughed throughout all the conversations he had had with Wyley and Miles about Wyley's plan, figuring it all for a joke. He said that the day after the burglary at the log house, they were all in the computer room and Wyley mentioned this plan he had about killing his father. "We thought it was funny," said Damian, not bothering to explain why a proposed assassination plan would seem merely humorous a day after a burglary plan had achieved reality. Miles, in fact, had said that he couldn't just drive up to the Kelgate garage on Route 295, that he'd have to park away from it—an embel-

lishment that, again, was intended to show the boys' imagination at work rather than any concrete planning. Damian testified that he saw Wyley on and off during the
remainder of that day, and each time he saw Wyley, Wyley
kept mentioning the plan. Damian said he was getting sick
of it, and told Wyley that it was dumb and that he should
drop it.

Regarding the conversation to which Ben Cooper had
testified, in which Damian had asked Cooper what he
thought about killing for money, Damian now implied that
the question had been hypothetical in nature and had been
asked principally because he knew that Cooper was interested in things like ninjas and people who profited from
killing. Damian flatly denied having said to Cooper that he
"wasn't above getting the gun."

Adams now turned to the night of the murders. Damian
testified that Wyley had knocked on his door and he had
let him in, locking the door behind them. He asked Wyley
why he was late, but Wyley just handed him the Walther
that he had taken from Damian after the target-practice
session at John Bailey's (Damian was not asked, however,
why the return of the Walther pistol had been effected so
wordlessly). Wyley then followed Damian down the hallway
to wash his hands, asking for a Band-Aid, which Damian
said that he provided.

Adams asked if there was anything unusual about the
gun, if it smelled of having been fired, and Damian said it
had not.

Damian then got his coat and told Wyley to hurry up.
They got into the car. Wyley turned to him and said, "I did
it." "Did what?" asked Damian, but Wyley did not respond.
A few minutes later, as they drove along Route 295, Wyley
repeated that he had done it, adding that he had killed
them, to which remark Damian responded by asking
"Who?" and Wyley said, "All of them." At that point, Damian
testified, he didn't really know what to think, that perhaps
Wyley had told him this just to get a rise out of him. Wyley
liked to tell him things, Damian explained; for instance,
before stealing the first computer from Chatham High

School, Wyley had told him he'd already stolen it just to see how he would react to the news. When, on Route 295, Wyley had told him that he "did" it, Damian hadn't really believed it. He had just sat back and watched him, he now testified. "How did he act?" asked Adams. "Completely normal," Damian replied. "He wasn't excited or anything." Furthermore, Wyley continued to act "completely normal" in the movies. "When it was funny, he laughed," Damian noted.

Leaving the movie house, they saw Miles and Matt Rueckheim waiting on line to get in. Damian testified that he gestured with his thumb toward Wyley, who was behind him, and said to Miles, "He said he did it." Returning home, he and Wyley played computer games until Wyley announced that he had to go home, which was around 10:30. But first, Wyley said he wanted to call home, because the last time he stayed out late he had gotten into trouble. He went to use the phone and then came back, saying that there hadn't been any answer. Damian testified that he let him out the front door and then went back upstairs to watch TV with his aunt and uncle.

Adams asked if he were thinking about what Wyley had said, but Damian replied that it wasn't something that had bothered him, adding, by way of explanation, however hollow, that he had been watching TV.

Some hours after Wyley's departure, the phone rang at the Joseph residence and Damian answered. A woman who identified herself as a member of the sheriff's department asked for instructions to the Joseph home, which Stanley Joseph provided and soon thereafter Investigator Cozzolino arrived at the house. Cozzolino told Damian that four people had been found dead at Wyley's house, and he wanted Damian to tell him anything that might help him. But Damian now testified that he did not, at that time, tell Cozzolino about the conversation with Wyley en route to the movies, or about the guns. Adams asked him why he hadn't told the police about the guns; and Damian explained that once Cozzolino had said that there were four people dead in East Chatham, all he could think was that he had all these *things* in his house—rifles in the attic, library books, a computer.

The next day, when he awoke, his uncle told him that the state police were in the house, and that they wanted him to come with them to headquarters for questioning. That afternoon, an agreement was made to turn over the stolen items.

At any time, asked Adams, did you ever intend to have Robert Gates, Sr., or Robert Gates, Jr., killed?

Damian replied that he had not, nor had he conspired to have Robert Gates, Sr., or Robert Gates, Jr., killed; nor, until the police came to his house, did he ever believe that Wyley Gates had been serious; nor when he broke into the Gates residence, had he intended to provide a weapon for the murders; nor when Wyley gave back the weapon to him on December 13, had he intended to conceal it.

Adams had no more questions. It had been a lengthy examination. Snyder's cross-examination, in contrast, was a brief peppering of questions, almost all of which Damian denied.

You and Wyley were pretty close friends, weren't you? Snyder asked.

Damian replied that they were.

Isn't it a fact that Wyley Gates first approached you regarding his plan to kill his father while at a football game?

Damian denied this. Similarly, in a tense exchange, he denied telling Ben Cooper that somebody had offered him a contract, and he denied as well that he had referred to the Walther automatic pistol as his "little toy."

Snyder then began a line of questioning based on information derived from tapes that Wyley had made for Dr. Marchionne. These tapes had been turned over to the prosecution in the Gates case as what is called *Rosario* material, meaning statements of a prior witness, in this case the witness being Marchionne. In the Gates case, the prosecution was at a disadvantage because whereas the prior statements of all the People's witnesses had to be turned over to the defense attorney before opening statements were made, the defense attorney only had to turn over the prior statements of his witnesses just before the beginning of cross-examination. Therefore, the D.A. in the Gates case only had minutes to review the forty hours of tapes and was denied the recess of several days he requested to review the tapes. Now, in the Rossney trial, Snyder was prevented from going any further than her peppering line of questioning because the statements she was relying on were hearsay. She could not play the tapes for the jury, nor call to the stand Dr. Marchionne, whose testimony could only be admitted in regard to Wyley's mental state. But a peppering line of questioning could conceivably have its uses in terms of swaying a jury, and so she forged ahead.

Isn't it true that you agreed to let Wyley take the Walther for a fee of three thousand dollars? Snyder demanded, citing a figure that Wyley had mentioned to Marchionne.

Damian denied that this was true and denied as well that he had offered to "rent" the gun to Wyley. He further denied the suggestion that when he and Wyley were incarcerated together at the Columbia County Jail he had sent a message to Wyley saying that he still wanted his three thousand dollars. Snyder demanded to know if it was true that on the Thursday before the murders Wyley called to tell him that he was going to do it and Damian said to call him back. Damian denied this as well, as he denied Snyder's charge that he had offered his help once again to Wyley on Saturday.

Snyder asked whether Wyley, when he picked up Damian on Saturday night, went into Damian's bedroom and said "I did it," but Damian said this was not true. And when Snyder asked Damian if he had said to Wyley, "How are you? Are you all right?", Damian said that he did not remember such a conversation.

Snyder had no more questions. The evidentiary portion of the trial had been concluded.

Like the opening remarks, the closing statements were unemotional and to the point. There were many things about this case that were bizarre, Adams told the jury. One thing that the prosecutor had to prove was that Damian Rossney had a conscious intent to kill. Where are you going to get that from in this case? he asked. If it was there at all, you would have to get it from Miles McDonald. McDonald said, "Oh yes, we had conversations," but McDonald "laughed it off as a joke"; "he didn't take it seriously"; "never in his wildest dreams." McDonald took it that way, charged Adams; why shouldn't another boy take it exactly the same way? The use of the word *joke* by Miles McDonald in his testimony may not have been in good taste or shown good judgment, Adams allowed, but that's the way he put it.

And how about the conversation between Damian and Ben Cooper about "offing" someone? Ben Cooper wanted to write about ninjas and so, Adams suggested, Cooper was an appropriate person to talk to about such a subject. If Damian had really been part of a conspiracy, would he have gone outside the tight circle of conspirators to talk about such a plan? Adams demanded of the jury. Was there one statement by Damian Rossney that convinced them beyond a reasonable doubt that he had an intent to kill? Adams asked. Each and every one of those boys, he maintained, took the murder plan as just so much loose talk.

And the same was true of the conspiracy, Adams charged. The intent just wasn't there. When you hear the word *conspiracy*, Adams suggested to the jury, what crosses your mind is people in dark rooms. But where did these conversations take place? Adams asked. In the lunchroom. In the computer room. In places where there were other people going back and forth. Some of it was ludicrous, laughable, Adams insisted. Imagine three boys filling a house with ether. Imagine three boys committing murders right out on Route 295. It didn't make sense. The reality of what happened at the Gates residence didn't fit in with what had been talked about.

Adams methodically attempted to defuse all the charges, and devoted particular attention to the matter of hindering prosecution. Ask yourselves this, he urged the jury. You are sixteen years old; you're there with the police; you know if you go back and get the gun, they will search the house and find all the other things you're not supposed to have. The prosecutor has to prove beyond a reasonable doubt that Damian's intent was to hinder prosecution, but the next day, through an attorney, the gun was given to the police. If he intended to hinder prosecution, Damian would have been out on the road at 2:30 in the morning, giving the gun his best throw into the woods. And remember what Miles McDonald told you, that the police came to him and he said nothing. Was Miles McDonald arrested? Adams demanded. Did Miles McDonald not do what anyone else would do at sixteen? A young boy, scared, not knowing what the police would do? He is a good measuring stick, Adams concluded, by which to measure the conduct of my client.

The closing remarks of prosecutor Nancy Snyder represented perhaps the strongest part of her case. They were well organized, well delivered, and possessed of a controlled anger. She asked the jury to remember Miles McDonald's testimony regarding the series of conversations that had taken place in the fall of 1986. The first conversation was a general one, she said, in which Wyley Gates said that he had a plan to kill his father and knew how to do it. The second conversation was much the same as the first, but this time both Wyley and Damian were doing the talking. *They* had a plan, and the two of them were intent on enlisting Miles. In the third conversation, both Damian and Wyley were discussing the shooting of Robert Gates and Robert Gates, Jr., and this time the plan included the participation of Miles, as the three of them would go up to the garage on Route 295. The fourth conversation was similar to the third, but this time featured Damian's idea of piling up tires at one of the doors, thus ensuring that Bob and Bobby would have to exit by the unimpeded door, where Damian and Miles would be waiting to ambush them. Finally, there were the two telephone conversations between Damian and Miles in which Damian told Miles how much he would be getting paid for the shooting.

Damian's version of the conversations tracked Miles's version remarkably well, charged Snyder, except in the spots where they implicated Damian. Damian's version said that all conversations before the burglary only involved burning down or blowing up the log house. Damian's version also limited any conversation regarding the shooting of Robert Gates to one conversation after the burglary, whereas Miles talked about at least two in which the plan was modified somewhat.

As for Damian's conversations with Ben Cooper, Damian had an explanation for everything except for his statement, which Cooper testified to, that he "wasn't above getting the gun." Snyder asked the jury what motivation Cooper would have for offering misleading evidence. After all, Ben Cooper had no reason to feel that he would be implicated.

As for the suggestion that the boys all thought of the murder plan as a joke, Snyder raised significant doubt here. Although Miles had received total immunity, there was still an obvious reason why he might not tell "the whole truth," and this reason, Snyder suggested, was because it was difficult for an eighteen-year-old boy to get up and tell the community that he had been a serious member of a plot to commit murder. For further proof of Miles's having taken the plot seriously, Snyder re-created that last scene in the computer room when Wyley had turned off his computer and Miles had called him names and said, "I'm not going to do it." He hadn't said, "You're bugging me," Snyder pointed out. He had said, "*I'm not going to do it*." And what had Wyley said to Damian on the way to the movies? "*I did it. I did it*." What had Damian said to Miles outside the Crandell Theatre? "*He did it*." If there wasn't a meeting of the minds about what went on here, Snyder demanded of the jury, what was there? These boys were serious; they knew what went on in each other's heads; they had it all down to a shorthand.

Snyder conceded, in her closing remarks, that she did have to prove that Wyley had committed the murders, and she felt that she had proven, without a doubt, that Wyley was the trigger man. She cited the cut on his thumb; the blood on the slide; and now, something that had been unavailable to them in the Gates trial, the confession that Wyley had made to Damian on the night of the murders. Another thing the jury might find strange, suggested Snyder, was the fact that the boys were late to the movies but when Wyley arrived at the Joseph house to pick him up, Damian took the time to lock the door behind him. If they were late, why would Damian have bothered to do this? She suggested that he wanted to get the details; the implication was that he wanted to do so without any unwarranted interruptions. Furthermore, Snyder said, reaching the crest of her argument, Damian said that he didn't know how to "take" it when Wyley said "I did it." If it was so perplexing to him, she wondered to the jury, then why did Damian simply say to Miles, "He did it." And why didn't Miles ask, "Did *what*?"

The questions—good ones, indeed—resonated in the courtroom as Snyder took her seat.

All that remained to be done was for Judge Zittell to charge the jury, which he did with painstaking care. As Judge Leaman had done in the Gates trial, Judge Zittell devoted particular attention to the details of the conspiracy charge and to the issue of reasonable doubt. So charged, the jury, after a seven-day trial that was like a weird digest of the Gates trial, went into deliberation. The citizens of Columbia County waited to see how justice would be served this time.

26

It took three days for the Rossney jury to come to a decision. When, on December seventh, the verdict was announced, it was exactly two years to the day since the target-practice session at John Bailey's house.

In those two years, some things had changed, some things had remained the same. Just a few days before the Rossney trial ended, Paul Groudas had been awarded $972,000 in a negligence suit relating to the injury he had sustained in 1981 while working for Hudson Handling, an injury that had required the amputation of his right foot. The irony that underscored this very large award was that part of the Gates family's motivation in seeking custody of Jason in the first place had had to do with the fact that Paul and Laurie Groudas, who were countering them in the suit, didn't have "much money" and "had a hard time . . . surviving on his business." Now, it was abundantly clear, there would have been more than sufficient money to support little Jason.

There had been changes in the legal community too. Paul Czajka, who had represented Wyley at the time of his arraignment, had succeeded Gene Keeler as district attorney. Gene Keeler, in turn, had assumed the office of public defender and had hired onto his staff, as an assistant public defender, Richard Hogle, who had admitted to being "green" at the time that he accompanied Wyley to Poughkeepsie for the polygraph examination. The passage of time, and the ensuing controversy over the Gates case, had evidently ripened Hogle considerably.

The house on Colane Road to which Damian had come with the hopes of enjoying a more fruitful high school career was no longer inhabited by Stanley and Sally Joseph, who, instead, were now operating a handsomely restored bed-and-breakfast establishment near Queechy Lake. But the house on Maple Drive—the house that Bob and Kristi Gates had built with their own hands, log by log—still remained empty, having been up for sale since 1987. "The events have placed a serious stigma upon the property, producing a negative effect on value which only time will cure," reported a July 1987 appraisal filed at surrogate court. In considerably plainer language, Dick Klingler said, "Nobody local would buy it knowing what happened there. I can't stand to even drive by it."

As the jury deliberated, the waiting time at the courthouse was scored with piped-in Christmas music. Vibraphone arrangements of "Jingle Bells." Dripping choral renditions of "Do You Hear What I Hear?" Andy Williams in an almost mocking promise of "I'll Be Home for Christmas." The routinized merriment of the courthouse's seasonal color clashed drastically with the tense vigil of family, police, reporters, and the curious retirees and court watchers who populated the smoke-filled hallways.

Unlike Wyley, Damian was not keeping the vigil alone; his family remained at his side. Generally, the Rossneys presented a staunch demeanor and, when things looked as if they might get out of hand, Damian's sister, tall and attractive, would authoritatively shepherd her little brother through the ranks of reporters.

As the vigil continued, there were all sorts of guesses made as to what the verdict would be, but there was really no calling it. Regarding Damian's own testimony, his attorney, Robert Adams, said that he felt it had been necessary to put his client on the stand not to convince anyone of his innocence but, rather, to make some details clearer. "I was very pleased with the testimony," Adams told the press. But many who observed Damian's testimony felt that nothing was gained for his case by his having taken the stand. In his litany of burglaries and petty crimes that he had committed, he conveyed a sense of having been capable of other, greater crimes.

The first night the jury deliberated until 10:30 P.M., asking for readbacks of testimony from Michael Lofgren, John Bailey, and Ben Cooper. The next day they deliberated until 11:40 P.M., asking to have the murder charges and the hindering prosecution charges read back, and asking as well for a legal dictionary, which request was denied. At 2:00 on the afternoon of December 7, the jury sent out a note that they had reached a verdict.

The courtroom filled quickly. The other shoe—that long-awaited other shoe—was about to drop. The foreman rose and announced that they had found the defendant not guilty on the charges of murder and hindering prosecution, but guilty on the charges of conspiracy and criminal facilitation.

Damian remained absolutely impassive, as did the rest of his family except for his sister, who broke down sobbing in the arms of her aunt, Sally Joseph. The jurors were polled individually, and each juror replied "Affirmed" when their names were called. Judge Zittell praised the jury for its diligence, and allowed Damian to remain free on bail until his sentencing on January 17. Damian was now facing eight and one-third to twenty-five years on the conspiracy conviction, and five to fifteen years for criminal facilitation, although it was agreed that the sentences should run concurrently.

Prosecuting attorney Nancy Snyder said, "I wanted 'guilty' on everything but I'm satisfied with the verdict. It was fair and well considered." Attorney Robert Adams allowed that he felt relief not to be pursuing appeal of murder charges but added, "I think I feel the same disappointment for him that he and his family have."

For his part, Charles Wilcox called a press conference on the day after the Rossney verdict was returned. With pathologist Dr. Jack Davies at his side, Wilcox announced that he was calling the press conference to remind the community that not all of the evidence concerning Wyley Gates had been heard at the Rossney trial. If it had been, he held, the Rossney jury would not have concluded that Gates was the murderer. He added that he believed that the real killer was still at large and all the possibilities had not been investigated properly. "With my heart I know we could investigate it thoroughly and if somebody could be found as the perpetrator, we would find them," he avowed.

The Columbia County Sheriff's Department disagreed. Through their spokesman, Undersheriff James Bertram, they now declared the case closed, barring discovery of any new evidence. "This verdict confirms what we have always known," he stated. "Wyley did it."

Surely the truth lay somewhere between "the real killer, still at large" to whom Wilcox alluded and Undersheriff Bertram's dogged belief that Wyley had gone it alone. But the unfortunate fact is that the truth will probably never be known. The worst crime in the county's history had failed to result in a conviction for murder. The worst crime in the county's history had resulted instead in two convictions for conspiracy to commit murder; as the murders had in fact been committed, these convictions now existed in a kind of strange relation to reality.

But what was the reality? Had Wyley cunningly involved these other boys with the idea that in so doing he would put up a smokescreen around the fact that he really had done it all by himself, the sole perpetrator? Or had the other boys preyed on Wyley's warped mind, causing, through their encouragement, the fantasies to fester into an ugly reality? Did Wyley, on the night of December thirteenth, pick up Damian at the Joseph residence shortly before seven o'clock and did they return together to Maple

Drive and did they go in together to the log house and did they share the killings? Did Damian stand by and watch as Wyley fired the Walther, or was it the other way around? Damian and Wyley claimed that they had arrived at the Crandell Theater in Chatham by 7:30, but no one at the theater would attest to their having been there. In fact, the only persons who could verify Damian and Wyley's proximity to the theater were Miles McDonald and Matthew Rueckheim, but who could verify Miles's whereabouts other than his "best friend"? And then, trying out another scenario, were there other boys involved? Was there a pickup truck on the road and, if so, who was in it? And if Wyley had committed the deeds by himself, and if these other boys were stained by his insidiousness, then why weren't these other boys—these cruelly framed boys—crying and screaming and flailing their arms? Why was Damian so stoic when faced with the prospect of serving at least eight and one-third years in prison for a crime he claimed not to have committed? Why had John Bailey been laughing in the hallways outside of the courtroom? Why were none of these boys exhibiting any pity for the victims? Why were they without any sign of human emotion and feeling that would serve to indicate that they were people who would not ruthlessly and unfeelingly commit murder?

The questions were everywhere and they were endless. "I said to my son one night, 'I would give anything, it would make me feel so good inside, if this kid would just open up his mouth and spit it all out and let everyone know, even if he did shoot them,' " said juror Mary Meyer. "Just let it rip and let everyone know who all was involved. I'd love it. I mean, it would be like frosting on the cake for me at this point. But the additional problem is that once you've gone through the list of possible scenarios—Mr. Plum, in the parlor, with the candlesticks—then there are all the questions about motive. Had an habitually isolated Wyley offered up his family in a kind of rite of initiation that would gain him admittance into this fraternity of aggressive boys? Or had he suffered for years in silent retreat from the abuses, however unrevealed, that he endured at the hand of a martinet father? Had he been born a "bad seed" as claimed by those who remembered the icy detachment with which he had turned his back on religion at the tender age of thirteen? Or was this some kind of revenge killing on behalf of a mother who had largely disappeared from Wyley's life when he was all of ten years old, a depressed mother whose lack of affect was perhaps the model for his own lack of affect? Had he, in her absence, internalized her and, consequently, did the rage he felt for Cheryl, a rival in the home, finally explode?

Wild, sinister theories emerged throughout the course of the trial. The theories had no foundation in fact, but this did nothing to keep people from circulating them. Images of satanism and the black arts were evoked; the Dungeons and Dragons business was hauled out regularly. The theories circulated primarily because people were at a loss for reasons and so were desperate in their inventions. The other reason for the loss and the desperation people felt in confronting this crime was that it seemed, unfortunately and frighteningly, part of a bigger problem, the corruption and perversion of our young people, which stood as a chilling wave of the future. "I think there is a kind of substantial segment of the adolescent community which is truly indifferent to things that the next generation values," said Dr. Marchionne. "Whether it be people or family or friendship or closeness. And I think that the adolescents know that they've gone a little beyond just the superficial show of the differences between generations. It began with the way they danced and the way they dressed and that was supposed to be kind of the statement that they made which said, 'Hey, I'm independent.' And I think that process now is unfortunately being accepted and tolerated by the majority culture. The school system says, 'Yes, you want to come dressed as an Indian, come on in.' I think they've gone further now, at least some of them have, to make that impact, that shock, where you come up with these bizarre issues—killing friends, killing some derelict downtown, killing families."

Already, just in the short time since these two trials took place, there have been, in this immediate area, more horrifying crimes of this nature. In Poughkeepsie, a sixteen-year-old boy was arrested for killing his father, his mother, his eight-year-old brother, and critically wounding his sister. The alleged reason? A dispute over homework. Police found in the room of this boy, who nicknamed himself "Rambo," dozens of Rambo posters, army packs, smoke grenades, and ammunition pouches. "Brian wore camouflage outfits," said a neighbor, "but he didn't seem any different from other kids." And, on the heels of this atrocity, two young female graduates of the Ichabod Crane School, located in Valatie, which neighbors Chatham, were charged with the murder of their stepmother, found with a hundred stab wounds. The woman, according to the girls, had kicked the family poodle and this had been the last straw.

And then, after you've asked all the questions about whodunit and why they did it, then you have to ponder the reasons why justice, in the opinion of most people who live here, was not served. Some disillusioned members of the community have linked the Gates verdict to the verdict in the case of New York City subway "vigilante" Bernhard Goetz. The term *nullification* has been invoked, meaning a principle by which a jury is empowered to ignore both the facts and the law in rendering its verdict. The most famous historical instance of nullification is to be found in the case of John Peter Zenger, who was tried for seditious libel in 1735 when his newspaper criticized the royal governor. The judge in that case held that mere publication was sufficient to sustain a conviction, whether the information printed was true or false. In fact, the printed information was true, and Zenger had been charged and jailed for several months pending the trial. The defense attorney, Alexander Hamilton, urged the jury to ignore the judge and to decide for itself whether publication of the truth should be considered a crime. The panel voted to acquit the defendant, even though Zenger had been guilty of publishing the information, the only issue legally before the jury.

In an opinion related to the nullification principle and rendered by the Court of Appeals on an appeal brought by the attorney for Bernhard Goetz, the court wrote, "While there is nothing to prevent a jury from acquitting although finding that the prosecution has proven its case, this so-called mercy-dispensing power ... is not a legally sanctioned function of the jury and should not be encouraged by the court."

Some in Columbia County felt that the nullification principle was in effect in the Gates trial, that the jury, in fact, had decided to overlook the preponderance of evidence indicating the guilt of Wyley Gates in favor of sending a message to the law-enforcement authorities that they did not approve of the way business had been conducted. But, if this was so, it would be a difficult thing indeed to rationalize how a jury came to such a decision. The police in the case of Wyley Gates were generally thought of as "good guys"— "Cozzy," "Shooky," the hometown team. What would cause a jury to reject the behavior of these good men for the sake of a Wyley Gates?

"I just don't know," Gene Keeler said. "It just shows you how the form can be held over the substance of something." It remains Keeler's belief that, in those issues where somebody is guilty of a crime, to hide behind a procedural matter that protects the individual is wrong. Beyond this, there is always the possibility of a jury simply being confused by the judge's charge. "Every trial you have jury instructions," said Keeler after the trial. "Generally speaking, getting a good grip on those things is very difficult and I've had twelve years' experience in the business. I can imagine the way a jury just comes in and sits down and doesn't know any law, doesn't have any experience, sits there, and you read through a charge real quick. It's a joke to think they can comprehend it."

For Wilcox, however, the outcome was a triumph of the system. "The surprise of it was that the jury was able to do it. As much as we believed in the case, as much as we believed we could make it happen, from a realistic standpoint and experience, its happening was another question alto-gether," said Wilcox, who felt that with all the publicity it was unlikely that the jury was going to withstand what he referred to as "a stampede of horses." In terms of finding juries that will see themselves as protectors of the Constitution, it has been Wilcox's experience that this is unlikely. He has found that when presented with a Constitutional argument in favor of the defendant, most juries will look for another way to convict. Indeed, they will initially put aside that testimony as tainted and go on to look through the whole thing, and if they can't come up with anything else, they will then go back to the tainted evidence and try to untaint it somehow. They will reincorporate this evidence if that's all they have to work with, and they will say, "Well, it really isn't our decision, what do we know about the Constitution?" In this case, Wilcox found a decidedly less resistant jury, and he believed that their lack of resistance had to do with what he termed the "basic unreliability" of the evidence.

Judge Leaman, in a sense, agreed. Some jurors described that alleged barring motion that Salmon directed toward Hogle as the "pivotal" moment for them, but Judge Leaman said, "I think you have to take it as part of a continuum. If that had been the only negative piece of evidence concerning the police, I don't think anyone would have thought about it." Leaman, however, pointed to a long line of evidence that, if it was believed, compromised the credibility of the police, starting as early as when, in the grandmother's presence and in her house, they asked Wyley Gates to go with them with bland assurances and then, the instant they got outside the door, they began reading him his *Miranda* rights. "Now that has a certain unattractive look to it, or could be construed as having such an unattractive look," said Leaman. "You start with that and you go on with many other instances that could be construed—not that I necessarily do—but that could be construed by a jury in a negative way as reflecting poorly on the police and call into question what the thought processes were."

As for the prosecution of the case, the judge was more forgiving. "In terms of Mr. Keeler and the case of the prosecution, what can one do except to deal with the circumstances as they were?" he pointed out. "There were some tests that were going to be done, I think, by law-enforcement agencies, whether of powder stains on clothing, things of that sort; the clothing was taken for that purpose and the tests were never done. And I'm afraid, as I say, in simply looking at what the jury did and trying to deduce what led them to that result—I don't presume to second-guess to any great extent—but I suppose that if the case essentially consists of an alleged confession and if you find the confession unworthy of belief and credibility, which the jury obviously concluded, and there was a lack of corroborative evidence that might have given the jury greater confidence in the so-called confession down in Poughkeepsie—which, for example, whatever scientific tests that might have been done were done and were corroborative of the confession—who's to say what the result might have been?"

There is no one who can say, and so the questions will linger on. In an extraordinary way, these murders in this community offer an almost laboratory-like situation by which to gauge the effects of violence on a community. The sister towns of Chatham and Canaan have suffered a wound on their wound: first, it was the violence, so utterly aberrant, and then it was the lack of resolution, the failure, in the minds of many, of the justice system. It will take many years for the wounds to heal, for the community to recover from what one of its members termed "the whole tragedy of errors." In fact, in some crucial ways, Chatham and Canaan may never be the same. A loss of innocence has occurred, and innocence, like brain cells, cannot regenerate. "You've found your little quiet nowhere where you can get away from everything," said juror Robert Jensen, "and you can't get away from everything. It follows you. A certain amount of decadence follows us wherever we go. Wherever people are, something follows eventually."

On top of all this, the smallness of the town makes the memories inescapable. Everywhere in town are allusions to this ugly thing that has happened here. One day it's the husky kid in the Chatham Auto Parts store who turns out to be Matt Rueckheim, Miles McDonald's "best friend." Another day, at a truck stop off Peaceful Valley Road, it's Miles himself in a green twill work suit, employed as a mechanic. After all this, one can't help thinking, Miles has gotten himself the kind of good, honest job of which Bob Gates would have approved.

But, for all the decadence creeping in and all the inescapable memories, there's a glue here that manages to hold everything together. It's a fast and powerful glue, made up of family connections; neighbor connections; the land; the smell of the cows in the fields; the Little League games; the firehouse bingo; the postmaster who gives lollipops to the kids. It is, in fact, a glue that, if it touches you, makes you stick to the place. When I started work on this book, I was living in Manhattan and raising my children there. Now, as I end it, I have become a "full-timer." Nothing that I uncovered in my writing of this book has made me want to leave the town. I uncovered no strangely indigenous rot or evil. What I found here is the same dark side of the moon that is found everywhere. And, in a world in which decadence follows you everywhere, this small part of the world remains, for many and for me, a place where you have a fighting chance against it all, a good place to be.

On February 7, 1989, Damian Rossney was sentenced to the maximum term of eight and one-third to twenty-five years for conspiracy and five to fifteen years for criminal facilitation, the terms to run concurrently. Robert Adams cited the case of *People* v. *Cruikshank* in requesting youthful-offender status for his client, but Judge Zittell maintained that the *Cruikshank* case involved "hasty and thoughtless acts," whereas, in the case at hand, the actions were "articulated, considered, and deliberate." As before, Damian betrayed no sign of emotion, nor, this time, did any member of his family.

Damian was returned to the Columbia County jail awaiting transfer to a state facility, which occurred almost immediately. By the afternoon of February 10, Damian had been taken to the Elmira State Correctional Facility, where his friend Wyley was serving out his sentence.

A spokesman for the State Department of Correctional Services had earlier stated that it was very unlikely that

Damian would be assigned to the same prison as Wyley. Spokesmen, however, have been known to be wrong. In fact, there are few maximum-security facilities geared for the younger offender. But, more than that, it is just possible that the destinies of these two boys were to remain, in the end, inextricably and inalterably entwined.

By the time Damian arrived at Elmira, the Christmas decorations had been taken down. The red stone buildings stood unadorned and somber. The only bow to a force in life other than a grim functional existence—so strange now for these two boys who had shown so much promise and enjoyed so much opportunity—was a statue on the front lawn before the main building. Cast at Elmira in the 1930s, and, all things considered, a rather misguided sculptural conceit for a penal institution, it showed two boys in fig leaves, their arms around each other. The inscription at the base read "Builders of Men." In the light that was dying so early on this cold February afternoon, the two boys still cast a long and cold shadow.

AFTERWORD

Destinies for us are naught,
but there will always be we two
who travel on the shores of hope,
searching for what was promised,
but has been forever lost.
We two, who share, will never be
what youth had promised us to be
in the time of childhood memory.
We search for destiny.
We find reality.
But not each other.

We who were one. We who are one,
lost forever. How could we be lost,
together, forever searching,
for each other, for ourselves?
We were. We are.

          —WYLEY GATES, *"Gemini"*

In southern California, the country near the town of Gorman is remarkably rugged. There are ravines and gullies where the terrain is steep and irregular, rising and falling sharply. The soil is alternately rocky and sandy, covered with thin grasses, scrub oaks, and desert bushes. In the summer, the temperature can be fiercely hot; at night, it can drop sharply. The landscape seems almost primitive.

On the morning of June 10, 1983, Glen Fischer was headed toward Gorman in his Ford pickup. The alarm had gone off at six o'clock, and by seven Fischer was moving east along Route 126. He was feeling good, and even the heat could not dampen his enthusiasm. He poked at the controls on the air conditioner, the cool air barely filling the cab.

Owner and operator of a company called Fischer Apiaries, he was looking for a remote canyon where he could store his one hundred twenty beehives. His mission was to find a place rich with sage and buckwheat, where his bees could forage unmolested and produce gallons of golden honey, which he hoped to sell at a considerable profit.

With temperatures rising into the high nineties, it was important that he get his day's work done quickly. His shirt already lacquered to his back by sweat, Fischer was uncomfortable from the heat, and it was barely two hours after sunrise. He tried to coax more cool air from the air conditioner as he passed through the sleepy towns of Fillmore and Piru. At the Saugus junction, he turned north on Interstate 5, and now he was heading toward Gorman.

Fischer called this section of the interstate the ridge road. It rose sharply from Saugus to an elevation of more than four thousand feet, and there it continued on toward Bakersfield. Fortunately for him, Fischer was not headed that far. All he had to do was drive partway up the ridge road, where he was to pull off and wait at a designated wide spot in the frontage road. There, at eight-thirty, he was to meet a park ranger, get into her truck, and scout out possible bee sites.

The ranger, a pretty, well-spoken woman named Lynn, arrived, and Fischer proceeded north on the interstate in her truck. They were in what was called lower chaparral country, an area of small, low-lying scrub oaks, greasewood, and manzanita, a chaparral plant with distinctive red bark and a lovely grayish leaf. This was not forest; on the contrary, it looked more like desert than anything else.

At the Hungry Valley exit, they turned off, continuing north on a frontage road, then east into a narrow canyon on a poorly maintained dirt road, called, on some older maps, Caswell Canyon Road. A quarter mile east of the frontage road, it abruptly ended. It was ten-thirty when the ranger stopped the truck and Fischer jumped out.

"This looks very good," he said. All he could hear was the faint hum of freight trucks rumbling along the interstate.

Stepping out of the truck, Lynn said she thought it would be perfect for the bees; and, of the half-dozen sites Fischer had looked at on the topographical map, this one was not used by any other beekeepers.

"You'll be alone here," Lynn said.

With its steep washed-out sides, the narrow pass where the road ended was like a box canyon. There appeared to be only one way into the canyon, and Fischer could not imagine anyone else following the same road to this exact spot. He figured his bees would be safe here.

"I really think this is perfect," Fischer said, wiping the sweat off his forehead with a handkerchief. But as he headed away from the truck, his feet crunched on something, and he noticed a number of broken beer bottles and smashed cans. Stepping back, he saw piles of spent bullet casings littering the ground.

"Looks like someone's idea of a target range," he said, kicking at one of the shells with the point of his boot. It seemed like a long way to go just to fire off a gun.

The ranger said she agreed, noting that target shooters had trampled through a lot of the valleys in the area. She said she wanted to see if she could go farther up into the canyon, and she turned and moved away from the truck. As she left him, Fischer began walking back down along the edge of the road, toward a narrow, rocky gully. What he was looking for was a flat, open area of perhaps a half acre in size.

He was about a hundred yards from the truck when he smelled something truly horrible. Something's dead, he thought.

This alarmed him, not because he was afraid of coming across a dead animal, but because he needed to be certain there was nothing living in this canyon that would upset his hives. Like a bear, for instance.

Jesus, it really smells, he thought, thinking maybe a cow had wandered into the box canyon and been eaten by coyotes.

He walked in fifteen or twenty feet, toward the far side of the dry wash, and when he came around a greasewood bush he saw a hand sticking up toward the sky, with two fingers extended and partially separated, in the manner of a sixties peace sign. The flesh was yellow, the color of skin stained by nicotine.

Momentarily stunned, he stood and stared. It was clearly a human hand; there was no getting around that.

He slowly approached the hand, and as he got closer, he could see it was attached to some blue cloth. He could make out legs, or rather the shape of legs under more blue cloth, and the other arm and a portion of the top of a head, with a shock of brownish hair. He stopped again, staring at the ground in front of him.

Fischer stood trying to answer all the questions popping into his head. He did not know whose body he was looking at, but he was certain it did not belong here. This was no hiker who fell off a cliff, he thought. Or a hunter who had somehow shot himself. The blue cloth—a suit, perhaps—seemed to indicate that these fetid remains were those of a businessman. The rank odor indicated they had been here a long time, baking in this sun, picked at by predators. It seemed upon closer inspection that only a fraction of the original body was still there and the rest had melted away into the earth, the hand protruding as the body receded.

This was the first such body he had ever seen. He tried very hard to remain calm. At least the chance of confronting whoever it was that had left the body here was remote.

He inched a bit closer, his eyes focused on what was left of the head. One side of the face was mostly gone, leaving a portion of the skull on top and the jawline at the bottom. There was nothing in between but stained earth.

Jesus Christ, he thought, deliberately averting his eyes. The head had been destroyed, blown away. The body seemed to have crash-landed against the bush. Suddenly, Fischer pulled back. Overcome by the stench and the grotesque condition of the body, he turned quickly and went to find the ranger.

"There's a body in there," he said, out of breath.

Lynn was stunned. "What should we do?"

"There's no hurry. It won't do him any good. He's been dead a long time."

They left and went to the nearest ranger station, about two miles south at Pyramid Lake. There, the sheriff's office in nearby Gorman was called, and Fischer was told to wait so that he could escort a detective to the scene.

By early afternoon, the box canyon was crawling with Los Angeles County sheriff's deputies. This was a crime scene, so nothing was touched, not the corpse nor the ground around it, while the deputies waited for homicide detectives from Los Angeles to show up. Those who went over to examine the remains did so with handkerchiefs across their mouths.

Toward the middle of the afternoon, two homicide detectives arrived, Willi Ahn and Carlos Avila. Stout and muscular, with a calm, contemplative disposition, Avila had seen enough crime scenes in his career not to be sickened by this one. He stood over the remains and stared, and immediately noticed that buttons had been pulled off the front of the suit coat.

Must have been a struggle, Avila thought. Probably more than one shooter. Then they blasted him in the head, maybe six or eight times, a goddamn free-for-all. The whole side of his face, from the temple to the jaw, was sheared off, as if by a buzz saw. Considering the condition of the skull, it was certainly possible that a shotgun had been fired at point-blank range, sending the body reeling backward into the greasewood bush.

God, that hand, someone said. Just sticking up like that.

Like he'd been praying, someone else said.

Late in the afternoon, the sun retreated, casting long shadows into the box canyon. After Avila and Ahn were satisfied they had taken note of every detail, the Los Angeles County Medical Examiner's office removed the remains. Later, they were found to weigh only seventy pounds, confirming the theory that the victim had been dead a long time.

A check by Avila of the Los Angeles Police Department's computer records of missing persons cases revealed a month-old case concerning the disappearance of a New York theatrical producer named Roy Alexander Radin. The suit found in the canyon matched the one Radin had worn on the night he disappeared. Avila needed dental records to make a positive identification, and that would take several days. There was not much in the police department file to go on. Some names, some addresses—that was about it.

On the evening of May 13, twenty-eight days earlier, Roy Radin had been seen getting into a limousine in front of the Regency Hotel in Los Angeles with a beautiful woman from Miami named Karen DeLayne Jacobs. They were going to dinner in Beverly Hills. He was never seen alive again.

BAD COMPANY—THE NEWEST ADDITION TO THE TRUE CRIME LIBRARY, COMING IN NOVEMBER FROM ST. MARTIN'S PAPERBACKS